During his remarkable career, David Hill has been chairman then managing director of the Australian Broadcasting Corporation; chairman of the Australian Football Association; chief executive and director of the State Rail Authority; chairman of Sydney Water Corporation; a fellow of the Sydney University Senate; and chairman of CREATE (an organisation representing Australian children in institutional care).

He has held a number of other executive appointments and committee chair positions in the areas of sport, transport, international radio broadcasting, international news providers, politics, fiscal management and city parks.

David came from England to Australia in 1959 under the Fairbridge Farm School Child Migrant scheme. He left school at 15, then returned to complete his Master's degree in economics while working as an economics tutor at Sydney University.

After graduating in 2006 in classical archaeology from the University of Sydney, David became an honorary associate at the university in the departments of archaeology, classics and ancient history. He is also a visiting fellow at the University of New South Wales. Since 2011 he has been the manager of an archaeological study of the ancient Greek city of Troizen. He has for many years been a leading figure in the international campaign to have the Parthenon sculptures returned from the British Museum to Greece.

David is the author of the bestsellers *The Forgotten Children* (2006), *1788* (2008), *The Gold Rush* (2009) and *The Great Race* (2011).

Also by David Hill

David
HILL

The Making of
AUSTRALIA

WILLIAM HEINEMANN: AUSTRALIA

A William Heinemann book
Published by Random House Australia Pty Ltd
Level 3, 100 Pacific Highway, North Sydney NSW 2060
www.randomhouse.com.au

Penguin
Random House
RANDOM HOUSE BOOKS

First published by William Heinemann in 2014
This edition published in 2015

Random House Books is part of the Penguin Random House group of companies whose addresses can be found at global.penguinrandomhouse.com.

National Library of Australia
Cataloguing-in-Publication entry (paperback)

Hill, David– author

The making of Australia/David Hill

ISBN 9781742757674 (paperback)

Australia – History
Australia – Colonization
Australia – Social life and customs
Australia – Politics and government

994

Cover design by Luke Causby, Blue Cork
Internal design by Midland Typesetters, Australia
Typeset in 12/15pt Sabon by Midland Typesetters, Australia
Printed in Australia by Griffin Press, an accredited ISO AS/NZS 14001:2004 Environmental Management System printer

Random House Australia uses papers that are natural, renewable and recyclable products and made from wood grown in sustainable forests. The logging and manufacturing processes are expected to conform to the environmental regulations of the country of origin.

CONTENTS

To my son, Damian

CHAPTER 1

BEFORE THE BRITISH

It is not yet determined whether it is an island or a main continent; but I am certain that it joins neither to Asia, Africa, nor America.

AUSTRALIA MAY NEVER HAVE BECOME A BRITISH COLONY IF ANY one of a number of other European powers that had journeyed to the continent years before any British explorer, had decided to settle the land first.

In the 200 years before the first British convict settlement in 1788, various European countries had sent expeditions to explore the mysterious Great South Land in the hope of finding new riches. However, expedition after expedition returned with reports of an inhospitable, waterless and seemingly infertile land, whose exploration would yield nothing in the way of worthwhile resources. It appeared that the original owners, who had lived there for thousands of years, were the only ones who could thrive in the local environment and adapt effectively to its vagaries.

The first documented European visits to Australia were in 1606 by a Dutch explorer, Willem Janszoon, and, a few months later the Spaniard Luís Vaz de Torres. There is, however, persuasive evidence that other Europeans had arrived years before this, including maps that some are convinced are copies of those used by Portuguese sailors who may have explored the Australian coast as early as the first half of the 1500s. The British explorer Matthew Flinders, who navigated the coast two hundred years later, was among those who believed the Portuguese could have made it as far south as the island continent. He said of the surviving maps, 'the direction given to some parts of the coast, approaches too near the truth, for the whole to have been marked by conjecture alone'.[1]

Yet it is entirely possible that such maps were works of imagination rather than the result of actual discovery.[2] There are no original surviving Portuguese maps from the sixteenth century that depict a large land mass; nor are there any original journals or written accounts of any Europeans sailing along the coast of Australia before 1606.[3]

Another claim tested in recent years is that the Chinese could have reached the east coast of Australia around the time of the Han dynasty (206 BC – AD 220), if not before.[4] This theory argues that ancient maps suggest Chinese navigators charted parts of the east coast of Australia even up to a century before the Portuguese.[5]

*

The first recorded European landings in Australia were certainly Janszoon's and Vaz de Torres's. No log or journal of

Janszoon's expedition has survived, but copies of his charts of the voyage show that he sighted land near the mouth of what we now call the Pennefather River, about 130 kilometres south of the Cape York Peninsula on the Gulf of Carpentaria side. He proceeded south for about 230 kilometres along the eastern coast of the gulf (though still considered to be New Guinea), until he reached current-day Weipa, then returned to Java in June 1606, without the riches his sponsors, the Dutch East India Company, had hoped to reap from this new part of the world.

We know equally little about Luís Vaz de Torres, who found the strait separating the northern tip of Australia from New Guinea a few months after Janszoon had been in the vicinity. Most of the information we have about Torres's voyage comes from a letter he wrote to the King of Spain in 1607 and from a later account written by one of his fellow officers, Don Diego de Prado y Tovar. We do know that Torres was commander of one of three Spanish ships that left Callao in Peru in December 1605 to search for the much discussed, mysterious Great South Land, which had appeared on early French maps known as the Dieppe maps.

After sailing for six months Torres's ship, the *San Pedrico*, and the third ship became separated from the flagship. Torres nevertheless continued to search for the Great South Land and was able to navigate both vessels through the treacherous reef that separated the north of Australia from New Guinea. What he did not know was that as he passed through the strait, he was sailing along the northern side of the very land for which he was searching. He recorded only seeing some 'very large islands' to the south.[6]

The Spanish kept Torres's discoveries a secret from their European rivals for the next 150 years, when the British got hold of evidence of Torres's discovery and the existence of the passage became more widely known. In 1769, the Scottish geographer Alexander Dalrymple included the strait in a map and named it after its discoverer.

In the years that followed, other Dutch sailors journeyed along swathes of the western and southern coasts of Australia. In October 1616, having set a course for Batavia (now Jakarta) but then sailing further east than he meant to, Dirk Hartog landed at the entrance of what later became known as Shark Bay, Western Australia, on the *Eendracht*. Then, in 1627, in the *Gulden Zeepaerdt* (Golden Seahorse), Pieter Nuyts sailed for nearly 2000 kilometres from the south-west tip of Western Australia to present-day Ceduna in South Australia. Nuyts named two islands along the coast St Peter and St Francis Islands, which are the oldest European names for parts of South Australia.

*

Significant additional stretches of the Australian coast were discovered by another Dutchman, Abel Tasman, during his two great voyages of discovery in 1642 and 1644. Tasman was sent by the Dutch East India Company to the Great Southern Ocean in search of a new sailing route east to South America and for sources of new wealth and trade.

He and his crew were the first Europeans to discover the southernmost tip of a new continent, on 24 November 1642, and he named it Van Diemen's Land. Tasman's men explored the small island and found it had good timber, drinking water and plants that could provide sustenance. On 3 December, Abel Tasman claimed legal ownership of Australian territory on behalf of his country.

The expedition found little of trading value on his voyage, but the Dutch East India Company paid Tasman and his crew a bonus for their other achievements after they returned to Batavia in June 1643.

In February the following year, Tasman was sent with three small ships on a second voyage of discovery to the south of the East Indies. According to the charts of his journey, he sailed east in the direction of the Torres Strait to the western side of Cape York Peninsula, near where fellow Dutchman Janszoon had begun his journey in the Gulf of Carpentaria nearly forty years earlier. Sailing south and west around the gulf, Tasman then continued west around the north of today's Northern Territory and south along the current-day North West Cape. His ships covered around 5000 kilometres – by far the longest naval exploration of Australia's coastline yet. Tasman again failed to find any sources of new wealth or trading opportunities for the Dutch East India Company, and after his expeditions Europeans showed no further interest in exploring the lands to the south of the East Indies. However, as a result of his and other explorations, by the middle of the 1600s the Dutch were able to produce a map of much of the north, west and south of what became Australia. On these Dutch maps the Great South Land carried the name 'New Holland' for nearly two hundred years, until the publication of Matthew Flinders' maps in 1814.[7]

*

The first Englishman known to have visited the Australian mainland was William Dampier. Pirate, navigator, writer, natural historian, naval officer and adventurer, Dampier was the first person to circumnavigate the globe three times, and he visited Australia twice, landing there first in January 1688, forty years after Tasman and more than eighty years before Captain James Cook.

Dampier and the crew of the pirate ship *Cygnet* reached the Australian mainland almost exactly a hundred years before Captain Arthur Phillip founded the British colony in New South Wales. They landed in a cove in the Kimberley region of north-west Australia at the mouth of the Fitzroy River after nearly nine years pirating in the Atlantic, Caribbean and the Pacific.[8]

Dampier and his men were on shore for two months – the longest known stay by Europeans in Australia up to that time. Dampier was convinced that the huge tract of land was a separate continent: 'It is not yet determined whether it is an island or a main continent; but I am certain that it joins neither to Asia, Africa, nor America.'[9]

Dampier eventually returned to England and wrote of his discoveries. More than ten years later, the Royal Navy sent him back as commander of the *Roebuck* to assess the potential for annexing New Holland as part of the British Empire. On his second voyage, he again reached New Holland, on 25 July 1699. The expedition passed Dirk Hartog Island and entered a large inlet that Dampier named Shark Bay. His men spent two weeks exploring the inlet, making sketches and collecting plants, many of which Dampier pressed between the pages of his books. Dampier then sailed north along the coast for 1000 kilometres, where he came across a group of islands near current-day Karratha now known as the Dampier Archipelago.

After a journey of thirty-two months, William Dampier returned to England in August 1700, disappointed that his expedition had yielded so little immediate potential for the British Empire. His career as a captain in the Royal Navy came to an inglorious end when he was court-martialled and sacked for beating and jailing his deputy in Rio de Janeiro almost two years earlier. Dampier was bitter about the conviction but his dismissal from the navy did not stop him writing the two-volume *A Voyage to New Holland*, which was published in 1703 and 1709.

In 1715, Dampier died in London aged sixty-four, but during the next twenty years, seven editions of his books were published and translated into Dutch and French. The books greatly influenced writers such as Daniel Defoe, Samuel Taylor Coleridge and Jonathan Swift, and scientists and navigators such as James Cook, Matthew Flinders and Charles Darwin. However, at the time, the British must have been disappointed that Dampier's expedition had yielded so little apparent bounty for the British Empire to exploit.

*

More than half a century passed before any European nation again ventured to the Great South Land. Then, in 1768, the British sent Lieutenant James Cook on a voyage to the Pacific to observe the transit of the planet Venus.

The transit of Venus is similar to the moon's solar eclipse and occurs when Venus moves across the face of the sun when viewed from the earth. Observing such transits helped scientists calculate the distance of the earth from the sun and other planets, which in turn was helpful in navigation. Transits of Venus are predictable phenomena that come in pairs – eight years apart – and each pair of eclipses occurs about every 100 years. A transit had occurred in 1761 and Cook was sent to observe the second of the pair.

Only after successfully witnessing the transit of Venus, was Cook to look for parts of the Great South Land, which was thought to surround the South Pole and had been 'formerly discovered yet . . . imperfectly explored'.[10]

The Royal Geographical Society had recommended that the Scottish geographer Alexander Dalrymple lead the expedition, but the Admiralty was strongly opposed to having anyone but an experienced naval officer commanding one of their ships. Cook was chosen because he had previously impressed the naval hierarchy with his navigation skills.

James Cook was born in Yorkshire in 1728 into relatively humble circumstances. His father, a farmer, was Scottish and his mother was from Yorkshire. Cook grew up on the farm where his father worked as a labourer, and he attended a village school. At eighteen, he took an apprenticeship on a merchant ship that sailed from Whitby to the Baltic Sea. In 1755, he joined the Royal Navy as a master's mate on the *Eagle* and two years later was promoted to master on the *Pembroke*, sailing with the Channel fleet.

In 1758, aged twenty-nine, he served in the Seven Years War (1756–63) and was part of the successful siege of Fort Louisburg on the St Lawrence River in Canada, which opened the way for the British to take Quebec the following year and end French rule in North America. By the time Cook arrived back in England in 1762, he was recognised for his superior navigating and mapping skills, which he'd developed in Newfoundland and Nova Scotia, and on the St Lawrence River. In a letter to the secretary of the Admiralty, Admiral Lord Colville recommended Cook for 'greater undertakings' and referred to his 'genius and capacity'.[11]

Cook's first great voyage, which resulted in the establishment of New South Wales and led to the British settlement of Australia, is his most celebrated and is widely regarded as his most momentous. Cook left England on 26 August 1768 on the *Endeavour*. The expedition reached Tahiti on 10 April in plenty of time for astronomer Charles Green to observe the transit of Venus on 3 June. The *Endeavour* then sailed south-west, looking for the great continent. Finding nothing, Cook headed for New Zealand and became the second European after Abel Tasman to reach its south coast. Cook spent the next six months charting the New Zealand coast and confirmed that it consisted of two major islands. Then he headed west to look again for the east coast of New Holland.

At 6 am on 20 April 1770, he found it, when his second lieutenant, Zachary Hicks, who was on watch on the *Endeavour*, sighted land. Cook decided 'to follow the direction of the coast northward'.[12] The voyage of more than 3000 kilometres would take him five months.

Ten days into the journey, Cook entered a large bay that was later named Botany Bay after botanist Joseph Banks and his team collected hundreds of plants and seeds from the area. Cook stayed seven days in the bay, long enough to collect fresh water and wood, and for Banks to collect his specimens, before heading off to the north. Cook could have had no inkling that the British would later choose Botany Bay as the location for Australia's first convict colony.

At the northern tip of the coast, Cook successfully navigated his way through the Torres Strait, whereupon he claimed the entire east coast of Australia for Britain on 22 August 1770:

> notwithstanding I had in the name of His Majesty taken possession of several places upon this coast, I now once more hoisted English colours, and in the name of His Majesty King George the Third took possession of the whole eastern coast ... by the name of New South Wales ... together with all the bays, harbours, rivers, and islands, situated upon the said coast; after which we fired 3 volleys of small arms, which were answer'd by the like number from the ship.[13]

Cook was well aware that, while he may have been the first to chart and claim the east coast of Australia, the west had long before been mapped by others:

> on the western side I can make no new discovery, the honour of which belongs to the Dutch navigators, but the eastern coast from the latitude of 38 degrees South, down to this place, I am confident, was never seen or visited by any European before us . . . [14]

Cook's mapping of more than 3000 kilometres of what was the world's longest remaining stretch of unknown coast had enormous and far-reaching consequences, opening the way for British colonisation and the eventual establishment of what would become the country of Australia.

*

In 1779, almost ten years after James Cook's visit to Botany Bay, the British House of Commons established an inquiry to solve the nation's problem of escalating convict numbers. Botanist Joseph Banks appeared before the committee and, when asked where the convicts might be sent, had no hesitation in recommending Botany Bay:

> *Joseph Banks* Esquire, being requested, in case it should be thought expedient to establish a Colony of convicted felons in any distant part of the Globe, from whence their escape might be difficult, and where, from the fertility of the soil, they might be enabled to maintain themselves, after the first year, with little or no aid from the mother country, to give his opinion what place would be the most eligible for such settlement . . . that the place which appeared to him best adapted for such a purpose, was Botany Bay, on the coast

of New Holland, in the Indian Ocean, which was about seven months voyage from England; that he apprehended there would be little probability of any Opposition from the natives, as, during his stay there, in the year 1770, he saw very few, and did not think there were above fifty in all the neighbourhood, and had reason to believe the country was very thinly peopled; those he saw were naked, treacherous, and armed with lances, but extremely cowardly, and constantly retired from our people when they made the least appearance of resistance . . . in this bay in the end of April and the beginning of May 1770 . . . the weather was mild and moderate; that the climate, he apprehended, was similar to that about Toulouse in the South of France . . . the proportion of rich soil was small in comparison to the barren, but sufficient to support a very large number of people; there were no tame animals, and he saw no wild ones during his stay of ten days, but he observed the dung of what were called kangourous, which were about the size of a middling sheep . . . and difficult to catch; some of those animals he saw in another part of the bay, upon the same continent; there were no beasts of prey, and he did not doubt but our oxen and sheep, if carried there, would thrive and increase; there was a great plenty of fish, he took a large quantity by hauling the seine, and struck several stingrays, a kind of skate, all very large; one weighed 336 pounds. The grass was long and luxuriant, and there were some eatable vegetables, particularly a sort of wild spinage; the country was well supplied with water; there was an abundance of timber and fuel, sufficient for any number of buildings, which might be found necessary. . .[15]

Banks's glowing report of Botany Bay to the parliamentary committee was at odds with his own, less enthusiastic journal entries made during his visit to the bay. Following an inland expedition four days after the *Endeavour* arrived at Botany Bay on 29 April 1770, Banks had recorded in his journal: 'Where we went a good way in to the country which in this place is very sandy and resembles something of the moors of England, as no trees grows upon it but everything is covered with a thin brush of plants about as high as the knees.'[16]

Why Banks's evidence to the parliamentary committee was so 'strangely at variance'[17] with his original journal entries is puzzling. It has been suggested that his desire to shape the future British Empire 'caused his memory to play tricks'.[18] It is also worth noting that Banks stood to gain from any British settlement on the east coast of Australia. When he visited Botany Bay on the *Endeavour*, he had collected many botanical species and would benefit from ships returning with more specimens. Banks's influence was so great, sheds were installed on the decks of British ships to store botanical samples.

Lieutenant James Cook had recorded his own views of Botany Bay when he had landed there back in 1770, and they, too, differed from Banks's submission to the committee. Cook had said that the land was uncultivated and produced virtually nothing fit to eat. However, while Banks was giving his evidence to the House of Commons Committee, it was not yet known in London that Cook had been killed, and was not in a position to shape events in England.

Cook had died in February 1779 while searching for the passage linking the Pacific and Atlantic oceans. When he had anchored in Kealakekua Bay, Hawaii, he and his men had initially established good relations with the locals. However, when a dispute followed the theft of one of the small boats belonging to the English, Cook led a party back to shore. In the fight that followed, Cook was cut down and killed in a spray of 'daggers and spears'.[19]

Despite Joseph Banks's recommendations, the British Government made no decision with regard to where to send the convicts for another six years. By then there were complaints of 'overburdened' prisons and hulks, and a fear of 'epidemic distemper' breaking out of the jails and into the wider community. Nevertheless, while 'parliament, press, pamphlet and pulpit' were all calling for something to be done, the British Government continued to procrastinate.[20] In April 1785, an increasingly frustrated House of Commons held another inquiry that again heard of the system's failures and what was seen as the need to transport some of the convicts overseas.

More than a year later, in June 1786, the British Cabinet considered a number of sites, including Canada, the West Indies and Africa, but for various reasons most options were ruled out. Finally, the home secretary, Lord Sydney, announced in August 1786 that the destination would be New South Wales, which was very much the last resort:

> The several gaols and places for the confinement of felons in this kingdom being in so crowded a state that the greatest danger is to be apprehended, not only from their escape, but for infectious distempers, which may hourly be expected to break out among them, His Majesty, desirous of preventing by any possible means the ill consequences which might happen from either of these causes, has been pleased to signify to me his royal commands that measures should immediately be pursued for sending out of this kingdom such convicts as are under sentence or order of transportation . . . His Majesty has thought it advisable to fix upon Botany Bay.[21]

The man chosen to lead the expedition to Botany Bay and become the first governor of Britain's new colony of New South Wales had nothing particularly outstanding in his career to recommend him. But although Captain Arthur Phillip was nearly fifty years of age and living in semi-retirement at his Hampshire farm when he was appointed, he would nevertheless prove to be a good choice.

The circumstances of what was to be such an important appointment are somewhat mysterious. Like James Cook before him, Arthur Phillip was an example of how, at that time, men from relatively modest backgrounds could progress through the ranks of the British Navy in a way far less likely in the British Army, where class and connections were still more dominant.

Arthur Phillip was born in London in 1738. He entered Greenwich boys' naval college after the death of his father, who had come from Germany as a language teacher. Phillip had some help getting into the school – his mother's first husband was a naval officer, Captain Herbert, who was from a well-connected family.

Young Arthur Phillip spent his first two years on a merchant ship before transferring in 1755 to the British Navy as a captain's servant on the *Buckingham*. Later that year, he became an able seaman, then a yeoman corporal, before sailing the following year from the West Indies to the Mediterranean, where he was involved in a battle with French ships off the island of Majorca on 20 May.

Over the next few years, Phillip served on a number of British warships and saw action on the *Aurora* at the Battle of Quiberon Bay in the Bay of Biscay in 1759. In 1760, he was promoted to master's mate, continuing his steady climb up the naval promotional ladder. But after the Seven Years War, Phillip was pensioned off by the navy at half-pay (fairly standard practice when hostilities subsided), and became a farmer near Lyndhurst in Hampshire. There he married a widow, Margaret Charlotte Tybott. The couple had no children and, over the next forty years, there was an almost total absence of references to his marriage in any reports, letters or journals.

In 1774, with the approval of the Admiralty, Phillip became the commander of Portuguese warships in the renewed war between Portugal and Spain. He served for more than three years, leaving in 1778 with high praise from the Portuguese for his bravery.

After returning to England, Phillip was again largely idle and regularly wrote to the Admiralty in search of further appointments. There has been much speculation but little evidence as to why Phillip was eventually asked to take the convict fleet to New South Wales. His appointment did not please the first lord of the Admiralty, Lord Howe, who said that the little knowledge he had of Phillip would not have led him 'to select him for a service of this complicated nature'.[22]

It may have been Evan Nepean, then an assistant to the colonial secretary Lord Sydney, who influenced Phillip's appointment. Nepean knew Phillip well from when Phillip had been attached to the Portuguese Navy and Nepean was responsible for British Navy spies and intelligence. Perhaps Phillip did have a certain amount of influence with the right people after all.

The transport of convicts overseas was an experiment in social engineering that was breathtaking in its scope and ambition. It involved the forced exile of an entirely unwanted strata of society – the growing convict class – to a remote spot on the other side of the globe about which practically nothing was known.

The First Fleet that sailed from England in 1787 was, at the time, the largest overseas migration the world had ever seen. The expedition took with it two years' supply of food and the tools and equipment to build a new life and become self-sustaining. Over the following seventy years, Britain would send almost 170,000 convicts to Australia, and in so doing both rid itself of a social problem and add a number of new colonies to its growing empire.

The fleet of eleven tiny, wooden ships that sailed from Portsmouth in the early hours of Sunday 13 May 1787, carried more than 1400 people, including nearly 800 convicts, and several hundred seamen, navy officers, marines, and some wives and children. The convicts loaded onto the transports were not chosen with any regard to their fitness for the long voyage or their suitability for building a new settlement once they got there. Only those too frail to walk were excluded, and fourteen pregnant convicts were boarded who would give birth during the voyage. The youngest convict was John Hudson, who was nine years old when sentenced for theft; the oldest was Dorothy Handland, who was believed to be eighty-two when the fleet sailed. Almost 60 per cent of the prisoners had been convicted of stealing food or other goods of relatively little value.

A captain of the First Fleet marines, Watkin Tench, recorded the convicts' fear and apprehension, which they conveyed in the last letters written to their families: 'The . . . constant language [of the letters] was an apprehension of the impracticality of returning home, the dread of the sickly passage and the fearful prospect of a distant and barbarous country.'[23]

On the first morning, as the ships passed the Isle of Wight, Tench, who was aboard the *Charlotte*, went below decks to register the mood of the convicts. He noted that among them some felt 'the pang of being severed, perhaps forever, from their native land [which] could not be wholly supressed'.[24]

Conditions on the convict transports were appalling. The largest of the ships was barely 30 metres long and carried 200 prisoners, plus stores and provisions. Many of the convicts had already spent years in cramped, over-crowded prisons and hulks in Britain and would now spend eight more months locked up in the bowels of the trans-ports in even more cramped quarters. When the convicts were allowed on deck for exercise, they were restricted to a few metres. In their quarters, there were no portholes and no candles – due to the risk of fire – meaning they spent most of the time in the dark with limited fresh air. The heat was particularly unbearable in the tropics, espe-cially given that the short supplies of drinking water were strictly rationed.

Rats, bed bugs, lice, fleas and cockroaches thrived on all ships. A constant threat to health came from the bilges, which were the lowest part of the vessels, where all the excess liquids, including urine, tended to drain.

While crossing the Atlantic, the number of ill convicts on one transport, the *Alexander*, increased dramatically. When Chief Surgeon John White inspected the ship, he complained that the level of the toxic bilge water was rising so fast that the silver buttons on the officers' uniforms 'were turned nearly black'. White said that, when the hatches above the convict quarters were removed, 'the stench was so powerful that it was scarcely possible to stand over them'.[25]

When the fleet reached the Dutch-controlled port of the Cape of Good Hope on 13 October, it replenished its stock of water and food for the last long leg of more than 10,000 kilometres across the Great Southern Ocean to the coast of New South Wales. It also took aboard more plants, including fig trees, bamboo, sugar cane, quince, apple, strawberry, oak and myrtle. On the decks of the already overcrowded ships, the carpenters built wooden stalls, and more than 500 animals were boarded, including cows, bulls, pigs, horses, ducks, chickens, sheep, goats and geese.

Finally, on 13 November, the fleet set out on the long haul, which would take more than two months in the worst sailing conditions it had yet encountered. Soon, in high seas and strong winds, the livestock began to die, and in the middle of November there was an outbreak of dysentery among the convicts that soon spread to the marines. The epidemic lasted for six weeks but, despite the large number of serious cases, only one marine died.

Two weeks after leaving the cape, Arthur Phillip decided to split the fleet, taking the fastest four ships ahead. He intended to scout out the best location on the New South Wales coast and start constructing the new settlement before the bulk of the fleet arrived. Joseph Banks's journals would have been available to Phillip, the navy and the government. Perhaps aware of Banks's earlier, more negative assessment of Botany Bay, Phillip may have wanted the time to explore other possible sites.

Captain Phillip took off with the fastest four ships, leaving the slowest seven to follow under the command of his deputy, John Hunter. It was the height of the southern-hemisphere summer, but both fleets were sailing at high latitudes, where it was icy cold, the seas high and the weather bad. It was tough sailing.

Arthur Bowes Smyth, a surgeon on one of the slower ships, the convict women's transport the *Lady Penrhyn*, described the conditions:

The sky blackened, the wind arose and in half an hour more it blew a perfect hurricane, accompanied with thunder, lightning and rain . . . Every other ship in the fleet except the *Sirius* sustained some damage . . . During the storm the convict women in our ship were so terrified that most of them were down on their knees at prayers . . . [26]

The four faster ships also met heavy weather, and when they reached Botany Bay on the afternoon of 18 January 1788, their passengers were surprised to see Hunter's seven ships all arrive during the following forty hours.

It had been a remarkably successful voyage despite the ordeal. The First Fleet had sailed to the other side of the world without the loss of any ships and with fewer deaths than most of the later convoys that brought convicts to Australia over the next fifty years. Only sixty-nine convicts had died, most while the ships waited to leave Portsmouth or on the first leg to the Canary Islands. This suggests that Arthur Phillip's claim that the general health of the convicts improved during the voyage was probably correct.

However, Phillip quickly realised that Botany Bay was unsuitable for settlement. As Watkin Tench wrote:

we set out to observe the country, which, on inspection rather disappointed our hopes, being invariable sandy and unpromising for the purpose of cultivation . . . Close to us was the spring at which Mr. Cook watered, but we did not think the water very excellent, nor did it run freely. In the evening we returned on board, not greatly pleased with the latter part of our discoveries . . . [27]

After only three days searching the shores of Botany Bay, Phillip decided to set out in search of a more suitable site.

In his journal, he recorded, 'we at daylight in the morning weighed with a light breeze . . . [and] steered along the shore N-N-E and . . . about two to three miles from the land and abreast the bay of harbour wherein there appeared safe anchorage, which I called Port Jackson.'[28]

It was at Port Jackson that Captain Phillip established the first European settlement in Australia, naming the settlement Sydney, after Britain's home secretary, Lord Sydney.

The emerging European and American concepts of democracy and liberalism would for years have no place in Sydney or the colony of New South Wales. Until 1824, the military governors of the colony were absolute rulers, with almost unlimited powers to impose order and inflict punishment, including executions. But, for all Arthur Phillip's powers, during his years leading the fledging settlement he would confront the threat of disaster again and again, as miserable harvests and declining food stocks took Sydney Town to the brink not only of failure but also of starvation.

Chapter 2

The Early Days of Struggle

Hope is no more, and a new scene of distress and misery opens our view . . . For all the grain of every kind which we have been able to raise in two years and three months would not support us for three weeks.

THE TINY BRITISH SETTLEMENT OF SYDNEY STRUGGLED TO survive in the first two years of its existence, and it was only thanks to the arrival of the second fleet in June 1790 that the settlement's inhabitants avoided starvation.

From the very beginning, the English found the New South Wales climate harsher than anything they had previously experienced. In addition to the hot summer winds, which resembled a 'blast from a heated oven', they were confronted by tumultuous summer storms, the like of which they had never encountered in Britain.[1] The struggle to build a new home in the harsh and unfriendly Australian bush took years, and most of the settlers – particularly the convicts – lived largely on the rations they had brought with them. For some years, many lived without a chair to sit on, a table to eat at or a cot or a bed to sleep in.

The tough Australian scrub, which came right down to the water's edge, was difficult to clear. The settlers found that their wood-cutting tools were not strong enough for the gnarled hardwood gum trees, and Phillip complained that it could take a day to cut down each tree, which 'splits and warps' and was 'useless' for building.[2]

The fleet encountered Aboriginal people on the first day it landed in Botany Bay, and again when it came to Port Jackson, but there was no violence, which gave Phillip and his colleagues confidence that the locals were as peaceable as Banks had assured the House of Commons Committee. The British Government had made it clear in its instructions to Phillip that, if possible, it wanted good relations with the locals. However, interactions between the new settlers and the local Aboriginal people were characterised by a mutual incomprehension that gradually worsened. The settlers had virtually no knowledge or understanding of the local inhabitants beyond the brief observations of Cook and Banks, who had stayed barely a week in Botany Bay almost eighteen years earlier.

After some initial encounters, the new settlers had little further interaction with the Indigenous people, who for some months stayed clear of them. As the year progressed, however, there were a number of incidents in which both whites and blacks were killed, causing increased hostility between the European and the Aboriginal people.

Chief Surgeon John White believed that the increased attacks against the settlers were retaliatory:

30th [May 1788] Captain Campbell of the marines, who had been up the harbour to procure some rushes for thatch, brought to the hospital the bodies of William Okey and Samuel Davis, two rush-cutters whom he had found murdered by the natives in a shocking manner . . . What was the motive or cause of this melancholy catastrophe we have not been able to discover, but from the civility shewn on all occasions to the officers by the natives, whenever any of them are met, I am strongly inclined to think that they must have been provoked and injured by the convicts.[3]

Within a few months of the First Fleet's arrival, food stocks declined and, with the failure to grow food locally, the struggle to establish the settlement became a full-blown crisis. Sydney Cove may have had a stream of fresh water and a good harbour, but the soil proved to be as poor as that at Botany Bay. Before the coming of winter, Phillip wrote home in a sombre tone:

The great labour in clearing the ground will not permit more than eight acres to be sown this year with wheat and barley. At the same time the immense number of ants and field-mice will render our crops very uncertain. Part of the live stock brought from the Cape, small as it was, has been lost, and our resource in fish is also uncertain.[4]

Only a few months later, Phillip had to report to England that the first harvest had been an almost total failure and had yielded only enough food to support the colony 'for a few days'. Consequently, none of the grain was fed to the settlers but was instead saved as seed for the following year's sowing:

it was now found that very little of the English wheat had vegetated and a very considerable quantity of barley and many seeds had rotted in the ground, having been heated in the passage, and some much injured by the weevil. All the barley and wheat, likewise, which had been put on board the *Supply* at the Cape were destroyed by the weevil.[5]

Despite the colony's dire predicament, Phillip tried to be optimistic about its long-term prospects, saying that, eventually, it would 'prove a most valuable acquisition to Great Britain'.[6] The head of the marines in Sydney, Major Robert Ross, strongly disagreed and wrote a letter at the same time as Phillip:

with respect to the utility of a settlement upon this coast . . . it never can be made to answer the intended purpose or wish of Government, for the country seems totally destitute of everything that can be an object for a commercial nation, a very fine harbour excepted, and I much fear that the nature of the soil is such as will not be brought to yield more than sufficient sustenance for the needy emigrants whose desperate fortunes may induce them to try the experiment.[7]

Already harsh, life in the colony got progressively worse during the first year of settlement. Hundreds of convicts living on reduced rations were crowded into poor accommodation made of canvas tents or strips of bark. Clothing was also wearing out and replacements running short. By the time the first winter approached, many of the settlers, including the marines, had worn out their shoes and were forced to go about their business barefoot.

News of the crisis in Sydney reached London on the First Fleet ships, which returned to England in early in

1789. The government reacted quickly. In April 1789, Lord Sydney wrote to the Admiralty to say King George had authorised the urgent dispatch of a supply ship to relieve the colony:

> The letters which have been received from Captain Phillip, Governor of New South Wales, representing that a great part of the provisions sent out with him to the settlement . . . had been expended, and that there is an immediate occasion for a further supply, together with certain articles of clothing, tools, and implements for agriculture, medicines &c. . . . his Majesty has given orders that one of his ships of war of two decks, with only her upper tier of guns, shall forthwith be got ready to carry out the said provisions and stores.[8]

Five months later, in September 1789, the *Guardian*, commanded by twenty-seven-year-old Captain Edward Riou, left Portsmouth with almost 1000 tonnes of supplies. The ship made good time to Cape Town, arriving on 24 November, where it stayed three weeks to restock food and load some additional livestock for Sydney.

The ship left the Cape on 11 December and sailed south across the Great Southern Ocean, catching the strong westerly winds. However, on Christmas Eve, it smashed into a giant iceberg. The *Guardian* was listing badly and part of its top deck was already under water, but Captain Riou and the remaining crew stayed on board, pumping to keep the ship afloat.

About half the crew scrambled onto five small lifeboats, but only one made it to safety. Its fifteen survivors were rescued when it was spotted about 400 kilometres off the coast of Natal by a passing French ship on its way from India to Cape Town.

Almost two months after hitting the iceberg, the *Guardian* was still being pumped by a desperate crew when, on 21 February 1790, a Dutch ship on its way back to Europe from Batavia saw it drifting in the Indian Ocean south of Madagascar. The Dutch helped tug the *Guardian* to the Cape of Good Hope. The following April, the ship was torn off its moorings and broken up by a gale.

Meanwhile, back in Sydney, unaware that the British had sent the *Guardian*, still less that it had been wrecked, the settlers were in a state of crisis. As Marine Lieutenant Watkin Tench wrote, all attention was on where the next meal would come from:

> Famine . . . was approaching with gigantic strides, and gloom and dejection overspread every countenance. Men abandoned themselves to the most desponding reflections, and adopted the most extravagant conjectures. Still we were on the tiptoe of expectation . . . every morning from daylight until the sun sunk, did we sweep the horizon, in the hope of seeing a sail. At every fleeting speck which arose from the bosom of the sea, the heart bounded and the telescope was lifted to the eye . . . all our labour and attention were turned on one object – the procuring of food.[9]

In April 1790, John White wrote to a friend in London to say that the settlers had not been able to produce any food. 'Hope is no more, and a new scene of distress and misery opens our view . . . For all the grain of every kind which we have been able to raise in two years and three months would not support us for three weeks.'[10]

Finally, two and a half years after the arrival of the First Fleet, when all hope had gone, the signal flag was broken out on Port Jackson's South Head. At half past three in the afternoon on 3 June 1790, a ship's sail was sighted. It was the *Lady Juliana*, the first ship of the Second Fleet, bringing more convicts and, more importantly, food. Tench captured the excitement:

> I was sitting in my hut, musing on our fate, when a confused clamour in the street drew my attention. I opened my door, and saw several women with children in their arms running to and fro with distracted looks, congratulating each other, and kissing their infants . . . [I] instantly started out, and ran to a hill, where, by the assistance of a pocket glass, my hopes were realized. My next door neighbour, a brother-officer, was with me, but we could not speak. We wrung each other by the hand, with our eyes and hearts overflowing.[11]

Four more ships arrived during the next few weeks, carrying between them enough food to end the crisis that had threatened the early convict settlement. However, the arrival of the Second Fleet was also an infamous episode in the early history of Australia and one of the worst chapters in maritime history. Of more than 1000 convicts who in England boarded the three largest transports – the *Surprize*, the *Neptune* and the *Scarborough* – nearly a quarter had died on the voyage. Of the remaining 756 who arrived alive, 486 were immediately hospitalised in hastily erected tents. A hundred and twenty-four would die during their first days in the colony. Unlike the First Fleet, on which the convicts were well fed and granted limited exercise, the prisoners on the Second Fleet were confined, mostly in chains, below decks for the entire voyage, and had not been fed properly.

Arthur Phillip wrote to London complaining that 'it would be a want of duty not to say that it was occasioned by the contractors having crowded too many on board those ships, and from their being too much confined during the passage'.[12]

After the arrival of the second and subsequent fleets with more provisions, the food crisis began to abate. Over the next decade, with the arrival of regular supplies and with the increased agricultural production west of Sydney and on Norfolk Island, the colony gradually began producing enough food to subsist.

*

After almost five years in the colony, Arthur Phillip returned to England on the *Atlantic* on 11 December 1792. He had wanted to leave earlier, having first requested to be relieved more than two years before, in April 1790. In his letter to Lord Sydney, he had given no sound reason for his request, but, in a separate letter to Admiralty Secretary Evan Nepean, he had made a rare reference to his wife, saying he thought she was dying and that their affairs needed attending to.[13] However, the government was well aware that the settlement was still struggling and rejected his application, saying:

I am much concerned that this situation of your private affairs should have been such as to render this application necessary at a time when your services in New South Wales are so extremely important to the public. I cannot, therefore, refrain from expressing my earnest hope that you may have it in your power so to arrange your private concerns that you may be able, without material inconvenience, to continue in your Government for a short time longer.[14]

In his five years as governor, Phillip had done a good job. He had successfully brought the First Fleet to New South Wales and established a new colony. After initial harvest failures, he had overseen productive farms west of Sydney and on Norfolk Island. He had kept a cool head and sensibly rationed food, and steered the colony through its profound first crisis.

After Phillip left to return to England, it would take nearly three years before his successor, John Hunter, reached Sydney. Part of the delay was due to the British Government being preoccupied with France, whose revolution had started in July 1789. John Hunter was appointed in January 1794 and commissioned to sail two months later, in March. However, there were delays to his departure and he did not leave until March 1795, arriving in Sydney six months later, on 7 September.

During the delay between governors, the colony was left in the hands of the most senior officers in the Marine Corps. For the first two years, thirty-four-year-old Major Francis Grose was in command, and when he returned to England it passed to Captain William Paterson. Over those few years, the marines' control over the colony's economy became entrenched, and their growing political power plagued the colony's administration for the next two decades.

In the two years that Grose was acting as governor, he established military rule in New South Wales and strengthened the authority of the marines. He abolished civilian courts and put all magistrates under the authority of Captain Joseph Foveaux, a military colleague. After the poor crops of 1793, he cut the rations of the convicts, but not those of the Marine Corps, overturning Phillip's policy of equal rations for all.

First under Grose and then under Paterson, marine officers were given generous land grants and free convict labour to work their farms. The restriction of the trade in alcohol – namely spirits – was relaxed and eventually become monopolised by the military, which earned it the nickname the 'Rum Corps'. New South Wales, like many British territories at the time, was short of coins, so rum also became a form of currency.

Early in his term, Grose wrote to Britain's colonial secretary Henry Dundas to explain that giving economic control to the Marine Corps was the only way the colony could prosper: '[The Corps officers are] the only description of settlers on whom reliance can be placed . . . their exertions are really astonishing . . . I shall encourage their pursuit as much as is in my power.'[15]

One of the beneficiaries of the generosity of the military governors was Lieutenant John Macarthur, whom Grose appointed to the position of director of public works when Macarthur was twenty-five. Grose also granted him some of the best available land for farming. A man driven by vexation and greed, Macarthur saw 'plots and insults everywhere' and 'spent half his life in imbroglios'.[16] Variously described as arrogant, forceful and cunning, Macarthur hounded and attempted to intimidate every governor from Phillip to Macquarie, and was at the heart of the conspiracy that overthrew Governor William Bligh in 1808.

Twenty-three-year-old Macarthur had arrived on the Second Fleet of convicts in June 1790. His father had been a draper and mercer, who had somehow managed to obtain an ensign's commission for his fifteen-year-old son, John, in the Marine Corps. John Macarthur was trained for the American War of Independence, but when the war ended he was retired on half-pay and for the next five years lived and worked on a farm in rural Devon. In 1788, he was stationed in Gibraltar and the following year earned a promotion to the rank of lieutenant by agreeing to transfer to the New South Wales Marine Corps destined for Botany Bay in 1789.

Macarthur sailed on the *Neptune* with his wife of one year, Elizabeth, and their infant son, Edward. In contrast to her irascible husband, Elizabeth Macarthur was widely popular and gracious in manner. She was the first educated woman to arrive in Australia and was for some time the only female to be received at the governor's table.

At the start of the voyage to New South Wales, Macarthur argued with the ship's master, Captain Gilbert, resulting in a duel – though when it was fought neither man was injured. After Macarthur continued to disagree with Gilbert, he, his wife and son had to be transferred to the *Scarborough* before the fleet reached Cape Town. After Cape Town, Macarthur became seriously ill with what was thought to be rheumatic fever and lumbago. Though he recovered, he would experience recurring symptoms throughout his life.

Upon his arrival, Macarthur was posted to Rouse Hill, west of Sydney, where his aggressive conduct brought him into conflict with Arthur Phillip. Described as 'incorrigibly haughty', Macarthur was accused in the early days of treading a path 'strewn with minor hostilities', which led to his withdrawal from all social intercourse at Government House after a reprimand from Governor Phillip.[17]

Francis Grose was acting governor of New South Wales for two years. Debilitated by wounds he'd suffered in the American War of Independence more than a decade before, he returned to England in December 1794. Still awaiting the arrival of a new governor, the administration of the colony was now in the hands of its next most senior military officer, Captain William Paterson.

Thirty-nine-year-old Paterson had a passion for alcohol and for botany, and had written a book about the flora of southern Africa, which he had dedicated to Sir Joseph Banks. It is believed that Banks was influential in his appointment to New South Wales. The captain had first arrived in Sydney in October 1791 with his wife, Elizabeth, and the following month had been sent away for the next two and a half years to be the head of the marine detachment to Norfolk Island.

Paterson returned to Sydney in 1793 and with the departure of Francis Grose became the second acting governor in December 1794. During his nine months of running New South Wales, he managed to grant nearly 5000 more acres (2023 hectares) of land, largely to marine colleagues, and at the same time did nothing to curtail the growing role played by the officers in controlling the local economy. He also promoted John Macarthur to the rank of marine captain, thus consolidating Macarthur's power in the colony. By the time John Hunter arrived as the replacement for Arthur Phillip, Captain Macarthur, while still in the marines, had become one of the colony's biggest farmers. After Hunter took over as governor, Paterson returned to England.

Captain John Hunter had been born in Leith, Scotland, in 1737, the son of a ship master. He had gone to sea as a sixteen-year-old captain's servant before becoming an able seaman, then a midshipman. He became a lieutenant in 1770, but he was not given his commission for another decade, in 1780. During his naval career, he had served in a variety of places, including North America during the War of Independence, the West Indies and the East Indies, before being appointed Phillip's deputy on the First Fleet. So this was Hunter's second tour of duty to New South Wales. In 1789, he had taken the *Sirius* and circumnavigated the globe to fetch grain for the starving colony from Cape Town. The following year, he was in command of the *Sirius* when it was wrecked on Norfolk Island and was stranded there for nearly a year until the next ship arrived to take him back to Sydney.

Sailing to Sydney with Hunter in 1795 on the *Reliance* was a young naval lieutenant, Matthew Flinders, and a naval surgeon, George Bass, who, with Hunter's blessing and very little available shipping, would achieve some remarkable exploration feats.

At the time Hunter became governor, the population of the colony was a little over 3000 people. There were only a dozen or so free settlers, and about 60 per cent were convicts. The remainder were ex-convicts, military and civilian personnel. Hunter did not turn out to be entirely effective in governing the colony, but he was more successful in ordering the exploration of vast stretches of the Australian coastline. When he arrived, the map of the New South Wales coast extended only thirty kilometres north and south of Sydney. It had not yet been confirmed whether the east coast, called New South Wales, and the west coast, named New Holland, were part of the same land mass or separated by a strait or a sea.

Hunter tried to rally support in England for more exploration, but, owing to the long and costly wars with France, there was little interest in the discovery of any territory surrounding a tiny convict colony on the far side of the globe. He also tried to enlist the support of the highly influential Sir Joseph Banks, who replied that further British commitment to Australian exploration was currently out of the question:

> the situation in Europe is at present so critical & his Majesty's Ministers so fully employed in business of the deepest importance, that it is scarce possible to gain a moment's audience on any subject but those that stand

foremost in their minds; & colonies of all kinds, you may
be assured, are now put into the back ground.[18]

Still, with only limited resources, Hunter managed to
organise the exploration of the coast of New South Wales
for more than 1000 kilometres north of Sydney and an
even greater distance to the south. In 1795 and 1796, he
authorised Flinders and Bass to explore as far south as
Lake Illawarra in a tiny, three-metre dingy they named
Tom Thumb.

The following year, without Flinders, Bass sailed south
for 1000 kilometres in a whaleboat crewed by six sailors,
and charted Western Port and other parts of what is
now the Victorian coast. Between the end of 1797 and
the beginning of 1798, Flinders and Bass, together in the
slightly larger *Norfolk*, circumnavigated Van Diemen's
Land, thus proving it was separated by a strait from the
mainland. At Flinders' suggestion, Governor John Hunter
agreed that it be named Bass's Strait.

Shortly after their important discovery, George Bass
abruptly left the navy to become a merchant. He returned
to London, married and went back to sea, and was last
seen leaving Sydney in 1802 on his ship the *Venus*. Many
attempts over many years have failed to find any trace of
what happened to Bass when he headed east from Sydney
bound for Chile.

At Hunter's behest, Matthew Flinders conducted other
explorations of the New South Wales coast, including that
of Moreton Bay, which was named by James Cook and
later became the site of the city of Brisbane.

*

Hunter was less successful in his attempts to break up the military control of the local economy, and ultimately was unable to break the marines' stranglehold on farming and commerce, the currency of rum remaining largely 'at the mercy of the monopolistic trading practices of the military hierarchy'.[19] His attempts to challenge the authority of the Rum Corps brought him into conflict with the officers of the New South Wales Corps, including the powerful John Macarthur.

Macarthur had already written to the home secretary, the Duke of Portland, complaining about Hunter. In the letter, he charged Hunter with extravagance in the spending of government money and granting land to men who were incapable of cultivating it. He also complained of the moral condition of the colony and that 'vice of every description was openly encouraged'.[20]

Hunter was angered and hurt by the attacks and also wrote to the Duke of Portland, pointing out that Macarthur earned money from traffic in spirits and that the officer's ring was partly responsible for the moral state of the colony.[21] The following year, Hunter wrote to Philip Gidley King, who had been his immediate subordinate on the First Fleet in 1788 and would be his successor as governor of New South Wales. In the letter, Hunter accused Macarthur of 'horrible depravity and wickedness' and said his business interests were a source of his difficulties: 'There is not a person in this colony whose opinions I hold in greater contempt than I do this busybody's, because I have ever observed that under the most specious and plausible of them there has always been covered a self-interest.'[22]

A month later, he wrote again to the Duke of Portland to reiterate that he thought Macarthur's conduct concealed 'a degree of malevolence' and, 'I have long been of the opinion that his troublesome turn of mind should've been made known much sooner than it has.'[23]

The Duke of Portland replied to Hunter demanding a response to Macarthur's allegations, which he said 'highly affects the credit of your administration and the general character of the Government'.[24] Macarthur's other allegations included the claim that goods in the colony under Hunter had 'doubled in price' and 'that spirits and other articles are purchased by officers of His Majesty's forces in New South Wales and retailed by them at most exorbitant prices to the lowest orders of settlers and convicts'. Most damaging of all was the charge 'that this sort of traffic is not confined to the officers, but is carried out in the Government House'.[25] Hunter's position was weakened by the discovery that many of his own staff were corrupt, including his steward Nicholas Franklyn, who committed suicide after being accused of orchestrating an illegal trading operation in rum.

Hunter attempted to defend himself further, but the government had made up its mind. At the end of 1800, the London authorities sent Philip Gidley King to Sydney carrying a letter to Hunter from the Duke of Portland telling the governor he was sacked:

Having now made all the observations which appear to me to be necessary . . . it is with very sincere concern that I find myself obliged to add that I felt myself called upon by [a] sense of duty . . . to express my disapprobation of the manner in which the government of the settlement has been administered by you in so many respects – that I am commanded to signify to you the King's pleasure to return to this kingdom by the first conveyance which offers itself after the arrival of Lieutenant-Governor King, who is authorised by his Majesty to take upon him the government of that settlement immediately on your departure from it.[26]

The avuncular Hunter was widely liked and respected but had struggled in the role of governor. Devastated, he left Sydney on the *Buffalo* and arrived back in England in May 1810, demanding an inquiry into his management of the colony. He was not only denied the chance to clear his name but was also given the cold shoulder by the British Government and denied an audience with the secretary of state. Two years later, he published his own account of his governorship and was subsequently granted a pension. In 1804, despite being nearly sixty-seven years old, he was given the command of the *Venerable*, a seventy-four-gun warship in the Channel fleet. In 1807, he was appointed rear admiral and in 1810 vice admiral. In his last years, he lived alone in Hackney in London and died in 1821, aged eighty-three.

CHAPTER 3

THE SETTLEMENT OF
THE SOUTH

*It was reported to me after the French ships sailed that
a principal object of their voyage was to fix on a place
at Van Diemen's Land for a settlement . . . Under these
circumstances I judged it expedient to form a settlement at Risdon Cove in the River Derwent.*

WHEN FORTY-TWO-YEAR-OLD PHILIP GIDLEY KING ARRIVED
back in Sydney to take over as governor from Hunter, he
was the first man known to have travelled from England to
Australia three times. He had come out on the First Fleet
in 1788 and, after arriving in Sydney, had been ordered by
Arthur Phillip to settle Norfolk Island. The British wanted
to secure the island, which had been noted by Cook on his
voyage eighteen years earlier, because it was believed to

produce a flax plant that could be used to make superior sails and canvas – both vital for the Royal Navy.

King had set sail for Norfolk Island only three weeks after the arrival of the First Fleet. He left on the tiny tender *Supply* with perhaps the smallest ever party to establish a colony of the British Empire. His group of twenty-three included a surgeon, a carpenter, a weaver, two marines, eight male convicts and six female convicts. For two years, King supervised the little settlement, and, because of the fertile soil, he was able to report favourably on the island's prospects. However, they were never successful at growing the flax there.

Among the convict women who had been taken to Norfolk Island was Ann Inett, who, at the relatively mature age of thirty-one, became Philip Gidley King's housekeeper and lover. She had been convicted in 1786 in the Worcester Court for stealing a petticoat, two aprons, a pair of shoes, five handkerchiefs, a silk hood and other clothing, with a total value of a little under one pound.

After two years on Norfolk Island, King returned to England in 1790 at the request of Arthur Phillip to report on the difficulties of settling New South Wales. As the first officer to have returned with experience of living in Britain's new colonial possession, he was able to meet with men significantly more senior in rank, including Lord Grenville and Sir Joseph Banks.

In England, thirty-three-year-old King was promoted to the rank of commander on 2 March 1791, married his twenty-six-year-old cousin Anna Coombes on 11 March and, four days later, sailed back to Norfolk Island with his new bride. Six weeks after arriving, Anna gave birth to Phillip Parker King, the first of five children they would have together. (King did not abandon the two sons he had with the convict Ann Inett and arranged for the boys to be educated in England. Both later became officers in the navy.)

In 1796, and suffering severe gout, King returned again to England, where three years later he was appointed John Hunter's successor. King was ambitious and had wanted the job, despite his deteriorating health. He had regularly corresponded with Sir Joseph Banks, who was a valuable supporter and probably an influence in King gaining the appointment.

King arrived back in Sydney for the third time in October 1799 but did not take over as governor from Hunter for almost another year, on 28 September 1800. He was younger than both his predecessors when he became governor (Phillip had been forty-nine and Hunter fifty-nine). However, by the time he returned to Sydney, a combination of gout and rheumatism had 'ravished both his appearance and his character' and he became known for a 'violent and intemperate temper'.[1]

Even before he took over the running of the colony, he wrote complaining of the widespread laziness, drunkenness and child prostitution he had found there:

> Vice, dissipation, and a strange relaxation seems to pervade every class and order of people . . . Cellars [of rum], from the better sort of people in the colony to the blackest character among the convicts, are full of that fiery poison. The children are so abandoned to misery, prostitution, and every vice of their parents, and, in short, nothing less than a total change in the system of administration must take place immediately . . . [2]

King proved to be an effective governor. His first task was to attack the monopolist rum traders, and by imposing port and price controls on the trade he managed to reduce the amount of imported spirits compared to what had come in under Hunter. To bring down prices of other goods, King established public warehouses that sold imported items at a lower profit. He tried, with mixed success, to control wages, interest rates and hours of work. He limited the number of servants working for each officer to two. He successfully increased the acreage under cultivation on publicly owned farms and raised the amount of land granted for private farms. Consequently, the number of farmers who needed to supplement their food by drawing on the public stores fell from 25 per cent in 1800 to less than 10 per cent in 1806.[3]

It was while King was the governor that the exploration of the Australian coastline was completed. He was governor when the British settlements were established on Van Diemen's Land and at Port Phillip, both of which had less to do with Britain's colonial ambitions and much more to do with that country's rivalry with France. For 200 years, starting with Willem Janszoon's 1606 charting of several hundred kilometres of the eastern Gulf of Carpentaria, scores of other Europeans had mapped parts of the coast. The Dutch had charted much of the north, west and south-west of New Holland in the first half of the 1600s, which included Abel Tasman's two voyages in 1642 and 1644, and the naming of Van Diemen's Land. More than 100 years later, Cook had mapped the east coast and named the land beyond it New South Wales.

However, by the end of the 1700s, and even after the First Fleet of convicts arrived in 1788, large parts of the coast remained unexplored. By 1800, the largest uncharted section, referred to as the 'unknown coast', stretched from current-day Ceduna, on the southern Australian shore, 3000 kilometres east to Western Port in current-day Victoria. In 1800 and 1801, the French and the British sent out expeditions with almost exactly the same instructions: to chart the unknown coast to determine whether there was a strait or river separating the east and west; and to complete the first map of Australia.

The French expedition departed first. Personally authorised by Napoleon Bonaparte, and commanded by Nicolas Baudin, two French ships – the *Géographe* and the *Naturaliste* – left Brest in October 1800. The English expedition, led by Matthew Flinders, set sail from Portsmouth eight months later, in June 1801, on the *Investigator*. Flinders had already made the important discovery three years earlier that Van Diemen's Land was a separate island from the Australian mainland, and he would later earn a reputation as one of Britain's greatest explorers. By all accounts, he was a calm, determined and talented navigator, and, in keeping with the expectations of an officer of his times, he always applied himself seriously to the task at hand and rarely displayed a sense of humour.

The French expedition was better equipped than the English. Forty-six-year-old commander Nicolas Baudin took twenty-four scientists, including botanists, zoologists, mineralogists, artists, gardeners, geographers and astronomers. Flinders and the English ship took only six scientists. Baudin was ordered to examine 'in detail the coasts of New Holland ... some of which are still entirely unknown' and to make 'a special search along the mainland coast to discover if there is some large opening to a large river'.[4]

Despite their nine-month head start over the English expedition, the French squandered their lead and reached the unknown coast after Flinders. Baudin was already running late when he reached the south-west tip of Western Australia at the end of May 1801, and he was afraid it was too close to winter to continue along the south coast. So he headed north along the Australian west coast to reach Kupang in Timor in September 1801. After replenishing supplies, the French left Timor in November before heading back south along the western coast of Australia and across the Southern Ocean to Van Diemen's Land, from where Baudin planned to explore the south coast the following year. He reached the D'Entrecasteaux Channel near current-day Hobart in mid-January 1801, and in February sailed north to chart the east coast of Van Diemen's Land, before heading across Bass Strait to at last begin exploring the south coast of the Australian mainland from the east, early in 1802.

However, Baudin didn't know that Flinders was already on his way to explore this stretch of the unknown coast from the west. Flinders was able to chart the unknown coast first, confirming that the two gulfs towards the east did not split New Holland and New South Wales, as 'neither . . . seemed to belong to a channel capable of leading us into the Gulf of Carpentaria'.[5] He named the gulfs the Spencer Gulf, after the Princess of Wales' great-grandfather, George John Spencer, 2nd Earl of Spencer, and the Gulf of St Vincent, after a prominent English naval earl. It was a momentous discovery. After 200 years of European exploration, Flinders had proved Australia was one major land mass. With his new charts and those of earlier explorers, it would now be possible to draw a complete map of the island continent.

After his great discovery, Flinders continued east on his explorations, until the onset of winter, when both Baudin's *Géographe* and Flinders' *Investigator* returned to Sydney to replenish their food and water, and repair their ships. Shortly afterwards, in June 1802, the second French ship, the *Naturaliste*, arrived back in Sydney, and for some weeks the English and French were there together.

Flinders said that, 'as soon as the anchor was dropped', he called on the governor of New South Wales, Philip Gidley King, who had by now replaced Flinders' friend and supporter of his earlier explorations, John Hunter. Flinders was able to develop an equally good relationship with King, who would become a strong supporter of his later explorations around Australia.

King, who spoke good French, also enjoyed the company of the French commander Nicolas Baudin while he was in Sydney, and on a number of occasions hosted dinner parties at Government House for both the French and British officers. It was at one of these dinner parties that a junior French officer made no secret of his resentment that the French expedition had been more focused on natural history than exploration, which had allowed the English to overtake them. According to Flinders, French sub lieutenant Henry Freycinet complained to him at one of Governor King's dinners, 'Captain, if we had not been kept so long picking up shells and catching butterflies in Van Diemen's Land, you would not have discovered the south coast before us.'[6]

Shortly after Baudin left Sydney to resume his expedition, Governor King was alarmed to hear a rumour from Captain William Paterson – who was still in the colony and now the deputy – that the French intended to establish their own colony on Van Diemen's Land.

During the preceding ten years, the French had paid it a number of visits, which would have fuelled British fears of their designs on the place. Before reaching Sydney in June 1802, Baudin had sailed around the island, staying for some weeks in the south at the mouth of the Derwent River and charting much of its east coast. A decade before Baudin, the Frenchman d'Entrecasteaux had stayed twice in Van Diemen's Land when searching for the lost explorer

La Perouse. On both visits, in 1792 and again ten months later in 1793, d'Entrecasteaux had made extensive maps and named Bruni Island (now Bruny Island) and the D'Entrecasteaux Channel.

Concerned that his friend Baudin had made no mention of this rumour, Governor King hastily dispatched the naval captain Charles Robbins on the *Cumberland* with letters for Baudin, which were delivered to the Frenchman while he was anchored in the Bass Strait off King Island to the north-west of Van Diemen's Land:

> You will be surprized to see a vessel so soon after you . . . but this has been hastened by a report communicated to me soon after your departure, 'that the French intended to settle in Storm Bay [Van Diemen's Land] . . . and that it was recommended to you by the Republic . . .'[7]

Baudin responded with two letters – one official and the other private – which Robbins took back to King. In the official letter, Baudin said the rumour King had heard was baseless and that, if they had been instructed by the French Government to settle somewhere in Van Diemen's Land, he would still be there and not hundreds of kilometres further west.

In the private letter, Baudin gave his friend further assurances but also made some poignant observations about the injustice of European settlement on Aboriginal land:

> I now write to you as Mr. King, my friend, for whom I shall always have a particular regard . . . To my thinking, I have never been able to conceive that there was justice and equity on the part of Europeans in seizing, in the name of their Governments, a land seen for the first time, when it is inhabited by men who have not always deserved the title of savages or cannibals . . . [8]

Baudin went on to describe, with extraordinary pre-
science, how white settlement was devastating Aboriginal
civilisation:

> If you will reflect upon the conduct of the natives since the
> beginning of your establishment upon their territory, you
> will perceive that their aversion for you, and also for your
> customs, have been occasioned by the idea which they
> have formed of those who wished to live amongst them.
> Notwithstanding your precautions and the punishments
> undergone by those among your people who have ill-
> treated them . . . the hope of seeing them mix with you is
> lost, and you will presently remain the peaceful possessors
> of their heritage, as the small number of those surround-
> ing you will not long exist.[9]

There is no record of King's response to Baudin's letter –
Baudin was preparing to return to France, so it's likely
none was written. King may have been assured that his
friend was not about to establish a settlement south of
Sydney, but Baudin's letter left room for anxiety about the
intentions of the French Government in the future. This
fear may have been inflamed by Baudin's simultaneous
assertion that French claims on the territory had greater
merit because they had been the first to seriously explore
southern Van Diemen's Land:

> I have no knowledge of the claims which the French
> Government may have upon Van Diemen's Land, nor of
> its designs for the future . . . However, if it were sufficient
> (according to the principle you have adopted) to have
> explored a country in order to vest it in those who made it
> known first, you would have no claims. To convince ones
> self well that it was not the English, it is but necessary to

cast eyes at the ideal maps prepared by your geographer, Arrowsmith, and compare them with those of Beautemps Beaupré, which leave nothing to be desired.[10]

(The British Arrowsmith maps were largely based on the chart Matthew Flinders had made when he circumnavigated Van Diemen's Land in 1798 with George Bass. As Baudin pointed out, the earlier and more extensive maps of southern Van Diemen's Land had been made by Beautemps-Beaupré, who had sailed on the d'Entrecasteaux expedition six years earlier.)

King remained suspicious of the French Government's intentions and advised the British Government that he was sending a party to occupy the Derwent River. On 9 May 1803, he wrote to Evan Nepean, the Admiralty secretary:

It was reported to me soon after the French ships sailed that a principal object of their voyage was to fix on a place at Van Diemen's Land for a settlement, and that the French officers who had talked of it had pointed out a particular place, what the French call Baie du Nord [North West Bay] in Storm Bay Passage [D'Entrecasteaux Channel] . . . Under these circumstances I judged it expedient to form a settlement at Risdon Cove in the River Derwent . . . [11]

The man chosen by King to lead the expedition was twenty-three-year-old navy lieutenant John Bowen, who was ordered to go to Risdon Cove 'with men, women, stores and provisions', where he was to select a 'space for the building of a town' and clear the ground for 'the cultivation of wheat and other grains'.[12] Governor King ordered him to take a small party to settle the cove, which included twenty-one male and three female convicts, members of the New South Wales Marine Corps and some free settlers and their families.

In separate, 'confidential' instructions, Bowen was specifically told he was to stop the French establishing a settlement:

> In case any French ships, or ships of any other nation, should attempt to form an establishment anywhere in the neighbourhood of where you are settled ... you will endeavor to prevent them carrying their intention into effect, but without any act of hostility, if it can be avoided.[13]

Bowen and his small band of settlers left Sydney on two small ships, the *Lady Nelson* and the *Albion*. The *Lady Nelson* reached Risdon Cove on 8 September and the *Albion* five days later.

Governor King did not know that, at the time he was establishing the settlement in the south of Van Diemen's Land, the British Government in London was making a decision to establish a second convict settlement in Australia. In early 1803, motivated by the same concerns that the French intended to settle somewhere to the south of Sydney, the British Government commissioned forty-seven-year-old David Collins as the lieutenant governor to establish a sizeable settlement in Port Phillip, on the south coast of New South Wales, in what is now the state of Victoria.

Port Phillip had been visited in early 1802 by naval lieutenant John Murray, who had been sent by Governor King to conduct a more thorough survey of this stretch of the south coast following the earlier explorations of George Bass in 1798 and James Grant in 1800. The recommendation to establish a settlement there had come from King in a letter to the Duke of Portland on 21 May 1803: 'From accounts given by Acting Lieutenant Murray and Captain Flinders, the goodness of the soil and the natural advantages of Port Phillip in Basses Strait, I beg to suggest the propriety of a settlement being made at that place.'[14]

The man chosen to head the new British migration, David Collins, had been to New South Wales previously when he sailed on the First Fleet to serve as New South Wales' first judge. Collins had stayed in the colony for nine years – the longest term of any of the First Fleet officers. He could have returned from Sydney to England as early as 1791 but had extended his term to help the acting governor after Phillip had gone home, and then John Hunter when he became governor in 1795.

Collins had eventually reached England in June 1797 on the *Britannia* to find his wife, Maria, in poor health. Over the next two years, he wrote the two-volume *Account of the Colony of New South Wales*, which provided more detail of the history of the early years of the colony than had previously been published. Despite being promoted to the rank of lieutenant colonel in 1798, he did not secure a substantial role until he was commissioned to become the lieutenant governor of the proposed new convict colony at Port Phillip and was instructed to choose an area around the port in which to establish it.

Although not on as grand a scale as the first convict fleet of 1788, Collins' expedition was similar in design. The *Calcutta* and the *Ocean* sailed out of Spithead on 24 April 1803 with a total of 466 people, including Collins, the Reverend Robert Knopwood, a number of senior officials, a judge advocate, two surgeons, forty-eight marines, nineteen settlers, twenty-six settlers' wives and children, 299 convicts, plus twenty-nine convicts' wives and children. [15]

Arthur Phillip had written to Lord Sydney in London in 1789 complaining that the convicts he had on the First

Fleet had few of the skills that were needed to build a new settlement.[16] His views were clearly heeded because Collins' convict party included men who had some connection with sailing or ship repair, nine sawyers, four carpenters, four bricklayers, twelve shoemakers, eighteen clothes makers, and a number of bakers and butchers.[17]

For the establishment of the settlement, Collins was given instructions similar in many respects to those given to Phillip fifteen years earlier. He was to grow food, put the convicts to work, make land grants to 'non-commissioned officers, and privates of the marines, to settlers and to emancipated convicts', live harmoniously with the Aboriginal inhabitants and instruct the settlers in the Anglican faith.[18]

After sailing via Rio de Janeiro and Cape Town, the *Calcutta* and the *Ocean* landed at Port Phillip on 16 October 1803 at a spot on the western side of the bay that Collins named Sullivan Bay, after John Sullivan, the then undersecretary of war and the colonies. Almost immediately, Collins and his officer colleagues found Port Phillip unsuitable for settlement – just as Phillip had found Botany Bay unsuitable when he had first arrived there. Three weeks after arriving, Collins wrote to Governor King in Sydney saying that a 'more minute survey' had confirmed their first impressions of the place. He said the soil was too sandy, the vegetation 'thinly clad with miserably stunted timber' and the only place with enough soil for planting crops 'entirely destitute of that great essential, fresh water'.[19]

The letter was sent on a small cutter and King received it in Sydney only two weeks later. The governor responded quickly. On 26 November, he sent a letter back on the *Ocean* suggesting to Collins that he move his new settlement to Van Diemen's Land – either to Port Dalrymple on the Tamar River in the north of the island (near current-day Launceston) or to Risdon Bay on the Derwent in the south of the island (near current-day Hobart). King laid out the relative benefits of both places but left the decision to Collins.

Collins opted for the Derwent simply because John Bowen's tiny Risdon settlement was already there, saying to Governor King that 'the advantages which I must derive from establishing myself in a place already settled had certainly great weight with me'.[20] He added that he thought the Derwent was preferable because it was as a sea port used by traders and whalers and was thus better adapted to commercial purposes.

The settlement at Port Phillip was abandoned on 30 January 1803 and, after an uncomfortable voyage on the *Ocean* in 'strong gales and squally conditions' and 'with a heavy shower of sleet', they reached the Risdon Bay settlement on 15 February and found John Bowen and his party, who had settled there five months before.[21] As they approached, the Reverend Robert Knopwood recorded in his journal that the Derwent River was 'much better supplied with fish and birds than . . . Port Phillip', including ducks, teal, snipes and woodcock.[22]

Nevertheless, the very next morning, Collins and his colleagues quickly decided that Risdon Bay had insufficient fresh water and was 'unsuitable for a town'.[23] The following day, they explored what they thought was a better site on the other bank of the Derwent to the south-west, and Collins, who was senior in rank to Bowen, ordered the moving of the settlement to the new location. He named the new settlement Hobart Town, after Lord Hobart, who was the secretary of state for war and the colonies at the time. It had an extensive plain and continually running water from a large mountain the earlier French explorers had named Table Mountain. (Twenty years later, after the Battle of Waterloo, the British renamed it Mount Wellington.)

Bowen did not stay in Hobart long after Collins arrived. According to the Reverend Knopwood, he decided to leave immediately 'with an intention of going to England'.[24] He returned to Sydney and then sailed back to England in early 1805 on the *Lady Barlow* to resume his naval career. While in Van Diemen's Land, he had lived with Martha Hayes, the daughter of a convict, and together they had had two children: Martha Charlotte, in 1804, and Henrietta, who was a small baby when he left. He did not take any of them with him when he resumed his naval career, which was an all too common occurrence in the early days of the Australian convict settlements.

The landing of more than 400 people and their supplies that began on 20 February was not marked with the same celebrations and drinking that had accompanied the arrival at Sydney Cove in 1788. But the struggle to establish the convict settlement in Hobart Town had many similarities to the earlier experiences of the First Fleet in Sydney. The convicts were unqualified to work in the wilderness and the English tools were not strong enough to cut through the tough Australian hardwood trees that needed to be cleared for the settlement. A year later, Hobart Town was still dominated by tents and wooden huts and the timber Government House, which 'was no more than a cottage'.[25]

Van Diemen's Land was, however, more fertile than New South Wales, as Charles Darwin noted when he compared the two places on his visit on the *Beagle* in 1836:

The climate here is damper than in New South Wales, and hence the land is more fertile. Agriculture flourishes; the cultivated fields look well, and the gardens abound with thriving vegetables and fruit-trees. Some of the farmhouses, situated in retired spots, had a very attractive appearance. The general aspect of the vegetation is similar to that of Australia; perhaps it is a little more green and cheerful; and the pasture between the trees rather more abundant.[26]

The building of the settlement and the start of a government farm at Cornelian Bay near Hobart Town were slow. Collins had brought enough food to last for a year, but with losses and damage the rations were cut within months to near starvation levels. The settlement was critically dependent on the hunting of kangaroo and emu for the next two years, but hunting parties risked clashes with hostile Aboriginal groups and escaped convicts.

The food shortages were made worse because no supply ships were arriving. According to Collins' deputy, Lieutenant Edward Lord:

> the whole settlement was called upon to endure hardships of no ordinary kind. The Governor himself, the officers, and the entire settlement for eighteen months, were without bread, vegetables, tea, sugar, wine, spirits, or beer, or any substitute, except the precarious supply of the wild game of the country.[27]

In a report of the colony dated 30 June 1806, the settlement had 327 convicts, of whom only six were emancipists. There were forty-nine free settlers, including their families, and ninety-nine civil officers or marines, including their families. After more than two years, 465 of approximately 480 people in the settlement were still dependent on the government stores, which consisted mainly of what the settlers had brought with them from England.[28]

Occasionally, Collins was able to buy supplies from a passing whaler or trading ship, but he could not rely on the irregular provisions sent from Sydney. During the eight years he was the head of the British settlements in Van Diemen's Land, not one of his dispatches to London was replied to; in fact, he received rebukes for what were seen as 'excessive demands' from the governor in Sydney. Collins was not consulted when the British Government sent 550 convicts from Norfolk Island, which in one year almost doubled Hobart's dependent population.

Only nine months after David Collins had joined John Bowen's party on the south of the island, Governor King ordered the settlement of Port Dalrymple in the north. Again, trepidation about French intentions was the primary motivation, as it was thought that in the event of war France might attempt to establish a foothold on the coast of Bass Strait. Another factor was the desire to find somewhere to relocate the remaining settlers on Norfolk Island, since administration of the island had become too expensive and the British were looking for an alternative.

King's deputy, William Paterson, was chosen to lead the expedition. It was Paterson who, two years before, had told Governor King of the rumour that the French explorer Nicolas Baudin had intentions of colonising Van Diemen's Land. Paterson and his party left Sydney for Dalrymple on four small ships – the *Buffalo*, *Lady Nelson*, *Integrity* and the *Francis* – on 1 October 1804. He took with him his wife, Elizabeth, a captain, two subalterns, four sergeants, two drummers, fifty-eight privates and seventy-four convicts.[29] For the next eight years the British maintained two settlements under separate command in the north and the south of Van Diemen's Land.

Paterson's expedition had first left Sydney in June 1804, but after being buffeted in heavy weather had returned to wait for the end of winter.[30] On this second attempt they reached Dalrymple on 5 November. A few days later, they 'hoisted His Majesty's colours', and began to erect buildings and clear the land.[31] The following day saw the first recorded hostile incident with the locals. Paterson said that one of his sergeants had been threatened, prompting a guard to fire, which killed one of the Aboriginal men and wounded another. The incident was a small precursor to three decades of violence that would result in the effective extermination of the Aboriginal people of Van Diemen's Land.

Within a year, Paterson – a weak man and a heavy drinker who was severely afflicted with gout – was complaining that the new settlement was struggling. The convicts, he said, were averse to work, the marines insubordinate, the shoes falling to bits and the tools not strong enough for the task.[32] Two years later, in 1806, he began moving them from the western arm of the river across to a new site, which would later become the city of Launceston.

By the end of 1806, there were a total of 747 white people struggling to survive in Van Diemen's Land, either in Hobart Town or Port Dalrymple, and, in a report to London, Governor King said that almost all of them still needed provisions from the government stores.[33]

Paterson finally left Port Dalrymple to return to Sydney on 1 January 1809, where he was required to act as governor because the New South Wales governor, Captain William Bligh, had just been deposed. Overwhelmed by the pressures of office and drinking heavily, Paterson stayed until the new governor, Lachlan Macquarie, took up office on 1 January 1810. He returned to England on the *Dromedary* the following May but died at sea on 21 June as the ship was rounding Cape Horn.

Meanwhile, in Hobart Town, David Collins had taken up living with a seventeen-year-old convict girl, Margaret Eddington, and they had two children together. His wife was in England, and he had already had two other children, a boy and a girl, while living with a convict woman called Ann Yeats in Sydney.

Collins died suddenly in Hobart on 24 March 1810 of a stroke while sitting in a chair after offering his doctor refreshments. He was buried with full military honours on the site of what would become St David's Church. He was fifty-six years old. When he died, the population of Hobart Town was 1062 and another 259 lived in Port Dalrymple.

By this time, Philip Gidley King had returned to England, having completed his term as New South Wales governor. He had served for almost six years, which was slightly longer than both of his predecessors, Arthur Phillip and John Hunter. During his rule, the colony had strengthened and diversified, and the threat of starvation that had stalked the early settlement had now passed. King's term had coincided with Matthew Flinders' completion of the charting of the Australian continent. However, despite King's undeniable achievements, he had not broken the insidious power of the New South Wales Marine Corps, which, three years after his departure, would depose his successor in Australia's first and last military coup.

CHAPTER 4

WILLIAM BLIGH AND AUSTRALIA'S COUP D'ÉTAT

This rebellious act was done so suddenly, that in about five minutes from the first time we knew of it, Government House was surrounded with troops, Major Johnston having brought up in battle array above 300 men under martial law, loaded with ball to attack and seize my person ... they marched to the tune of the 'British Grenadiers'; and, to render the spectacle more terrific to the townspeople, the field artillery on parade was presented against the house where I became arrested.

PHILIP GIDLEY KING WAS REPLACED AS GOVERNOR OF NEW South Wales in 1806 by survivor of the mutiny on the *Bounty*, Captain William Bligh. Bligh was appointed because he was tough and was considered to have the strong disciplinary record needed to straighten out the corrupt colony. Included in his written instructions was a specific direction to break up the illegal rum trade, which was run largely by the colony's Marine Corps officers and other corrupt officials.

William Bligh was born in 1754 near Bodmin, Cornwall, the son of a Plymouth customs officer. At seven years of age, with the help of family connections, he was signed on with the navy as a 'captain's servant', which was a common method for young gentlemen to start their career.[1] It is not known at what age Bligh first went to sea, but he was able seaman on the *Hunter* by the time he was fifteen and, a little over a year later, was promoted to midshipman on the *Crescent*, where he began learning navigation and seamanship. From the *Crescent*, he was moved to the *Ranger*, which searched for contraband among merchant ships on the Irish Sea.

In 1776, at the age of twenty-two, Bligh was appointed sailing master on Captain Cook's *Resolution*, which, along with the *Discovery*, went on Cook's fateful last voyage. It was in the third year of the four-year voyage to the Pacific that Cook was killed in Hawaii on 14 February 1779. (It is believed that Bligh witnessed Cook being murdered.) The survivors of Cook's expedition, including Bligh, arrived back in England in October 1780.

In 1781, Bligh married Elizabeth 'Betsy' Betham, the daughter of wealthy trader and collector of customs Richard Betham, who was friends with Scottish philosopher David Hume and the economist Adam Smith. Together, William and Betsy would have four daughters and twin sons, although both boys died very soon after birth. After his marriage, Bligh returned to sea and served on a number of warships – at the time, England was at war with Spain, France and the Netherlands. Bligh subsequently saw action at the Battle of Dogger Bank against the Dutch in 1781, and with Lord Howe in the siege of Gibraltar against the French and Spanish in 1782. With declining hostilities in Europe and North America, Bligh then signed off from the navy on half-pay and, with the approval of the Admiralty, sailed merchant ships for the next five years.

In 1787, he was given command of the *Bounty*, with instructions from Lord Sydney to explore the South Pacific Ocean. Bligh had been offered the job following an intervention by the influential Joseph Banks after Banks had been lobbied by the prominent shipowner Duncan Campbell, who was the uncle of Bligh's wife.[2] After the appointment was confirmed, Bligh quickly wrote to thank Banks, who would remain a faithful supporter throughout Bligh's turbulent career.

Bligh would be sailing the *Bounty* to the South Pacific to collect samples of the breadfruit plant (a large, round, starchy fruit of the Pacific Islands) and take them to the West Indies, where it was hoped the fruit could be grown as a cheap source of food for slaves working on the sugar plantations. The English had first been made aware of the breadfruits by the English pirate William Dampier 100 years before, and later by Captain Cook on his first voyage to the South Pacific in 1768:

> Whereas the king, upon a representation from the merchants and planters interested in His Majesty's West India possessions that the introduction of the bread-fruit tree into the islands of those seas, to constitute an article of food, would be of very essential benefit to the inhabitants, hath, in order to promote the interests of so respectable a body of his subjects (especially in an instance which promises general advantage) thought fit that measures

should be taken for the procuring some of those trees, and conveying them to the said West India islands.[3]

It was three weeks after leaving Tahiti to deliver the breadfruits to the West Indies that the *Bounty*'s crew mutinied, on 28 April 1789. Bligh and eighteen of his loyal crew were put over the side of the ship into a small cutter with a sextant, compass and time-keeper. Without maps, they somehow managed to navigate nearly 7000 kilometres to Kupang, Timor, arriving six weeks later. In Kupang, Bligh bought a small schooner and sailed for the Dutch East Indies capital of Batavia, where he took the next passing ship to the Cape of Good Hope. He finally reached Portsmouth almost a year after the mutiny, on 14 March 1790.

After deposing Bligh and throwing the breadfruit cargo overboard, the mutineers had sailed back to Tahiti, where sixteen of the crew decided to leave the *Bounty* and settle into the local community. Fletcher Christian, the master's mate and the most senior of the mutineers, and the eight remaining crew, left Tahiti and sailed the *Bounty* another 1400 kilometres through uncharted waters to settle on remote Pitcairn Island. They brought with them eighteen Tahitian women and six men and later burnt the *Bounty*, which Fletcher Christian thought might be seen by any British ships sent to search for them.

Determined not to leave the mutiny unpunished, the British navy sent Captain Edward Edwards on the *Pandora* to hunt down the *Bounty*'s crew and bring them to justice. Arriving in Tahiti eighteen months after the mutiny, in April 1791, Edwards captured fourteen of the crew (two had died on Tahiti) and imprisoned them in a small makeshift cell on the deck of the *Pandora*. Of the fourteen captives, four drowned when the *Pandora* was shipwrecked on the western end of the Great Barrier Reef as the ship was sailing back to England. Edwards managed to bring the other ten back to England for trial. Three were hanged, four were acquitted and three pardoned, but Fletcher Christian and the remaining mutineers on Pitcairn Island were never caught.

Much has been written about the causes of the mutiny on the *Bounty*, including that Bligh was intolerant and too severe with his crew. Bligh believed the mutiny was caused by the sailors having enjoyed themselves too much among the women of Tahiti and being reluctant to return to their unhappy lives in England:

> It will be very naturally asked, what could be the reason for such a revolt? In answer I can only conjecture, that the mutineers had flattered themselves with the hopes of a more happy life among the Otaheitians, than they could possibly enjoy in England ... The women ... are handsome, mild and cheerful ... possessed of great sensibility, and have sufficient delicacy to make them admired and beloved ... It is ... scarcely possible to have been foreseen, that a set of sailors, most of them void of [family] connections, should be led away ... to such powerful inducements.[4]

After returning to England, Bligh was court-martialled but cleared of any wrongdoing. He was sent again to collect the breadfruits with two ships – the *Providence* and *Assistant* – and this time given the security of a marine detachment to ensure the crew was kept in order. On a voyage that lasted more than two years, Bligh had on his crew the seventeen-year-old Matthew Flinders, who would of course later play a major role in charting the Australian coast.

Following the delivery of the breadfruits, Bligh returned to naval service and saw more action, including under

Vice Admiral Nelson at the Battle of Copenhagen against the Danish and Norwegian fleet in 1801.

In 1805, and again with the support of the influential botanist Sir Joseph Banks, Bligh was offered the position of governor of New South Wales. Banks had been asked by the secretary of state for war and the colonies, Lord Camden, to recommend someone 'who had integrity unimpeached . . . firm in discipline, civil in deportment and not subject to whimper and whine when severity in discipline is wanted to meet emergencies'.[5] Britain was at the time totally preoccupied with the war against Napoleonic France, and it would have made sense to seek advice from Banks, who was the recognised authority on the Australian colony. Banks had no hesitation in recommending fifty-one-year-old Bligh, who took the offer of the appointment at the reasonably comfortable pay of £2000 a year and the promise of a pension of £1000 a year. (By way of comparison, an ordinary seaman at the time earned around £12 a year.)

Bligh left England in February 1806 with his twenty-three-year-old daughter Mary and her fiancé, Lieutenant John Putland, whom Bligh had appointed to his staff so his daughter could escort him to Australia. Bligh's wife, Betsy, stayed in England with the couple's remaining daughters. She was fifty-two and had an 'extreme horror of the sea', which Bligh felt 'would be her death'.[6]

John Putland later married Mary, though he was already in the early stages of tuberculosis and died eighteen months later in Sydney. Mary would play a prominent role in her father's life in New South Wales. In a later account by Judge Ellis Bent in Sydney, she was described as having a

very small, nice little figure, rather pretty, but conceited and extremely affected and proud. God knows of what!

Extremely violent and passionate, so much as now and then to fling a plate or candlestick at her father's head . . . everything is studied about her, her walk, her talking, everything . . . and you have to observe her mode of sitting down . . . dressed with some taste, very thinly, and to compensate for the want of petticoats wears breeches or rather, trowsers.[7]

Arriving in Sydney in August 1806, Bligh was well received and so was Mary, who came to function as the colony's first lady in the absence of her mother. The *Sydney Gazette* reported that the colony was 'extremely happy [that Bligh] is accompanied by his amiable daughter . . . a circumstance which conveys the greatest pleasure'.[8]

William Bligh's first impressions of the Sydney settlement were not favourable: 'The settlers in general, and particularly those from prisoners, are not honest, have no prudence, and little industry, besides being burdened with debts; great chicanery is used in all their dealings.'[9]

At the time of his arrival, the colony's economy remained overwhelmingly controlled by the military and ex-military officers – and in particular John Macarthur. The free settlers were too few in number and had insufficient social weight to counter the economic power of the military. The army men still had a monopoly on home-grown produce, because they had been bestowed with land grants and free convict labour to work their farms. They also controlled most of the imports by buying up entire ships' cargoes, using bills drawn up against officers' wages in London, and then on-selling to the locals at exorbitant profits.

The heart of the economic power of the military remained the rum trade, which, in the absence of sufficient coinage, had become an acceptable form of currency – indeed, it had effectively replaced money.

Bligh was soon in dispute with Macarthur. Five years before Bligh arrived, Macarthur had been sent back to England to face charges for having shot his superior officer William Paterson in the shoulder during a duel. Not only were the charges dismissed, but Macarthur had also managed to persuade the British Government of the superiority of New South Wales wool and had been promised 5000 acres (2023 hectares) on his return, to expand the Australian sheep industry. Macarthur had returned to Sydney in June 1805 and, by the time of Bligh's arrival the following year, had become the colony's most successful entrepreneur and cattle and sheep farmer.

Macarthur insisted on determining where his promised 5000 acres would be, but Bligh refused, shouting at Macarthur that, as governor, he was 'in command' in the colony.[10] In another case of a dispute with his debtors, Bligh found against Macarthur.[11] In a further incident, Bligh ordered the confiscation of two spirit 'stills' that had been imported into the colony by Macarthur.

Things came to a head in June 1807 when a prisoner being conveyed on one of Macarthur's ships managed to escape. As a result of the lapse in security, Bligh insisted the ship's bond of £900 be forfeited to the government. Rather than pay the fine, Macarthur declared that he had abandoned the vessel. The issue escalated when the colony's judge advocate, Richard Atkins, demanded an explanation and Macarthur refused an issued warrant for his arrest. Atkins was a dishevelled drunk who had been known to pass the death sentence intoxicated. Even Bligh described him as 'weak' and 'a disgrace to human jurisprudence'.[12]

Macarthur insisted he had no involvement with the ship in question and claimed Atkins' 'summons' was improperly drawn up. Atkins took Macarthur's reply to Bligh, who had a team of four magistrates, including Atkins, hear the matter. They voted to arrest Macarthur.

In a letter sent to her mother, Bligh's daughter Mary complained that dealing with Macarthur was causing her father a great deal of stress:

> Papa is quite well, but dreadfully harassed by business and the troublesome set of people he has to deal with. In general he gives great satisfaction, but there are a few that we suspect wish to oppose him . . . Mr. Macarthur is one of the party, and the others are the military officers, but they are all invited to the house and treated with the same politeness as usual.[13]

The date of Macarthur's trial was set down for 25 January 1808. The night before, the head of the marines, Major George Johnston, hosted a large officers' mess dinner in Sydney and invited his close friend Macarthur as a special guest, along with a number of other prominent civilians, all of whom shared a dislike of Bligh.

Forty-three-year-old Johnston had first arrived in the colony twenty years earlier, as a young lieutenant on Arthur Phillip's First Fleet. In 1804, he cemented his reputation for toughness by putting down Australia's first and only major convict uprising at Rouse Hill, north-west of Sydney. In what became known as the Battle of Vinegar Hill, Irish radical Phillip Cunningham and more than 200 convicts planned to march on Parramatta and then on to Sydney, overthrow the British authority, then commandeer ships and sail back to Ireland.

When news of the uprising reached Sydney, Major Johnston led soldiers and armed volunteers on an overnight march to meet the rebels. After a brief attempt at negotiations failed, Johnston's troops opened fire, and the rebellion was put down, with more than twelve of the rebels killed.

In the dispute between Macarthur and Bligh, it was inevitable that the militaristic Johnston would side with his old army colleague; indeed, he would lead the overthrow of the governor.

At the start of Macarthur's trial, the judges agreed with Macarthur's objection to being tried by Atkins. The trial fell into farce when Atkins withdrew but said the court must not proceed without him; the other judges simply ignored him, then released Macarthur on bail.

On hearing the news, Bligh was enraged, and he ordered the provost marshal William Gore to re-arrest Macarthur the next day. Bligh also summoned Johnston to Government House, but Johnston said he was unwell at his farm at Annandale, having fallen off his horse on the way home from the officers' mess dinner two nights before. At the same time, the six marine officers who had made up the court for Macarthur's trial met and reapplied to Bligh to have someone other than Atkins hear the case. Bligh refused and ordered the six marine officers to answer for their conduct.

Meanwhile, Major Johnston, miraculously recovered from his injuries, arrived back at the Sydney barracks around 5 pm on 26 January, where he was given a petition signed by John Macarthur and seven other prominent men of the colony, including D'Arcy Wentworth, the colony's principal surgeon:

On my arrival at the barracks, I saw all the civil and military officers collected . . . the gentlemen who had assembled . . . entreated me to adopt decisive measures for the safety of the inhabitants . . . In a short time after, a letter was presented to me imploring me instantly to put

Governor Bligh in arrest. This letter was also approved of by all the officers of the Corps present . . . [14]

The petition, signed by 151 citizens, claimed that Bligh was a threat to the life and liberty of everyone in the settlement:

> Sir,
> The present alarming state of this Colony, in which every man's property, liberty, and life is endangered, induces us most earnestly to implore you instantly to place Governor Bligh under an arrest and to assume the command of the colony. We pledge ourselves, at a moment of less agitation, to come forward to support the measure with our fortunes and our lives. [15]

Johnston immediately ordered his troops to arm and directed four officers to accompany him to Government House to arrest Bligh. When the marines reached the front of the house, Bligh's daughter Mary blocked their way. Mary was already distressed following the death of her husband two weeks before from tuberculosis. An eyewitness reported:

> regardless of her own safety and forgetful of the timidity peculiar to her sex, her extreme anxiety to preserve the life of her beloved father prevailed over every consideration and with uncommon intrepidity she opposed a body of soldiers who, with fixed bayonets and loaded firelocks, were proceeding in hostile array to invade the peaceful and defenceless mansion of her parent, her friend, her protector, and as she then believed, to deprive him of his life. She dared the traitors to stab her to the heart but to spare the life of her father. The soldiers themselves, appalled by the greatness of her spirit, hesitated how

to act and that principle of esteem and respect which is inherent in the breast of every man who sees an amiable woman in distress, and is not himself a most consummate villain, deterred them from offering any violence to her.[16]

Two soldiers marched on either side of the governor with their muskets at the ready as they took him captive, in what would later be known as the Rum Rebellion. Bligh's clothing was covered with dust, which Mary attempted to wipe off, and another soldier, Captain Sims, took his naval sword. A few months later, Bligh gave an account of his arrest to Home Secretary Lord Castlereagh:

> This rebellious act was done so suddenly that in about five minutes from the first time we knew of it, Government House was surrounded with troops, Major Johnston having brought up in battle array above three hundred men under martial law, loaded with ball to attack and seize my person and a few friends, some of whom were magistrates, that had been at dinner with me. Their colours were spread, and they marched to the tune of the 'British Grenadiers'; and, to render the spectacle more terrific to the townspeople, the field artillery on the parade was presented against the house where I became arrested . . . [17]

In the course of the arrest, Major Johnston gave Bligh a letter accusing him of crimes that made him unfit to continue as governor:

> Headquarters, 26th January 1808
> Sir,
> I am called upon to execute a most painful duty. You are charged by the respectable inhabitants of crimes that render you unfit to exercise the supreme authority another

moment in this colony; and in that charge all the officers under my command have joined ... I therefore require you, in His Majesty's sacred name, to resign your authority, and submit to arrest which I hereby place you under, by the advice of all my officers, and by the advice of every respectable inhabitant in the town of Sydney.

I am, &c., George Johnston, Major commanding N.S.W. Corps[18]

Much has been argued about Bligh's immediate reaction to his arrest. Johnston implied that Bligh was in the toilet when he said that, at first, Bligh 'was nowhere to be found' but that after a 'rigid search [he] was discovered in a situation too disgraceful to mention'.[19] This allegation was based on rumours at the time – a political cartoon of the day showed Bligh being pulled from under the bed, the inference being that he was hiding. However, there has never been any solid evidence to suggest he acted in a cowardly fashion. The arrest was totally illegal. Bligh had been appointed by the British Government on the authority of the King, and his commission could only be revoked by order of the British Government.

Johnston assumed command of the colony using the title of lieutenant governor, and a regime of reprisal followed. He began by dismissing all the officers of the Bligh government and replacing them with Macarthur's supporters. Macarthur was overjoyed, and wrote on the evening of the coup to tell his wife, Elizabeth:

I have been deeply engaged all this day in contending for the liberties of this unhappy colony, and I am happy to say I have succeeded beyond what I expected ... The tyrant is now no doubt gnashing his teeth with vexation at his overthrow. May he often have cause to do the like![20]

For more than a year after he was overthrown, Bligh was held captive in Government House, which was then an unpretentious structure standing within a small area situated at the top of Bridge Street in Sydney:

> From the 26th of January, 1808, until the 20th of February, 1809, at which time I got possession of my ship, in which I was proclaimed, or rather, I was proscribed, as an outlaw, and every person in the colony was ordered, upon pain of punishment, not to supply me or my family with any food or article whatever. I was completely outlawed; and in this situation I remained till about the middle of January, 1810 . . . [21]

In July 1808, six months after the coup, control of the colony had passed into the hands of Joseph Foveaux, who had arrived to take up the position of lieutenant governor. Finding Bligh under arrest and control of the colony in the hands of George Johnston, as its most senior officer Foveaux took command of the colony, but decided against reinstating Bligh. Two months after arriving, Foveaux wrote to Colonial Secretary Lord Castlereagh saying that nothing but Bligh's removal had prevented insurrection in the colony.[22]

He also wrote to Lieutenant Colonel William Paterson, who was establishing the settlement in Van Diemen's Land at Dalrymple, appealing to him as the most senior officer in the colony to return to Sydney and take command.[23] A reluctant Paterson finally reached Sydney on New Year's Day 1809 and officially took control of the colony on 9 January. He too refused to reinstate Bligh, and after ten weeks in charge wrote to Lord Castlereagh making claims about Bligh's tyrannical disposition.[24]

Paterson offered to release Bligh, provided he agreed to leave the colony immediately and return to England, which he refused to do, insisting that he was still legally the governor and could only be relieved of office by order of the British Government.[25] Then, in February 1809, he did agree to the conditions but on boarding the *Porpoise* reneged, saying that the commitment had been extracted from him by force.

Instead, Bligh sailed on the *Porpoise* with his daughter Mary to Hobart, hoping for the support of David Collins. At first, Collins treated Bligh with every courtesy, but he could only offer the most modest accommodation. Government House in Hobart was a tiny dwelling of three rooms, which Bligh described as a 'miserable shell'. Mary stayed there, but Bligh decided to return each night to sleep on the *Porpoise*. Bligh was also offended that fifty-three-year-old Collins, whose wife was still in England, was living with the seventeen-year-old Margaret Eddington – a convict's daughter – and was openly seen 'walking with his kept woman (a poor, low creature) arm-in-arm about the town'.[26]

Eventually, the relationship between Bligh and his host broke down:

> He [Collins] acknowledged my authority, he was very happy to see me, and we remained there on the best terms a week or a fortnight; when a Gazette containing a proclamation was sent down from Colonel Paterson at head-quarters, proscribing me and my family, and prohibiting all descriptions of persons from having any communication with me. Colonel Paterson wrote at the same time to Colonel Collins in such a way, that nothing I could say to him could prevent his mind being alienated from me.[27]

For the next six months, Bligh stayed on the *Porpoise* at the mouth of the River Derwent. He stopped all ships approaching Hobart to read any messages they were carrying from London and also to restock his own ship with food. Finally, in January 1810, almost two years after the coup, he sailed for Sydney upon hearing of the impending arrival of the new governor, Lachlan Macquarie.

Macquarie was carrying orders for Bligh that said he was to be reinstated as governor for twenty-four hours 'to confirm the King's writ', before Macquarie was to assume the governorship himself: 'when liberated from arrest, you are not to proceed to the general exercise of the functions of Governor, but the day after . . . you are to receive Colonel Macquarie as your successor . . . and you will swear him into office'.[28] Macquarie was also instructed to declare void all of the appointments made after Bligh's arrest, and to restore all of Bligh's officers to their offices, except the drunkard magistrate Richard Atkins.

Macquarie at first offered Bligh 'every respect and attention in my power' but would not become involved in the arguments about Bligh's overthrow. Macquarie complained in his journal that, when Bligh came ashore with Mary, 'I invited them to dinner, but they declined.' In a letter to his brother, Macquarie was more direct:

> Bligh certainly is a most disagreeable person to have any dealings, or public business to transact with; having no regard to his promise or engagements, however sacred, and his natural temper is uncommonly harsh, and tyrannical in the extreme . . . and he is certainly generally detested by high, low, rich and poor, but more specially by the higher classes of people.[29]

Having been ordered by London, Bligh finally agreed to return to England. He arranged to leave Sydney in May 1810, nearly two and a half years after the coup. Shortly before the ship sailed, Mary, who had already loaded her bags on the *Hindostan* for the voyage home, announced to her father that she would not be coming. In the short time they had been back in Sydney, the now twenty-six-year-old widow had met and fallen in love with Colonel Maurice Charles O'Connell, and they wanted to marry. The forty-two-year-old bachelor O'Connell was in command of Governor Macquarie's 73rd Regiment, which had arrived in Sydney with Macquarie the previous December, only weeks before the Blighs returned from Hobart.

In a letter written later by Bligh to his wife in England, he explained that he was taken by surprise but felt he did not have any choice in the matter:

> I at the last found what I had least expected – Lt. Col. O'Connell commanding the 73rd Regiment had, unknown to me, won her affections. Nothing can exceed the esteem and high character he has. He is likewise Lt. Gov. of the territory – a few days before I sailed when everything was prepared for her reception, and we had even embarked, he then opened the circumstance to me – I gave him a flat denial for I could not believe it – I retired with her, when I found she had approved of his addresses and given her word to him. What will you not, my Dear Betsy, feel for my situation at the time, when you know that nothing I could say had any effect; at last overwhelmed with a loss I could not retrieve, I had only to make the best of it. My consent could only be extorted, for it was not a free gift. However, on many proofs of the Honour, Goodness and high character of Colonel O'Connell and his good sense, which had passed under my own trial I did, like having no alternative, consent to her marriage . . . [30]

The wedding took place on 8 May 1810, the week before Bligh sailed from Sydney. Bligh gave his daughter away, and Governor Macquarie and his wife, Elizabeth, hosted the wedding party at Government House. The day before the nuptials, Macquarie gave O'Connell a grant of 2500 fertile farming acres west of Sydney as a wedding present. William Bligh left Sydney – and his daughter – on 14 May and arrived in England on 25 October 1810.

The following year, his usurper, Major George Johnston, was tried for mutiny at a court martial held at the Chelsea Hospital from 7 May 1811.

The trial was of great interest to its participants and to the colony of New South Wales, but it made little impression on the British public or the government in London. At the time, Britain had been at war with France for almost twenty years and was struggling with rising prices, falling wages, poverty, strikes and civil disorder. With Napoleon almost at the peak of his success, the events in a remote and relatively insignificant penal outpost generated only limited local concern.

The charges against Johnston were that he did:

> begin, excite, cause, and join in a mutiny, by putting himself at the head of the New South Wales Corps . . . seizing and causing to be seized and arrested, and imprisoning and causing to be imprisoned, by means of the above-mentioned military force, the person of William Bligh . . . Governor in Chief in and over the territory of New South Wales.[31]

In a statement defending his decision to sack Bligh as governor, Major Johnston told the trial that he feared there would be an insurrection and Bligh would be murdered by the mob if he did not act.

The trial lasted thirteen days and finished on 4 June, evidence having been taken from forty-two witnesses.

After hearing the evidence, the judges took less than an hour to reach a verdict. Johnston was found 'guilty of the act of Mutiny'. But, rather than being sentenced to death, he was simply 'cashiered', or dismissed from the army. The court justified the lenient sentence by referring to the 'novel and extraordinary circumstances' surrounding the case. However, most of the fourteen judges were, like Johnston, senior army officers. The president of the judges was Lieutenant General William Keppel, five of the others were also lieutenant generals, two were major generals and two lieutenant colonels.

Johnston had been dismissed from the army but had suffered very little and was able to return to Sydney. He still owned considerable farmland in the colony, which he had acquired from land grants while still in the Marine Corps. For more than a decade, he lived a successful and wealthy life as a farmer at Sydney's Annandale and Bankstown, and he died in 1823 aged fifty-eight.

Bligh, while vindicated by the guilty verdict, was not avenged, and he 'damned' the court for its leniency.[32] On hearing the decision, the Prince Regent, who was the ruling monarch during the illness of his father, King George III, remarked that the sentence was 'so inadequate to the enormity of the crime of which the prisoner has been found guilty' that the court's decision subverted 'every principle of good order and discipline'.[33]

John Macarthur had also travelled voluntarily to England in order to defend himself. But on legal advice it was argued that, as a civilian, he could not be charged and tried in England along with Johnston. Secretary of State for War and the Colonies Lord Castlereagh wrote to Governor Macquarie in Sydney, saying that if Macarthur returned to Sydney he should be tried before the criminal court of the settlement:

as Gov'r Bligh has represented that Mr. Mcarthur has been the leading promoter and instigator of mutinous measures . . . you will, if examinations be sworn against him . . . have him arrested thereupon and brought to trial before the criminal court of the settlement.[34]

To avoid the risk of being tried if he went back to the colony, Macarthur remained in England for the next eight years. He was given permission early in 1817 to return, after protracted negotiations in London, on condition that he should in no way participate in public affairs.[35]

At the time of Johnston's trial, Bligh was fifty-seven years old and a senior captain in the navy. He was due another promotion but this had been held back pending the outcome. Four weeks after Johnston's guilty verdict, Bligh was promoted to rear admiral of the blue, which was backdated to July 1810. Bligh's wife, Betsy, who had been ill for some time, died the following year, in April 1812. Bligh was twice more promoted before retiring and living with his four unmarried daughters in Farningham, Kent. On 7 December 1817, he collapsed and died. He is buried alongside Betsy at Lambeth. His epitaph reads:

Sacred
to the Memory of
William Bligh
Esquire, F.R.S.
Vice Admiral, of the Blue,
the celebrated Navigator
Who first transplanted the Bread fruit tree
From Otaheite to the West Indies,
Bravely fought the battles of his country
And died beloved, respected, and lamented
On the 7th day of December 1817,
Aged 64.

There is no mention of him having been the governor of New South Wales. But Lachlan Macquarie provided some more personal insights as to conditions in the colony under Bligh in a private letter to Lord Castlereagh. Macquarie said he could not find any act by Bligh that warranted the overthrow. On the other hand, he said, Bligh had seemed erratic and untrustworthy:

> I have taken particular pains to discover the cause which gave rise to ... the mutinous conduct of Lt.-Colonel Johnston and the New South Wales Regiment, and find it extremely difficult to form a just judgment on this delicate and mysterious subject ... But, in justice to Governor Bligh, I must say that I have not been able to discover any act of his which could in any degree form an excuse for, or in any way warrant, the violent and mutinous proceedings pursued against him ... On the other hand, there cannot be any doubt but that Governor Bligh's administration was extremely unpopular, particularly among the higher orders of the people; And from my own short experience, I must acknowledge that he is a most unsatisfactory man to transact business with, from his want of candour and decision, in so much that it is impossible to place the smallest reliance on the fulfilment of any engagement he enters into.[36]

CHAPTER 5

LACHLAN MACQUARIE: 'THE FATHER OF AUSTRALIA'

At my first entrance into this colony, I felt ... that some of the most meritorious men of the few to be found, and who were most capable and most willing to exert themselves in the public service, were men who had been convicts. I saw the necessity and justice ... towards these people, namely ... of extending to them ... the same consideration and qualifications, which they would have enjoyed ... had they never been under the sentence of the Law.

AFTER THE TURBULENCE OF THE COLONY'S EARLIER YEARS AND the overthrow of William Bligh, the man sent 'to restore order and tranquillity' in the colony was a Scottish army officer, Lachlan Macquarie.[1] A visionary and a man of action, Macquarie began transforming the convict settlement into a free society, laying the foundations of modern Australia. For this, he earned the ire of the British Government, which remained focused on the threats posed by the Napoleonic Wars and wanted to keep New South Wales purely as a penal colony – and one that would not be a drain on the public purse.

Macquarie was more fortunate than his predecessors: he arrived with his own regiment, the 73rd, which was a distinct advantage as it made him both military commander and governor. All four of his predecessors – Phillip, Hunter, King and Bligh – were navy officers who had had to deal with an uncooperative and at times hostile Marine Corps that was commanded independently by army officers. With the arrival of Macquarie and the 73rd, the New South Wales Corps was recalled to England 'because of the share it had in the [Bligh] revolution'.[2]

At the time of his appointment in 1810, Lachlan Macquarie was approaching fifty years of age and, after a military career spanning more than thirty years, must have judged himself soon destined for retirement. He had been born in 1762 on the island of Ulva, off the west coast of Scotland, into a landowning family. At the age of fourteen, he joined the British Army and was sent in 1777 as a new recruit to take part in the American War of Independence. Initially stationed at Halifax, Nova Scotia, he was promoted five months later to ensign. In 1781, he was promoted to lieutenant and served in North America and Jamaica before being posted to India, where he would serve for the next sixteen years.

In 1787, he served in the Indian Army in Egypt and was present at the capture of Alexandria and the final expulsion of the French Army from the country. In 1793, the thirty-one-year-old Macquarie married twenty-year-old

Jane Jarvis, the daughter of the former chief justice of Antigua, but within a year Macquarie's new bride had been diagnosed with tuberculosis. On medical advice, Macquarie took his sick wife on a sea voyage, but she died fifteen days after arriving in China in July 1796, aged twenty-three. Devastated, he brought her remains back to India, where she was buried in Bombay's European cemetery the following January. Macquarie arranged for a 475-word epitaph to be engraved on the tomb, extolling her virtues:

> Here lie interned the much honoured and beloved remains of Mrs Jane Macquarie ... aged 23 years and 9 months ... she possessed in a most eminent degree all the virtues that adorn the female character, and render it worthy of universal admiration ... She was mild, affable and polite ... sweet and even ...

After several more years in India and becoming the commander of his regiment, Macquarie finally returned home to England in March 1807. Later in the same year, he married for a second time, to twenty-nine-year-old Elizabeth Campbell. Macquarie had first encountered Elizabeth, a distant cousin, nearly twenty years before, when she was only ten years old, then had met her again in 1804 when he was on leave from India in England. He recorded in his journal at the time that she was a 'most amiable agreeable and sensible girl'[3] and later 'this girl is quite a heroine ... What an excellent soldier's wife she would make – and happy – in my mind – will that man be whose good fortune it may happen to be to get her'.[4]

The following year he visited Elizabeth, who was staying with an aunt in London, and 'finding her alone' made a 'full avowal to her of my sentiments, and of my sincere love and ardent affection for her'.[5] When she accepted his proposal of marriage, he recorded his 'infinite joy and delight that she had most kindly consented to be mine'.[6] Elizabeth would become a very influential partner in her husband's long period as New South Wales governor, and have many streets and landmarks named after her in New South Wales and Van Diemen's Land.

The following October, Macquarie became a father for the first time at forty-eight, when Elizabeth gave birth to a daughter – but the child died only days later. In September the following year, Elizabeth gave birth to another baby daughter, whom they named Jane Jarvis, but the infant died after only three months. Over the next five years, Elizabeth suffered at least seven miscarriages before giving birth to their only surviving child, a son, Lachlan, in 1814.

Lachlan Macquarie was not the first choice to replace William Bligh as governor of New South Wales. The job had initially been given to forty-year-old Miles Nightingall, a veteran army officer who had fought in India, the West Indies and Portugal. Macquarie was given the position of second in command as lieutenant governor, and his role was to take the 73rd Regiment to New South Wales to replace the Rum Corps. At first, he did not like the idea of being sent to Australia, and in a letter to his old friend Charles Forbes in Bombay he described the appointment as:

> not fair, it not being our tour by roster to be sent thither, having already served 25 years in India – and only two years yet at home. We are however, now in a great degree reconciled to our banishment and I am determined from the first to accompany my regiment thither – Mrs. Macquarie of course goes out with me, and we must endeavour to make ourselves as happy as we can in our exile for 3 or 4 years, at the end of which they will allow

me to return home again to my native country. Do not be greatly surprised if Mrs. Macquarie and myself should pay you a visit at Bombay . . . once we become tired of our exile at Botany Bay.[7]

However, only a month before the ship sailed for Australia, Nightingall withdrew, citing crippling rheumatism that was so violent he complained he could not even hold a pen to write. In the end, Macquarie lobbied to be his replacement. He was promptly appointed governor on 1 May 1809.

On 22 May 1809, Macquarie and his wife sailed with his troops from Portsmouth on the *Dromedary* via Rio de Janeiro and Cape Town, on a voyage that would last seven months. The ship arrived in Port Jackson on 28 December to a welcome salute fired from Dawes Point,[8] and Lachlan Macquarie officially took up office on 1 January 1810.

*

Macquarie had been given detailed instructions from Secretary of State for War and the Colonies Lord Castlereagh about cleaning up the colony.[9] 'Macquarie was to restore officers who had been sacked by the rebel government, revoke any land grants and pardons the previous government had made, and declare their trials invalid. Judge Richard Atkins was to be sent back to England and replaced by Ellis Bent, who had come out on the *Dromedary* with Macquarie. The two men liked each other and remained friends for the next few years.

At a New Year's Day ceremony in front of the lines of the newly arrived regiment, Macquarie made clear His Majesty's 'utmost regret and displeasure on account of the late tumultuous proceedings' and 'mutinous conduct'[10] towards his predecessor Bligh:

I am sanguine in my Hopes, that all those Dissentions and Jealousies which have unfortunately existed in this Colony, for some time past, will *now* terminate forever, and give way to a more becoming Spirit of Conciliation, Harmony, and Unanimity, among all Classes and Descriptions of the Inhabitants of it.[11]

But he was clever to avoid becoming involved in the mess of his predecessor; nor did he give any public sign of the parlous state in which Bligh had left the colony. Instead, he gave Bligh a splendid farewell party before he left for England:

On Monday last a farewell Fête was given by his Excellency in honour of Commodore Bligh and his Daughter . . . on which occasion a numerous party of Ladies and Gentlemen were invited, among whom were most of the Officers Civil, Military, and Naval. Government house was neatly decorated, and brilliantly lighted; the ball-room hung round with festoons of flowers, encircling the initials of [Mary Bligh] and Commodore Bligh in a very neat device. In the Evening a Ball was given, which was supported with uncommon vivacity until 'the twinkling stars gave notice of approaching day'; a handsome firework was also displayed on the occasion, between the hours 10 and 11; and no single circumstance was omitted that could convey an idea of the respect entertained by His Excellency for the distinguished persons in compliment to whom the Entertainment had been given.[12]

*

Macquarie's first priority was to restore orderly, lawful government. Although his arrival marked the beginning of the end of the corrupt monopoly on the rum trade by officers of the Marine Corps, many ex-marines who had become businessmen and farmers inevitably resented his autocratic style of governing, and their opposition would only increase in the years that followed.

In the first year of his rule, he began to transform Sydney into an orderly town. Sydney's streets had previously been called old 'rows' or had odd names such as High Street, Sergeant Majors Row – or no name at all.[13] Macquarie named George Street after King George III, who was still alive but too ill to reign, and York, Gloucester, Kent, Clarence, Cumberland and Sussex Streets after the royal dukes. He named Pitt Street after the British prime minister who had served a total of twenty years and who had died in 1806, and after his predecessors as New South Wales governors he named Phillip, Hunter, King and Bligh Streets, and Macquarie Street and Elizabeth Street after himself and his wife.

He ordered that all the city's streets be made at least 50 feet (15 metres) wide. New houses could not be built on them without the governor's approval, and old houses that encroached on the new, wider road were moved back in line at government expense.[14] Macquarie named Harrington Street after his former military commander in London, Argyle Street for his native county, and Castlereagh Street for Lord Castlereagh, who became British foreign secretary in 1812 and a senior representative at the Vienna Convention at the end of the Napoleonic era.

He also built the main road to Parramatta and the main road to South Head, and named the farming towns that had sprung up along the Nepean and Hawkesbury Rivers to the west of Sydney Wilberforce, Pitt Town, Windsor, Castlereagh and Richmond.

To promote better public hygiene, clothing could no longer be washed in the Tank Stream, which was the city's principal source of drinking water, and it was forbidden to bathe in the nude off the government wharf in the daytime.

Macquarie faced an almost total absence of public infrastructure at a time when convict numbers were continuing to increase. At the end of his term, he listed 265 public works built during his tenure, including many that survive today. The more impressive structures include the Mint (1811–16), the new barracks in Macquarie Street (1819), and the church St James' (1819–24).

His largest and most controversial project was the building of a new Sydney hospital on Macquarie Street. Sydney needed a new hospital. The colony's first had been a collection of tents on the western side of Sydney Cove to accommodate the sick convicts arriving on the First Fleet, and the much higher numbers of sick and dying who arrived on the second and subsequent fleets. Macquarie's new, two-storey hospital was designed to be 95 metres long, nine metres deep and 12 metres high, 'with a veranda round each storey 3 metres wide'. The pillars of the lower storey were to be stone and the upper storey wood. It was to cover seven acres (three hectares) of land and include two surgeons' barracks.[15]

The contract to build the hospital was awarded to Garnham Blaxcell, Alexander Riley and the colony's principal surgeon, D'Arcy Wentworth. Riley was a prosperous trader and Blaxcell a former ship's purser and a business partner of John Macarthur. To pay for the building, Macquarie gave the men a monopoly over the import of rum into the colony as well as free convict labour to build it. Initially, the contract allowed them to import 45,000 gallons of rum, but this was later increased to 60,000 gallons.

The contract was signed in November 1810 and the hospital took nearly five years to build. Towards the end of its construction, it was inspected by the convict architect Francis Greenway, who found that because of poor workmanship it 'must soon fall into ruin'. Indeed, under Greenway's supervision, the hospital needed substantial renovations throughout the 1820s.

London was highly critical of Macquarie's public-works spending. Early in his term as governor, he was told that Britain, financially exhausted by years of wars, could not afford to pay for the convict colony's public buildings. In Macquarie's second year, the colonial secretary Lord Liverpool severely criticised the governor for overspending. He pointed out that, in Governor King's last year, only £13,873 had been drawn against the British Government. In Governor Bligh's last year, it was £31,110. After Bligh's overthrow, it was £23,163 in 1808 and £49,514 in 1809.

By contrast, Liverpool pointed out bluntly to Macquarie that the expenditure in his first year of £72,600 was totally unacceptable. He ordered that the spending be cut and that Macquarie not undertake any new works without prior approval from London:

> I am to repeat to you the positive commands of His Royal Highness that while you remain in charge of the colony of New South Wales you use the most unremitting exertions to reduce the expense at least within its former limits, that you undertake no public buildings or works of any description without having the previous sanction of His Majesty's Government for their construction, or without being enabled to prove most clearly and satisfactorily that the delay of reference would be productive of serious injury to the public service.[16]

Liverpool said that Macquarie should raise the money locally from free traders for 'erecting quays, wharfs and bridges . . . streets and roads' because they were 'to receive the immediate benefits from these improvements'.[17] But Liverpool saved his most damning criticism for the way Macquarie had paid for his new hospital by giving the rum monopoly to Wentworth, Blaxcell and Riley, and for forgoing the normal import duty that was collected from all rum landed in the colony:

> Many objections might be urged to an engagement of this nature under any circumstances . . . I am surprized that you did not foresee the embarrassment which would inevitably be occasioned in the execution of this contract . . . It would have been adviseable that an engagement of this kind had not been entered into, until you had an opportunity of learning the sentiments of His Majesty's Government . . .[18]

Macquarie was 'depressed and discouraged'[19] by such a severe reprimand and wrote back to Liverpool expressing 'the sincere sorrow and mortification . . . on account of the severe censure and strong animadversions on my conduct'.[20] However, Lord Liverpool was no longer colonial secretary. He had become prime minister following the assassination of Spencer Perceval in the House of Commons on 11 May 1812. Liverpool's successor as colonial secretary, Lord Bathurst, proved to be 'more equable and reasonable';[21] he occasionally called for greater economy in the New South Wales finances but otherwise left Macquarie to pursue his public-works programs.

In November 1811, Macquarie visited Hobart Town with his wife Elizabeth. The governor's party left Sydney on 4 November on the *Lady Nelson* and, after nineteen days' sailing and much seasickness, reached the Derwent. Macquarie described in his diary how they were welcomed by cheering crowds and saluting guns:

the Town was very handsomely illuminated, and large Bone-fires were made by the Troops, the free Inhabitants, and Convicts, in compliment to my arrival at this Settlement. – Some of the Houses were very fancifully and prettily illuminated, and the Inhabitants & Troops & Convicts continued singing and dancing around their Bone-fires to a late hour.[22]

Macquarie was appalled at what he thought was a ramshackle town and quickly set about designing the layout of the city, including a major street to be named after Hobart's founder, David Collins, who had died eight months before. The Macquarie plan remains the outline of the city of Hobart today:

I pointed out to the Inspector of Works this morning where the new Military Barracks & Hospital are to be built on Barrack Hill, a little South East of the Town. – Also where the new Genl Hospital and County Jail are to be built – on an eminence to the Westward of the Town and near the West Bank of the River. I had the names of the great square and principal streets painted on boards and this morning erected on posts at the angles of the square and streets to define and mark out their respective limits and direction; naming them as follows: viz. George's Square – Macquarie (Main) Street – Liverpool Street – Argyle Street – Elizabeth Street – Murray Street, Harrington Street – and Collins Street; being 3 long and 4 cross streets as per Plan of the Town.[23]

Thirty kilometres outside Hobart, in the district of New Norfolk, Macquarie ordered the building of the town to be named Elizabeth, 'in honour of my dear good wife'.[24] On his tour of Van Diemen's Land, the governor had no qualms about naming sites and landmarks after himself: Macquarie Street, Governor Macquarie's Resting Place, Macquarie River, Macquarie Springs and Macquarie Plains.

The party then travelled overland to the northern settlement of Launceston (the first overland trip by Europeans from north to south had been achieved in 1807). This was the longest land journey of any New South Wales governor to date – the Blue Mountains, west of Sydney, would not be penetrated for another two years, in 1813. Macquarie was impressed by the vista:

> The grand view, and noble picturesque landscape, that presented themselves on our first coming in sight of Launceston and the three rivers and fertile plains and lofty mountains by which they are bounded, were highly gratifying and truly sublime; and equal in point of beauty to anything I have even seen in any country.[25]

He was not completely impressed by his inspection of Launceston but nevertheless ordered each soldier to be rewarded for his duty to king and country:

> At 11 a.m. I inspected the Detachment of the 73d. Regt. stationed at Launceston and found them in good order. – I afterwards proceeded to inspect the Men's Barracks and Hospital –; the former I did not find so clean as they ought to be, and the latter fortunately is empty, there being no sick either Military or Civil to occupy. – I then visited the Public Stores, and Military & Civil Officers Barracks. – The latter were clean & neatly kept, but the former in many respects, require improvement and better arrangement. I issued some Genl Orders respecting the Inspection of the Troops, and directed Half a Pint of Spirits to be issued to each Soldier to drink the King's Health.[26]

While Macquarie and Elizabeth had been travelling overland from Hobart to Launceston, the *Lady Nelson* had sailed around and was waiting in the Tamar River to take them back to Sydney on 20 December 1811, after a tour of five weeks.

Macquarie's impact on the design of both Hobart and Launceston would have an even longer-lasting impact than his influence on Sydney. Before he left Van Diemen's Land, he instructed that a number of public works be built in the two towns – and also in George Town – including courthouses, barracks for prisoners, hospitals, and houses for judges, convict supervisors, surgeons and officers.

On the voyage home to Sydney, the Macquarie's celebrated a successful visit, and, on Christmas Day in the Bass Strait, they 'ordered a good Dinner with some Drink for the Sailors'.[27]

*

Back in Sydney, William Bligh's daughter Mary gave birth to her first child, Maurice Charles (junior) O'Connell, in January 1812. By now, Macquarie was growing increasingly aware that some of the discontent in the colony originated from Mary's resentment of the people still there who had contributed to her father's overthrow. In 1813, he wrote to the colonial secretary Lord Bathurst asking for the withdrawal of the 73rd Regiment and its commanding officer, Colonel O'Connell:

> Mrs O'Connell . . . naturally enough, has imbibed strong feelings of resentment and hatred against all those persons and their families who were in the least inimical to her father's government . . . for, tho' Lieut. Colonel O'Connell is naturally a well disposed Man, he allows himself to

be a good deal influenced by his wife's strong-rooted prejudices against the old inhabitants ... it would most assuredly greatly improve the harmony of the country ... if the whole of the officers and men of the 73rd Regiment were removed from it ... .[28]

Macquarie had other reasons for wanting the 73rd Regiment transferred. On the night of 13 June 1813, two drunken lieutenants, Archibald McNaughton and Phillip O'Connor, got into a fight and killed a civilian, William Holness. Charged with murder, the two officers were tried by a military court that consisted of Judge Advocate Ellis Bent and six regimental colleagues. They were acquitted of murder and found guilty of manslaughter. Each was fined a shilling and imprisoned for six months.

The extraordinarily lenient treatment of the two officers led Macquarie to write to Bathurst criticising the constitution of the court:

The sentence being in direct variance with what was generally expected, and particularly by several of those who had been eye witnesses of this disgraceful scene, but were not called on in the prosecution ... excited a public sensation of strong surprize and much indignation. Neither could the popular sentiment be suppressed or restrained that 'little justice could be expected towards the poor, whilst the court consists of brother officers to prisoners at the bar' ... .[29]

In asking Bathurst for the regiment to be transferred, Macquarie said that 'an alarming degree of licentiousness' had for a long time 'marked the general conduct' of the 73rd. No doubt alluding to the trouble his predecessor William Bligh had had with the New South Wales Corps,

Macquarie also suggested that in future no regiment remain in New South Wales for more than three years.[30] The British Government agreed, and the first men of the 73rd began leaving Sydney for Ceylon on 17 January 1814 on the *Earl Spencer*. The first replacements of the 46th Regiment began arriving a few weeks later in Sydney on the *General Hewitt*.

The 73rd Regiment, under the command of Bligh's son-in-law Maurice O'Connell, stayed for more than sixteen years in Ceylon before returning to England, where Maurice was promoted to major general in 1830. In 1834, the O'Connells were posted to Australia when Maurice was again appointed to command the New South Wales forces. Their eldest son, Maurice, who was now twenty-two years old and a captain in the army, came as his father's military secretary.

*

It was under Macquarie that the hinterland of Australia was opened up for farming, when the Blue Mountains, 50 kilometres to the west of Sydney, were finally crossed by the settlers. For more than twenty years since the arrival of the First Fleet, the New South Wales settlement had been limited to a small coastal plain, as it was felt that the mountain range was impassable. As late as 1812, the explorer Matthew Flinders told a House of Commons Committee that the mountain range 'cannot be penetrated from Port Jackson'.[31]

By Macquarie's time, with a growing population, the shortage of fertile land was becoming a major problem, and the colony was still dependent on the importation of a wide range of foods. However, in May 1813, with Macquarie's blessing, three colonists found a passage through the range. Thirty-eight-year-old William Lawson, thirty-four-year-old Gregory Blaxland and twenty-three-year-old William Charles Wentworth (the son of D'Arcy Wentworth, and a man who would have a great influence on the colony's government in his later years) became the first white men to cross the Blue Mountains.

A number of earlier attempts at crossing the range had failed, including one by Matthew Flinders' close friend and exploring colleague George Bass, ten years before, and two by Gregory Blaxland himself. The three men were aware of the routes taken in the earlier failed attempts. They also knew that those who had kept to the ridges rather than the valleys had penetrated furthest, including botanist George Caley, who had reached what became Kurrajong almost a decade earlier, in 1804.

Wentworth, Blaxland and Lawson, together with four servants, four horses and five dogs, set off from Blaxland's farm and took twenty-one days to reach the other side. Blaxland recorded in his journal that they found plenty of good 'grassland, sufficient in extent . . . to support the stock of the colony for the next thirty years'.[32] As with all European explorers before and after, Blaxland did not register any awareness that opening up the interior for farming would have devastating consequences for the local Aboriginal people who had lived off the land for thousands of years.

Five months after Blaxland, Wentworth and Lawson's find, Macquarie sent the government surveyor George Evans to confirm the route through the mountains and to try to find the best place for settlement and farming.[33] Evans left Sydney with three convicts and two free men, including James Burns, who had been with Blaxland's party a few months before. By 9 December 1813, they had retraced Blaxland's route and gone west 'ninety-eight and a half miles further',[34] finding what Macquarie described as 'beautiful and champion country of very considerable extent and great fertility, through which a river of large size, abounding in large and very fine fish, takes a westward course'.[35]

When Evans returned from the west and reported his find, Macquarie immediately decided to build a road to the new country. The road was built in a remarkably short time by a group led by forty-nine-year-old William Cox, a former marine who had first come to the colony in 1800 with his wife and four sons. The 160-kilometre road, some of it through steep terrain and dense, hardwood Australian bush, had to be levelled and made 3.7 metres wide to allow a four-wheeled vehicle 'to negotiate the surface without difficulty or danger'.[36]

Cox started building on 18 July 1814 and, remarkably, finished five months later, on 21 January 1815, three months ahead of the most optimistic forecast. To help him, he had five free men, thirty convicts, who were promised emancipation at the end of the project, and an escort of eight marines. Their equipment included a horse, six bullocks, two carts and an assortment of axes, saws, hoes, picks, sledgehammers and crowbars.[37] When they reached the site of present-day Bathurst, 225 kilometres from Sydney, they hoisted the first British flag west of the mountain range.

A grateful Macquarie rewarded Cox with a payment of £300 and the first land grant west of the ranges. By any measure, the project was an extraordinary achievement. While there have been many extensions and deviations, Cox's original road was the basis of the main modern highway that runs west from Sydney and across the Blue Mountains.

Excited about the potential of the opened-up farming land, Macquarie decided in April 1815 to go and see for himself. He took a party of thirty-seven people, which included his wife, Elizabeth, the surveyor general and explorer John Oxley, and artist and government botanist John Lewin. It was unusual for the wife of a senior British colonial official to travel with her husband, but Elizabeth accompanied Macquarie on most of his long trips. On this trip, she left behind their only child, baby Lachlan, who had been born the year before. Macquarie wrote in his journal: 'At 8 o'clock this morning Mrs. Macquarie and myself, after having taken leave of our beloved infant, set out in the carriage on our long projected journey to visit the new discovered country to the westward of the Blue Mountains.'[38]

After ten days, they reached their destination, and Macquarie named it Bathurst after Lord Bathurst, the British secretary of state for war and the colonies between 1812 and 1827. Macquarie said:

> The Bathurst Plains ... extending for many miles on both sides of the Macquarie River, and surrounded at a distance by fine verdant Hills, is truly grand, beautiful and interesting, forming one of the finest landscapes I ever saw in any Country I have yet visited. The Soil is uncommonly good and fertile, fit for every purpose of Cultivation and Pasture, being extremely well watered, and thinly wooded.[39]

*

With the economy expanding during Macquarie's term, there was a growing shortage of British currency, which was made worse by the outflow of sterling currency to pay for imports. In 1813, Macquarie ingeniously introduced a new currency, minted from the Maria Teresa Spanish silver dollar. The previous November he had purchased 40,000 Spanish dollars from the visiting merchant ship the *Samarang* and had each of the coins hollowed out. The outside ring was known as the colonial dollar and valued at five English shillings. The small inside coin was called the 'dump' and valued at fifteen pence, or a quarter the value of the dollar. The dump was re-struck with a crown in the centre and the words 'New South Wales' around the edge. In 1816, despite reservations from the Colonial Office in London, Macquarie pressed on and created Australia's first bank, the Bank of New South Wales.

But of all the reforms of the Macquarie era, the most revolutionary and the one that would eventually cause his downfall was his attitude towards convicts who had completed their sentences or earned pardons. According to Macquarie, once a man fitted either description, his 'former state should no longer be remembered, or be allowed to act against him'.[40] He outlined his views in his third dispatch to Lord Castlereagh:

> I have, nevertheless, taken upon myself to adopt a new line of conduct, conceiving that emancipation, when united with rectitude and long-tried good conduct, should lead a man back to that rank in society which he had forfeited, and do away, in as far as the case will admit, all retrospect of former bad conduct.[41]

When Macquarie arrived in the colony, convicts who had finished their sentences, or been given 'tickets of leave', were free to work in any endeavour of their choice. However, they were rarely ever appointed to government posts and were never accepted into higher colonial society. By offering ex-convicts greater opportunity and social acceptance, Macquarie was defying the rigid British class system and ultimately putting himself out of step and out of favour with his London superiors.

He had not always held such radical, reformist views and years later, when under attack, he explained that he changed his opinions after arriving in Sydney. He acknowledged that he had taken the policy much further than his predecessors:

> At my first entrance into this colony, I felt as you do, and I believe I may add, every one does; at that moment I certainly did not anticipate any intercourse but that of control with men who were, or had been convicts; a short experience shewed me, however, that some of the most meritorious men of the few to be found, and who were most capable and most willing to exert themselves in the public service, were men who had been convicts! I saw the necessity and justice of adopting a plan on a general basis which had always been partially acted upon towards these people, namely, that of extending to them generally the same consideration and qualifications, which they would have enjoyed from the merits and situations in life, had they never been under the sentence of the Law, and which had been partially or rather individually adopted towards them by my predecessors.[42]

Macquarie's promotion of ex-convicts not only put him at odds with London but also alienated him from the colony's 'exclusives', who were horrified that he would appoint any ex-convict or 'emancipist' to a government post without regard to their criminal background or social origins. The exclusives were composed of local aristocrats, military and civilian officials, and a number of gentlemen squatters, farmers and businessmen. They felt threatened by the idea of large numbers of ex-convicts who could now become full members of society. The growing class of emancipists were those who had served their prison terms, become free and were now settlers.

In 1814, Ellis Bent was instrumental in having his older brother Jeffrey appointed as judge to the newly constituted Supreme Court. From the date of his arrival, Jeffrey, who was a hard-line exclusive, was in conflict with the colony's administration. Among the issues was his refusal to allow two former convicts to act in his court. Increasingly, Macquarie became estranged from both brothers, and, in 1814, he successfully urged Lord Bathurst to have them dismissed as judges. (At any rate, a few months later, Ellis, who had been ill since his first voyage to Sydney from England in 1808, died. As he left behind a wife and five young children with no wealth to fall back on, Macquarie managed to persuade the British Government to award his widow with a pension.)

Another persistent critic of Macquarie was the Reverend Samuel Marsden. As well as being the colony's leading chaplain, he was a successful farmer and magistrate, whose punishments were so cruel and severe as to attract the nickname the 'Flogging Parson'. Marsden had already been in the colony for sixteen years when Macquarie arrived. Born in Farsley, Yorkshire, in 1765, the son of Thomas Marsden a blacksmith, he became a man of strong personality and deep religious conviction. After limited schooling, he was apprenticed to his father, a blacksmith. By adulthood, he was said to have developed the 'ox-like' features of many blacksmiths.[43] Young Samuel developed a strong interest in religion and, under the guidance of William Wilberforce, attended Cambridge University before becoming ordained.

Marsden arrived in the colony on 10 March 1794. He took up the position of assistant to the colony's original chaplain, Richard Johnson, who had arrived with Arthur Phillip on the First Fleet six years earlier. When Johnson returned to England in 1802, Marsden became the senior clergyman in the colony. In addition to his pastoral duties, he steadily acquired land. By 1802, he had more than 400 acres (162 hectares) of land and 480 sheep, and had become a prominent and wealthy farmer. Three years later, his landholdings exceeded 1700 acres (688 hectares) and he owned more than 1000 sheep, as well as hundreds of pigs and cattle.

It was as a magistrate that Marsden developed a fearsome reputation for ordering extremely severe and excessive punishments, including illegal floggings as a form of torture to attract confessions from suspects. He had a particular hatred of Irish Catholics:

> The number of Catholic convicts is very great . . . and these in general composed of the lowest class of the Irish nation; who are the most wild, ignorant, and savage race that were ever favoured with the light of civilization; men that have been familiar with . . . every horrid crime from their infancy . . . [they are] always alive to rebellion and mischief, they are very dangerous members of society . . . they are extremely superstitious, artful and treacherous, which renders it impossible for the most watchful & active government to discover their real intentions.[44]

His first serious clash with Macquarie came within months of the new governor's arrival in Sydney. Marsden was alarmed to read in the *Sydney Gazette* that he was to become a director of the new toll road to Parramatta but that two of his co-directors were ex-convicts. Later, he said he was totally opposed to Macquarie's policy of promoting former convicts: 'To unite the free and convict population [was to] raise one class and lower another, and to bring bond and free to a common level.'[45]

In 1814, Marsden found himself again at odds with Macquarie when the government issued an order that magistrates refrain from excessive flogging:

the governor recommends in the strongest manner to the magistrates, to inflict corporal punishment as seldom as possible; but to substitute in its stead confinement to the stock for petty crimes, and either solitary confinement, or hard labour in gaol gang, according to their judgment of the degrees of offence; still keeping in view the general conduct and character of the delinquents.[46]

He was further incensed by Macquarie's insistence that no magistrate sitting alone could inflict more than fifty lashes. Marsden regularly ordered several hundred lashes.

The hostility between the two men continued for years, with Marsden regularly challenging the governor's decisions. By 1818, Macquarie had come to believe that Marsden was sending reports back to London complaining about the colony's administration:

Although the name of the author of these gross calumnies is withheld, I have good reason to suppose it proceeded from the pen of the Reverend Samuel Marsden, as I firmly believe he is the only person, in the character of a gentleman in the whole colony, capable of writing and making such unfounded and malicious representations with a view to injure me in the opinion of His Majesty's Minsters.[47]

On 8 January 1818, Macquarie summoned Marsden to Government House and, in front of witnesses, presented him with a letter accusing him of disloyalty and under-mining the governor's reputation in England:

> I have long known, Mr. Marsden, that you are a secret Enemy of mine and as long as you continued only a secret one, I despised too much your malicious attempts to injure my character to take any notice of your treacher-ous conduct; but now that you have thrown off the mask, and have openly and Publickly manifested your hostile and factious disposition towards me, I can no longer, con-sistently with what I owe to my own high station, and the tranquillity of the Country I have the honour to Govern, pass over unnoticed, a recent most daring act of insolence and insubordination, of which you have been guilty.
>
> . . . I consider, Sir, that act of yours, not only as most insolent and impertinent as it respects myself Personally; – but also as highly insubordinate and seditious; . . . such conduct, on your part tends to inflame the minds of the Inhabitants, excite a clamour against my Government, bring my administration into disrepute, and disturb the General Tranquillity of the Colony. Such conduct, Sir, would be highly Criminal in any man; but still much more so in you as being both a Magistrate and a Clergyman who ought to be the first to set an example of loyalty, obedience, and proper subordination! . . . I cannot help deeply lament-ing, that, any man of your Sacred Profession should be so much lost to every good feeling of Justice, generosity and gratitude, as to manifest such deep rooted malice, rancour, hostility and vindictive opposition towards one who has never injured you – but has, on the contrary, conferred several acts of kindness on both yourself and Family![48]

Undeterred, Marsden and other exclusives complained to London about Macquarie's liberal attitude towards convicts. Like most of the governors before him, Macquarie's noble ideals were undermined by harsh realities and constant opposition. In 1816, he had enforced a new proclamation he had drawn up against trespassing on the government's Domain by having three free settlers flogged who had been found on the land. This incident was among several that Jeffrey Bent and others reported to the British Government as examples of Macquarie's authoritarian excesses. As a result, Macquarie was censured by Lord Bathurst, and in 1817 Bathurst ordered an inquiry into the colony's administration.

The man chosen to travel to Australia and undertake the task was thirty-two-year-old judge John Thomas Bigge. In addition to the criticism that Macquarie was too autocratic, conversely, it was also widely believed in England that Macquarie's humanitarianism had gone too far and that 'amongst the criminal classes . . . being sent as a convict to New South Wales was preferable to being unemployed in England'.[49] Before Bigge left England, Lord Bathurst made it clear to him that the primary purpose of the convict colony was severe punishment, and that compassion for the convicts could not work properly:

> you will . . . constantly bear in mind that Transportation to New South Wales is intended as a severe Punishment applied to various Crimes, and as such must be rendered an Object of real terror to all classes of the community . . . if . . . by ill-considered Compassion for convicts, or from what might under other circumstances be considered a laudable desire to lessen their sufferings, their Situation in New South Wales be divested of all Salutary Terror, Transportation cannot operate as an effectual example on the community at large, and as a proper punishment for those Crimes . . . against . . . which His Majesty's Subjects have a right to claim protection . . .[50]

Bigge arrived in Sydney on 26 September 1819, took thousands of pages of evidence in New South Wales and Van Diemen's Land, then returned to England in 1821 to write three reports, which he presented to the House of Commons: 'The State of the Colony of New South Wales' (19 June 1822); 'The Judicial Establishments of New South Wales and of Van Diemen's Land' (21 February 1823); and 'The State of Agriculture and Trade in the Colony of New South Wales' (13 March 1823). In the reports, he made it clear that he was largely in agreement with the exclusives' complaints, and he criticised Macquarie's emancipation policy and his public-works program.

Macquarie had first attempted to resign a year before Bigge was appointed. In December 1817, he qualified for the pension he had been promised if he completed eight years as governor, and he offered his resignation the following month. At first it was not accepted by Lord Bathurst, but, after repeated requests and some major differences with Bigge, who was by then in the process of preparing his report, Macquarie finally received notification from Lord Bathurst on 31 January 1820 that his resignation had been accepted.

At the beginning of 1821, he began preparing for his return to Britain, but he had to wait until 11 June to discover who his replacement would be. Sir Thomas Brisbane would be taking up the post, having been recommended by the Duke of Wellington, with whom Brisbane had seen service. (In 1824, a convict settlement was named after him, which became today's capital of Queensland).

Despite the disapproval from sections of the local society and from London, Macquarie and his family were greatly appreciated and widely liked in New South Wales. They were given a splendid farewell when they finally left Sydney on the *Surry* to sail home to Scotland on 12 March 1822:

About noon His Excellency Major General Macquarie, Mrs. Macquarie, Master Macquarie . . . took final leave of Government-house . . . The Band played '*God save the King!*' The Regiment presented arms, and the Officers saluted, in honour of the beloved Major General. At about half-past 12, His Excellency and family embarked in the governor's barge . . . a salute of 19 guns was fired from Dawes' [Point] Battery. Launches . . . and wherries, were seen crowded with those who appeared determined on catching a parting glimpse of the object of their profound veneration and fondest regard . . . Never did Sydney Cove look so attractive and gay, as upon this occasion; and the shores were lined with spectators innumerable; but each countenance was indicative of sombre feelings too big, too sincere for utterance; – and yet, who witnessed the scene, and could repress the inward sigh? Australia saw her Benefactor, for the last time, treading her once uncivilized and unsocial shores – and felt it too . . . [51]

After arriving back in England on 5 July 1822, for much of the next year, the family undertook a grand tour of France, Italy and Switzerland, which was hoped would improve Elizabeth's deteriorating health. The following year, while in London defending himself against Bigge's charges, Macquarie had a recurrence of a bowel illness that had troubled him since his army service in India. He died in his London lodgings on 1 July 1824, with Elizabeth at his side.

Macquarie's reputation continued to grow after his death, especially among emancipists and their descendants, who were the majority of the Australian population until the gold rushes began in 1851. His public-building and town-planning programs had established a solid infrastructure for the colony. Exploration had reached deep inland, and the settlement and agriculture that followed took the colony closer to self-sufficiency.

Many locations still carry his name throughout New South Wales, including Lake Macquarie, between Sydney and Newcastle; the Lachlan and the Macquarie rivers in western New South Wales; Mount Macquarie near Blayney in western New South Wales; Port Macquarie on the mid-north coast of New South Wales; and Macquarie Pass, traversing the Illawarra escarpment to the New South Wales Southern Highlands. In Sydney, Macquarie Street, Macquarie Place, the suburb of Macquarie Fields and Macquarie Lighthouse on the south side of Sydney Heads all bear his name. In Tasmania, he appears in the names of Macquarie Island, between Tasmania and Antarctica; Macquarie Street in Hobart, Macquarie Harbour on the west coast and the Macquarie River. Important later institutions that adopted his name include Macquarie University, Macquarie Hospital and Macquarie Bank.

Lachlan Macquarie is also responsible for the official adoption of the name Australia. Matthew Flinders had wanted to use Australia rather than Terra Australis but did not have enough influence to persuade the British authorities. Flinders' chart and journal, which included a reference to the name Australia, was not published until 1814, and copies did not reach Macquarie in Sydney till 1817. On 21 December 1817, Macquarie first used the name Australia in an official dispatch to the British under-secretary for war and the colonies, Henry Goulburn.

Gradually, the appellation replaced Terra Australis, and in 1824 the name Australia became official when the Admiralty used it on their maps.

Today, Macquarie is regarded as the most enlightened and progressive of all the early colonial governors, and responsible for transforming Australia from a prison camp into a country. His grave in Mull, Scotland, is inscribed with the words 'The Father of Australia'.

Chapter 6

The Aboriginal People

The injuries we have inflicted, the oppression we have exercised, the cruelties we have committed, the vices we have fostered, the desolation and utter ruin we have caused . . . Every law of humanity and justice has been forgotten or disregarded. Through successive generations the work of spoliation and death has been carried on.

Within half a century of British settlement, local Aboriginal communities in areas of colonisation had been decimated.

When Arthur Phillip sailed from England in 1788 with the First Fleet to establish the British convict colony, he carried instructions signed by King George III ordering:

You are to endeavour by every possible means to open an intercourse with the natives, and to conciliate their affections, enjoining all our subjects to live in amity and kindness with them. And if any of our subjects shall wantonly destroy them, or give then any unnecessary interruption . . . it is our will and pleasure that you do cause such offenders to be brought to punishment according to the degree of the offence.[1]

Shortly after reaching Sydney in early 1788, Phillip made it clear to his colleagues how the British should treat the local people:

The Governor gave strict orders, that the natives should not be offended, or molested on any account, and advised that wherever, they were met with, they were to be treated with every mark of friendship. In case of their stealing anything, mild means were to be used to recover it, but on no account to fire at them with ball or shot.[2]

But, from the start, Phillip's colleagues saw little to justify the respect he wanted shown to the Indigenous people. Many recorded negative views, and when their journals were published back in England, they would help to shape a European view of the Aboriginal people that would last for the next two centuries. Surgeon Arthur Bowes Smyth believed the Indigenous people were 'stupid and lazy',[3] and Seaman Jacob Nagle on the *Sirius* said they were the 'most miserable . . . that I ever saw'.[4]

Not all the first assessments were negative. Marine Lieutenant Watkin Tench said he acknowledged that the lack of 'advancement and acquisition' might support the view that they 'were the least enlightened and ignorant on earth' but argued that, on more detailed inspection, they 'possessed acumen, or sharpness of intellect, which bespeaks genius', citing some of their tools and weapons that 'display ingenuity'.[5]

Initial contact between the first settlers and the Aboriginal people was friendly enough, but within a few months there were increasing numbers of violent incidents. Towards the end of the first year, Phillip acknowledged a further deterioration in relations when he recorded that the locals were increasingly avoiding the settlers:

> The natives now avoid us more than they did when we first landed, and which I impute to the robberies committed on them by the convicts, who steal their spears and fizgigs, which they frequently leave in their huts when they go out a-fishing ... This the natives revenge by attacking any straggler they meet, and one convict has been killed ...[6]

In April 1789, there was an outbreak of smallpox in the Sydney settlement that was to kill a large number of Aboriginal people. Some estimates suggest that as much as half the local population died, but only one European perished – a sailor from the *Supply*.[7] Midshipman Newton Fowell, who sailed with the *Sirius* on the First Fleet, described the hundreds of bodies of dead Aboriginal people around Sydney:

> every boat that went down the harbour found them laying dead on the beaches and in the caverns of rocks ... They were generally found with the remains of a small fire on each side of them and some water left within their reach.[8]

Smallpox was a greatly feared disease, and an outbreak could spread quickly and kill many people. Its first symptoms included a fever, headaches, joint and muscle pain, and a feeling of exhaustion, followed by frequent vomiting. After several days of shivering, a rash developed and the skin blistered. In severe cases, the blisters became so dense as to coalesce into giant pustules. If the individual survived, the pustules left scars or 'pocks', which resulted in the disease being called the 'speckled monster' in the eighteenth century. Death was slow, painful and probably came as a relief for those who were severely affected. Those who were weaker, the very young and the very old died swiftly.

The process of eradicating smallpox began when it was learnt that survivors could never contract the disease a second time. This led to the process of 'variolation', whereby a healthy person would deliberately infect someone with the disease in the hope of inducing a mild case of infection and therefore immunity.

The Aborigines had no exposure or resistance to the disease, and it would devastate their population. Arthur Phillip said the disease 'must have been spread to a considerable distance, as well inland as along the coast'.[9]

The white settlers could not account for the outbreak, although it must have been brought into the area by the First Fleet. If it had been carried by one of the new settlers, why had it taken so long to appear – almost fifteen months after their arrival? And why wasn't it evident among any other of the Europeans? One possibility is that the disease was released from one of the vials the surgeons had brought as a source of variolation, but the surgeons denied this at the time.

Arthur Phillip had no idea of its cause and speculated that the French could have brought it, even though La Perouse and his ships had left more than a year before:

Whether the small-pox, which has proved fatal to great numbers of the natives, is a disorder to which they were subject before any Europeans visited this country, or whether it was brought by the French ships, we have not yet attained sufficient knowledge of the language to determine. It never appeared on board any of the ships in our passage, nor in the settlement, until sometime after numbers of the natives had been dead with the disorder . . .[10]

Over the coming decades, the Aboriginal population was ravaged by a number of other European diseases, including measles, tuberculosis, cholera, whooping cough, influenza, venereal disease and alcoholism. By the 1840s, for example, more than 90 per cent of the Aboriginal women in Victoria's Loddon Valley were found to have been afflicted with venereal diseases.[11]

Towards the end of the first year of British settlement, Arthur Phillip decided to take action at what Watkin Tench described as the 'petty warfare and endless uncertainty' that now prevailed between the British and the local Aboriginal people by abducting some of the locals, who, it was hoped, would bridge the gap between the two cultures.[12] On New Year's Eve 1788, a Lieutenant Henry Ball, Lieutenant George Johnston and some marines were sent down to Manly Cove, where some Aboriginal men had been seen on the beach. The British seized two men but the locals fought back with spears, stones and firebrands. Firing their muskets, the marines lost one of their captives but managed to hold the other as they beat a hasty retreat down the beach to their boats and back to Sydney.

When the men reached Sydney Cove, the captive caused a lot of excitement as he was brought out of the boat tied up: the 'clamourous crowds . . . flocked around him'.[13]After many unsuccessful attempts to learn his name, he was called Manly after the name of the beach from which he had been abducted. Tench, who helped bathe, dress and feed Manly, recorded the episode in considerable detail:

> he appeared to be about thirty years old, not tall, but robustly made . . . his hair was closely cut, his head combed and his beard shaved. To prevent his escape, a handcuff with a rope attached to it was fastened around his left wrist; which at first highly delighted him . . . but his delight changed to rage and hatred when he discovered its use.[14]

The next morning, New Year's Day, Manly was taken in a boat down the harbour 'to convince his countrymen that he had received no injury'. When a number of people came down to ask him why he didn't jump from the boat 'he only sighed and pointed to the fetter on his leg, by which he was bound'.[15]

Perhaps to compensate for his abduction, Manly was given much more to eat than the standard ration, including duck and fish. He was offered but would not eat bread or salted meat. He only drank water and would not drink alcohol. Over the next months, Manly settled down and managed to communicate his real name – Arabanoo – but his continued detention failed to cause any significant improvement in the relationship between the settlers and the locals, which, as Lieutenant Tench wrote, had been the entire justification for the abduction:

> One of the principal effects which we had supposed the seizure and captivity of Arabanoo would produce, seemed yet at as great a distance as ever; the natives neither manifested signs of increased hostility on his account, or attempted to ask any explanation . . . of their countryman who was in our possession . . .[16]

Following the outbreak of smallpox that devastated the local Aboriginal population, Arabanoo asked to be released so he could go to the aid of his people. The fetter was removed from his leg so that he could move around the area, but he too was soon struck down with the disease and died six days later. By this stage he had become popular among the settlers. He was buried in the governor's garden, and Phillip and all the officers of the settlement attended the funeral.

After the death of Arabanoo, the settlers sought a replacement and conscripted two Aboriginal men, Bennelong (also known as Beneelong) and Colbee, into their service. The two men joined two Aboriginal children, Abaroo and Nanbaree, who had been taken into the settlement after their parents had died during the smallpox epidemic.

Bennelong was to adjust to the white man's environment better than his fellows. For most of the time he seemed happy to live among the English. He wore their clothes and was an effective liaison between his people and Governor Phillip. He also enjoyed drinking 'the strongest liquors, not simply without reluctance, but with eager marks of delight'.[17] He went to live in a little house built by the settlers for him in Sydney Cove at a point that later became known as Bennelong Point – the eventual site of the Sydney Opera House around 180 years later.

Bennelong fled back to his own people early in 1790. Some months later Phillip was told that Bennelong had been seen, and the governor took a boat with armed marines to recapture him at Manly Cove, while the Aboriginal people were feasting on a beached whale.

With the rowers sitting in the boat, Phillip went ashore with his fellow officers, carrying gifts for the locals. As a gesture of friendship, Phillip withdrew a knife from his belt and threw it on the ground, but it frightened one of the Aboriginal men, who quickly lifted his spear with his foot and threw it at Phillip. The four-metre lance went through Phillip below the shoulder blade and the barb came out of his back.

Phillip and his colleagues hurriedly stumbled down the beach towards the boat. One of the marines, Lieutenant Waterhouse, tried to pull the spear out, but, realising it would cause more damage that way, broke off the shaft instead. As they pulled Phillip onto the boat, the crew fired off a round from their muskets to aid their escape.

It took two hours to row back up the harbour. Phillip lay on the floor of the boat, conscious but bleeding, and his colleagues expected him to die. When they reached Sydney Cove, it was thought at first by surgeon William Balmain that an artery of Phillip's had been severed, but after treating the wound the injury didn't seem as serious as had been first thought.

Bennelong expressed concern at the incident and began calling at Sydney Cove to ask after the welfare of the governor. Eventually contact was re-established and Bennelong moved back to Sydney Cove.

When Phillip returned to England in 1792, he took Bennelong and another Aboriginal, named Yemmerrawanne, with him. Yemmerrawanne was reportedly unhappy in London and became ill and died, but Bennelong seemed to enjoy himself, initially at least. He wore laced shirts and embroidered waistcoats and was a novel figure in British society. It is believed that Bennelong may have met King George III at the Theatre Royal in Covent Garden. In London he learnt to box, skate and smoke, and some English manners, including the use of a knife and fork, bowing and drinking toasts.

After more than two years, Bennelong longed to go home, and eventually he returned to Sydney in September 1795. By now he was drinking heavily and constantly fighting, which resulted in him losing the respect of many of his own people. He died a sad figure aged about 50 in 1813.

The failure of the Aboriginal people and the Europeans in Australia to understand each other was caused by fundamental differences in their respective societies. The Aboriginal people accepted that different groups have rights to different territory. The Europeans treated all the land as their own: by their law, it now belonged to King George III and his heirs and successors.

Survival in the harsh Australian environment required a sensitive relationship between the people and the land and the sea, and this world would not survive the intrusion of more than 1000 European settlers who had no understanding of the delicate ecological balance. The First Fleet took everything they could, depleting the natural food supply and chasing away many of the other animals. The Aboriginal people shared what they had, but the English, committed to the idea of individual property, saw them as scavengers when they asked for food.

Over the next 200 years these fundamental differences would disrupt and destroy a civilisation and culture that had survived thousands of years.

*

During the first two decades of settlement, there were repeated violent incidents between the newcomers and the Indigenous occupants of the land. Much of the conflict arose from the spread of settlement, as emancipated convicts were increasingly granted land west of Sydney along the fertile banks of the Hawkesbury and Nepean rivers and became farmers. The European settlers had already taken a large proportion of traditional sources of food around the Sydney basin by fishing and hunting kangaroos, wallabies and birds. As the farms spread westwards, many of the traditional owners were forced off their land and, driven by a need for food, began to steal farm crops, which inevitably provoked violent responses from the farmers. Following an outbreak of clashes between farmers and local Aboriginal tribes west of Sydney in 1804, Governor Philip Gidley King conducted his own inquiry:

> Wishing to be convinced myself what cause there was for these alarms, three of the natives from that part of the river readily came on being sent for. On questioning the cause of their disagreement with the new settlers they very ingenuously answered that they did not like to be driven from the few places that were left on the banks of the river, where alone they could procure food; that they had gone down the river as the white men took possession of the banks; if they went across white men's grounds the settlers fired upon them . . .[18]

Despite this apparent understanding of the hunger of the alienated Aboriginal tribes, King had no hesitation in dispatching armed troops to shoot at them if farms were threatened.[19]

Many of the raids on settlers' farms were led by Pemulwuy, a local Aboriginal leader who was believed to have been born around 1750 on the northern side of the Georges River.[20] In December 1790 Pemulwuy speared Governor Arthur Phillip's gamekeeper, John McIntyre, who later died from the wound. From 1792, for the next decade, Pemulwuy led raids on settlements in a wide arc around Sydney at Prospect, Toongabbie and Parramatta and along the Hawkesbury River. In 1795 Judge David Collins described him as the most active enemy of the settlers. In that year, after Pemulwuy had led an attack on a government farm at Toongabbie, a punitive expedition tracked him down and shot him, along with about fifty other Aboriginal people.[21] Hospitalised with seven buckshot wounds to the head and body, Pemulwuy survived and managed to escape, even though his legs were chained. Finally in 1802 and after a succession of close escapes, he was caught and shot dead. His head was cut off and sent to Joseph Banks in England for study.

In the early years, the dispossession of traditional hunting lands was limited to the coastal areas, but following the crossing of the Blue Mountains in 1813 and the spread of farming to the hinterland, the savage clearing of the local Aboriginal people continued. For more than a century, the spread of British settlers involved cases of widespread abductions and rape of Aboriginal women, and the indiscriminate killings of the locals by settlers across the hinterland, and by escaped convicts and sealers along the vast Australian coastline.

The impact of settlement was even more savage in Britain's second colony, Van Diemen's Land. Having survived thousands of years, the entire Aboriginal population had been killed or exiled within thirty years of the arrival of the British. At the time of the first British settlement in 1803, it was estimated that between 4000 and 7000 Aboriginal people were living on Van Diemen's Land. For the first two decades of British settlement, there were relatively few reported killings of either Indigenous people or the white settlers by one another. However, as new farms spread, the locals were robbed of their traditional sources of food and increasingly raided settlements as the only means of keeping alive. Since the authorities were unable to provide all the remote settlements with protection, the farmers were left to defend themselves with guns – in much the same way as was occurring at about the same time on the American frontier.

From around 1825, there was a steady increase in the number of attacks on farms, and over the next seven years an estimated 170 British settlers were killed – and a similar number of Aboriginal people. In 1830, on the orders of the lieutenant governor, George Arthur, an attempt was made to round up all the Aboriginal men on the island. Arthur called upon every able-bodied male colonist, convict or free, to form a human chain, which then swept across the settled districts, moving south and east for six weeks. Some 3000 men and 550 soldiers spread out to form this 'black line' across the island to push all the hostile tribes into the south-east corner. The plan was to corral the Aborigines onto the Tasman Peninsula by closing off Eaglehawk Neck (the isthmus connecting the peninsula to the rest of the island), where Arthur hoped these Indigenous peoples could live and maintain their culture and language. The manoeuvre was inevitably impossible to carry out, and many of the locals easily slipped through the white men's net and disappeared into the surrounding bush.

Two years before the failed 'round-up', George Arthur had appointed George Augustus Robinson to try to conciliate the remaining Aboriginal people in the colony. Thirty-seven-year-old Robinson had migrated from London to Hobart in 1824 and established a profitable building business. Well educated and very religious, he spent the next few years extensively travelling around Van Diemen's Land, consulting with all the surviving Aboriginal tribes in the colony. Robinson managed to persuade the now fewer than 200 people to leave Van Diemen's Land and move to a new settlement called

Wybalenna on Flinders Island, about 54 kilometres off the north-east of Van Diemen's Land in Bass Strait. In agreeing to move, the relatively few surviving Aboriginal people were promised good housing and food, and freedom from interference. By September 1834, Governor Arthur was able to report to London that all but a handful of the Aboriginal inhabitants of Van Diemen's Land had been moved to Flinders Island.

However, the resettlement was also a failure, and none of the promised benefits to the Aboriginals eventuated. The island was exposed to strong winds, there was insufficient water and little good land for growing crops. The food ration was inadequate and the Aboriginal people would not eat the oatmeal that was provided. They were also forced to live in groups of twenty to thirty in each of the stuffy, crude huts, which made them vulnerable to pulmonary illnesses.[22]

Charles Darwin arrived in Van Diemen's Land in 1836, and in his account of his journey, *The Voyage of the Beagle*, he pointed out that European colonisation almost inevitably led to the destruction of indigenous populations:

Besides these several evident causes of destruction, there appears to be some more mysterious agency generally at work. Wherever the European has trod, death seems to pursue the aboriginal. We may look to the wide extent of the Americas, Polynesia, the Cape of Good Hope, and Australia, and we find the same result. Nor is it the white man alone that thus acts the destroyer; the Polynesian of Malay extraction has in parts of the East Indian archipelago thus driven before him the dark-coloured native. The varieties of man seem to act on each other in the same way as different species of animals – the stronger always extirpating the weaker.[23]

Accounts of the mistreatment of Aboriginal people in the early nineteenth century angered humanitarians and missionaries, and ultimately led to a House of Commons Parliamentary Inquiry. On 9 February 1836, the British House of Commons ordered that a select committee be appointed to review the state of affairs with respect to the treatment of Aboriginal people by British subjects throughout the Empire. The inquiry was chaired by Thomas Fowell Buxton, a humanitarian and Quaker, who had been active in the campaign to abolish the slave trade.

At the time of the inquiry, about one-sixth of the world's inhabitants were part of the British Empire, which was still expanding. Also at that time in Britain, there were great forces promoting humanitarianism, social and political reforms. The Whig government headed by Earl Grey had abolished slavery throughout the Empire in 1833 and had stopped sending convicts to New South Wales in 1840. The committee was to inquire into and propose measures that would secure justice for Aboriginal peoples, protect their rights, promote the spread of 'civilisation' among them and 'lead them to the peaceful and voluntary reception of Christianity'.

The committee published an interim report in 1836, and a final report was presented to the British House of Commons in 1837. It was one of the most damning ever written about the devastating impact of British colonisation on Indigenous peoples:

> Too often, their territory has been usurped; their property seized; their numbers diminished; their character debased; the spread of civilization impeded. European vices and diseases have been introduced amongst them, and they have been familiarized with the use of our most potent

instruments for the subtle or the violent destruction of human life, viz. brandy and gunpowder.[24]

The report pointed out that aspects of colonisation were at odds with Britain's claims to be an enlightened country that valued freedom and liberty:

The injuries we have inflicted, the oppression we have exercised, the cruelties we have committed, the vices we have fostered, the desolation and utter ruin we have caused, stand in strange and melancholy contrast with the enlarged and generous exertions we have made for the advancement of civil freedom, for the moral and intellectual improvement of mankind, and for the further-ance of that sacred truth, which alone can permanently elevate and civilize mankind . . . Every law of humanity and justice has been forgotten or disregarded. Through successive generations the work of spoliation and death has been carried on . . .

Most damaging was the report's catalogue of evils that had been inflicted on the Aboriginal Australian popula-tion by the British:

The inhabitants of New Holland, in their original con-dition, have been described by travellers as the most degraded of the human race; but it is to be feared that intercourse with Europeans has cast over their original debasement a yet deeper shade of wretchedness . . . from the planting amongst them of our penal settlements . . . very little care has since been taken to protect them from the violence or the contamination of the dregs of our countrymen. The effects have consequently been dreadful beyond example, both in the diminution of their numbers and in their demoralization.

During the inquiry, the committee heard evidence from Bishop William Broughton, the head of the Anglican Church in Australia. Broughton had first sailed to Australia with his wife and two daughters eight years before, in 1829. He said that, in addition to the atrocities committed against them, the local Aboriginal tribes were in decay after being 'contaminated' by the Europeans:

> they are, in fact, in a situation much inferior to what I supposed them to have been before they had any communication with Europe . . . It is an awful . . . appalling consideration, that, after an intercourse of nearly half a century with a christian people, these hapless human beings continue to this day in their original benighted and degraded state . . . While, as the contagion of European intercourse has extended itself among them, they gradually lose the better properties of their own character, they appear in exchange to acquire none but the most objectionable and degrading of ours.

Broughton added that, around Sydney and Parramatta:

> The natives . . . are represented as in a state of wretchedness still more deplorable than those resident in the interior . . . they go about the streets begging their bread, and begging for clothing and rum. From the diseases introduced among them, the tribes in immediate connexion with those large towns almost became extinct; not more than two or three remained, when I was last in New South Wales, of tribes which formerly consisted of 200 or 300.

The situation was equally bleak in Van Diemen's Land, where the committee noted that 'it appears that not a single native now remains'. The decline of the Aboriginal population of Van Diemen's Land had been so obvious that in 1830, seven years before the House of Commons report, Colonial Secretary Sir George Murray had warned that the entire race would become extinct:

> The great decrease which has of late years taken place in the amount of the Aboriginal population, render it not unreasonable to apprehend that the whole race of these people may, at no distant period, become extinct . . . it is impossible not to contemplate such a result of our occupation of the island as one very difficult to be reconciled with feelings of humanity, or even with principles of justice . . . having for its avowed, or for its secret object, the extinction of the native race . . .[25]

The committee described how, in the recent British settlements in the north of Australia and in Western Australia, the Aboriginal people were also treated violently and with no justice; and that, in the soon-to-be-settled South Australia, land had been taken for British settlers to farm, with no regard for the traditional owners.

As a result of the parliamentary report, the Aborigines' Protection Society was formed in London. It included five of the fifteen members of the parliamentary committee that had conducted the inquiry. One of the objectives of the society, which was to operate in all British colonies, was the idealistic, if not patronising:

> To encourage and develop, not to damp or destroy their native ardour and energy; to direct and not to weaken their physical character; to enlighten their minds by

reason, and not to darken their understanding by decep-
tion and mystification; to help, and not to oppress ...
[which] would infallibly lead them to be moral, intelligent, peaceful and happy . . .[26]

For some time, the Aborigines' Protection Society had an
impact on British colonial policy. On 18 December 1838,
seven white stockmen were hanged for massacring twenty-eight Aboriginal men, women and children earlier in
the year at Myall Creek, near Inverell, New South Wales.
It was very rare for whites to be punished for killing
blacks, and it was believed the sentences were carried
out because the Aborigines' Protection Society 'had lately
aroused much concern at home about what the colonists
of Australia were doing to the native inhabitants'.[27]

Whatever the effectiveness of the Aborigines' Protective
Society in its early years, it did not have any lasting benefit
for Indigenous Australians. From the 1840s, the colo-
nisers continued to spread across the hinterland, taking
up farmland with no regard for the traditional owners.
The dispossession, violence, rape and disease continued.
By 1850, the number of Indigenous people had fallen dramatically, and with the discovery of gold and the influx
of hundreds of thousands of migrants, the number would
fall further. By 1861, Australia's Indigenous population of
around 180,000 was barely half its estimated total when
Arthur Phillip landed just over seventy years before. Over
the rest of the century, and for the first four decades of the
twentieth century, the population would steadily fall to
below 100,000.[28] It was only after the Second World War
that the decline would stop, but the numbers have never
recovered.

Nor were the Aboriginal people allowed to be part of
the process of building the modern Australian nation.

When the nation of Australia was born in 1901, the country's new constitution stated that 'Aboriginal natives shall not be counted' as citizens and, just to make sure, the *Commonwealth Franchise Act* of 1902 stated that 'no Aboriginal native of Australia' would be entitled to vote. It was not until 1967 that the Australian constitution was amended and Aboriginal people were given the same rights as other Australian citizens.

CHAPTER 7

THE FOUNDING OF THE
OTHER AUSTRALIAN COLONIES

*As the French discovery ships may possibly have in view
the establishment of a settlement on some part of the
coast of this territory, it should be made clear . . . that
the whole of New Holland is subject to His Britannic
Majesty's Government.*

AFTER DAVID COLLINS ABANDONED HIS ATTEMPTS TO ESTABLISH
a large settlement on Port Phillip Bay in 1803, that stretch
of what was then the southern coast of New South Wales
was left alone by the British for the next twenty years. In
1824, though, two explorers became the first Europeans
to reach it overland from Sydney. Twenty-seven-year-old
Hamilton Hume was a farmer who had already explored
a small part of New South Wales near current-day

Goulburn. Thirty-eight-year-old William Hovell was a retired English sea captain who had arrived in New South Wales in 1813 as a free settler. The two men were authorised by the New South Wales governor, Sir Thomas Brisbane, to explore the unknown country from the west of Sydney 1000 kilometres south to Bass Strait. Brisbane was interested in knowing whether there was land suitable for farming, and the explorers were interested in finding out more about the colony's inland river systems. Hume and Hovell largely self-financed their expedition, with Brisbane's government providing a few supplies, such as tents, guns and ammunition.

They took with them more than 500 kilograms of flour, 350 kilograms of pork, sugar, coffee, tea, salt and 30 litres of rum, loaded on packhorses and carts. Leaving Appin, outside Sydney, in early October 1824, each with three servants, the men began a gruelling trek that would take sixteen weeks. On the way, they had to cross swollen rivers, including traversing the Murray, near the later site of Albury, which took three days. Towards the end of December, they finally crossed the southern end of the Great Dividing Range, short of food and with the last of their meat rotten. They arrived at Corio Bay, near current-day Geelong, though they thought they were at Western Port. The Hume and Hovell expedition was of enormous importance and led to the opening up of vast areas of farmland in southern New South Wales from Sydney to Bass Strait.

When the explorers finally reached the southern coast they were surprised to see a number of European habitations. From the late eighteenth and for most of the nineteenth century, hundreds, possibly thousands, of Europeans lived along the southern coast of the continent. They were never officially recognised and never included in any population census but were scattered along the shore for thousands of miles from New Holland to New South Wales, and through the Bass Strait islands. Mainly sealers and whalers, they built little shacks and even small villages, kept livestock and planted crops and vegetables. Others were escaped convicts who lived in lawless isolation, moving along the coast, sometimes abducting Aboriginal women from the mainland or Van Diemen's Land.

Two years after the Hume and Hovell expedition, Lieutenant Edmund Lockyer noticed the same thing when he was sent to establish a tiny British settlement in the continent's south-west corner. Lockyer said there were Europeans regularly camped along the coast for about 3500 kilometres from Rottnest Island to Bass Strait:

> From what I have learned and witnessed they are a complete set of pirates going . . . along the southern coast of New Holland from Rottnest Island to Bass's Strait, having their chief resort or den at Kangaroo Island, making occasional descents on the main[land] and carrying off by force females . . .[1]

In 1826, British anxiety about the French was fuelled by the arrival in Western Port of the *Astrolabe*, captained by the explorer Jules Dumont d'Urville. Ralph Darling, who had taken over from Sir Thomas Brisbane as governor of New South Wales the previous year, warned that the French were 'understood to have been preparing for these seas' and 'possibly have in view the establishment of a settlement on some part of the coast of this territory'.[2] He sent a small party under the command of a forty-one-year-old Captain Samuel Wright to build a settlement in Western Port and deter the French:

should it so happen that the French have already arrived, you will ... signify that their continuance, with any view of establishing themselves or colonisation, would be considered an unjustifiable intrusion on His Britannic Majesty's possessions; and you will warn them immediately to desist from any such attempt, as their perseverance must be attended with unpleasant consequences ...[3]

The settlers included Hovell, forty-one soldiers from the 3rd and the 57th Regiments, a handful of officials and thirty-four convicts, including a carpenter, sawyers, a blacksmith and a brickmaker.[4]

The first of the new settlers sailed from Sydney on the brigs the *Fly* and the *Dragon*, and arrived at Western Port on 24 November 1826, to find that d'Urville had left four days earlier and was heading for Sydney.[5] After setting up a battery and planting a vegetable garden, the British built a small government house with brick chimney and shingle roof, a barracks for the soldiers and the convicts, and a hospital, storehouse and stables.

Despite the success of the building program, Captain Wright was damning about the area as a site to support a permanent settlement. In a report to Governor Darling, he described the soil as 'sterile, swampy and impenetrable' and said the area did 'not possess sufficient capabilities for colonisation on a large scale'.[6]

After a little more than a year, when it was clear the French had no intention of establishing their own settlement in Bass Strait, Governor Darling authorised the British to withdraw. In February 1828, Captain Wright and his colleagues were taken back to Sydney and the site was abandoned.

*

In November 1834, Edward Henty became the first person to cross Bass Strait from Van Diemen's Land to begin farming on Crown land on the mainland. Edward Henty's father, Thomas, had been a farmer in Sussex until 1829, when he had sold up and taken his wife, Charlotte, and seven sons and a daughter to the newly opened colony on the Swan River in Western Australia. However, after two years of struggling with poor soil there, the family abandoned the west and sailed for Launceston. Unfortunately for the Hentys, the system of free land grants in Van Diemen's Land had recently been replaced by sale to the highest bidder, so their move was not initially fruitful.

The Hentys, along with other Van Diemen's Land farmers, had been petitioning the New South Wales governor and the British Government in London for the right to farm across Bass Strait when Thomas Henty started farming there anyway. His initiative led other farmers in Van Diemen's Land to quickly follow suit, including a man called John Batman, who had had his official application to farm on the mainland first rejected in 1827. Batman crossed Bass Strait with sheep and cattle in 1835 and began farming on the north shore of Port Phillip between current-day Geelong and Melbourne. In agitating for his right to do so, Batman, along with a number of other prominent men in Van Diemen's Land, was instrumental in establishing the Port Phillip Association, an organisation designed to develop farming in the Port Phillip district.

Batman left Van Diemen's Land on the 30-tonne schooner *Rebecca* on 10 May 1835 and landed in Port Phillip on 29 May. A week later, at Merri Creek (near current-day Northcote), he purchased 60,000 acres (24,280 hectares) of land from eight local Aboriginal chiefs, paying for it with an assortment of knives, tomahawks, scissors, cloth, clothing and a large quantity of flour.[7] Two days later, before making a return trip to Launceston for more livestock and supplies, he rowed up the Yarra Yarra River and decided on an area for settlement. This would become the site of Melbourne.

The following month, on 6 July 1835, three of Batman's team, who were in a camp at Indented Head on the western arm of the entrance to Port Phillip, noticed an abnormally tall man wearing kangaroo skins and carrying Aboriginal weapons approaching them. The three – William Thompson, William Todd and James Gum – were shocked to see it was a white man. His name was William Buckley and he was an escaped convict from the first ship that had landed in Western Port in 1803 as part of David Collins' settlement, which had subsequently shifted to the Derwent River in Van Diemen's Land.

Buckley had been in the wild Australian bush for more than thirty years and now had difficulty speaking English. He began to understand the settlers when they offered him bread. He said they called it by its name and 'a cloud appeared to pass from over my brain'.[8]

Buckley had escaped with four other convicts, taking with them some bread, meat, cooking pots and a stolen rifle. It appears they had a notion that they could walk to Sydney, but Buckley had become separated from his colleagues, of whom nothing more was ever heard. For some weeks, Buckley wandered the coast, living on small shellfish and eating the tops of plants. He said that he had come across a spear in a mound of earth and later was found sleeping with it by some local Aboriginal women. The women befriended him after recognising the spear as belonging to a relative who had recently died. Thinking he was the spirit of the dead owner of the spear, they invited him back to their camp. He was warmly welcomed into their tribe: the Wathaurung people. (In fact, Buckley had taken a spear used to mark a grave for use as a walking stick.) 'They called me Murrangurk, which I afterwards learnt was the name of a man formerly belonging to their tribe, who had been buried at the spot where I had found the piece of spear I still carried with me.'[9]

For the next thirty years, Buckley lived with the Aboriginal people. He is believed to have married two of them and had a daughter with one. One of his wives was said to have been killed by the tribe for preferring a non-Aboriginal man, but it was also reported that Buckley said he gave her up in order to prevent unrest among the men. According to Buckley, warfare was a central part of life among the Australian hunter-gatherers. He said he had often witnessed wars, raids and blood-feuds.

John Batman was fascinated by Buckley's story and managed to arrange a signed pardon for him from Lieutenant Governor George Arthur in Hobart. Buckley left the south coast and sailed for Hobart on 28 December 1837. He landed in January to see an established township for the first time since he'd left England, on a convict ship almost thirty-five years before. In Van Diemen's Land, he became assistant storekeeper at the Immigrants' Home and then gatekeeper at the Female Factory. He got married in 1840 and retired in 1850, aged seventy. He died in Hobart on 30 January 1856.

After Batman arrived on this stretch of coastline and began farming, more unauthorised settlers began to pour into the countryside around Port Phillip. These included John Pascoe Fawkner, who landed at Hobsons Bay in Port Phillip in October 1835 and established a pub and hotel. In 1838 he also founded the settlement's first newspaper, which was called the *Melbourne Advertiser* and was handwritten until he was given a press. With that, in

February 1839, he launched the *Port Phillip Patriot and Melbourne Advertiser*. Fawkner later became a member of Victoria's first parliament and was an influential and idealistic member of the colony. As his entry in the *Australian Dictionary of Biography* reads, 'His triumph over heredity and early experiences and his struggles with autocracy, convictism and corruption, demonstrated the strength of his purpose, and his rehabilitation and later career were remarkable.'[10]

The New South Wales governor of the time, Richard Bourke (from December 1831 till December 1837), initially declared the land grabs by the farmers unlawful, because they had not been authorised by His Majesty's Government.[11] However, faced with a fait accompli, he then urged that the areas around Port Phillip be allowed to be permanently settled, and the Colonial Office in London agreed and let him decide how best the area should be governed. So, in September 1836, he sent Captain William Lonsdale to provide 'the general superintendence in the new settlement of all such matters as require the immediate exercise of the authority of the government'.[12]

Lonsdale arrived at the mouth of the Yarra in Port Phillip on the *Rattlesnake* on 29 September 1836, with his wife, children and two servants, to find a township of more than 200. A month later, three surveyors, two customs officials, a clerk, thirty soldiers and thirty convicts followed. Lonsdale's duties, with their help, were 'to send in returns and reports, take a census particularly noting land occupation, protect and conciliate the Aboriginals and try to induce them to offer their labour in return for food and clothing, employing as the medium of communication with them "the European named Buckley".'[13]

In 1837, Richard Bourke came from Sydney to see the new settlement for himself. He arrived at the beginning of March and stayed for four weeks. The local population – by then over 500 – had doubled since the previous November.[14] On his visit, he named the port of Williamstown after King William IV and the site Melbourne, after the British prime minister at the time.

The new settlement, at that point officially part of New South Wales, grew rapidly, and the British Government in London decided a more senior man was needed to oversee it. The man chosen to be the settlement's new superintendent was thirty-eight-year-old Charles Joseph La Trobe. He was an unusual appointment: he had no army or navy training, as all earlier governors and lieutenant governors had, nor did he have extensive administrative experience. He would nevertheless prove an effective choice and would serve in Melbourne for fourteen years – longer than any other governor or lieutenant governor sent to any of the Australian colonies in the eighteenth and nineteenth centuries.

La Trobe came from a Huguenot family that had escaped persecution in France by fleeing to England in 1688; Charles was born in London in 1801. His father had been a missionary who had worked in southern Africa while young Charles was educated in Switzerland, where he then worked as a tutor. He became an accomplished mountaineer and wrote two books about his adventures. In 1838, he was knighted, and in January 1839 he was appointed as superintendent of the Port Phillip district.

He arrived in Port Phillip on 30 September 1839 with his wife and daughter, two servants and a prefabricated house. By this time, the local population had grown rapidly to about 10,000 people as farming spread on the fertile lands north of the coast.

By the time of La Trobe's arrival, a Separation Association had been formed by the settlers of the district, which demanded that Port Phillip and its environs become independent of New South Wales. Those agitating for separation complained that too little of the proceeds from Crown land sales was being applied to local public works. A bridge was desperately needed over the Yarra, the roads were in very poor condition and there was no piped water supply.

The first petition for the separation of the Port Phillip district from New South Wales was drafted in 1840 by Henry Fyshe Gisborne. Gisborne was born in England and educated at Harrow, then Eton and Trinity College, Oxford. He had sailed for Australia in 1834 and on his arrival became private secretary to the then governor, Richard Bourke. When Bourke left the colony in 1837, Gisborne took the position of police magistrate in western New South Wales before being appointed commissioner for Crown lands in the Port Phillip district in 1839. He enjoyed a lively social life and was instrumental in establishing Melbourne's horseracing at Flemington.

In Sydney, the new governor, George Gipps, took a dim view, writing to Gisborne to say that 'it brings discredit on the Government to see Gisborne's name figuring in the newspapers as a Steward at Races and at Balls when he ought to be otherwise employed'.[15]

Gisborne resigned, which freed him up to work in support of the growing number of locals who were calling for Port Phillip to become autonomous from New South Wales. In 1840 his draft petition calling for 'responsible government' separate from New South Wales 'with all the exigencies of a state' was unanimously adopted at a public meeting of 600 settlers at Melbourne's St Patrick's Hall. With his health failing, Gisborne presented the petition to Gipps in Sydney before heading back to England. He died on the journey home in April 1841, aged twenty-seven.

Throughout the 1840s, the calls for a separate colony increased as the Port Phillip district quickly developed: the first timber bridge opened across the Yarra in 1844; in 1846 the *Argus* newspaper began publication; and in 1847 Melbourne was proclaimed a city. In 1850, the population of the settlement had reached almost 100,000 people, and in August Queen Victoria signed assent to the *Australian Colonies Government Act*, which made Victoria a colony in its own right the following July.

In 1851, gold was discovered to the north-west of Melbourne, and the rush that followed caused the fledgling colony's population to surge. Within a year of the news reaching the northern hemisphere, five and more ships a day were arriving in Port Phillip to unload thousands more people. Many of the ships were stranded as their crews deserted to join the race to the diggings. Within a decade, Victoria's population had overtaken that of New South Wales, and it would stay higher for the next forty years.

*

South Australia's settlement began in 1836. It was the only Australian colony to be established by free settlers and without convicts.

Part of the southern coast of Australia had been seen by the Dutch seafarer Pieter Nuyts 200 years before, when he became the first European to sail from the south-west tip of Western Australia to current-day Ceduna. However, it was not until 1803 that the English explorer Matthew Flinders completed a detailed exploration and charting of the 'unknown coast', including Spencer Gulf, the Gulf of St Vincent and the large offshore island he named Kangaroo Island.

Flinders did not find the coast inviting. For more than 3000 kilometres, he recorded in his diary sandy, infertile soil, lack of animal and even bird life, and a shortage of fresh water. He sailed close to but did not see the mouth of what was later named the Murray River, which is where Australia's largest river system reaches the sea. The inland rivers were not discovered by Europeans until Charles Sturt explored several of them early in 1830.

Charles Sturt was born in 1795 in Bengal, the son of an East India Company judge. At five years of age, he was sent to relatives in England and educated at Harrow and Cambridge before joining the army. At thirty-one, he sailed as captain of the regiment of marines on the *Mariner* to the convict colony in Sydney, arriving in May 1827. In 1828, he was given permission to explore the inland river systems of New South Wales, and early the following year charted the Darling River, which he named after the governor, Sir Ralph Darling. The Darling runs for more than 1400 kilometres from the north to the south of western New South Wales, and with its tributaries is the largest river in Australia.

The following year, on a second expedition, Sturt headed south-west of Sydney and followed the Murrumbidgee River to the lower Darling and into the 'broad and noble' Murray River, which he named after Colonial Secretary Sir George Murray. By following the Murray, he found that it opened into a great lake, which he named Alexandrina, after the Princess Alexandrina, who seven years later would become Queen Victoria. (Sturt was not the first European to see the lake. It was first sighted in 1828 by sealers based on Kangaroo Island, and a letter about the discovery, addressed to the Colonial Secretary, Sydney, was written by Captain Forbes of the schooner *Prince of Denmark* in January 1829. Unfortunately, this letter did not reach Sydney until May 1830, shortly before Sturt returned from his journey down the river.)

Unlike the earlier coastal explorers, who saw little fertile land from the sea, Sturt found the terrain appealing:

> Hurried . . . as my view of it was, my eye never fell on a country of more promising aspect, or of more favourable position, than that which occupies the space between the lake [Alexandrina] and the ranges of the St Vincent's Gulf, and . . . stretches away, without any visible boundary.[16]

Attracted by Sturt's discovery, Governor Darling sent forty-seven-year-old Captain Collet Barker the following year to undertake a more thorough survey. Barker's party sailed to South Australia on the *Isabella* and began exploring in April 1831. Over the next two weeks, he climbed Mount Lofty and sighted the Port River inlet, which would become the later location of the city of Adelaide. On 29 April, he reached the mouth of the Murray and swam across its narrow channel before climbing over a sand dune. He was never seen again. A few days later, his party learnt that he had been killed by local Aboriginal people, who had mistaken him for a whaler or a sealer.

Based on Barker's expedition and his own earlier findings, Charles Sturt argued in 1833:

> it would appear that a spot has, at length, been found upon the south coast of New Holland, to which the colonist might venture with every prospect of success . . . All who have ever landed upon the eastern shore of St Vincent's Gulf agree as to the richness of its soil, and the abundance of its pasture.[17]

The discovery coincided with the emergence of a movement in Britain that was promoting a scheme for free settlers to migrate to Australia. Edward Gibbon Wakefield was an early advocate of establishing free settlements in the region. He had written his original proposal in Newgate Gaol in London, where he was serving a three-year prison sentence for abducting a fifteen-year-old girl.

Wakefield had been schooled at Westminster and Edinburgh High Schools, and at eighteen became secretary to the British envoy in Turin, Italy. Two years later, while back in England, he eloped and married seventeen-year-old heiress Eliza Pattle. Together, Eliza and Edward had a daughter and a son before Eliza died in 1820, leaving Wakefield with a substantial inheritance.

In 1826, Wakefield, by now thirty years old, abducted a fifteen-year-old heiress called Ellen Turner. He had sent a servant in a carriage to Ellen's school in Liverpool with a message that her father was ill and must see his daughter immediately. Instead, he took her to Manchester and then to Scotland's Gretna Green, where they were married, before fleeing to France. Pursued by Ellen's enraged family, the pair was finally caught in Calais, where Ellen was induced to return to England. Wakefield was charged, convicted and sentenced to three years' jail on 14 May 1827.

In prison, he began writing his proposed migration scheme, and his first publication, 'Sketch of a Proposal for Colonizing Australasia', appeared anonymously in 1829. In it, Wakefield argued that, as an alternative to convict settlement, Crown lands should be sold to free settlers. The revenue raised could then be used to attract emigrant workers, preferably young married couples, thus relieving population pressures on Britain and ensuring prosperous colonies.

Over the next few years, Wakefield pressed his case in a constant flow of letters and articles to newspapers, pamphlets and books.

In 1829, the National Colonization Society was formed in London, which promoted a plan for the settlement of South Australia. Then, in 1833, the South Australian Association came into being in London: it wanted to attract free settlers to a new colony. Leaders of the movement included member of parliament and classical historian George Grote, and rising politician William Molesworth, and it attracted the support of the hero of Waterloo, the Duke of Wellington. The association proposed that Crown land be sold at a fixed price per acre to free settlers and that some of the money raised pay the passage of migrants.

In 1834, the British Parliament passed the *South Australian Constitution Act*, which established the British province of South Australia, an area of 802,511 square kilometres, about the size of France and Germany combined. The new law established a 'colonisation' commission, which advertised the sale of land to free settlers, including the offer of free passage to the colony:

For His Majesty's Province of
SOUTH AUSTRALIA
Selling orders for Town and Country sections
LAND
The Commissioners are also prepared to receive
applications from such intending settlers as may wish
to have their servants and labourers conveyed to the
colony
FREE OF COST

Also in 1834, the South Australian Company was formed by British businessmen to buy large tracts of land at a wholesale discount for on-sale in smaller parcels to farmer settlers. The company combined 'the higher order of moral and religious views – the extension of civilization and the truths of Christianity – with the practical objects of commercial enterprise'[18] and in its prospectus avowed to 'have no connections with any persons of dissolute habits or immoral principles or whose former actions could not undergo a strict examination'.[19]

In February 1835, the first migrant ships sailed, and in August the pioneers reached Kangaroo Island aboard the *Duke of York*, *Emma*, *Lady Mary Pelham* and *John Pirie*. Not all were happy with what they saw, including twenty-eight-year-old Charles Hare, who arrived on the *Emma*:

> Kangaroo Island is a place in which you were grossly deceived; there's no timber fit for houses or ships; there are not 500 acres of good land on the island; there are the most impenetrable masses of jungle here that I have ever met . . . With all these difficulties, I thank God to take courage. I do not fear making this a prosperous settlement and the company doing well . . .[20]

Hare also complained about the threatening behaviour of some of the other settlers: 'The men [brought out by the Company] have been most infamous in previous character and conduct. They have threatened Mr Stephens's, Mr Beare's and my own life since I have been here and we have been obliged to walk about with loaded pistols in our pockets.'

According to twenty-six-year-old Charles Powell, who arrived on the *Duke of York*, another problem was the prevalence of cheap grog:

> There was not much teetotalism in those days and rum was very cheap, only 4s 6d a gallon. Had I drunk as heavily of it as some did I should not be here now. I have seen men drink pannikin after pannikin of it until they appeared to be more dead than alive. . . I was on the island for nearly two years.[21]

Within two months, and after an inspection of the land by the colony's new surveyor general, Colonel William

Light, it was decided that the resources of Kangaroo Island were insufficient to support a large colony, and the settlers moved to the mainland, where other migrants were already arriving. However, Charles Powell argued that the island was productive. He worked on a South Australian Company vegetable garden on Kangaroo Island for the first two years before the company closed its operations and moved to the mainland:

> I commenced my gardening operations and soon had many kinds of seeds in the ground and the headway they made and the site attained in comparison with what have been the case in England under similar circumstances were remarkable. The inhabitants of the island could not consume the vegetables raised and the surplus was sent in boats to the mainland. The fruit trees and vines also did well . . .[22]

The first governor of South Australia was fifty-two-year-old Sir John Hindmarsh, who had spent almost forty years in the navy, including a period as a lieutenant on Admiral Nelson's *Victory*. Hindmarsh sailed in August 1836 from England on the *Buffalo* and reached Holdfast Bay (which is now a beachside suburb of Adelaide) in late December. Eight ships of migrants, including the pioneers who had first gone to Kangaroo Island, had reached the new colony before him. On 28 December 1836, under a huge tree and in front of about 200 settlers, South Australia was proclaimed, the British national anthem sung and 'Rule Britannia' played by the band.[23]

Two days after the proclamation ceremony, Hindmarsh was taken by Colonel William Light to inspect the site he had chosen for the new capital, which he named Adelaide after the queen of the ruling monarch King William IV.

(William IV was the king from 26 June 1830 to 20 June 1837, between the reigns of King George IV and Queen Victoria.)

South Australia's tiny population of only 546 people in its first year had risen to 14,630 a decade later. However, between 1850 and 1860, it more than doubled in size, from around 60,000 to over 125,000, and for the next quarter of a century it was the third-largest colony after New South Wales and Victoria.

*

More than a decade before the free settlers established South Australia, the first attempt was made to colonise what would become the Northern Territory, some 3000 kilometres to the north.

From 1824, there were three separate attempts to establish a permanent military and commercial port in the 'top end' on the far north coast of the continent, but all of them were abandoned.

The first push came from British merchants trading in the East Indies, who complained to the British Government that the Dutch were imposing heavy duties on non-Dutch traders. In February 1824, thirty-eight-year-old Captain James Bremer was sent with instructions from Colonial Secretary Lord Bathurst to take possession of 'that part of the said coast contained between the western shore of Bathurst Island [one of the Tiwi Islands, north of current-day Darwin] and the eastern side of the Cobourg Peninsula [the spit of land to the east of Darwin], including the whole of Bathurst and Melville Islands'.[24]

Sailing from England on the warship *Tamar*, Bremer reached Sydney in June 1824, where Governor Brisbane provided stores, thirty marines, forty-four convict volunteers, about ten of whom are believed to have been women, and a few free settlers. Nearly half the convicts had professions that would help build the planned settlement, including carpentry, stonemasonry, blacksmithing, bricklaying and cabinet-making. The convicts were offered the inducement of a ticket of leave after twelve months if they behaved. The handful of free settlers had been offered free passage to the new settlement and allowed rations for six months after their arrival, provided that for half the period they devoted their services to the Crown.

Melville Island was at the time slightly to the west of the limits of the territory of New South Wales claimed by the British when Arthur Phillip had arrived to settle with the First Fleet. A year later the British Government simply extended their claim to the territory of New South Wales a further six degrees westwards to include both the Cobourg Peninsula and Melville Island.

Bremer arrived in September 1824 at Port Essington, on the Cobourg Peninsula. The navy's Phillip Parker King had named the port after Admiral Sir William Essington while charting the north coast in 1818. On 26 September, Bremer 'unfurled the British Flag and formally took possession of the territory . . . in the name of King George the Fourth'.[25] However, citing a lack of available fresh water, he and his men abandoned Port Essington after only three days and instead decided to build the settlement on nearby Melville Island.

On 2 October, work began on building the first permanent settlement in Australia north of the Tropic of Capricorn. Trees were felled and a fort built that was 70 metres long, 50 metres wide and was surrounded by a three-metre-deep ditch. A storehouse and jetty were also built, and gardens cleared and planted.

The settlement, named Fort Dundas, struggled from the start. After two months, Bremer was ordered to sail for India, and its command passed to Lieutenant Charles Cartwright. Most of the settlers who remained were in a permanent state of poor health. Tropical illnesses, poor diet, food shortages and the failure of the vegetable gardens meant that scurvy was prevalent. In the first year, almost every convict was registered as sick, and three died. The settlement failed to attract traders and investors, British political interest waned and, after less than four years, it was abandoned.

Despite the difficulties of living deep in the tropics, the British remained 'spurred on by . . . trade with the rich East Indies'.[26] A year before Melville Island was officially abandoned, another settlement was being attempted. The second one was also ordered by Colonial Secretary Bathurst. The new settlers were to be taken from Sydney under the command of James Stirling, a captain who had been in the navy for well over twenty years, having entered service at the age of twelve. Stirling was given a new ship, the *Success*, his second command, and was sent from England to Sydney in July 1826 with a supply of new coins. He had been given instructions to then proceed to the struggling settlement on Melville Island to remove it to a more suitable site on the mainland.

Stirling was waylaid in Western Australia for some time, but when he finally made it up to the north and assessed the land around the Van Diemen Gulf, he decided to build the new settlement of Fort Wellington at Raffles Bay on the Cobourg Peninsula. The settlers he had with him from Sydney included commandant Captain H. G. Smyth, a surgeon, a storekeeper, thirty soldiers, fourteen marines and twenty-two convicts, seven of them women. In addition to food rations, the *Success* took with it from

Sydney some livestock, seeds and plants for the development of a local farm.

This new settlement also struggled. Over the next year, it failed to attract any trading ships and many of the settlers became ill, including its commander Captain Smyth. On 1 November 1828, after fewer than eighteen months, the new secretary of state for war and the colonies, Sir George Murray, ordered its abandonment, citing lack of any substantial trade, widespread sickness and the difficulty of supplying the settlement with provisions:

> The . . . settlement . . . was undertaken upon representations from the East India Trade Committee, who hoped that the possession of establishments in that quarter would lead . . . to a trade with the islands of the Eastern Archipelago. These hopes as you are aware, have been disappointed . . . the settlements have proved unhealthy, difficulty is found in supplying them with provisions, and much annoyance is experienced from the natives . . . I do not think that there is . . . any prospect of advantage sufficiently strong to warrant a continuance . . . [27]

Almost ten years after the closure of Fort Wellington, a third attempt was made at establishing a viable community and port in the top end when James Bremer was sent to try again. Once more, fear of the 'French who were thought to have covetous eyes' prompted the British to order another impractical settlement on a remote spot on the Australian coast.[28]

On 27 October 1838, Bremer landed at Port Essington and began building. This time, he had with him only marines – no free settlers and no convicts. A year after he had landed at Port Essington this third time, Charles Darwin arrived on the north coast of Australia aboard the *Beagle* and anchored in Shoal Bay, about 40 kilometres south-west of Port Essington. While the *Beagle* was at anchor, its commander, Lieutenant John Stokes, rowed further down the bay and named Port Darwin. However, it would be another thirty years before it was finally settled.

Meanwhile, the settlement at Port Essington was experiencing the same difficulties as the earlier townships. Only a year after it was opened, on 25 November 1839, it was demolished by a cyclone, which killed twelve people and drove the ship HMS *Pelorus* aground. In tropical heat, soldiers and marines sweated in thick uniforms to rebuild this settlement in the untamed north, this time naming it Victoria after their young queen. The new town included some stone and brick buildings, constructed with the assistance of a brickmaker who had been shipwrecked during the storm.

It enjoyed one moment of fame with the unexpected arrival of the overland explorer Ludwig Leichhardt at the end of 1845. Leichhardt had left the Darling Downs, west of Brisbane, on 1 October 1844 on a privately funded exploration, and headed north then west across the base of the Gulf of Carpentaria. After fourteen months and 4800 kilometres, he and his team reached Port Essington on 17 December 1845. Nothing had been heard of Leichhardt for well over a year, and news that he had reached Port Essington alive was enthusiastically reported in the Melbourne and Sydney papers:

We have the highest satisfaction in announcing to our readers that Dr. Leichhardt has returned to Sydney, from his overland expedition to Port Essington . . . [the] difficulties to be overcome were neither few nor light, but with an energy and courage rarely to be met with he succeeded in overcoming them all, and has the high honour of being the first man who crossed from the eastern to the western side of Australia . . . Dr. Leichhardt has done that which must cause his name to be enrolled among the benefactors of Australia . . .[29]

Finally, in 1849, Port Essington met the same fate as the two previous attempts: it was abandoned. In the eleven years of the settlement's existence, its population had never exceeded eighty people. Its demise saw the end of British attempts to occupy the north coast for another twenty years.

In 1862, the explorer John McDouall Stuart succeeded in traversing central Australia from south to north. The following year, the north was formally taken in as part of the colony of South Australia, but it was not until 1869 that a town was built up there that would actually survive, when the South Australian surveyor general George Goyder established a tiny settlement on the spot that the crew of Darwin's *Beagle* had named Port Darwin thirty years before.

There was considerable public scepticism at Goyder being sent to make yet another attempt at settling in the far north, which was by now described in the press as a 'white elephant':

George W. Goyder . . . has been selected by the Government to carry out the onerous task of surveying the much talked of Northern Territory, which unfortunately, as far as South Australia is concerned, has been truly 'a white elephant'. Mr. Goyder has by his energy raised himself to his present high official position, and during his career has drawn upon himself no small share of unenviable notoriety in the discharge of his duties, especially in carrying out the very difficult and invidious task of valuing the runs of the colony . . . however, be this as it may, it appeared that there was no one so well fitted for the onerous post of selecting and surveying the future colony of North Australia. It is to be hoped that success will attend his efforts. Of one thing we are certain, if this fourth attempt prove a failure, it will not be the fault of Mr Goyder, but the result of circumstances beyond his control.[30]

Starting with 135 men and women, the town was named by Goyder as Palmerston, after the British prime minister Lord Palmerston, who had died in office three and a half years earlier. Again, the settlement struggled from the start. The long grass 'held no nourishment for European animals [and] the shallow leached ironstone soil held no nourishment for European plants'.[31] In the first five years, many of the farmers who had bought Crown land demanded their money back and were offered more land as an encouragement to stay.[32]

In 1911, when the population of the top end was still barely 3000, Palmerston's name was changed to Darwin. For more than half a century, the settlement grew very little, and it was not until the mid-1930s that its population reached 5000, and by the late 1950s the non-Indigenous population had reached almost 10,000.

*

Western Australia was another part of the continent that was claimed by the British because of concerns the French might attempt to build their own settlements there. In the late eighteenth and early nineteenth centuries, there had been a number of French explorations along the west coast. In 1772, Louis Aleno de St Aloüarn had sailed the west coast and landed at Shark Bay and Dirk Hartog Island, and staked France's claim there. Twenty years later, Bruni d'Entrecasteaux had landed in Western Australia and Van Diemen's Land in his circumnavigation of Australia while looking for La Perouse, who had disappeared after leaving Botany Bay four years before. After that, there was something of a lull in French exploration of the region until after the Napoleonic Wars – apart, of course, from Baudin's southern-coast expedition of 1802.

British suspicions of France's territorial ambitions were again aroused in 1826 by the appearance of another French ship exploring the Australian coast. It was the *Astrolabe*, commanded by Jules Dumont d'Urville, which had sailed from Toulon in April 1826 and reached the south-west coast of Australia later that year. D'Urville had sailed on a regular route to the Pacific from Europe, via the Cape of Good Hope and across the southern ocean to Australia, where he surveyed and charted the Swan River (the later site of Perth), which had been named after the local black swans by Dutch East Indies commander Willem Vlamingh in 1696.

Even though d'Urville had no instructions to settle the territory, the renewed French interest spooked the British, and on hearing of his expedition, British colonial secretary Lord Bathurst wrote to New South Wales governor Darling in March 1826, instructing him to head off any French territorial ambition by establishing a settlement in New Holland and extending the British claim to include the whole of Western Australia, or about one-third of the Australian continent.[33]

On receiving Bathurst's letter, Darling ordered Major Edmund Lockyer to hasten from Sydney to Western Australia to thwart any French territorial ambition: 'As the French discovery ships may possibly have in view the establishment of a settlement on some part of the coast of this territory, it should be made clear ... that the whole of New Holland is subject to His Britannic Majesty's Government.'[34]

Lockyer left Sydney on 9 November 1826 on the *Amity* with a detachment of twenty marines and twenty-three convicts, and orders to take over the almost two million square kilometres of land that stretched from the west coast to the closest inhabited area of southern Australia. On Christmas Day, the *Amity* landed at King George Sound, which had been named thirty-five years before by the British explorer George Vancouver on his way to explore the north-west coast of America. Lockyer began building a settlement and planting a vegetable garden on the coast near the later site of Albany. Shortly after arriving, he learnt from passing sealers that d'Urville had been in the sound two months before and had made some scientific measurements, but the French explorer had not attempted to claim the territory or construct any settlement before leaving for Sydney.

In April 1826, James Stirling had been sent from Britain to Australia with his instructions to remove the settlement on Melville Island in the north. When he reached Sydney in December – by which time Lockyer was on his way to King George Sound – he met d'Urville, who had only recently left Western Australia. In Sydney, d'Urville showed Stirling his detailed charts of the Swan River, which d'Urville believed was inaccessible as a port and lacked sufficient fresh water for a settlement. Stirling, however, felt it might prove 'a suitable site for a garrison or for another settlement to open trade with the East Indies',[35] and succeeded in persuading Governor Darling that shifting the Melville Island settlement could wait until he had surveyed the Swan River.

Stirling sailed on the *Success* from Sydney on 17 January 1827 and anchored at the mouth of the Swan River, off Rottnest Island, on 3 May 1827. After surveying the Swan, he enthusiastically reported to Governor Darling that the river was easily navigable and would provide a good harbour. He also claimed that the land was as good as, if not better than, that of New South Wales.[36] Darling, in turn, reported to London that it should become a British settlement, and that it was 'of great importance that so advantaged a position should not be taken possession of by the French'.[37]

The British Colonial Office was at first unpersuaded, believing that such plans 'always ended in becoming sources of expense to the mother country'; it said it 'trembled at the thought of the expense involved'.[38] But Stirling persisted with his plan. After returning to Sydney, he finally sailed for Melville Island, where he claimed and named Raffles Bay as a new British possession. He left the northern Australian shore in July 1827 and, when he reached England in January 1828, he further argued his case for the settlement of Western Australia.

In London, the influential secretary for the Admiralty, Sir John Barrow, was initially against the idea, pointing out that, as the Dutch had discovered two centuries before, the west Australian coastline was dangerous for shipping. However, when he learnt from the British Embassy in Paris that the French were indeed looking to establish their own penal colony in Australasia, Barrow was persuaded and urged that the settlement go ahead: 'The French having turned their head to that quarter makes it absolutely incumbent on us to take possession of Swan River, Geographe Bay and King George Sound.'[39]

Such was the sensitivity of the British to French intentions that approval was given to send British settlers in

October 1828, and the first ship left England with three years' supply of food bound for the Swan River on 6 February 1829. Stirling led the expedition to secure for Britain 'all those parts of New Holland not included in New South Wales'.[40]

The first ship to reach what was to be named the Swan River Colony was the *Challenger*, under the command of Captain Charles Fremantle, who declared the territory for Britain on 2 May 1829. Stirling arrived with his heavily pregnant wife on the *Parmelia* later in the month and the following August, three more ships – the *Calista*, *St Leonard* and *Marquis of Anglesea* – arrived with more settlers and supplies.[41]

The earliest accounts from the new colony reported that the settlers were struggling. In December 1829, the *Lotus* reached Sydney, after it had dropped off some of the first settlers at Swan River the previous October, with reports that were printed in the eastern colonies' newspapers: 'The accounts received by the *Lotus* from Swan River are most melancholy, and calculated to produce a disappointment to the sanguine emigrants who have ventured there, fully as violent and sudden as their ill-grounded expectations.'[42]

The report said there was not enough grass or water for the cattle and sheep, and 'even had there been grass, there is no fencing timber', and that the livestock brought by the settlers from 'England or the Cape' are 'daily straggling into the bush and for ever lost to the owners'. The report also criticised the choice of Swan River as the site of the new settlement:

The river, which has been made so principal a feature in the imaginary picture of this modern Arcadia, is not deep enough for a Thames wherry. The mud flats are, in one part, of a mile and a half extent, and gentlemen and ladies must all jump into the water to lift the boat over, which occupies several hours.[43]

It said that the government food supplies were 'to cease the last day of the year' and 'after that the poor wretches of settlers must live on their own supplies'. Over the next few years, more settlers and more supplies were sent, but by 1832, when the colony changed its name to Western Australia, the population had reached barely 1500 people. After twenty years, the total population of the entire colony was still below 6000, settled mainly around Perth and Albany, or on the relatively narrow fertile coastal strip in the south-west of the colony that would support farming. Perth, which became the capital of the colony, was established by Stirling 25 kilometres upstream on the Swan River, and was given its name by the Scottish-born British secretary of state for the colonies Sir George Murray.

Western Australia grew more slowly in the nineteenth century than any of the other colonies. After sixty years, the population of the entire west was still below 50,000. Only after the discovery of gold in Coolgardie in 1892 and later in Kalgoorlie did the population surge. From 58,000 in 1892, it rose to almost a quarter of a million a decade later.

*

Queensland was the first territory to be discovered by European explorers but the last colony to be established.

The first recorded European landing in what became Queensland was by Willem Janszoon of the Dutch East India Company, at Cape York Peninsula in 1606. In the same year, the Spanish explorer Luís Vaz de Torres sailed through the strait that separated New Guinea from the northernmost tip of Australia. It was not for another 160 years that Europeans sailors were next recorded as being in the region when in 1768 the French explorer Louis-Antoine de Bougainville got within 160 kilometres of the Queensland coast. He was sailing west from the New Hebrides but was forced to turn back when he was unable to penetrate the corals of the Great Barrier Reef.

Two years after Bougainville, Englishman James Cook became the first to sail northwards along almost the entire east coast of Australia. When he reached what he called Possession Island, off the northernmost tip of Australia, he claimed the 3000-kilometre coastline on behalf of Britain and King George III, naming it New South Wales.

During the voyage, Cook named many of the coastal features of what would become the Queensland coast. These included: Moreton Bay, the later site of Brisbane, which was named (and later misspelt) after the Earl of Morton, president of the Royal Society; Wide Bay; Hervey Bay, after the Earl of Bristol; Keppel Island, after Viscount Keppel; Whitsunday Island, which Cook passed on what he believed was Whitsunday, 4 June 1770 (although it was actually Whit-Monday); Magnetic Island – 'the compass did not traverse well when near it'; Dunk Island, after the Earl of Halifax; and York Cape (Cape York), after Prince Edward Duke of York. Cook also named the Endeavour River, where his stricken vessel was beached for six weeks for repairs, having been smashed on the Great Barrier Reef.[44]

Almost thirty years later, in 1799, Matthew Flinders was sent from Sydney by Governor John Hunter and spent six weeks charting the coast between Moreton Bay and Hervey Bay. (Despite spending fifteen days exploring Moreton Bay, Flinders did not find the Brisbane River.) More than twenty years after that, Moreton Bay was decided on as the site for particularly recalcitrant convicts.

It had been recommended by the experienced surveyor and explorer John Oxley.

Oxley had arrived in New South Wales more than twenty years before. Born into a moderately well-off family in Yorkshire in 1784, he joined the navy as a fifteen-year-old midshipman and made his first voyage to Sydney in 1801. Over the next five years, he was involved in a number of coastal surveys of Van Diemen's Land and the southern coast of New South Wales. Oxley was in Sydney at the time William Bligh was deposed as governor but denied having been a supporter of Bligh's nemesis, John Macarthur. In 1812, Oxley became engaged to Macarthur's daughter, Elizabeth, but the marriage was called off, allegedly because of Oxley's unpaid debts.

As an officer, Oxley benefited from some generous land grants and became a sizeable landholder, farmer and businessman. He also became a prominent explorer as the colony's surveyor and, following the crossing of the Blue Mountains, led expeditions that opened up vast regions of grazing country to the west and north-west of the hinterland of Sydney.

In 1823, Oxley was sent by New South Wales governor Sir Thomas Brisbane to find a suitable site for a strict prison settlement. Finding Port Macquarie unsuitable, he pressed on to Moreton Bay, which he recommended. The following year, he accompanied Lieutenant Henry Miller and a small party of soldiers and convicts to establish a settlement in Moreton Bay on 14 September 1824. The settlement operated as a prison for only fifteen years until 1839, during which time around 2500 convict men and 145 convict women were sent there.[45]

Moreton Bay, like Norfolk Island and Port Arthur, in Van Diemen's Land, became notorious for its brutal treatment of convicts. In 1830, an inmate, E. S. Hall, wrote to the English member of parliament and prison reformer Fowell Buxton pleading on behalf of the 'unpitied and neglected' prisoners in the jail.[46] Hall claimed that the 'minds and bodies of all the felons' were 'utterly broken down and debased' by ill-treatment, 'illegal punishments' and a shortage of food. In a long statement, he gave a number of examples of prisoners who died as a result of the brutality. The first involved a fifty-year-old:

He had been a soldier and had been wounded. Hence he walked lame, and used a stick ... No allowance, however, was made on this account ... He became ill with the dysentery ... and sent ... to the hospital ... The commandant ... 'believed the man was feigning sickness'. He was ordered to a gang of men, whose work [hauling large stones] was the severest on the settlement ... The man was incapable of the ... work [but] the commandant ... ordered him to be tied up ... fifty lashes were administered ... He was taken to the hospital, and died that day week.

Another case involved a fifteen-year-old boy:

He was unwell on his landing in the settlement. He was sent to one of the gangs whose business it is to break up ground with the hoe. It was reported to the commandant that the boy did not do his work. He was sentenced to solitary confinement for eight days [where] he received a quarter of a pound of bread a day ... After five or six days, the sentry reported the boy did not eat his mess. He was ordered up to the office of the commandant, who enquired, why he had not done his work? The boy said, he could not do it on account of being ill ... He was taken to the hospital, and died next day. When he died, his irons were on his legs.

Four years after the establishment of the settlement, Allan Cunningham, a botanist, explorer and colleague of Oxley's, found a way through the mountain range to the west and thus opened the route to the fertile Darling Downs. From the late 1830s, the convict settlement dwindled. The land to the west of Moreton Bay was increasingly opened up by farmer settlers, and the township of Brisbane was established.

By 1850, with the settlement's population at fewer than 10,000, the first public meetings were held calling for the establishment of a separate colony. The push came mainly from squatters on the Darling Downs, who wanted the new colony to reintroduce convict transportation as a source of cheap labour for their farms. On 23 July, at Drayton, in the Darling Downs, a meeting agreed to petition the British for a new colony in the north, and the following January a group of leading citizens met in Brisbane and devised a petition to send to Queen Victoria. The petition sought a separate colony 'similar to those granted to the neighbouring colonies' with the 'seat of the new government' to be 'the central port and town of Brisbane'.[47]

After three years of agitation, which included sending a deputation of the 'Moreton Bay and Northern Districts Separation Association' to London, the British Government in July 1856 noted the 'strong and repeated representations' from the 'inhabitants of the northern districts' and agreed to grant a separate colony.[48]

1856 was also the year Van Diemen's Land was officially named Tasmania, the change having been approved by Queen Victoria the year before. The locals wanted a new name to help remove the stigma of having been a convict colony: Van Diemen's Land had continued to take shipments of convicts until 1853, many years after transportation to the other colonies ended.

Three years later, on 6 June 1859, the district of Moreton Bay became the colony of Queensland, named after Victoria, who had already been on the throne for more than twenty years. It became the only Australian colony that started with its own parliament instead of first spending time as a Crown colony.

The separatists did not get all they wanted. The new territory did not include the New England farming districts or the coastal area near the Macleay River, which remained in the north of New South Wales. Nor did the new colonists persuade the British to resume convict transportation.

Queensland, which came into being with a population of barely 25,000 people in 1859, soon found itself in the depths of economic depression. The Bank of Queensland closed its doors; there was little money in the colonial Treasury; the public works, including the first railway line linking Ipswich and Brisbane, were abandoned; and the unemployed were protesting in the streets of Brisbane.

Then, in 1867, gold was discovered in Gympie, some 160 kilometres north of the capital. This saved the colony and set it on the road to great prosperity. At the time of the gold discovery, the population of Queensland was barely 100,000. Within thirty years, it would exceed half a million.

CHAPTER 8

W. C. WENTWORTH AND SELF-GOVERNMENT

Gentlemen, I beg to announce to you that it is my intention to offer myself as a candidate for the honour of representing your City in the first Session of the new Legislative Council . . . A son of the soil myself, it must be almost needless to add, that my whole interests, feelings, and prejudices, are identified with the prosperity of my country.

AUSTRALIA'S LONG JOURNEY FROM A CONVICT SETTLEMENT TO A succession of self-governing colonies was greatly influenced by 'Australia's greatest native son', William Charles Wentworth. Barrister, explorer, newspaperman, landowner and politician, Wentworth commanded the Australian political stage for several decades until his death in 1872.[1]

Variously described as a 'firebrand' and a 'dangerous revolutionist', Wentworth was a bear of a man with
a 'mass of grizzled hair' who stood six feet, five inches
(196 centimetres) and had a commanding presence.[2] In
1849, a newspaper described him as:

> With [a] heavy, loose, drab coat . . . there is something
> of the commanding ruin in Wentworth . . . In his public
> speaking there is an inexcusable slovenliness and disre-
> spectful bearing which would never be tolerated . . . if
> he did not possess superior intellect . . . There are times
> which witness him rise to the stature of a giant over his
> compeers. Few have equal power . . . to demolish an
> opponent's arguments; and none can command more
> forcible and original language . . . The tones of his voice
> are discordant and grating, sometimes running into a
> loud, harsh, impatient and decided drawl . . . His action
> is inelegant and random. His personal appearance is tall
> and athletic [but] slightly stooped . . . His countenance is
> florid and marked by courage and determination.[3]

William Charles Wentworth was born in 1790, the son
of Catherine Crowley, a seventeen-year-old convict who
had been found guilty of stealing clothing and sent on the
convict ship *Neptune*, which arrived in Sydney in June
1790. Catherine was lucky to have survived the voyage.
The *Neptune* was part of the notorious Second Fleet, on
which many convicts died. Of the 502 convicts who sailed
on the *Neptune*, 141 men and eleven women died during
the voyage to Sydney, and a further 269 were sick when
they landed.

William was born on the *Neptune* after the ship reached
Sydney and was bound for the colony's second convict
settlement, at Norfolk Island, where young William

would spend the first six years of his life. His father was D'Arcy Wentworth, the ship's surgeon on the *Neptune*, who would later become superintendent of police and a leading member of the New South Wales colony. There is some conjecture about William's paternity because D'Arcy had only boarded the *Neptune* the previous December at Portsmouth and young William was believed to have been born the following August. Although this was less than nine months after he met Catherine Crowley, D'Arcy acknowledged the boy as his. Despite having a prominent father in the colony, the fact that young William was a 'bastard' would come back to haunt him in later life.

D'Arcy was a distant relative of the British aristocratic Fitzwilliam family and lucky not to have been sent to Australia as a convict himself. On four occasions, he had been charged with highway robbery but was acquitted or escaped conviction each time. It has been suggested that he only avoided being transported by virtue of his family connections and his timely enlistment as surgeon aboard the second convict fleet.

When William was ten years old and had moved to live in Sydney, his mother Catherine died, and D'Arcy gave William, and his younger brother and sister, the surname Wentworth. Two years later, in 1802, the increasingly prosperous D'Arcy sent William and his younger brother D'Arcy (junior) to school in England. The Wentworth boys first went to Bletchley and later to Greenwich, where William benefited from a traditional British private-school education. After nearly seven years of this schooling, William returned to Australia on 24 March 1810, only four months after the arrival of the new governor, Lachlan Macquarie.

Now a strapping twenty-year-old, Wentworth cut a striking figure around Sydney with his 'tall frame, thick shoulders, Roman head, and auburn hair, his rugged and untidy person'.[4] The year after he returned, Governor Macquarie appointed him to the post of provost marshal, with responsibility for organising the courts, and arranging hangings and the public-speaking engagements of the governor. The post of provost was normally filled by Major Francis Grose, but he was away in London giving evidence against Lieutenant George Johnston for the overthrow of Governor William Bligh. The appointment of a man so young to the position caused 'a good deal of muttering', not least because William's father, D'Arcy, by now had become a leading member of the local society.[5]

The following year, William Wentworth's name became etched in Australian history when he teamed up with thirty-eight-year-old William Lawson and thirty-four-year-old Gregory Blaxland and they became the first white men to cross the Blue Mountains.

In 1816, at the age of twenty-six, Wentworth returned again to London, where he studied law. He spent six years in England and a year living in Paris. In 1819 in London, he published a book about Australia with the impossibly long title *A Statistical, Historical and Political Description of the Colony of New South Wales and its Dependent Settlements in Van Diemen's Land: With a Particular Enumeration of the Advantages Which These Colonies Offer for Emigration, and Their Superiority in Many Respects over Those Possessed by the United States of America*. It was the first book written about Australia by someone who had been born there, and had a big impact in both England and Australia. Wentworth admitted in the preface to the book that he had written it as an unapologetic promotion of Australia:

[My] aim in obtruding this hasty production on the public, is to promote the welfare and prosperity of the country . . .

[of my] birth ... attempting to divert from the United States of America to its shores, some part of that vast tide of emigration, which is at present flowing thither from all parts of Europe [and] describ[ing] the superior advantages of climate and soil possessed by the colony ...[6]

For many years, Wentworth's book became the primary text for colonists who envisaged political independence. In arguing for New South Wales to have more say in its own government, Wentworth added the warning that Australia might follow the 'terrible' American route to revolution by being 'goaded into rebellion', which was 'neither so problematical nor remote, as might otherwise be imagined'.

The book was also very popular among emancipists for describing 'exclusives' as 'whores and rogues and vagabonds', and reflected much of Wentworth's vision for Australia, including his desire for an elected parliament, equal rights for emancipated convicts, trial by jury, an end to press censorship and no taxation without representation. The book sold well at twelve shillings a copy and netted a much-needed £120 for the heavily indebted Wentworth, being reprinted in 1820 and again in 1824. (By comparison, a farm labourer in England was earning about ten shillings a week in 1824.)[7] It promised Australia as a land where one could easily become rich from growing fine wool, and did much to stimulate immigration to the continent.

In England, Wentworth became close friends with the founder of the Australian wool industry, John Macarthur, and his sons, who were also living in England at the time. William wanted to marry Macarthur's daughter Elizabeth, but her father advised him to first complete his studies. Then, after a subsequent quarrel with the Macarthurs, the marriage was called off, possibly because the Macarthurs did not want their daughter marrying the illegitimate son of a convict. Over the next decades back in Australia, the relationship between the Wentworth and Macarthur families would become increasingly acrimonious as William Wentworth promoted social reform and an acceptance of ex-convicts, which the more conservative Macarthur opposed.

William finished his law studies and was admitted to the Bar in 1822. He was now thirty-two years old and still heavily in debt. He decided to return to Australia, expressing his primary aim as serving his country:

> I am actuated by a desire of better qualifying myself for the performance of those duties, that my birth has imposed – and, in selecting the profession of law, I calculate upon acquainting myself with all the excellence of the British Constitution, and hope at some future period, to advocate successfully the right of my country to a participion in its advantages.[8]

He arrived back in Sydney on 15 July 1824, vowing 'to hold no situation under government'. He said that he believed he might one day lead the colony 'as a mere private person', saying that, 'as a servant of the Governor I could only conform to his whims, which would neither suit my tastes nor principles'.[9]

Sydney had changed dramatically in the seven years Wentworth had been away. The 'rum' hospital and the large convict barracks on Macquarie Street had both been built, as had St James' Church with its impressive spire, and a row of new wharves along the foreshore of Sydney Harbour.

Also, in 1823, the British Government had passed a law for 'the better administration of Justice in New South Wales and Van Diemen's Land'. Within the act, there was provision for the governor to appoint a council 'not exceeding Seven and not less than Five' to advise him. Until then, all power had been vested in the governor, who had no obligation to consult with anyone else. With Macquarie's successor, Governor Thomas Brisbane, presiding, the new Legislative Council of six (the governor, lieutenant governor, chief justice, colonial secretary, principal surgeon and surveyor general) held its first meeting at the then Government House on 25 August 1824, just a month after Wentworth had returned to Sydney.[10]

Wentworth had sailed home from England with an English friend, Robert Wardell. Both men would become successful barristers, newspaper publishers and farmers. Wardell was three years younger than Wentworth, a graduate of Trinity College, Cambridge, and had previously owned the *Statesman* newspaper in London, which he sold so he could start the *Australian* newspaper in Sydney with Wentworth. The paper, which began on 14 October 1824 – only three months after the two men arrived in Sydney – sold for one shilling, and the first edition of 625 copies sold out. The hard-hitting editorial of the first edition asserted: 'A free press is the most legitimate, and ... powerful weapon that can be employed to ... frustrate the designs of tyranny.' For the first time the colony had a voice independent of officialdom.

The earnings from the successful paper provided Wentworth and Wardell with vital income while they were establishing their legal practices. Wentworth was co-founder of and journalist for the newspaper. He later left to focus on his legal career, but Wardell remained as editor and continued to support Wentworth's political campaigns. This came to an untimely end in 1834, when Wardell was shot dead by a runaway convict on his farm at Petersham in Sydney. He was only forty years old.

In May 1825, Wentworth took on a case involving a young woman, Sarah Cox, who was born in Sydney in 1805 to convict parents. She was suing ex-convict Francis Cox for breach of promise of marriage. Wentworth won the case and damages of £100, and became Sarah's lover.

In 1827, Wentworth's father, D'Arcy, died, leaving him his Homebush estate and a number of sheep farms. In the same year, William bought a property from Captain John Piper at Vaucluse, on the south side of Sydney Harbour, which he later enlarged, replacing the small house with a stately mansion (it survives to this day as Vaucluse House). The large estate of 515 acres (208 hectares) is almost ten kilometres east of the city of Sydney and was one of the first major buildings seen by ships entering Sydney Heads.

William and Sarah's first daughter, Thomasine, was born in 1825 and their first son, William Charles, in 1827. They moved into the new Vaucluse estate in 1829 with their two children and were married later in the year, when Sarah was pregnant with their third child, Fanny. They had ten children, born over a twenty-three-year period from 1825 to 1848. None of the ten died in infancy and four lived well into their seventies, which augured well for the spawning of the Wentworth clan in Australia. (Wentworth could also have fathered another child. On 4 November 1830, Jemima McDuel, who was then married to Wentworth's friend Edward Edgar, gave birth to a baby boy. More than a decade later, it was revealed that the baptism papers said the father of the child was William Charles Wentworth.)[11]

At thirty-seven, a prominent lawyer and wealthy land-owner, Wentworth represented the colony's new nobility and ruling class. However, despite becoming one of the wealthiest and most powerful men in the colony, he and his wife were social outcasts for more than thirty years because of their convict heritage and having had their first two children out of wedlock.

Eighteen years after their marriage, in 1847, the colony's chief justice, Sir Alfred Stephen, objected when Lady Mary FitzRoy included Wentworth and his wife on the Government House guest list. The fact that Sarah had lived 'in sin' with William Wentworth for some years and borne him two children before they married had not been forgotten, which was hinted at in the *Sydney Morning Herald* at the time:

> It has been generally supposed, that the Court gives the tone to the manners of the Country. If it does not do so . . . it is not only worthless, as not fulfilling the only practical use of a Court, but . . . absolutely mischievous, by giving its sanction to the public, to regard with indifference and contempt, the . . . established virtues, and decencies, of life . . . Whenever a woman falls, she falls for ever. No after repentance,–no expiation in her, or in any human power, can restore to her the place, she has lost . . .[12]

*

By the 1820s, the colony was still deeply divided between the 'exclusives' and the 'emancipists'. From early after his arrival, Wentworth took up the fight for the 'emancipists', which put him at odds with Sir Ralph Darling, who had become governor in December 1825, replacing Sir Thomas Brisbane. Darling was unequivocally for the 'exclusives' and treated the 'emancipists' as a kind of serf class. He had previously been the governor of Mauritius, which the British had taken from the French eight years earlier, and was an able administrator but an arch conservative, who found it difficult to accept that this was a colony rapidly in transition from a penal settlement to a free society, and a place in which there were calls for increasing self-government.

He was not receptive to Wentworth's reformist zeal, particularly his support for emancipists or his calls for elected parliaments and trial by jury. The relationship between the two men had totally broken down by the time of what became known as the 'Sudds and Thompson case', in which two marine privates were convicted of stealing a small quantity of calico.

At the time, it was common for lowly soldiers to commit small crimes to get out of the army, complete a short, easy sentence working on farms, and then become private citizens, able to prosper in the young, growing colony. Darling was well aware of this popular method of escaping military duty and had warned his troops that any further cases would be made examples of.

Joseph Sudds and Patrick Thompson were convicted and sentenced to seven years' hard labour on 22 November 1826. Darling ordered they be heavily chained around their ankles and necks, which Wentworth's *Australian* newspaper claimed prevented the soldiers from 'lay[ing] their heads down to rest'.[13] A week later, Sudds died and Governor Darling was immediately under attack from all quarters. The colony's chief justice, Sir Francis Forbes, said the punishment was 'contrary to law' and army captain Robert Robinson publicly stated the irons around the men's necks were far too heavy to carry. The most stinging attacks, however, came from Wentworth's *Australian*.

Darling complained to London about Wentworth's acrimonious conduct, and, alluding to his convict parent-age, said:

I should observe that, from the first he has evinced a feeling of hostility without my being able to discover any cause.

I have endeavoured to conciliate him by courtesy and attention; but he is a vulgar, ill-bred fellow, utterly unconscious of the common civilities, due from one gentleman to another. Besides, he aims at leading the Emancipists, and appears to have taken his stand in opposition to the government.[14]

Darling also complained that Wentworth and his lawyer partner Robert Wardell regularly used the courtroom to attack the governor: 'both Mr. Wentworth and Dr. Wardell are in the habit of indulging in the most indecent invectives against the government and the measures of the government in open court, without comment or observation from the bench.'[15]

In the face of increasingly hostile attacks from the *Australian*, Darling introduced a tax of fourpence on each copy of the paper sold and launched a number of libel suits against it. Wentworth retaliated and on 1 March 1829 wrote a huge, 25,000-word submission to the colonial secretary accusing Darling of murder and calling for his dismissal:

I felt that it would be obvious, to his Lordship . . . that he had been guilty in the punishment, which he had inflicted on Joseph Sudds, of a high misdemeanour at least, if not of murder . . . the collar of the set of irons placed on the deceased Sudds [was] too tight for his neck . . . and the basils too tight for his legs.[16]

London had little choice but to continue to publicly support Darling, who only had a little over a year left of his five-year term. The colonial secretary Lord Viscount Goderich wrote to say that the punishment was appropriate, since eight other soldiers had already used the same ploy to get out of the army and an example had to be made. He also said that there would not have been any fuss but for the death of Sudds:

> The death [of Sudds] ... appears to have given a complexion to this affair, which, had it not been for that unfortunate circumstance, would in all probability have excited comparatively little attention.[17]
>
> [It] certainly was very desirable that every proper step should be taken to discourage the repetition of such proceeding ... a perfectly proper and judicious measure ... there is certainly no ground upon which you could be justly accused of having exercised any undue severity in this case ...

So Darling stayed another year until his term expired, leaving Sydney for England with his wife and children on the *Hooghly* in October 1831. The day Darling sailed, Wentworth advertised an open party at his harbourside mansion in Vaucluse and 4000 people turned up to enjoy the free food and wine, and jeer and cheer as Darling sailed past the house from Sydney Cove towards the heads of Sydney Harbour:

> upwards of 4,000 persons ... assembled at Vaucluse to partake of Mr. Wentworth's hospitality, and to evince their joy at the approaching departure. The scene of the fete was on the lawn in front of Mr. Wentworth's villa, which was thrown open for the reception of all respectable visitants, while a marquee filled with piles of loaves, and casks of Cooper's gin, and Wright's strong beer, was pitched a short way off ... On an immense spit ... a bullock was roasted entire. Twelve sheep were also roasted in succession; and 4,000 loaves completed the enormous banquet ... By 7 p.m. two immense bonfires were lighted

on the highest hill . . . rustic sports . . . speeches, etc., etc., whiled away the night; and morning dawned before the hospitable mansion was quitted by all its guests.[18]

Darling's replacement as governor was fifty-four-year-old Sir Richard Bourke, who arrived in Sydney in December 1831; he would have passed his predecessor on the high seas as Darling headed back to England.

Born in Dublin in 1777 and educated at Westminster School and Oxford, Bourke had served in the Grenadier Guards in South America and against Napoleon in the Peninsular War, reaching the rank of colonel by the age of forty. Before being appointed to New South Wales, he had been the lieutenant governor of the eastern side of the British colony in the Cape of Good Hope.

Bourke was warmly welcomed by Wentworth and other 'reformists' because of his commitment to enlarging the role of emancipist jurors, repealing Darling's anti-press laws and using some of the proceeds of Crown land sales to promote immigration. However, he was soon in conflict with the 'exclusives', who found him far too 'liberal'.

His time coincided with a period of strong economic growth in the colony. In the six years he was governor, between 1832 and 1837, government revenue and exports doubled. Bourke was politically progressive and in 1833 recommended to the British Government that the colony be given elective government, with half the members of parliament to be appointed and the other half elected locally. However, to the disappointment of the locals, who were discontented with the unrepresentative system of government that ruled the colony, Bourke's proposals were 'pigeon-holed' by the Colonial Office in London.[19]

In 1835, a meeting of landowner, middle-class and professional men established the Australian Patriotic

Association, which agitated British parliamentarians for self-government of the colony, among other issues. Among the group's most notable leaders were W. C. Wentworth; Sir John Jamison, a surgeon and founder of the Agricultural and Horticultural Society; and William Bland, a prominent emancipist doctor.

Richard Bourke was becoming increasingly out of step with the colony's more conservative 'exclusives', and he resigned as governor in January 1837 and returned to England. Wentworth's relationship with the next governor began well. Forty-seven-year-old Sir George Gipps was another British Army officer and veteran of the Napoleonic Wars with colonial administration experience in the West Indies, who had been knighted before being appointed to administrate New South Wales. He arrived with his wife and son in Sydney in February 1838.

Gipps was aware of Wentworth's standing in the local community and wanted to appoint the now forty-nine-year-old to the colony's Legislative Council. In March 1839, he wrote to London to reassure them that Wentworth was no longer the firebrand and opponent of government he had been:

> He is . . . a man of vast influence in the Colony, as well as of vast possessions, of great knowledge . . . though in former days he was extremely violent in his opposition to the government, he has for a long time past, and especially since his retirement from the Bar, become moderate in his politics . . . it would . . . be . . . sound policy to attach such a man to the government by placing him in the Council . . .[20]

However, a year later, the relationship between the two men collapsed when Wentworth undermined the government's negotiations regarding the colonisation of New

Zealand by Britain, and land sales there. On 14 January 1840, while New Zealand was under the shadowy jurisdiction of New South Wales, Governor Gipps issued a proclamation forbidding future land sales, except to the Crown.

But Wentworth and John Jones of Sydney had made an agreement with Maori chiefs for the purchase of land in New Zealand on 15 February 1840. When seven chiefs from the South Island failed to turn up at the appointed hour in Sydney to sign the treaty that would formally hand over the balance of New Zealand territory to the British Empire, it was discovered that Wentworth had secretly paid them more for the land. The deal involved about twenty million acres and included virtually the whole of the South Island: the territory that is now Otago, Southland, Canterbury, Nelson and Marlborough, together with Stewart Island and part of the North Island. Wentworth signed and sealed the agreement in red wax, and the Maori chiefs signed with their 'mokos'. The contract made Wentworth the world's largest private landholder.

Gipps complained to London that Wentworth knew the government had reached the agreement before he ruined it with his secret deal with the Maori chiefs:

At the conclusion of [our] conference, a present of ten sovereigns was made to each of the chiefs, and they all promised to attend on the next day but one, to sign the paper. On the day appointed however, none of them appeared ... it subsequently appeared that ... Mr. Wentworth ... and after the issue of my proclamation, in conjunction with four or five persons purchased the whole of the ... island ... from these very natives, paying for it £200 in ready money, with a promise of a like sum per annum, as long as they shall live.[21]

An enraged Gipps was adamant that Wentworth could not keep the land:

> he [Wentworth] will never get one acre, one foot, one shilling for the land which he bought under the proclamation; and . . . he is not yet safe from prosecution for a conspiracy . . . all the jobs . . . that have taken place since the expulsion of the [royal] Stuarts . . . would not equal this job effected by Mr. Wentworth . . . who purchases a whole island at the rate of four hundred acres for a penny.[22]

In a speech to the New South Wales Legislative Council, Governor Gipps attacked Wentworth for trying to cheat the government:

> Talk of corruption! Talk of jobbery! Why if all the corruption which has defiled England since the expulsion of the Stuarts were gathered into one heap it would not make such a sum as this; if all the jobs which have been done since the days of Sir Robert Walpole were collected into one job, they would not make so big a job as the one which Mr. Wentworth asks me to lend a hand in perpetrating – the job of making him a grant of twenty millions of acres at the rate of one hundred acres for a farthing!

To make sure Wentworth gave up the land, Gipps had the *Lands Claims Act* passed in the New South Wales Parliament, which retrospectively declared all purchases of Maori land invalid.[23]

Meanwhile, the years of agitation by Wentworth and others for a representative parliament in the colony continued. By 1840, the population had grown to around

130,000 people. The development of industry and farming – particularly relating to wool – had attracted more free settlers, and the proportion who were convicts had fallen to around 30 per cent. The last shipment of convicts to the east coast of Australia was in late 1840 and followed a House of Commons enquiry in 1838 that strongly criticised transportation. Sir William Molesworth, a social reformer who was the chairman of the House of Commons Select Committee, argued transportation was uneconomic, inefficient and discouraged decent free settlers from migrating to the colonies:

> It is difficult to conceive how any man . . . merely having the common feelings of morality, with the ordinary dislike of crime, could be tempted, by any prospect of pecuniary gain to emigrate with a wife and family to one of these colonies, after a picture has been presented to his mind of what would be his probably lot. To dwell in Sydney . . . would be much the same as inhabiting the lowest purlieus of St Giles's in London where drunkenness and shameless profligacy are not more apparent than in the capital of Australia . . . every kind and gentle feeling of human nature is constantly outraged by the perpetual spectacle of . . . the lash, by the gangs of slaves in irons, by the horrid details of the penal settlements; till the heart of the emigrant is gradually deadened to the sufferings of others, and he becomes at last as cruel as the other gaolers of these vast prisons . . . the whole system of transportation violates the feelings of the adult, barbarizes the habits and demoralizes the principles of the rising generation . . .[24]

Transportation continued to Van Diemen's Land until 1853. The last shipment of convicts to Australia disembarked in Western Australia in 1868. In October 1840,

Governor Gipps announced to the New South Wales Legislative Council that transportation had ceased. Many in the colony welcomed the move, which would begin to remove the stigma of the 'convict colony'; however, plenty of the wealthy farmers disagreed, because convict transportation had provided a cheap source of farm labour.

General discontent with the unrepresentative system of government was growing, and in 1842 a great breakthrough was finally made. At last, the continuing demands for self-government resulted in the British Parliament passing the *New South Wales Constitution Act* – the first step towards representative government. The new law provided for the membership of the Legislative Council to be increased from the previous maximum of seven to thirty-six. Of greater significance, and for the first time, twenty-four of the thirty-six were to be elected. Of the twenty-four, six were to be elected from the Port Phillip District, which later became the separate colony of Victoria.

Wentworth was widely credited for the breakthrough, and his contribution was acknowledged even by the rival newspaper the *Sydney Morning Herald*:

Mr. WENTWORTH has ... been the strenuous and untiring champion of his country's cause. We have often differed with him on public questions; but we are not, on that account, the less sensible of the services he has rendered to the community, nor the less willing to acknowledge the claim he has thereby established to the suffrages of the electors.[25]

In the new political order, the governor still had more power than the new parliament. If the governor did not agree with the decisions of the Legislative Council, he could dissolve it and refer the matters to be determined by London. Nevertheless, it was undoubtedly a big first step towards parliamentary representative democracy in Australia.

Australia's first election campaign began in earnest on New Year's Day 1843, when the new law signed by Colonial Secretary Lord Stanley arrived by ship in Sydney. There were eighteen electoral districts for the twenty-four members, as some of the seats elected two members. The elections were spread over different days so it was possible for an unsuccessful candidate to have another run at a later date.

Of the more than 160,000 people in the colony at the time, fewer than 10,000 were entitled to vote. Voter eligibility was limited to men over twenty years of age who owned property valued at more than £200 or who occupied a property with a rent of more than £10 a year. This limitation was not a problem for Wentworth, who had never been an advocate of universal suffrage. In the book he had written more than twenty years earlier calling for local representative parliament, he had argued that landed property was 'the only standard' by which voting 'in any country could be regulated'.

The first election for the two members in the seat of Sydney was held on 13 June 1843. Wentworth was one of the candidates and was strongly supported by the *Sydney Morning Herald*:

Mr. WENTWORTH . . . an Australian by birth, has strong claims upon the gratitude and support of his countrymen. He was the first to bring the true state and prospects of the colony before the British public . . .

Certain it is . . . Mr. Wentworth must be returned for some place. His eloquence, his learning, his ample experience in every branch of colonial enterprise, his thorough knowledge of the resources, the capabilities, and the wants of the country – independently of the valuable services to which we have been referring – render it impossible that he should be spared from the counsels of our Legislature.[26]

The other candidates for the seat of Sydney were Wentworth's running mate Doctor William Bland; Sydney's mayor John Hosking; George Nichols, a wealthy merchant; Maurice O'Connell, Captain William Bligh's grandson, and his running mate, James Cooper.

At the beginning of the campaign, Wentworth reminded the voters of his long-held ambition for Australia to have its own political rights:

GENTLEMEN, I beg to announce to you that it is my intention to offer myself as a candidate for the honour of representing your City in the first Session of the new Legislative Council. After having laboured among you for the last eighteen years, in concert with other friends of freedom, to obtain those constitutional privileges, which are the rightful inheritance of Britons and their descendants, in whatever quarter of the empire they may reside, I trust . . . that I may be permitted to found my claim to your support, on the part I have taken in procuring this important concession . . . A son of the soil myself, it must be almost needless to add, that my whole interests, feelings, and prejudices, are identified with the prosperity of my country . . .[27]

During the campaign, supporters of Wentworth and William Bland flew white banners with an eight-point star and a Union Jack on the top corner. It is the earliest known banner to bear a resemblance to the later Australian national flag.

On the afternoon of the Sydney poll, about 8000 people gathered near Macquarie Place, where Wentworth's opponents O'Connell and Cooper were declared the election winners on a show of hands. Wentworth successfully appealed the decision and a formal ballot was scheduled for two days later, on 15 June. On the second election day, an angry mob demolished one of Wentworth's campaign tents, the mounted police were called to restore order, the *Riot Act* was read, and many were injured and a man killed in the troubles. According to the *Sydney Morning Herald*, the offenders were supporters of Captain Maurice O'Connell:

> We are sorry to say, that there was some very riotous conduct displayed yesterday. About twelve o'clock, a mob of four or five hundred persons, with Captain O'Connell's colours, rushed up to the polling places of Gipps's Ward, tore down Wentworth and Bland's colours, and made a most furious attack upon their supporters, who fled in all directions . . . The same mob afterwards went to the other polling places, and tore down Wentworth and Bland's colours . . . We regret exceedingly that the first election in the colony should have been stained with such disgraceful scenes as took place . . .[28]

At the end of the day, Wentworth topped the poll with 1275 votes. His running mate William Bland was also elected, with 1261 votes. Among the unsuccessful candidates, O'Connell had tallied 733 votes, and his running mate Cooper 365.

Thus, fifty-three-year-old William Wentworth entered Australia's first elected parliament. It opened on 1 August 1843 in a new chamber built onto the northern end of the former Surgeon's Wing of the Macquarie Street Hospital, the first of many additions to the original building. Public interest in the parliament was intense. At the start of proceedings at 3 pm each day, a queue formed along the front veranda of the hospital next door and wound its way up a small spiral staircase to a little public gallery that held fifty people. So great was the interest that a new eight-seat gallery needed to be built above the speaker's chair for local reporters.

Wentworth wanted to be the speaker, which was regarded as the most senior position in the parliament. However, the *Sydney Morning Herald*, which had supported Wentworth, believed he lacked the temperament to be speaker:

> we object to Mr. Wentworth's appointment to the office of speaker, on the distinct ground that he is personally unfit for it. He lacks the two grand qualifications of temper and industry. The Speaker should be habitually cool and collected: everybody who knows Mr. WENTWORTH is aware that he is exactly the reverse. His blood is constitutionally hot, and but very little excitement will set it a boiling. His temper is like gunpowder: a spark of provocation will cause it to explode. Instead of keeping down the passions of the house, he would, when his own were roused – which would be very often – exasperate them to greater fury.[29]

Instead, the speakership went to seventy-six-year-old entomologist and public servant Alexander Macleay, whom Wentworth bitterly dismissed as a 'twice superannuated octogenarian'.[30]

Wentworth was a controversial and outspoken member from the start. Shortly after entering parliament, he demanded to know why Governor Sir George Gipps was paid a salary of £5000, the same amount as the president of the United States. On another occasion, he compared the Aboriginal people with orangutans. The comments were made when the attorney general unsuccessfully proposed a bill to allow an Aboriginal man, Davey, to give evidence in a case against eight white men accused of massacring twenty-eight Aboriginal people at Myall Creek near Inverell in the colony's north-west:

> It would be quite as defencible to receive as evidence in a court of justice the chatterings of the ourang-outang as of this savage race and [I] would as soon vote in favour of a Bill for that purpose as for the present measure.[31]

In parliament, Wentworth continued to agitate for greater self-government, and, over the next few years, there was considerable discussion between Sydney and London about the future. In 1847, Earl Grey, who had been appointed the colonial secretary the year before, sent some radical proposals to the British Government for increased local decisionmaking that would involve the creation of new, local district councils, or 'municipal corporations'. According to Grey, the proposed municipal corporations would 'keep in check the powers of the Legislative Council'.[32] Earl Grey proposed that the new structure of government apply to Van Diemen's Land, South Australia, Western Australia and a proposed new colony of Victoria. His package of proposals also included the first official suggestion of a national Australian parliament of all the colonies for 'the enacting of such laws' relating to issues of 'common interests', including post, tariffs, roads and railways – even though there were as yet no railways in Australia.

Rather than embrace Grey's proposals, the citizens of Sydney feared these municipal corporations would reduce what little power the people finally had. On Wednesday 19 January 1848, between 'three and four thousand' people packed the Victoria Theatre in Sydney's Pitt Street, where the stage, 'filled with gentlemen of high political standing', spoke and moved a series of resolutions hostile to Grey's proposals.[33] The resolutions described the proposals as 'repugnant', 'adverse to the interests of this community' and 'a theoretical experiment'. The first motion moved by the New South Wales legislative councillor James Norton expressed 'utmost apprehension' at the proposals, which he said would reverse many of the gains already made. He argued that the colony had achieved its own parliament and elected its own members. Now the elected representatives were to be replaced by unelected representatives from 'district councils', which 'will have the effect of depriving the colonists of the elective franchise'.

As William Wentworth rose to speak, he 'was loudly cheered'. He told the meeting the proposals would weaken the local parliament and that Britain should only consider changes to the local political system if asked to by the locals. Wentworth added that the proposals were 'wholly unfounded' and 'against the wishes of the entire community'. He said they would involve the repeal of one of the 'inalienable rights of the British Constitution' and would be a 'great detriment' to the colonies'. The earl's proposals, he said, were 'unprecedented, impracticable' and 'unwarranted'.

After eight months of often heated public debate, on 11 August 1848 the New South Wales governor, Sir Charles FitzRoy, sent all of the records of the debates to Earl Grey, telling him that the central source of the complaint was the fear that the proposals would reduce the local power.[34] Grey picked up the pieces and cobbled together the Australian Colonies Government Bill, which he introduced to the British Parliament in 1849. The bill provided for more elected representatives to the New South Wales Legislative Council and a relaxation of the property qualifications for eligible voters, which would increase dramatically the number of men entitled to vote.

However, the most important feature of the new law, which was given royal assent in 1850, was the separation of the Port Phillip district on the south coast of New South Wales, which would become the new colony of Victoria. Port Phillip had been settled by farmers crossing with livestock from Van Diemen's Land for well over a decade and, by 1850, had a population of 70,000 people and an estimated six million sheep. Six of the twenty-four elected representatives in the New South Wales Legislative Council were from the Port Phillip district, but the locals had been agitating for their own parliament. They were supported by Governor FitzRoy, who complained to London that the task of governing faraway Port Phillip from Sydney was made more difficult 'the longer separation is delayed'.[35] Under the new law, Victoria would get its own Legislative Council with thirty appointed and twenty-one elected members.

News of the *Australian Colonies Government Act* reached Melbourne in November 1851 (it had been enacted in July 1851) and was greeted with celebrations and fireworks that coincided with the opening of the first major bridge crossing Melbourne's Yarra River.

Nonetheless, according to Wentworth, the concessions made by the British in this latest act were not enough. On 8 April 1851, he drafted a 'Declaration, protest and remonstrance' that argued there were deficiencies in the new act. The basic thrust of Wentworth's latest proposal was that Britain end its power to tax people in the colony;

that tax collected in the colony belong to the colony; and that the government in the colony be totally controlled by the colony. In other words, self-government.

The New South Wales Legislative Council agreed with Wentworth and sent the declaration off to London, where Sir John Pakington, who had replaced Earl Grey as colonial secretary earlier in the year, effectively adopted the Wentworth proposal and invited the colonies to suggest how they wanted their future political systems to work. Pakington's dispatch to Sydney on 15 December 1852 was historic. It was an invitation to the Australian colonies to design their own system of government.

On receipt of the dispatch in May 1853, a delighted William Wentworth successfully moved in the New South Wales Legislative Council for the establishment of a select committee to draft a constitution for New South Wales. Wentworth was to be its chairman and guiding spirit. In less than two months, he had drafted his Constitution Bill and advocated a form of government similar to the United Kingdom's. It proposed two houses of parliament: a lower house, called a Legislative Assembly, and an upper house, which would be called the Legislative Council. The parliament would have power over all domestic matters, including taxation and the sale of Crown lands.

However, there was one aspect of Wentworth's draft that attracted universal hostility. He proposed for New South Wales an unelected upper house of hereditary peers, similar to the House of Lords. The opposition to the proposal was swift and strong. Throughout the long years Wentworth had spent in public affairs, he had become increasingly reactionary and conservative. A number of factors had led to his eventual desertion of the battler: the gradual waning of the hostility between the 'exclusives' and the 'emancipists'; his large inheritance after his father's death; and his acquisition of large landholdings. Although he'd started out as an egalitarian, he was now much more of an elitist. While he fought consistently for self-government, he never supported universal suffrage and continued to argue that only the minority of property owners be permitted to vote.

His hereditary peerage idea was slammed. The Melbourne *Argus* described the suggestion as 'grotesque' and scorned Wentworth as the 'Duke of Vaucluse' and the 'Marquis of Botany Bay'.[36] Wentworth was also attacked at a series of spontaneously called public meetings throughout the colonies. On 10 August, a meeting attended by between 200 and 300 people at Bathurst's Commercial Hotel condemned the idea with a resolution of 'indignant disapproval', and resolved to petition Queen Victoria, the House of Commons and the House of Lords against the proposal.[37]

Five days later, at a lively meeting in Sydney's Victoria Theatre, resolutions were passed condemning the peerage proposal as a flagrant attack upon public liberty. Wentworth was attacked by almost every speaker and the crowd was reported to have chanted 'Out with Wentworth. Out with Wentworth'. In a memorable speech, Daniel Henry Deniehy, a young, relatively unknown member of the New South Wales Legislative Council, famously derided the proposal for a 'bunyip aristocracy' and in a reference to Wentworth's birth said they did not want an Australian aristocracy whose membership included 'William the bastard'.[38] Deniehy had seconded Henry Parkes' protest resolution to the proposed Wentworth aristocracy.

Within a few weeks, the opposition was so overwhelming that Wentworth had to reluctantly agree to drop the idea entirely from his constitution. Having abandoned the hereditary peerage, the Legislative Council voted to embrace the rest of the constitution and it was sent off to London. Many years later, Henry Parkes, who did much to bring about the conglomeration of the colonies, said that Wentworth's draft constitution had laid one of the 'foundation stones' of the nation of Australia.

Having finally agreed on the constitution, the New South Wales Parliament then voted for Wentworth and another member of the Legislative Council, Edward Deas Thomson, to travel to England to sell the proposal to the British.

Deas Thomson was born in Scotland and educated at Edinburgh High School and Harrow, followed by two years at college in Caen, in Normandy, where he learnt to speak fluent French, which he kept up throughout his adult life. After working with a London law firm and spending a year in the United States, he took a job in New South Wales as clerk to the colony's Legislative Council, arriving in Sydney on 24 January 1829. He first worked with New South Wales governor Sir Ralph Darling, then his successor, Sir Richard Bourke. In 1833, he married Anne Maria, the daughter of Governor Bourke, and in 1837 was promoted to the office of colonial secretary. Despite the obvious nepotism, Thomson was highly regarded for his experience and ability.

In England, Wentworth and Thomson convinced the British Parliament to pass the *Constitution Act*, which included all of the fundamental aspects of Wentworth's design. After they had left for England, there were some further significant steps in Australia towards self-government. In 1856, the two chambers of the 'bicameral' parliament – the Legislative Assembly and the Legislative Council – sat for the first time in New South Wales, and on 22 January 1856 the governor, Sir William Denison, invited newly elected member of the Legislative Assembly Stuart Donaldson to become the first premier and to form a government. Forty-four-year-old Donaldson had difficulty commanding majority support in the parliament and lasted only eleven weeks before being replaced by Charles Cowper, who lasted only five weeks. Cowper was replaced by Henry Parkes, in what was to be one of five terms he served as New South Wales premier.

From 1856 to the end of the century, politics in New South Wales were highly volatile and governments short-lived. There were twenty-nine changes of premier in thirty-four years, although some served a number of times. Prior to the advent of the political party, individuals became premier by cobbling together enough votes, in return for which they usually needed to keep giving something to their supporters, or risk losing them to another aspirant.

Another major reform occurred in 1858: the number of people given the vote increased dramatically. Previously, the vote had been limited to landowners. Now, almost every adult male was eligible, provided he was born in the colony, was naturalised, or had lived in the colony for more than three years.

Wentworth did not return immediately to Australia to relish his final victory. After the great success, he and his family stayed in England and did not return to Sydney until 1861. Arriving on 18 April, after an absence of seven years, the seventy-one-year-old was greeted by more than 1000 people and most of the colony's senior officials, as well as a band playing at the wharf, which was 'gaily decorated with flags' and a banner that read 'Wentworth Welcome Home'.[39] During the welcoming speeches, a message was read from his parliamentary colleagues:

> your seven years' absence ... has [not] diminished our admiration of the many services which you have rendered

to this country. Your early and long continued labours for its advancement – your energetic struggles for true constitutional freedom – the distinguished ability which has marked all your efforts – are still fresh in our memory . . . Whatever may be the regard in which other public men of this country, past or present, may hereafter be held, we think that we are justified in considering that your position in your country's annals is already fixed, as that of a true patriot, whose manliness, ability, and independence of character have reflected credit both on himself and on the land of his birth.[40]

In September 1861, Wentworth was elected president of the Legislative Council, and on 23 June 1862 his statue was unveiled in the Great Hall of Sydney University, which he had helped establish a decade before. Then, in September 1862, the Wentworths finally received the ultimate social acceptance when the governor and his wife attended their ball at Sydney's Roslyn Hall – after more than thirty years as pariahs. Five weeks later, they left Sydney for the last time to return to England 'with the best wishes'.[41]

Throughout the 1860s, the family spent their time living both in London and in the country. On 20 March 1872, Wentworth died at the age of eighty-one in Merley House, near Wimborne, Dorset. In keeping with his wish, his body was brought back to Sydney so that he could be buried on Parsley Hill overlooking Vaucluse, and a few months later, the New South Wales Parliament decided to grant the colony's first state funeral, which was held on Tuesday 6 May 1873, when a public holiday was declared. It was estimated that more than 100,000 attended the funeral at St Andrew's Cathedral next to the Town Hall in Sydney's George Street. Most of the main streets in Sydney were closed from 10 am. The crowds filled all the available vantage points, with men climbing 'drinking fountains, gate-posts, verandahs and roofs' and 'long rows of legs dangled from every parapet'.[42]

After the service, thousands lined the streets to view the funeral cortege on the way to Vaucluse, and thousands more joined the procession in carriages and on foot.[43]

The colony's chief justice, Sir James Martin, summed up Wentworth's achievements when he delivered the eulogy:

> he came back in early manhood to his native country. That country was then little better than a large prison. It was without free institutions . . . its press was shackled; its Legislature consisted of Crown nominees with limited powers; its criminal juries formed exclusively of naval or military men . . . Mr. Wentworth's means, culture, position, and ability marked him out as one to whom it would have been more agreeable to ally himself with the governing classes than with the governed . . . To his own great personal inconvenience he preferred to take the part of the oppressed . . . Hereafter, in the not far distant future, when these colonies shall be the abode of many millions . . . the best and ablest of them all may gather lessons from the life of William Charles Wentworth, and catch perchance, some inspiration from his tomb.[44]

CHAPTER 9

GOLD AND THE
EUREKA REBELLION

*The [Ballarat Reform] League is not more and not less
than the germ of Australian Independence. No power
on earth can restrain the united might and headlong
strides for the freedom of people of this country*

THE DISCOVERY OF GOLD IN AUSTRALIA WAS ARGUABLY THE MOST
significant event of the country's post-settlement history,
transforming a small, poor, pastoral society into a large,
rich one. At the time gold was discovered in 1851,
Australia had a population of barely 200,000 people.
Within ten years, the population had doubled, and it
would double again. Melbourne started the 1850s with
barely 30,000 people; a decade later it was a major,
thriving city of half a million and accounted for half the

country's total population. It would overtake Sydney to become Australia's largest city for the next fifty years.

In 1841, an Anglican vicar, William Braithwaite Clarke, claimed to have found gold west of Sydney but said his discovery had been kept secret by officialdom for fear of destabilising the settlement. Clarke claimed that when he took samples to George Gipps at his country residence in Parramatta, the governor said, 'Put it away, Mr. Clarke, before we all have our throats cut.'[1]

But the rush was inevitable, and was eventually sparked when thirty-four-year-old Edward Hammond Hargraves found a few specks of gold 250 kilometres west of Sydney in February 1851 at the junction of two creeks near Orange, at a place that would take the name of Ophir. For making the discovery, he collected a government reward that had been offered in an effort to stem the flow of men from Australia to the Californian gold rushes, which had begun in 1849. (Without the threat of California, it is highly unlikely that the New South Wales Government would have offered this reward. Hargraves had in fact been one of about 6000 who had gone to California, where he had met with only moderate success as a gold miner.)

Within days of the announcement of Hargraves' discovery, Sydney, with a population of around 60,000, was caught in gold fever. 'Jack' was now richer than his master. As a result, the social order was threatened and, within weeks, a continuous line of men, women and children, carts, horses, drays and wheelbarrows had formed, stretching for 250 kilometres from Sydney over the mountains to the goldfields at Ophir.

Many of the diggers were totally unsuited for the hardships of gold mining and started out without any equipment at the beginning of winter: 'men who would hesitate to walk the length of George Street in a shower of rain are going, at the beginning of winter, to a district where the climate is almost English, and where they will not be able to get shelter in even the humblest hut'.[2]

Sydney was transformed:

Sydney assumed an entirely new aspect. The shop fronts put on quite new faces. Wares suited to the wants and tastes of general purchasers were thrust ignominiously out of sight, and articles of outfit for gold-mining only were displayed ... The pavements were lumbered with picks, pans and pots, and the gold washing machine, or 'Virginian cradle' ... became in two days a familiar household utensil.[3]

Charlotte Godfrey, who arrived in the city in 1853, complained that the only reliable source of domestic help was the 'unsuccessful digger, whose health has suffered, or who has no luck at all', resulting in a dire situation for the ladies of the better houses:

Hardly a man is to be found contented to remain where he is ... you hear endless stories of ladies who have been used to larger establishments, and giving parties, now obliged to give up all thoughts of appearance, and open the door ... themselves ... no servants are to be had, and many of the best and pleasantest families literally driven out of the country by it ... .[4]

The men who found gold were earning more in an hour than they'd earned in a year before the rush. And even the sight of failed diggers did little to dissuade those who caught the fever:

In my four days across the [mountains] I met, I calculate, about three hundred men returning, disheartened and disgusted . . . many having sold for next to nothing the mining equipment, tents, carts, cradles, picks, spades, crows, and washing dishes, which had probably cost them all they possessed in the world three weeks before . . . Mortified, half-starved, and crest-fallen fellows . . . Some looking so gaunt, savage, ragged, and reckless . . .[5]

Within three months of the arrival of the first diggers in western New South Wales, the *Sydney Morning Herald* predicted:

ships will come in abundance . . . full of merchandise and passengers . . . Population and wealth will flow in upon us . . . The largest, the strongest, and the swiftest steamers would come, railways would follow and the British capitalists vie with each other in hastening so happy a consummation.[6]

Only weeks after the beginning of the rush west of Sydney, a bigger gold discovery was made 1000 kilometres to the south, outside Melbourne in the Pyrenees Hills of Victoria.

Victoria's yield of gold would soon dwarf that of its northern neighbour. At the time, Victoria's population was less than 80,000, and most of Melbourne's population of around 23,000 lived in small, one-roomed wooden houses. Only Bourke, Collins and Elizabeth streets were paved; the rest were dirt lanes without footpaths, covered with deep dust, or with deep mud after rain. When news of the discovery of gold broke in the colony, it caused a huge disturbance. On 14 June 1851, *The Argus* reported:

The whole city was alive last evening with a report that a gold mine had at last been discovered . . . the locale of the mine is not given, but it is said to be within 25 miles [40 kilometres] of Melbourne.

The rush that followed was immediate, and businesses of all kinds were forced to shut down when the entire staff deserted. Banks were stripped of cash as depositors withdrew all their money to buy food and equipment and hurried to the goldfields. The governor of the tiny colony, Charles La Trobe, wrote to Earl Grey three months after the start of the rush on 11 October to say that gold was creating greater chaos than it had in Sydney:

> It is quite impossible for me to describe to your Lordship the effect which these discoveries have had upon the whole community . . . The discoveries early in the year in the Bathurst district of New South Wales unsettled the public mind of the labouring classes . . . The discoveries within our bounds . . . in comparative proximity to our towns, exercise a far wider influence upon our excitable population than did the discoveries in New South Wales . . .[7]

La Trobe complained that the 'mania' for gold resulted in men abandoning their jobs and families, towns being emptied and ships being deserted:

> Within the last three weeks the towns of Melbourne and Geelong . . . have almost been . . . emptied . . . the streets that were crowded with drays . . . are now seemingly deserted . . . Shopmen, artisans and mechanics of every description [have] thrown up their employments . . . leaving their employers . . . wives and families to . . . run off to the workings . . . and not a few of the superior classes have followed . . . Cottages are deserted, houses to let, business is at a standstill, and even schools are closed.

In some of the suburbs not a man is left . . . The ships in the harbour are, in a great measure, deserted . . .[8]

William Hall, who had migrated from England in 1838 and opened a general store in Elizabeth Street, Melbourne, described the mania:

I cannot describe the effect it had upon the sober, plodding, and industrious people of Melbourne . . . it . . . was so intense, so all-absorbing, that men seemed bereft of their senses; magistrates, and constables, parsons and priests, merchants and clerks, placemen and paupers, all hastened to Golden Point . . .[9]

The higher echelons of society were, as Charlotte Godfrey in Sydney had expressed, outraged. A local gentleman complained about the difficulty of trying to get by in Melbourne:

I cannot get a pair of boots made or mended in Melbourne if I were to give any money that might be asked . . . I pay 5 shillings for a load of water, and 30 shillings for a single horse load of wood . . . I cannot at any price get a man to chop my wood and I think myself fortunate if I can prevail on the black gins (natives) to work for half an hour.[10]

At the goldfields, what had only weeks before been either pristine wilderness or open grazing country was now populated by thousands of people. There were no roads or sewerage and the surrounding country was soon completely dug up:

It is now absolutely honeycombed with holes eight feet [2.4 metres] square, varying in depth from six to forty feet [1.8 to 12 metres] . . . The holes near the water are dangerous, as the earth falls in; one or two men have been killed in this way, one or two have been murdered . . .[11]

Since the arrival of the white man, the local Aboriginal people had already been decimated by alcohol, influenza, smallpox, measles, tuberculosis and venereal disease. Within a year, according to William Thomas, the guardian for the Aboriginal people of the Melbourne district, the gold rush had further ravaged the local Indigenous population, which, he said, was now on the brink of extinction:

The present condition of the aborigines has in no way improved, but lamentably deteriorated. The discovery of gold has greatly affected their moral condition . . . [they] generally speaking, appear to have become habitual drunkards, male and female . . . they . . . prowl about the public houses and vile avenues, where they are encouraged by the improvident gold diggers into drinking . . . On various occasions they have been found lying in the highways during the night . . . They have now been brought to an awfully dangerous state of degradation, so that the speedy extinction of the Melbourne and Barrabool tribes are inevitable.[12]

Within twenty years, the surviving members of these decimated tribes were living from the proceeds of odd jobs and occasional work for Europeans, the remnants hunter-gathering and begging on the fringes of land that was now occupied by the white man.

*

One of the first British people to reach the Australian goldfields from overseas was Lord Robert Cecil, who fifty years later was the Third Marquess of Salisbury and prime minister of Great Britain when Australia was federated. On his visit to the goldfields, Cecil developed a low opinion of Australians.

The young Lord Cecil heard of the New South Wales gold discoveries in Cape Town in July 1851, when the news was still on its way to London. Cecil had recently dropped out of law studies at Oxford owing to ill health, and had taken a long sea voyage on the recommendation of his doctor. On hearing the news of the gold, he boarded the next available ship from Cape Town to Australia. His ship first landed in Adelaide, which Cecil said had already been 'drained of its population by the mania' caused by the news of gold in Victoria.[13] When he finally reached Melbourne on 25 March 1852 he was unimpressed:

> [it was] thronged with ephemeral plutocrats, generally illiterate, who were hurrying to exchange their gold nuggets for velvet gowns for their wives and unlimited whiskey for themselves, and who made the streets and hotels clamorous with drunken revels which now and again culminated in crimes of audacious violence.[14]

After staying for twelve days at Passmore's Hotel on the corner of Lonsdale and Elizabeth Streets, Lord Cecil and his companion, Sir Montague Chapman, took a carriage to have a look at the goldfields. Cecil did not relish having to share a 'spring cart' with the low calibre of his fellow travellers – something he would never have had to do in aristocratic England. In the goldfields, he witnessed some unpleasant behaviour from the police: they would trick diggers without a miner's licence by promising to issue them one on the spot, but then arrest them when they came forth to claim it. Cecil's observation that practices such as these 'create more ill-will' was apt, since the heavy-handed and increasingly violent policing of licences was the major cause of the uprising at Eureka more than two years later.

As more and more ships began arriving in Australia, many lost their entire crews as soon as they weighed anchor as the men deserted to join the passengers in the rush to the diggings. By the middle of the first year of overseas arrivals, there were more than fifty ships stranded in Port Phillip, and many more in other ports, without enough crews for the journey home.

Throughout the 1850s, up to six ships a day arrived in Port Phillip Bay. William Howitt, who came in September 1852, calculated that 5000 to 6000 people were arriving every week.[15] Howitt complained that passengers were being charged exorbitant prices to be transferred from the ships in Port Phillip to smaller barges for the remaining passage into Melbourne. He said that it cost more to get his luggage ashore and into Melbourne than the freight cost for the journey from England to Australia.

The tens of thousands of gold-diggers in a hurry to reach Australia were to benefit from a revolution in sea transport that was occurring at the time of the rushes: the rise of the clippers, or 'tall ships'. From the 1830s, the Americans had begun building a radically different ship to the small, blunt-nosed vessels that had dominated shipping for several centuries. The clippers were bigger and had long, sleek, narrow hulls with extremely tall masts that carried huge amounts of square sail. They were also very fast. Before the clippers, 240 kilometres a day was considered a good speed for a sailing ship, but the newly designed ships could achieve between 400 and 600 kilometres a day.

The clippers also allowed a more adventurous and far quicker course to be sailed from Europe to Australia, called the Great Circle Route. Prior to 1850, the standard route from Britain to Australia involved sailing down the African coast to the Cape of Good Hope then across the Indian Ocean. The Great Circle Route allowed the bigger, faster and more seaworthy ships to sail in a huge arc across the Atlantic to about 20 degrees west then head well south of the Cape of Good Hope to much higher latitudes, around 50 degrees south, where the wind blew stronger. Before the clippers, the average sailing time to Australia was about 120 days. After the clippers, it came down to around seventy-five days.

*

Until the discovery of gold, almost all the white people coming to Australia were English, Scottish or Irish. During the period of convict transportation, more than 160,000 were sent out, of which about 70 per cent were English, five per cent Scottish and the remaining 25 per cent Irish.

England would continue to supply the largest number of diggers to the Australian goldfields, but the prospectors came from all over the world. Many came from Ireland in the aftermath of the Potato Famine, which had devastated the country from the late 1840s. The famine became worse when, from 1848, financially indebted landlords evicted more impoverished potato-farming tenants. Hordes of desperate Irish migrated to England and to America, where the Irish accounted for more than 40 per cent of the migrant population by 1850. The news of the gold discovery in New South Wales and Victoria in 1851 resulted in more than 100,000 Irish migrants turning to Australia in the next decade and a further 300,000 by the end of the nineteenth century.

The Irish would become a dominant influence on the cultural and political development of Australia. Peter

Lalor was one such mover and shaker. He arrived in Victoria in October 1852, during the first wave of migration from overseas, with his brother Richard. Peter was one of eleven brothers born to Patrick and Anne Lalor, who, until the Potato Famine, had been relatively prosperous on a large, leased farm of 700 acres (about 280 hectares). Peter was lucky to have received an education and studied as an engineer in Dublin. When he arrived in Victoria, he found work on the construction of one of Australia's first railways, from Melbourne to Geelong. In 1854, after his brother Richard had returned to Ireland where he would later become a member of the British Parliament and an advocate of Irish Home Rule, Peter headed off for the Ovens goldfields. A few months later, he moved to Ballarat, where he would become a major player in the bloody Eureka uprising later the same year.

The next biggest source of immigrant diggers was the Chinese, who would change the face of Australia. There were already several thousand Chinese workers in Australia before gold was discovered. They had come mainly from China's southern provinces to work on sheep farms at a time when the decline in convicts was causing a labour shortage. The stream of Chinese coming to Australia after gold was discovered was initially quite slow and did not pick up dramatically until 1854. Most overseas migration from China at the time was from around the southern province of Kwangtung (Guangdong), where at the time there was widespread political corruption, political turmoil, dynastic decline, floods, crop failures, banditry and inter-clan rivalry.

Much of the current-day Australian hostility towards Asians, xenophobia and suspicion of refugees can be traced back to the arrival of the Chinese on the Australian goldfields. No other group during the gold-rush era would suffer the same persecution, violence, murder and official discrimination as the Chinese. They were attacked in public and in the press, and branded as barbarians, pagans and impure. The Melbourne *Argus* described them as 'a social evil' that would contaminate and degrade the European race.[16] *The Sydney Morning Herald* published allegations that the Chinese were guilty of infanticide and 'unnatural crimes'.[17]

Most of the Europeans who made up the bulk of the white population of Australia had never seen a 'celestial' before they began to arrive in large numbers to hunt for gold, and many were threatened by their very appearance. They were small in stature; they shaved their hair from the temple across the front of the head and did not cut the back, which was gathered in a long ponytail, or 'queue', which was usually tied towards the end with a ribbon. They dressed very differently from European men, with loose, wide-sleeved tops and loose breeches, and wore soft slippers or sandals, or went about barefoot. They tended to travel in large groups and wore wide, circular, straw hats that peaked in the middle, and carried their possessions in two large baskets that were hung from the ends of a long pole resting over their shoulders. When moving, they took short, fast steps and appeared to be jogging very slowly.

The Chinese built separate villages with their own shops, tradesmen, vegetable gardens and farm animals. Very few women came, and those who did were mostly servants to the wealthier Chinese.[18] About 40 per cent of the men were already married and would eventually return to their villages and their families. Almost all lived in a tent with a friend or a relative and could rely on a network of support if they became ill or injured while working.[19]

The Chinese were noted for being industrious and would typically work on the diggings from sunrise until it was dark. However, they were also regarded with suspicion and hostility for their leisure pursuits, which included gambling, drinking spirits and widespread opium smoking. After the first ten years of Chinese arrivals, it was estimated there were fifty gambling shops and eighty opium dens in Ballarat alone, and that four out of every ten Chinese men were addicted to opium. It was feared it could contaminate the non-Chinese population, particularly women:

> The opium shops which stud the Chinese camp so thickly are also dens of infamy and immorality. In these are found abandoned European women, some of whom have got into the habit of smoking the pernicious drug; and there is every reason to fear that in the course of time the practice will gradually spread among the European population . . . All these shops should be well watched, and kept under the vigilant surveillance of the police.[20]

Opium was not illegal at the time and a thriving trade was done by British merchants selling it into China. It was not until the 1880s that the Australian colonies attempted collectively to curtail its use, and it was not outlawed until 1908. The Chinese brought most of their own opium to Australia and, far from trying to limit its trade, the Victorian Government saw it as a useful source of revenue, imposing a tax on it along with imported rice from 1855.

That the Chinese were almost entirely men gave rise to the widely held view promoted in the newspapers that they were sexually depraved, and similarities were drawn with the earlier convict times in Australia when there had been fewer women.[21] Intermarriage between Chinese men and European women was uncommon, though it did happen. In 1867, after well over a decade of Chinese immigration to the goldfields, it was reported that there had been between fifty and sixty mixed marriages in Victoria, producing about 130 children.

Within a year, violent assaults on Chinese miners became increasingly widespread. The newspapers' coverage was not altogether balanced:

> The serious evils that may any day arise from the presence of these strangers is plain from . . . the reports that reach us of their numbers in which they are already to be found at the different gold fields . . . we see . . . in the peculiarities of their language, dress and habits of life, there is enough to unite the suspicions of the other diggers.[22]

In March 1855, a Victorian Government report echoed the hostility to the Chinese that was appearing with increased frequency in the newspapers:

> This number [of Chinese], although already almost incredible, yet appears to be still fast increasing, and is likely to increase still more . . . The question of the influx of such large numbers of a pagan and inferior race is a very serious one . . . and . . . comprises an unpleasant possibility of the future, that a comparative handful of colonists may be buried in a countless throng of Chinamen.[23]

Over the next months, there was a clamour for action particular to be taken and, on 12 April 1856, the Victorian Government announced particular measures. The new law was the first of many race-specific laws that would be introduced in Australia aiming to keep Australia 'white' for the next century. It imposed a prohibitively high charge, or poll tax, on each Chinese person landing at a Victorian port of £10 per head. (Until the gold rush pushed up wages, a European labourer might earn £20 a year.) Practically none of the Chinese had any money and most had borrowed to pay for their passage to the goldfields. Certainly, they would not have possessed anywhere near this amount. No doubt, the colonial authorities knew this, so the tax was to be collected from the captain of each arriving ship.

This resulted in one of the most ingenious tax-avoidance schemes and one of the most remarkable migration treks in history. To avoid paying the £10 tax for each passenger, the masters of the ships from China with men destined for the goldfields simply sailed past Port Phillip, around the coast of Victoria, and unloaded their human cargo in the colony of South Australia, where the tax was not levied.

Initially, the ships landed in Adelaide, leaving the Chinese with a walk of nearly 800 kilometres to the Victorian goldfields, in an area where there were few tracks and no clear colonial borders. But after a few months, the ships instead began to drop off the Chinese at the little settlement of Robe on Guichen Bay, which was closer to the Victorian border. Over the next year, the village of Robe, with a population of barely 200 people, became a thriving port as more than 20,000 Chinese landed there before walking the 350 kilometres to Ararat, 400 kilometres to Ballarat or 450 kilometres to Bendigo.

Thomas Smeaton, a bank manager newly arrived in Robe, described the first Chinese arrivals:

Imagine yourself an inhabitant of Robe on Saturday 17 January 1857. No banks, no electricity: no electric telegraph: everything on a mitigated scale . . . when, those whose eyes happened to be open, perceived a ship! A ship actually coming into Guichen Bay!! And crowded with passengers!! Before many hours the population of Robe had doubled.[24]

On the overland trek to Victoria, the typical party of Chinese might number between 100 and 300, but some totalled up to 600. Each group, carrying their possessions on baskets at the end of a long pole and in single file, could extend several kilometres as it moved across South Australia towards Victoria.

The 'back door' of South Australia as a way into Victoria was closed at the end of 1857. Under pressure from Victoria – and local public opinion – South Australia introduced its own anti-Chinese legislation in June 1857, and by the end of the year no ships were arriving at Robe.

By the end of the 1850s, as a result of the poll tax and the decline in easily worked, shallow alluvial deposits, the number of Chinese on the Victorian goldfields began to drop from around 45,000 at the end of the 1850s to only 20,000 less than a decade later.[25] Many joined the other diggers and began to spread north across the border to New South Wales, where new fields were being discovered, and by 1858 it was estimated that 1000 Chinese were still arriving every week – from Victoria and from China.

In New South Wales, the European diggers were equally hostile to the Chinese. *The Bathurst Free Press* in June 1857 described the Chinese as 'a race with whom we have little more in common than with a race of baboons or a tribe of orang-outangs'. Over the next few years, there were regular reports of attacks against the Chinese, which included murder. Towards the end of 1860 and the beginning of 1861, there were an increasing number of riots and violent attacks on the goldfields of Lambing Flat (later named Young after the tragic 1861 riot between European diggers and the Chinese).

In July 1861, an eyewitness account of thousands of Europeans rioting and attacking the Chinese was published in *The Sydney Morning Herald*, ensuring it would forever be stamped in the annals of Australian history. The riot started when more than 1000 men armed with 'bludgeons and pick handles' marched on the Chinese to run them off the diggings:

> the Chinese took to their heels, but to no purpose, for they were caught, and several had their pigtails cut off . . . The mob, now between 2000 and 3000 crossed the main creek, and . . . made for the camp of the Chinese, who were working inside the boundary set apart for them . . . Tents by scores were set on fire; rice and stores of all kinds destroyed. For a distance of half a mile the burning tents showed the work of destruction. Not content with this, some men on horseback proceeded forward and overtook the Chinese – some 1200. They rounded them up the same as they would a mob of cattle, struck them with their bludgeons and whips . . . I noticed one man who returned with eight pigtails attached to a flag, glorying in the work that had been done. I also saw one tail, with a part of the scalp the size of a man's hand attached, that had been literally cut from some unfortunate creature . . .[26]

From 1856, every colonial parliament introduced anti-Chinese-immigration laws in an attempt to keep the Chinese from the diggings: South Australia in 1857; New South Wales in 1861; Queensland in 1877; Western Australia in 1886; and Tasmania in 1887. In 1901, the first year of the new Australian Parliament, the *Immigration Restriction Act* was introduced, applying to all the states and territories. The new law was the basis of what was known as the 'White Australia' policy, which effectively banned or limited non-European migrants and was not totally repealed until 1973.

*

From the start of the gold rush in both New South Wales and Victoria, there were tensions between the diggers and the governments over the mining-licence fee. It cost thirty shillings a month and had to be paid in advance, even if no gold was found. As proof of payment, it had to be carried at all times.

The official justification for the licence was that Australia, as a British colony, belonged to the Crown, and therefore any gold found in the land was owned by the Queen. As part of the British Empire, the colonies were administered by the Queen's representative, the governor, who was appointed by the monarch on the recommendation of the Colonial Office in London.

Most British subjects in Australia were loyal to Empire. However, the discovery of gold in Australia would attract thousands of men and women from a host of other countries who felt no allegiance to the British Crown and little or no respect for British authority. This was particularly the case among many of the Americans, who, seventy years before, had won their War of Independence against the British, and had not paid a tax to mine for gold in California only a few years before.

The Irish saw immigration to the Australian goldfields as liberation from British oppression at home. Added to the mix were thousands from various other countries of Europe that had experienced revolutions only a few years before, in 1848.

Many of the diggers who had made it to the goldfields from the other side of the world found themselves struggling in the remote Australian bush, having to contend with limited food, rough accommodation, high prices for everything, lack of women and family, tedium, fatigue and loneliness – all of which contributed to their resentment towards the licence tax, and the heavy-handed ways of the police who collected it.

The man responsible for the gold licence in Victoria was Sir Charles La Trobe, who had been appointed superintendent of Port Phillip District in 1839 and had been the most senior government official in the colony for more than twelve years before the discovery of gold. The first protest meeting against the licence tax in Victoria was organised two weeks after its introduction, at Buninyong, near Ballarat, on 25 August 1851. A sympathetic account of the meeting appeared in the *Geelong Advertiser* two days later:

> Thirty shillings a month, for twenty-six days work, payable in advance, is the impost demanded by our Victorian Czar. Eighteen pounds sterling per annum, per head, is the merciless prospective exaction on an enterprise scarcely fourteen days old. It is a juggernaut tax to crush the poor . . . why should a lawful occupation, promising so much, be strangled in its birth? . . . It is an insult to common sense . . . If such a thing as this tax be tolerated, it will be the first step to liberticide, for liberty cannot be where the foundation of all wealth is trammelled.[27]

The fifty or so reportedly present at the meeting carried what was to be the first of many resolutions that would be passed at numerous meetings leading up to the rebellion and massacre at nearby Eureka three years later.

The antipathy of the miners towards the tax and the authorities that collected it was made worse by the local police, whom the diggers believed were corrupt and harassing. While there was plenty of crime to address, the police were preoccupied with the enforcement and collection of the licence tax, which had become a lucrative source of revenue for the fledgling colony of Victoria. Raffaello Carboni, an Italian radical who arrived on the goldfields in late 1852, described how, in January 1853, he was harassed by the police for his licence:

> I was hard at work . . . I hear a rattling noise among the brush. My faithful dog Bonaparte would not keep under my control. 'What's up?' 'Your licence, mate.' was the peremptory question from a six-foot fellow in blue shirt, thick boots, the face of a ruffian armed with a carbine and a fixed bayonet.[28]

By May 1853, the opposition to the tax had grown and a big miners' protest was held at Agitation Hill at Mount Alexander. In June, an Anti-Gold Licence Association was formed at Bendigo, where more than 20,000 diggers from Bendigo, Ballarat, Castlemaine, Heathcote, Stawell and other diggings signed what became known as the Bendigo Petition, which detailed the miners' grievances. The thirteen-metre-long petition was taken to Melbourne, where it was presented to Governor La Trobe on 1 August. By the end of the year, thousands of miners had taken to wearing a red ribbon in their hats to mark their opposition to the fee.

A diggers' riot almost happened in New South Wales before it happened in Victoria. The diggers along the Turon River in central western New South Wales had first met to protest the fee at a mass gathering on 17 June 1851, and continued to agitate against the tax. Then, in December 1852, rather than reducing the licence fee, the New South Wales Government extended it to everyone on the goldfields, including storekeepers and tradesmen, even if they were not digging. Non-Britishers were to pay double the fee, and the penalties for not paying it were dramatically increased.

Opposition to the new measures was fierce. Early in the new year, open warfare was only narrowly averted when several hundred armed diggers marched to fife and drum on 8 February 1852 into the township of Sofala, near Bathurst, but were dissuaded from violence as more troopers from the 11th Regiment arrived to reinforce the small garrison already there. The situation was defused when the colonial secretary, Edward Deas Thomson, signalled that the government was prepared to amend the *Gold Fields Management Act* and Governor Sir Charles FitzRoy duly asked the parliament to amend the law to drop the aliens' tax, cut the fee and apply it only to those actually digging.

Back in Victoria, no such concessions were offered, and in 1854 the situation changed quite dramatically when a new governor was sent from England to replace Sir Charles La Trobe. Sir Charles Hotham was a far more senior appointment than La Trobe had been fifteen years earlier. In the late 1840s, Hotham had been knighted and appointed British naval commodore for the west coast of Africa, and in 1852 he was the head of the British mission negotiating a treaty with Paraguay. He came reluctantly to Australia. At the outbreak of the Crimean War, he had sought the command of a ship but was assigned the role of lieutenant governor of Victoria instead.

He and his wife, Lady Sarah, reached Melbourne on 22 June 1854, nearly seven weeks after the departure of La Trobe. On arrival, they were greeted with much pro-British pomp and ceremony, which would have disguised the deep-rooted resentment of authority felt by the diggers on the goldfields. Indeed, on his first visit to the goldfields of Ballarat, Bendigo and Castlemaine three months later, Hotham reported meeting overwhelmingly loyal and obedient diggers who flocked in the thousands to see him with 'shouts of loyalty to Her Majesty, and cries of attachment to the old country'.[29]

The only dissent was at Bendigo, where Hotham recorded 'a slight show of disaffection' over the licence fee when he was given a petition for its abolition by some of the leaders of the miners. Hotham said that, when he responded to the petition by telling the diggers that they must pay for 'liberty and order', he was 'loudly cheered' by the thousands present.

The Italian firebrand Raffaello Carboni, who witnessed the event, recorded a different impression. He said that, when Hotham met the diggers, he thanked them for the petition and declared, 'I shall not neglect your interests and welfare.'[30]

Back in Melbourne a month later, Hotham decided to clamp down on licence evasion and ordered that, rather than occasional searches, there would be systematic policing of the goldfields to find evaders twice a week. The police, or 'traps', as they were known, conducted stringent licence hunts that inflamed the miners, and tensions were running high by the first week of October 1854.

Then, shortly after midnight on 7 October, Scottish miner James Scobie and his mate stopped at the Eureka Hotel for a drink on the way back to their camp. In an ensuing brawl with the publican, an ex-convict named James Bentley, Scobie was killed. After a hastily convened inquiry, the stipendiary magistrate John D'Ewes, who was known to be a friend of the publican, released Bentley and his colleagues on the grounds of insufficient evidence.

Only three days after Scobie's death, Johannes Gregorius, a native of Armenia who spoke little English and suffered from a physical disability, and who was a servant of the Reverend Patricius Smyth, the priest of the Catholic Church at Bakery Hill, was beaten and arrested for not having a miner's licence. Emotions were running high, particularly among the Irish. A mass meeting was held at Bakery Hill in Ballarat on 15 October to protest the rough treatment of the servant by the police. Two days later, another mass meeting was held near the spot where James Scobie had been killed, and a resolution passed castigating the outcome of the inquiry into his death.

At the end of the meeting, a number of miners marched on the Eureka Hotel, and its owner James Bentley hurriedly rode off on horseback to the protection of local police. An additional force of thirty armed police was sent to the demonstration but was unable to restore order as the hotel was first stoned by the protesters and then set alight and burnt to the ground.

Unrest around Ballarat escalated. In the last weeks of October, more police reinforcements and a detachment of soldiers from the 40th Regiment arrived, as the authorities grew increasingly concerned at the developments on the goldfields.

On 21 October, Andrew McIntyre and Thomas Fletcher were arrested for burning the Eureka Hotel; a third suspect, Henry Westerbury, was arrested later. The diggers reacted by calling a mass meeting, where it was resolved that bail would be collected to get their colleagues out of jail.

On 11 November, miners at Bakery Hill decided to establish the Ballarat Reform League and elect a number of the diggers to draw up its charter. The charter was radical for its time, calling for universal suffrage, the abolition of property ownership as a requisite for becoming a member of parliament, payment of salaries to members of parliament, voting by ballot and short-term parliaments. The licence tax had been at the centre of the dispute, but it had also fuelled a wider political discord. The *Ballarat Times* commented: 'This League is nothing more or less than the germ of Australian Independence . . . No power on earth can now restrain the united might and headlong strides for freedom of people of this country.'[31]

November saw the emergence of a number of natural leaders among the diggers. Thirty-year-old John Basson Humffray was elected secretary of the Ballarat Reform League and later, along with radical Irishman Peter Lalor, would become their first parliamentary representative when he was elected to the Victorian Legislative Assembly in 1855.

As the tensions rose, Governor Hotham agreed to a new inquiry into James Scobie's death, and James Bentley and an accomplice, Thomas Farrell, were re-arrested and charged with murder. At the same time, Hotham was determined to maintain order in Ballarat. Within four days, 450 extra soldiers and police were sent to the gold-fields with orders 'to use force, whenever legally called upon to do so without regard to the consequences which might ensue'.[32]

Not long afterwards, Henry Westerbury, Thomas Fletcher and Andrew McIntyre were convicted and each sentenced to three years' hard labour for burning the Eureka Hotel. On 25 November, Gold Commissioner Robert Rede reported he had been told that the government camp would be burnt down if the convicted arsonists were not released. The next day, a police inspector advised his boss that he had heard the same thing, and that an attack was imminent.

The following morning, Monday 27 November, Hotham met in Melbourne with a deputation of three miners – John Basson Humffray, George Black and Thomas Kennedy – who hoped the government might make some concessions that would defuse the tensions at Ballarat. Things got off to a bad start when Hotham objected to the deputation, referring to the diggers' 'demands', and after more than half an hour's discussion refused to consider releasing the three men convicted of the arson attack on the Eureka

Hotel. He also said he was powerless to extend parliamentary representation as the decision rested with London. The deputation left Melbourne to return to the goldfields empty-handed, and arrived back at Ballarat only an hour before a mass meeting of 10,000 diggers, who angrily passed a unanimous, provocative resolution:

> That this meeting, being convinced that the obnoxious licence fee is the imposition of an unjustifiable tax, pledges itself to take immediate steps to abolish the same by at once burning all licences. That in the event of any party being arrested for having no licence, that the united people will, under the circumstances, defend and protect them.[33]

The diggers had thrown down the gauntlet. There was no longer any reference to 'every lawful means', which had been part of the resolutions of only months earlier. The meeting was now threatening to fight if the authorities continued to police the gold-mining licences. The resolution ended by calling for another mass meeting the following Sunday at the nearby Adelphi Theatre.

On Thursday 30 November, Gold Commissioner Rede ordered another licence hunt, but when the police reached what was known as the Gravel Pits, they were stoned by the miners and forced to retreat.

The Irishman Peter Lalor described how the situation rapidly deteriorated, leading to the attack on the Eureka Stockade, on Bakery Hill, Ballarat, early the following Sunday morning, 3 December. The twenty-seven-year-old Lalor had only become prominent the day before, when he had spoken at a mass meeting of the miners that resolved to meet the government with violence if necessary. He said that none of the regular leaders were there to speak when the meeting started, so he volunteered, mounting 'the stump' to proclaim 'liberty' for miners. Tensions continued to rise:

> Great excitement now prevailed throughout the diggings, and early next (Friday) morning, some armed diggers began to assemble on Bakery Hill, but on the military and police moving upon them in force, they dispersed. About seven o'clock in the morning, about 200 armed diggers from Eureka, of which I was one, marched to Bakery Hill and hoisted the Southern Cross. So great was the horror excited in the minds of the diggers by the unconstitutional and bloodthirsty attack of the previous day, that, in about two hours, we numbered about 1500 armed men. The rest of the day was spent procuring arms, electing the officers, and improving the organisation.[34]

The diggers organised themselves in a wooden stockade, which was a fencelike enclosure they made of timber planks and old carts. Lalor said they never intended waiting in the enclosure until they were attacked but had 'scouts and sentries' throughout the goldfields and were prepared to send a sizeable force anywhere in the diggings they might be needed.

Around midnight on Saturday, after two false alarms, many of the diggers wandered off to their tents to sleep, so when the government attacked in the early hours of Sunday morning there were less than 150 men still in the enclosure. The government had many spies in and around Eureka, and decided to mobilise more than 300 troops when the miners' defences would be at their weakest.

The police and soldiers surrounded and attacked the stockade. After an exchange of shots, the outnumbered diggers were outgunned and overrun. During the fighting, twenty-two miners and seven soldiers were killed, many were injured and more than 100 were rounded up and jailed.

Charles Ferguson, an American digger who had formerly been on the Californian diggings, had joined the miners' resistance and was in the Eureka Stockade at the time of the attack. He explained that a group of American miners had formed themselves into a company they called the 'California Rangers' after Peter Lalor had come to talk to them. The California Rangers were some 300 strong and were commanded by an Irish American called James McGill.

However, Ferguson was one of only a handful of Americans inside the stockade in the early hours of Sunday 3 December when the government forces attacked. He said the diggers fired first. They could see the soldiers advancing 'just as the light of day was breaking in the east' and could hear the officer giving orders when one of the men in the stockade, Captain Burnette, 'stepped a little in front, elevated his rifle, took aim and fired'. When it was clear the stockade was being overrun, Ferguson tried unsuccessfully to escape, but he was 'seized upon by several soldiers'.[35]

He was taken to a wooden cell at the government camp, which was so crowded there was no room to sit down. Later the same Sunday morning, Henry Seekamp, the owner of the *Ballarat Times*, was arrested and jailed with the others. He was charged with 'seditious libel' for publishing a series of stories during November and December that were believed to have incited the diggers.

On the Sunday morning of the massacre, when he was arrested in his printing office, Seekamp was typesetting an editorial that was to finish with the words, 'This foul bloody murder calls to High Heaven for vengeance, terrible and immediate.' When the edition of the newspaper was finally issued with the help of Seekamp's wife, it carried the later insertion, 'The Editor of the *Ballarat Times* has been arrested since the above was written.'

During the fighting at the stockade, a musket ball and two small bullets shattered Peter Lalor's left arm. Bleeding heavily, he was hidden under some wooden slabs and secreted away after the battle ended. Lalor was hidden by friends near Ballarat, where his shattered arm was amputated. He was taken to Geelong, where he was kept in hiding and cared for by his fiancée, Alicia Dunne. Word quickly spread that he was alive, and Governor Hotham agreed to post a reward for his capture.

After consulting with his colleagues, Hotham declared martial law in Ballarat the day after the rebellion, and a strict curfew was imposed across the goldfields. Very quickly, there were a number of public declarations in support of Hotham but also widespread criticism. The Melbourne *Age* newspaper published an editorial that questioned sending a military force from Melbourne to the goldfields: '[We] do not sympathise with revolt; but neither do [we] sympathise with injustice and coercion. [We] will not fight for the diggers nor will [we] fight for the government.'[36]

On 6 December, a public meeting was called outside St Paul's Church on Flinders Street in Melbourne, which attracted a reported 6000 people but failed to pass the expected resolution of support for the governor. Hotham attempted to defuse the situation by establishing an inquiry into the Eureka event, and the next day thirteen of those who had been arrested in Ballarat were charged with high treason and taken by coach to Melbourne for trial.

If the immediate aftermath of Eureka proved troublesome for the government and Hotham, the following year would be even more difficult. On 10 January 1855, the commission Hotham had established to inquire into

Eureka met with the governor and, even though the report was still two months off, tried to persuade him to grant an amnesty to all those charged over the affair. Hotham would not hear of it and insisted the trials of the thirteen go ahead.

Over the course of the next three months, all those charged were acquitted by the courts, and the commission of inquiry set up by Hotham recommended the 'obnoxious' gold licence fee be abolished. The commission was highly critical of the way the licence collection was policed, and it supported other demands of the diggers, including the extension of the voting franchise and for diggers to be represented in parliament. To further undermine the authority of the governor and the government, Peter Lalor was increasingly seen in public until eventually the government backed down and revoked the reward it had offered for his capture. Later in the same year, he stood unopposed as a member of parliament for Ballarat with fellow rebel leader John Basson Humffray, and they were elected as additional members of the Legislative Assembly when Victoria's new constitution came into force in 1856.

The Eureka uprising had a lasting impact on the political development of Australia. All the demands of the Ballarat Reform League ended up being introduced across the country – many of them years before being adopted in Britain. Ever since, Eureka has been seen as Australia's first great fight for democracy[37] and the 'battle cry' for a range of later political ideologists, including nationalists, republicans, liberals, radicals and communists.[38] At the same time, it must be recognised that the insurrection failed, and, if anything, British authority in the Australian colonies was consolidated after the rebellion was suppressed.

*

Throughout the 1850s, the Australian gold rush was largely limited to Victoria and New South Wales. But over the next forty years, new discoveries would be made that would also transform other Australian colonies and territories.

The gold rush in Queensland came in the nick of time for the fledgling colony. In 1867, with a tiny population of only 23,000 settlers and having gained independence from New South Wales only eight years earlier, Queensland was in the depths of a severe economic depression. The huge gold find in October 1867 by semi-literate loner James Nash at Bella Creek near Gympie, some 170 kilometres north of Brisbane, is widely believed to have been 'a golden gleam shot across the midnight sky of the colony's adversity' that prevented Queensland's collapse.[39] It sparked great excitement in Brisbane:

> In the following month, the town of Brisbane resembled a hive of bees at swarming time. Pushing and shoving. Lawyers, parsons, doctors, shopmen, shopkeepers, and everyone else who could walk, could be seen swaggering up with blankets, making their way across the hills and treacherous track . . . for the new diggings.[40']

The year after Nash's discovery, new goldfields opened up 1000 kilometres further north at Cape River and at Ravenswood – the biggest of the early fields – about 100 kilometres east of the Cape River. By 1868, this small town had more than 4000 people and more than fifty pubs. One of those who found his way there and ended up running a pub on the diggings was a twenty-eight-year-old Danish carpenter called Thorvald Weitemeyer, who had come to seek his fortune in 1861.

Weitemeyer had initially left the family home in Copenhagen, Denmark, and gone to Hamburg, Germany, to work in a furniture factory rather than follow his father into the building trade. One Sunday night, while walking the streets of Hamburg on his day off, he saw in a shop window a large placard on which was printed in red letters, 'Free Emigration to Queensland, Australia'.

At the time, Queensland was one of a number of Australian colonies looking to promote development and boost its population by offering assisted migration. Weitemeyer said that he knew little about Australia other than remembering being taught at school that nature was reversed there: how leaves hung downwards from trees instead of upwards, how the great rivers ran inland away from the sea, how the centre was a great lake of salt water and how the swans were black, not white.

After pondering for a few days, he joined 600 other Germans, Swedes, Norwegians, Finns and Russians who spoke and understood no English but shared the 'same spirit of recklessness and poverty', and boarded a ship to Australia. After working as a carpenter along the Queensland coast, Weitemeyer saved more than £100 and headed for the diggings at Ravenswood: 'At last I was on the goldfield. What a magic spell ... Runaway nuns dressed in men's clothing, princes working like labourers and labourers living like princes.'[41]

After unsuccessfully searching for gold, Weitemeyer moved closer to the new diggings at Charters Towers, where he opened a grog tent and was soon doing a roaring trade. However, after several months, and having made a small fortune, he was robbed of all his saved money, which he had hidden in a bucket buried in the ground. He then joined a fellow Dane named Thorkill and decided to head for the new gold that had been discovered almost another 1000 kilometres away, at the Palmer River in Far North

Queensland, deep in the heart of the tropics of Cape York Peninsula.

The Palmer River gold rush in Queensland was one of the wildest, most lawless and most dangerous the world had seen. It was characterised by mountainous terrain, hundreds of kilometres of jungle track, a dry season where a man could die of thirst and a wet season that could wash away entire settlements and leave men stranded to starve to death.

As well as the extreme environment, the Palmer also brought together the most volatile mixture of people yet seen in Australia, including desperate Europeans hardened from years of gold hunting in the south of Australia, hostile tribes of Aboriginal people, and the Chinese, who became a majority in the area.

Gold had been found first by William Hann, a farmer from the Burdekin River, which was at the time one of the colony's most northerly settlements, about 1000 kilometres north of Brisbane. Hann was sent by the Queensland Government in 1872 to explore 'as far north as the 14th parallel of latitude, the character of the country and its mineral resources with a view to future settlement'.[42] During the five-month expedition, Hann's team found gold but warned its location meant mining it was not viable: 'The prospects we obtained were certainly not payable.'[43]

Undeterred by the warning of slim pickings, Irishman James Venture Mulligan organised five of his mates to follow in Hann's footsteps to the Palmer River the following year, where they found 102 ounces (around three kilograms) of gold.

Tens of thousands headed north, first overland then, late in 1873, by ship to the Endeavour River followed by a 250-kilometre overland trek to the west. As had been the case with the earlier goldfields in the south, the Europeans carried guns for hunting and for security – but here they would also be used for killing the local Aboriginal people, the Chinese and each other.

The local Aboriginal tribes were less nomadic in the tropical north than they were in the south, and they resented the intrusion and the disruption caused by the newcomers. They tended to make permanent camps on high ground but near reliable sources of water. They also tended to fight back, and the Europeans were not used to that.

The Chinese who arrived in Far North Queensland would experience the same persecution and violence from white diggers that had occurred on the Victorian gold-fields and elsewhere in Queensland. By the end of 1875, the gold warden on the Palmer, P. N. Sellheim, reported that the Chinese outnumbered the Europeans by a ratio of more than three to one,[44] and in 1876 there were public meetings in Cooktown calling on the government to 'consider the desirability of preventing the influx of Chinese on the northern goldfields'.[45] In May 1876, the *Cooktown Herald* forecast widespread violence unless measures were taken to rid the Far North of the Chinese:

> It is no longer a question of repelling a coming invasion, so much as to defend, not alone our hearths and homes, but our very lives against the invaders who swarm around us. The danger is imminent and deadly, and unless the most strenuous measures be at once taken, it may be ere too long, one of the most disastrous and bloody chapters in Australian history will have to be recorded.[46]

In response to the growing hostility to the Chinese, the Queensland Parliament passed *The Chinese Immigration Regulation Act 1877*, which imposed a hefty poll tax on ships' captains for every Chinese digger landed at Cooktown.

As had happened more than twenty years earlier in Victoria, an attempt was made to evade the tax, and many Chinese were unloaded from their ships at other points along the north coast. Some were taken to the Bloomfield River, about 50 kilometres south of Cooktown, and left to walk overland for about 240 kilometres to 'China Camp', at Bryerstown, on the Palmer. Others were landed at Cape Tribulation, about 95 kilometres south of Cooktown, which left a trek of a little over 300 kilometres to the Palmer.

By the end of the 1870s, most of the alluvial gold along the Palmer and the other rivers of the Far North had been worked out, and the diggers drifted away. A few went even further north up the Cape York Peninsula to mine gold at Normanton. Some went to Mount Morgan, which opened in 1882, or over to Papua New Guinea. Many drifted back to where they had come from.

The gold rushes spread not only to Queensland from the 1860s but also to New Zealand and Tasmania. In the 1870s, several thousand Europeans and even more Chinese went to the Northern Territory, but the alluvial gold was largely worked out before the end of the decade.

South Australia was the only colony that did not experience a major gold rush. Gold had been found at Castambul, about 25 kilometres east of Adelaide, in 1846, from which a brooch was made and presented to Queen Victoria. However, the initial excitement turned to disappointment when the mine produced little gold. From 1851, there were other gold finds, but over the next thirty years none was big enough to attract large numbers of prospectors from other colonies or from overseas.

The presence of abundant gold in other colonies – particularly in neighbouring Victoria – was devastating for

South Australia. An estimated one-third of the colony's men left for the eastern goldfields in the early 1850s, which created a serious shortage of manpower. Lord Robert Cecil stopped in at Adelaide on his way to the Victorian goldfields in early 1852 and described how Adelaide was in desperate straits:

> In consequence of the immigration mania, excited by the discovery of the goldfields, the colonial revenue has for the time almost vanished. The customs, which used to produce £3,000 a week, have fallen to zero, land is unsaleable, and property on which £1,500 has been spent has sold for £43.[47]

Gold was later found in South Australia in smaller quantities, but the colony subsequently benefited from exporting grain to feed the diggers in Victoria and New South Wales. Its economy was also boosted by the men returning from the eastern goldfields with their gold finds, and by the arrival of the first waves of several thousand German migrants, who launched the Barossa Valley wine industry in the 1850s.

*

Western Australia's first gold rush started in July 1885 when Charles Hall and a party of six prospectors found a few ounces of gold in a dry riverbed in the Kimberley ranges, more than 500 kilometres inland from the tiny port of Derby on Australia's remote north-west coast. The site would take the name Halls Creek. Within a year, an estimated 10,000 prospectors had gone to Halls Creek, and by 1887 nearly 10,000 ounces (284 kilograms) of gold had been found, after which the diggings went into decline.

Yet, within a few short years, Halls Creek would be almost forgotten with the discovery of what would be the biggest and longest-lasting of all the Australian goldfields, almost 3000 kilometres further south in Western Australia around Coolgardie and Kalgoorlie.

The great Western Australian gold rush started when, one Sunday afternoon in June 1892, two veterans of the diggings in Queensland found gold in a remote spot of desert in what would become Coolgardie. Here, twenty-two-year-old Arthur Bailey and forty-year-old William Ford found over 500 ounces (14 kilograms) of gold. Nine months later, a lone Irish prospector, Paddy Hannan, found even more gold 40 kilometres further east, at what was to become Kalgoorlie.

The discoveries sparked a rush from around the world. Over the next few years, gold would be discovered in a wide arc covering hundreds of kilometres to the north and to the east of both Coolgardie and Kalgoorlie.

There had been some remarkable advances in technology in the forty years between Edward Hargraves finding gold at Ophir in New South Wales and the rush in Western Australia. However, all the progress was of limited value deep in the Western Australian desert, which enjoyed less than three centimetres of rain a year. There were no running rivers and the country supported very little vegetation or wildlife. It is unlikely that there has ever been a situation where so many people lived for so long with so little fresh water as occurred during the last decade of the nineteenth century on the Western Australian goldfields. John Marshall, a thirty-four-year-old Scot who joined the rush from New South Wales, said he learnt on his way to the diggings that there was too little water for washing:

At an accommodation house on the road, where we stopped for dinner, the landlady apologized for not being able to find us water in which to wash our faces, and informed us it was usual for travellers to . . . knock the dust off each other with a handkerchief, and wipe their faces with a hat.[48]

The concentration of a large number of men combined with the absence of water with no effective sewerage led very quickly to an unhealthy environment, leading to an outbreak of typhoid. According to Mrs Arthur Garnsey, who worked in the tiny tin and canvas hospital in Coolgardie, the staff was forced to use whisky instead of water for the treatment of patients:

> The difficulties of hospital work were . . . almost insurmountable for lack of water . . . and in despair, when the water supply ran out, nurses often tried to cool burning bodies by damping the sponge in whisky or brandy; two liquids of which Coolgardie never ran short.[49]

After more than a decade in which tens of thousands of people were forced to live with practically no water, these problems were finally overcome with the building of a huge water pipe from Perth.

By the end of the nineteenth century, the population of the gold regions outstripped that of the rest of Western Australia, which gave the miners a dominant voice in the affairs of the colony, continuing the great and lasting changes the gold rushes heralded in Australia.

CHAPTER 10

LINKING THE COLONIES

*I congratulate you on the junction today of the railway
line connecting New South Wales and Victoria, which
cannot fail to be of the greatest importance . . . I feel
confident that with the increased railway communication the necessity of intercolonial free trade will
become daily more apparent . . . and of establishing an
intimate union among all Australian colonies, for their
mutual welfare and common good.*

UNTIL 1850, MOST OF AUSTRALIA'S TINY POPULATION OF A FEW
hundred thousand people lived in barely more than a
handful of major coastal towns or in isolated hamlets and
farms scattered throughout the interior.

In the forty years following the first discovery of gold
in 1851, the population of the colonies soared to well
over three million. New towns and settlements sprang

up, the area of land under cultivation expanded dramatically, the number of farmed sheep increased to more than five million, and mining and manufacturing flourished. At the same time, the long economic boom provided the impetus for investment in the new technologies of telegraphy and railways, which brought the separate colonies closer together.

When the gold rush started, the first diggers took around four days to reach the goldfields of Ballarat and Bendigo from Melbourne on horse-drawn carts. Within four years, stagecoaches could complete the journey in only four hours.

Leading the stagecoach revolution was Cobb and Co., which in early 1854 ran the first fast and cheap coach services to the Castlemaine and Bendigo goldfields, with successful diggers happily paying several pounds for the express service to Melbourne. The company was run by four young Americans, all in their early twenties, who had worked for the Wells Fargo and other coach companies in the United States: Freeman Cobb from Massachusetts, John Peck from New Hampshire, James Swanton from New York and John B. Lambert from Kansas.

Cobb & Co. was the first to introduce to Australia the Concord coach, which came from New Haven in Connecticut. The coach was vastly superior to the old English ones, which were heavy, slow and bounced uncomfortably on their steel springs. The secret of the Concord coaches was that, instead of being mounted on metal springs, the body of the coach was hung, or suspended, on long leather straps made of layers of thick bullock hide, which reduced the impact of jolts and gave the passengers a relatively smooth ride. Cobb and Co. employed experienced American coach drivers and switched tired horses for fresh ones at coach stages roughly 15 kilometres apart, which allowed the coach to travel at an average of around 20 kilometres an hour.

The Cobb and Co. coaches were painted a vivid red with the company name inscribed in bright yellow on the side. The first service was a daily run that left the Creighton Hotel in Collins Street in Melbourne at 6 am and was bound for the Forest Creek and Bendigo diggings. There was also a coach that left from Forest Creek at the same time and came the other way. Soon, a number of coach companies were running services between Geelong and Melbourne and to the goldfields.

Freeman Cobb stayed in Australia for a little more than three years then returned to America, where he became a senator in Massachusetts before heading to South Africa to set up a coach business to service the diamond mines. The Cobb and Co. business in Australia was sold and, over the next few years, passed through a number of hands until it was bought in 1861 by another American, who'd come from New York to the Victorian goldfields via California. James Rutherford and his partners extended the Cobb and Co. services to Bathurst in New South Wales. In 1865, the company expanded from New South Wales and Victoria into Queensland and South Australia.

By the 1880s, Cobb and Co. was operating the longest network of coach services anywhere in the world. Its coach lines covered nearly 45,000 kilometres, from Normanton in the Gulf of Carpentaria all the way down the Far North Queensland coast, linking with New South Wales, Victoria and South Australia. Rutherford died in 1911 and the last Cobb and Co. coaches ran in remote parts of Queensland until the horse-drawn service ended in 1924.

The romance of the stage and mail coaches was captured in Henry Lawson's poem 'Roaring Days', which was published in *The Bulletin* in 1889 and describes the days of the gold rush:

> Oft when the camps were dreaming,
> And fires began to pale,
> Through rugged ranges gleaming
> Would come the Royal Mail.
> Behind six foaming horses,
> And lit by flashing lamps,
> Old 'Cobb and Co.'s', in royal state,
> Went dashing past the camps.

Stage coaches finally gave way to the railways, which proved to be faster and more comfortable, but also safer. The coaches had been easily held up and robbed by bushrangers, who needed only to block the road with a felled tree, take cover in the bush and then surround the stricken coach. Most of the coaches carrying gold from the diggings to the safety of the banks in the city were escorted by a separate troop of mounted and armed police, but even these were sometimes successfully held up by armed gangs.

*

Another momentous change that began in the middle of the nineteenth century and would bring the colonies closer together was the introduction into Australia of the telegraph. Previously, communication with Europe or America had taken several months, and with other colonies several weeks. With the telegraph, communication came down to a matter of hours or a matter of minutes.

In 1835, American Samuel Morse demonstrated that it was possible to send short and long beeps ('dots' and 'dashes', respectively), which represented letters of the alphabet, down a wire. The world's first telegraph communication was between Baltimore and Washington in 1844, and Australia's first line of 13 kilometres opened between Melbourne and the local port of Williamstown in 1853.

The 17-kilometre line was built by a twenty-five-year-old Canadian called Samuel McGowan under contract to the Victorian Government. By the end of 1854, with Victoria enjoying the gold boom, the line was extended to Geelong and Ballarat, and the following year to Queenscliff, on the south-west mouth of Port Phillip. Within three years, there were nearly 3000 kilometres of cables, linking all of Victoria's major towns and reaching Portland near the South Australian border.

At the time Victoria was laying its first telegraph line, in 1854, the neighbouring colony of South Australia sought help from London to develop its own. On the recommendation of the astronomer royal, young Londoner Charles Todd was appointed telegraph superintendent in South Australia. Todd was the son of a London tea trader. After finishing school, he joined the Royal Observatory in Greenwich, where he developed a strong interest in the new invention of telegraphy. After agreeing to take the job with the South Australian Colonial Government, he sailed from England with his eighteen-year-old wife, Alice, arriving in Adelaide in November 1855.

In addition to supervising the laying of the local telegraph in South Australia, Todd travelled to Melbourne in 1856 to meet with Victoria's Samuel McGowan, and the two men became lifelong friends. Together, they managed to persuade their respective governments to link Victoria and South Australia, and the colony of New South Wales.

By 1860, most towns in New South Wales were connected by telegraph, including Yass, which allowed *The*

Sydney Morning Herald to file daily reports of the violent anti-Chinese riots in the nearby Lambing Flat goldfields in June of that year.

Tasmania's first telegraph line opened in 1857, a year before New South Wales', when Hobart was connected by a 170-kilometre line to Launceston. Tasmania was first connected to Victoria with an underwater cable in 1859, which was laid by unrolling the cable from coils at the rear of a steamship sailing across Bass Strait. But the project, which cost £53,000 and was shared between the two colonial governments, was never a success because of recurring underwater faults, and it was abandoned in 1861.

Submarine telegraph cables needed a reliable gum or rubber to insulate the wire, and many of the early schemes encountered significant teething troubles, right from the failure of the first underwater cable between France and England in 1850. It was not until 1869 – when a more durable undersea cable link was laid from Tasmania to Victoria, via King Island – that a reliable connection was possible with the mainland.

Queensland began laying its own telegraph in 1860. In 1861, it reached Ipswich and later in the same year extended to the colony's border some 200 kilometres to the south-west, where it connected with Sydney. By 1870, Brisbane was linked to most of the north Queensland towns, including Bowen, Rockhampton and Cardwell.

Western Australia opened its first telegraph line between Perth and Fremantle in 1869. The following year, the line was more than 400 kilometres long – from Perth to the port of Albany, where most ships from England and Europe would call on their way to the eastern colonies.

*

Captain James Cook and the British were relative latecomers to Australia: in 1770, when Cook discovered the east coast and named it New South Wales, more than 60 per cent of the island continent had already been charted by other Europeans.

Aristocrat Joseph Banks was the politically powerful botanist on Cook's expedition and was a driving force behind the British decision to send the convicts to Botany Bay. He also brought his influence to bear on the appointment of several of the early governors to the new British colony.

Arthur Phillip was plucked from semi-retirement at nearly fifty years of age to command the largest overseas migration the world had seen, to establish a convict settlement at a relatively unknown spot on the far side of the world.

The British First Fleet of eleven ships abandoned Botany Bay after finding it lacked fresh water and fertile soil, and headed 12 kilometres further north to build the first convict settlement at Sydney Cove.

In 1802, John Bowen was sent from Sydney to Risdon Cove in Van Diemen's Land with forty-nine people, including twenty-four convicts, to establish Britain's second colony in Australia. Fear of French territorial ambitions drove his assignation: he was to 'prevent them carrying their intention into effect'.

In early 1803, and motivated by the same fear of the French, the British Government sent David Collins from England with 300 convicts, forty-eight marines and nineteen free settlers to establish another convict settlement in what is now the state of Victoria.

Marine Lieutenant John Macarthur arrived on the second fleet of convicts in 1790 and became the colony's richest and most powerful businessman and farmer. Driven by vexation and greed, he was a thorn in the side of all the early governors, and an instigator of the overthrow of Governor Bligh in 1808.

A decade after surviving the mutiny on the *Bounty*, Captain William Bligh was overthrown as New South Wales governor in Australia's first and only military coup d'état – on the twentieth anniversary of British settlement: 26 January 1808.

Lachlan Macquarie, a governor of great vision, oversaw New South Wales for a record eleven years, from 1810 till 1821. Macquarie fell foul of the British Government for employing and even socialising with ex-convicts, and for not maintaining the colony as a centre of 'severe punishment'.

For the first twenty years, British settlement was limited to a narrow coastal strip of New South Wales. The Blue Mountains to the west were believed to be impenetrable, but in 1813 Blaxland, Lawson and Wentworth found a way across, and the following year a road there was built, in only five months, which helped to open the vast Australian interior to farming.

FLOURISHING STATE OF THE SWAN RIVER THING

THE
SWAN
TAVERN

Yet another colony established because of a fear of the French was Western Australia, settled in 1829. The site of the Swan River settlement had been recommended by Captain James Stirling, who became its first governor, but early accounts reported the first settlers struggled to survive there.

A romantic depiction of the proclamation of South Australia, on 28 December 1836, by its first governor, Captain John Hindmarsh, at what became Glenelg near Adelaide. South Australia was the only Australian colony founded by free settlers and with no convicts.

FRESCOES FOR THE NEW HOUSES OF PARLIAMENT NO. V.
THE FIRST LAND SALE.

A satirical drawing from Melbourne's *Punch*. Within a few years of European colonisation, the Aboriginal population had been decimated by dispossession, rape, violence and disease. Aboriginals were excluded from the process of building the Australian nation, and denied citizenship and the right to vote until 1967.

W. C. Wentworth did more than any other to achieve the first elected parliament, and self-government, in New South Wales. Despite his great wealth and power, both he and his wife, Sarah, had had convict parents, and it took more than thirty years for them to be accepted into Sydney society.

MR. E. H. HARGRAVES.
THE GOLD DISCOVERER OF AUSTRALIA

In February 1851, Edward Hargraves found a few specks of gold 200 kilometres west of Sydney at Ophir, which sparked the great gold rush that would last fifty years and forever change Australia.

Before dawn on 3 December 1854, more than 300 armed troops and police attacked the gold diggers' stockade at Eureka near Ballarat. The Ballarat Reform League was described as 'the germ of Australian independence [that] no power on earth can restrain'.

CELESTIAL HAPPINESS.

A Melbourne *Punch* cartoon of 1855 depicted a widespread fear that the large numbers of Chinese lured to the Australian goldfields would come to dominate the white population. Xenophobia abetted the drive towards Federation, Australian nationhood and the 'White Australia' policy.

AN INTERRUPTION ON THE OVERLAND TELEGRAPH LINE

Camels carried poles and supplies for the construction of the Adelaide to Darwin telegraph. From the mid-nineteenth century, the previously isolated colonies benefitted greatly from the revolution in transport and communications.

The second half of the nineteenth century saw a boom in railway construction. In June 1883 the opening of the line between Sydney and Melbourne was celebrated at the grand new railway station in the border town of Albury.

The inconvenience of inter-colonial travel. This illustration from the *Australasian Sketcher*, 1887, shows frustrated travellers at Spencer Street Station in Melbourne waiting while their luggage is searched by customs officials.

At 79 years of age and in the twilight of his career, Sir Henry Parkes set in motion the first serious negotiations to unite the colonies when he delivered a speech at the northern New South Wales town of Tenterfield in 1889. Parkes was described by Alfred Deakin as 'jealous of equals, bitter with rivals and remorseless with enemies – vain beyond all measure . . . and . . . a doughty parliamentary warrior'.

1890. Sir Henry Parkes managed to persuade colleagues from other colonies and New Zealand to join him in Melbourne, where they organised a convention to plan a constitution for the nation of Australia.

Back row: Andrew Inglis Clark (Tasmania), Captain William Russell (New Zealand), Samuel Griffith (Queensland), Henry Parkes (New South Wales), Thomas Playford (South Australia), Alfred Deakin (Victoria), Stafford Bird (Tasmania), George Jenkins (Secretary to the Conference). *Seated*: William McMillan (New South Wales), John Hall (New Zealand), John Macrossan (Queensland), Duncan Gillies (Victoria), John Cockburn (South Australia), James Lee Steere (Western Australia)

1891. The first convention met in Sydney. It was a most impressive gathering of senior Australian figures, and included twelve premiers and ex-premiers.

Edmund Barton, who later was Australia's first prime minister, became the effective leader of the Federation movement after Sir Henry Parkes died. Regarded as brilliant, Barton nonetheless earned the nickname 'Toby Tosspot' for spending too much time at his club and 'his lazy love of good living'.

Victorian-born Alfred Deakin was thirty-four when he attended the 1891 conference as one of the Victorian delegates. He was a key figure in the Federation movement and eventually became Australia's second prime minister. A spiritual man, Deakin consulted 'sibyls' and other fortune tellers.

New Zealand's Captain William Russell. Invited to the first meeting of colonial leaders in Melbourne in 1890, Russell claimed New Zealand was 'fundamentally different' and would not be joining the other colonies to form the Australian nation. Russell told the Australians they 'knew nothing about native administration'.

Tasmania's Andrew Inglis Clark was described as 'small, spare, nervous, active, jealous and suspicious in disposition, and somewhat awkward in manner'. Before the convention, he circulated his own draft constitution bill, which included several aspects of the American constitution.

Welsh-born son of a preacher, Queensland's premier Samuel Griffith played a leading role in the drafting of the first Australian constitution. He later became the first chief justice of the Australian High Court.

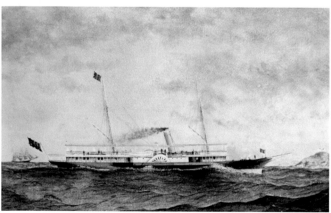

As the 1891 Easter long weekend approached, Samuel Griffith invited a key group of delegates aboard the Queensland government's luxury yacht *Lucinda* to complete the drafting.

Politician George Reid was described by Henry Parkes as 'the arch plotter against Federation'. Reid was a premier of New South Wales and went on to become Australia's fourth prime minister. He was disliked by many, including Deakin, who wrote of 'his immense, unwieldy, jelly-like stomach [and] his little legs apparently bowed under its weight to the verge of their endurance'.

In 1893 Ballarat solicitor John Quick helped to revive the issue of Federation by organising the first of a number of 'people's' conventions in the New South Wales border town of Corowa.

In response to the people's conferences, in 1895 the premiers met in the 'gentlemen only' Tasmanian Club in Hobart, where most agreed to hold elections to choose delegates to draft a new Australian constitution.

Seventy-one-year-old Scottish-born preacher, writer and feminist Catherine Helen Spence became the first woman candidate to stand for elected office in Australia when she, unsuccessfully, ran for election in 1897 as a South Australian delegate for the next constitution conference.

The next federal convention, in Parliament House, Adelaide, on 10 April 1897. Here, the popularly elected delegates begin a second attempt at drafting a national constitution.

A giant of a man, West Australian Sir John Forrest became a famous explorer. He was awarded the Royal Geographical Society's Foundation Medal before becoming the colony's first premier in 1890. The conservative Forrest baulked at the idea of Federation, and Western Australia was nearly left out of the union.

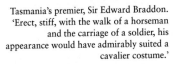

Tasmania's premier, Sir Edward Braddon. 'Erect, stiff, with the walk of a horseman and the carriage of a soldier, his appearance would have admirably suited a cavalier costume.'

Charles Kingston, head of the South Australian delegation to the 1897 constitution convention. Five years before, Kingston had challenged fellow South Australian delegate Richard Baker to a duel, and had been arrested for walking with a loaded revolver in his pocket on the way to the site he had nominated.

How to Vote

ON

Federation Day.

Saturday, June 4, 1898.

BALLOT PAPER.

Are you in favour of the proposed Federal Constitutional Bill?

" YES " ... ... ☒

" NO " ... ... ☐

This 'How to Vote' newspaper advertisement encouraged a 'Yes' vote, before the new constitution was put to the people for a vote.

THE GLORIOUS FOURTH.—" Watchman! What of the night?"

Referendum day in South Australia. Although 4 June 1898 was 'the glorious fourth' to supporters, anti-Billites claimed the bill 'would deprive you of your liberties and your employment'.

A campaign poster urging a 'No' vote at the referendum. The 'No' campaign in New South Wales said Federation was undemocratic because the colonies with small populations (Queensland, Tasmania, South Australia and Western Australia) would have the same number of federal senators as New South Wales and Victoria, which were more densely inhabited.

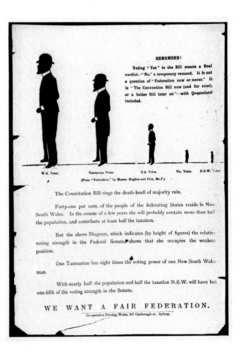

REMEMBER!

Voting " Yes" to the Bill means a final verdict—" No," a temporary remand. It is not a question of " Federation now or never." It is " The Convention Bill now (and for ever), or a better Bill later on "—with Queensland included.

W.A. Voter.   Tasmanian Voter.   S.A. Voter.   Vic. Voter.   N.S.W. Voter.
(From "Federation," by Messrs. Hughes and Dick, Ms.P.)

The Constitution Bill rings the death-knell of majority rule.

Forty-one per cent. of the people of the federating States reside in New South Wales. In the course of a few years she will probably contain more than half the population, and contribute at least half the taxation.

But the above Diagram, which indicates (by height of figures) the relative voting strength in the Federal Senate, shows that she occupies the weakest position.

One Tasmanian has eight times the voting power of one New South Wales man.

With nearly half the population and half the taxation N.S.W. will have but one-fifth of the voting strength in the Senate.

WE WANT A FAIR FEDERATION.

Co-operative Printing Works, 217 Castlereagh-st., Sydney.

Premier George Reid was accused of deliberately undermining the 'Yes' vote in New South Wales after promising to support it, and was dubbed 'Yes-No Reid' for his contradictory positions. Here he is shown in a *Bulletin* cartoon climbing two ladders labelled 'Yes' and 'No'.

In the 1899 campaign before the second referendum, Edmund Barton addressed a large open-air meeting in Sydney's Martin Place to urge on the 'Yes' vote.

COMBINE, AUSTRALIA!

Unple Punch. "You've done jolly well by combination in the Cricket Field, and now you're going to Federate at Home. Bravo, Boys!"

A *Punch* cartoon on 28 June 1899 encourages, 'Combine, Australia'.

"THREE MEN IN A BOAT."

Edmund Barton, Alfred Deakin and Charles Kingston, with their dog 'Persuasion', are depicted as heading for London in 1900 to press the British Government to agree to the Australian constitution.

Western Australia was not part of the original Commonwealth, but held a referendum on 31 July 1900, six months before the nation came into being. The overwhelming 'Yes' vote there was helped by the endorsement of the population in the eastern goldfields around Coolgardie and Kalgoorlie.

Crowds at Sydney's Centennial Park celebrated the inauguration of the Australian Commonwealth and the swearing-in of the first national government on 1 January 1901.

Unfinished business. The Duke of York (later King George VI) and the Duchess of York officially opened the new national parliament on 9 May 1927, exactly twenty-six years after the nation had been inaugurated. Australia started as a nation without a capital, a parliament, a flag, a national anthem, or a currency.

Australia's telegraph connection with the rest of the world began when the South Australian Colonial Government authorised Charles Todd in 1870 to construct a telegraph line from Adelaide to Darwin. Finding a route through the fierce desert of central Australia had only been made possible when Scottish explorer John McDouall Stuart managed to find a way through to northern Australia on his sixth attempt in 1862. An independent, hard-drinking explorer, forty-six-year-old Stuart led a party of nine men on horseback from Adelaide in September 1861 and trekked through some of the world's most inhospitable country before reaching Chambers Bay, east of Darwin on the Timor Sea, nine months later.

The responsibility for building the telegraph line fell to Todd. Using government-paid labour and private contractors, the project involved placing more than 30,000 iron poles at 80-metre intervals for 3200 kilometres from South Australia's Port Augusta to Darwin. Despite the enormity and difficulty of the task, the plan called for the laying of the line to start in September 1870 and to be finished in only fifteen months.

To complete the line within the highly ambitious timeframe, the construction was split between three teams: one starting in the south, one in central Australia and the third in the north. Each team worked for six days a week and was made up of a number of working parties that needed to be kept supplied with food, tools, equipment and medical stores. Todd's plan called for the erection of about twenty posts for each mile. Every posthole had to be dug by hand, using picks, the post installed, the wire hung and the land cleared around the pole, before moving on to the next one. Where possible, posts were made from local trees, but where no local timber was available one of the several thousand iron posts that had been made for the project was used.

The southern section of 800 kilometres from Port Augusta to north of Oodnadatta proved the least difficult, because all the land had been surveyed already and supplies were closer to hand.

A second team of eighty men sailed to Darwin and began to install poles on 15 September 1870. After they made a promising start, the wet season began in November and caused major problems: the supply carts became bogged and the supplies waterlogged and rotten. After the men went on strike, the contract was cancelled and Todd had to arrange for a new team. Six months later, a fresh team of 200 men, 170 horses and 500 bullocks arrived to resume the work.

The inhospitable 960 kilometres of the central section – the dead heart of Australia – stretched from Tennant Creek down through Alice Springs and also proved difficult. The shortage of water, the lack of local timber and the remoteness of the work gangs made supply lines hard to maintain. It was during construction of the line in March 1871 and towards the end of the relatively short wet season that surveyor William Mills found a water spring he named Alice Springs after the wife of Charles Todd, and the local river the Todd River.

In addition to the telegraph line, twelve relay stations were built about 250 kilometres apart between Adelaide and Darwin to receive the Morse code signal and resend it to the next section.

Despite being plagued by illness, food shortages, floods and water shortages, the line was finished in less than two years, on 22 August 1872. Charles Todd, who had managed the project, was unapologetic that the construction had exceeded the ambitious schedule:

Notwithstanding the delays and mishaps which have occurred on the northern portion of the work, we have this day, or within two years from the date it was commenced, completed a line of 2000 miles [around 3220 kilometres] long through the very centre of Australia, a few years ago a terra incognita, and supposed to be a desert, and I have the satisfaction of seeing the successful completion of a scheme I officially advanced 14 years ago.[1]

There was jubilation in Adelaide at the opening of the line, and the governor called a public holiday. Charles Todd, who at the time was still in central Australia at the Mount Stuart relay station, sent one of the first telegrams to Adelaide, stressing the significance of the line:

the Adelaide and Port Darwin Telegraph . . . an important link in the electrical chain of communication connecting the Australian Colonies with the mother-country and the whole of the civilised and commercial world, will, I trust, redound to the credit of South Australia, and amply repay her for the great outlay she had incurred in its construction by advancing her material interests and prosperity.[2]

In October 1872, the Darwin line was connected with a submarine cable to Java and on to Europe, and Australia was telegraphically connected with the world. Another public holiday was called in South Australia:

The demonstration, as an expression of the rejoicing of the people at the completion of the line and of their honour for those who had worked upon it, was a great success. Throughout the day the city wore a jubilant aspect. A public holiday was proclaimed, and everyone seemed desirous of honouring the occasion . . . A gay display of bunting floated from the towers of the General Post Office, the newspaper and Consular offices, as well as from various private buildings . . . At 6 a.m. the Albert bells commenced to send forth a merry peal, which was kept up, with short intervals, throughout the day. Sightseers and holiday-makers of both sexes thronged the principal streets, and vehicles of various descriptions rapidly passing to and fro increased the bustle of the scene. All classes seemed determined to contribute their quota to the rejoicings of the day. Large numbers of visitors from the country were to be seen bent on mirth and jollity, and everywhere proofs abounded that a gala occasion of unusual interest was being responded to by old and young.[3]

During the celebrations, the *South Australian Register* claimed the remote colony had achieved one of the world's 'greatest telegraphic achievements':

South Australia's demonstration in honour of the establishment of telegraphic communication with Great Britain, and in compliment to the men upon whom has devolved the task of carrying out her share of the enterprise, was an unequivocal success. It was fitting that the completion of a great work like the Anglo-Australian Telegraph, forming as it does a land mark in our national progress, and intimately bound up as it necessarily is with the future of this continent, should be made the subject of general rejoicings.

In December 1877, after three and a half years of construction, the connection was made from Albany in Western Australia across 1400 kilometres of the waterless Nullarbor Plain to Port Augusta in South Australia, which meant that all the colonial capitals were now connected with each other and with the rest of the world.

The governor of Western Australia, Sir George Ord, accurately predicted that the link would bring the colonies 'into closer union' and 'socially and commercially' create greater prosperity.[4] One of the first telegrams received in Perth after the connection was made was from the colonial secretary, the Earl of Carnarvon, in London on 20 December: 'The Queen has received your message with satisfaction, and continues to take a warm interest in the welfare of the colony.'[5]

*

Victoria beat New South Wales to the steam railway when it opened Australia's first rail line, a 16-kilometre link between Melbourne and Williamstown, on 12 September 1854, less than thirty years after the world's first railway between Stockton-on-Tees and Darlington had opened in England in 1825.

Work began on laying the line from the Flinders Street Railway Station in Melbourne in March 1853, and the first train ran eighteen months later to Sandridge (now Port Melbourne). Already, Victoria was being transformed by its gold from a remote backwater, and the local newspapers captured the excitement of this opening when huge crowds lined the streets along Melbourne's Flinders Street. As noon approached the Governor Sir Charles Hotham and Lady Hotham arrived and were presented with satin-bound copies of the railway timetable before boarding one of the first-class 'handsomely painted and varnished carriages' for the first train trip.[6]

Shortly after noon, two British warships in the harbour, the *Electra* and the *Fantome*, fired off their cannons in salute as the train left, drawn by the 'first locomotive constructed, not merely in Victoria, but in the southern hemisphere' by Robertson, Martin and Smith, a local firm that had assembled the engine from parts imported from England.[7] The 120-tonne locomotive, which drew 30 horsepower, took the first trainload of dignitaries at 15 miles per hour (24 kilometres per hour) past vast crowds that lined the route for the four kilometres to Sandridge. After arriving, the 300 official guests enjoyed a special banquet in a newly erected railway shed, 'an enormous hall . . . handsomely decorated for the occasion with evergreens and flags'.[8]

There was a big difference in passenger comfort on the early trains, depending on the class of travel. First class had large, leather-bound seats and windows, and the first-class carriage was always immediately behind the locomotive, so that the soot and cinders from the steam engine would fly overhead and catch the second- and third-class carriages. The second class had covered bench seating but the third had only uncovered wooden benches and no glass in the large window frames.

After Melbourne's first line was opened, others quickly followed elsewhere in the colony. In 1857, a service began operating on a seven-kilometre line between Melbourne and St Kilda. In 1859, a 65-kilometre line opened between Melbourne and the colony's second major port at Geelong, and in 1862 train services began to the gold centres of Ballarat and Bendigo. Being a smaller colony, Victoria was the first to reach the border with New South Wales when the Melbourne to Echuca line on the Murray River opened in 1864, and to Wodonga in 1873. It would take another eight years before New South Wales finished building the much longer railway line in the other direction from Sydney.

A year after the running of Melbourne's first train, New South Wales began operating a 20-kilometre rail service between Sydney and Parramatta in 1855. The Sydney Railway Company had been established in 1848 with private capital of £100,000 being raised. It planned to connect Sydney with its two largest hinterland towns of Goulburn and then Bathurst.[9] Both towns were more than 200 kilometres from the coast and the centre of major farming areas.

However, before the construction could start, the discovery of gold in 1851 caused a rush of manpower to the goldfields, and the consequent rise in labour costs threatened the entire railway project. According to the commissioner for railways, gold would harm railway construction for some years:

> The discovery of gold in the Bathurst country . . . upset the calculations both of the contractor and the directors, which threatened the former with ruin and entailed much anxiety on the latter from the sudden revolution in the price of labour and materials, which was destined for years to increase enormously the cost of carrying out railway and other works.[10]

In its first five years, the company managed to build only 24 kilometres from Sydney to Parramatta at a ruinous cost of more than £500,000. The extra money was paid by the New South Wales Government, which, in December 1854, took over the Sydney Railway Company before the running of the first train in September the following year. At the same time, the New South Wales Government also bought the Newcastle to Maitland private rail company, which was starting to build a line in the Hunter Valley. The Hunter line would later become the start of the Great

Northern Line, which would eventually stretch from Sydney to the Queensland border and link Sydney to Brisbane. The New South Wales Government Railways (NSWGR), as it became known, was to be 'Australia's mightiest corporation' for much of the nineteenth and twentieth centuries.[11]

The first train from Sydney to Parramatta, on Wednesday 26 September 1855, caused similar excitement as had occurred the year before in Melbourne: 'Never was a greater concourse assembled in New South Wales. People of many climes, of all ages, and representing every class of society congregated to witness the opening of the colony's greatest work.'[12]

According to the *Empire* newspaper, public offices, banks and most of the shops closed for the day, the ships in the harbour were 'gaily dressed with bunting' and flags were being flown along the railway route.[13] A little before the scheduled departure time for the first train, the New South Wales governor, William Denison, arrived at Central Railway Station (the first Central Railway Station in Sydney was near Cleveland Paddocks, south of the current station and on the way to Redfern) dressed in full 'Windsor Uniform'.[14] He was escorted by the Volunteer Yeomanry Corps and greeted with a flourish of trumpets and a salute of nineteen guns.

At 11.20 am, the train – with two first-class, four second-class and five third-class carriages – began the journey with a great rush of people 'literally diving in at the openings in the sides of the third class carriages . . . a mighty pushing and squeezing ensued in the second class. Nor with the exception of His Excellency, were the first class passengers exempt from the general strife.'[15]

After the opening of the Sydney–Parramatta line, more than 3000 additional kilometres of railways were built across New South Wales under the direction of one man: John Whitton. Thirty-five-year-old John Whitton became one of a long list of young English engineers to come out to the colonies to work on the new railways when he arrived in Sydney with his new bride, Elizabeth, in December 1856.

When Whitton started work in Sydney in January 1857, the New South Wales Railways had only 37 kilometres of track, four locomotives, twelve passenger carriages and forty rail wagons. When he retired in 1889, the network covered more than 3000 kilometres and reached 750 kilometres to the west of Sydney, across the Blue Mountains to Bourke, in the far north-west of the state, on the Darling River. To the north, the railway stretched for nearly 700 kilometres from Sydney through Newcastle and the New England Ranges to Wallangarra, in Queensland, where, in 1888, it connected with Queensland's railway to Brisbane. To the south, the railway reached Goulburn in 1869, Junee in 1878 and Albury, more than 500 kilometres from Sydney and on the colony's southern border with Victoria, in 1881.

In addition to laying the track, Whitton designed and built bridges and many railway stations himself. On the Blue Mountains, west of Sydney, he built the great zigzags down the western slopes, and, in 1887, he tried unsuccessfully to promote the building of a Sydney Harbour Bridge, which was not completed until 1932.

South Australia opened its first railway in 1856, when a 14-kilometre train service opened from the city of Adelaide to Port Adelaide. The following year, a 50-kilometre line opened to the north to Gawler and then extended to the copper-mining town of Kapunda and then to Burra, 160 kilometres north of Adelaide, in 1870. The first intercolonial connection was in 1887, when the South Australia line reached the Victorian border, 300 kilometres to the south-east of Adelaide, and connected with the trains to Melbourne.

Queensland became independent of New South Wales in 1859 and opened its first railway six years later, in 1865, with trains running 30 kilometres from the upriver port of Ipswich to Grandchester, in the foothills of the Darling Downs. It was the only colony that started building its railway from outside the capital city, and the construction was marked as a major event in the young colony's history. At a ceremony on the northern side of the Bremer River on 25 February 1864, huge crowds from surrounding districts and from Brisbane came to watch the wife of the governor, Lady Bowen, turn the first sod.

The line was extended 70 kilometres west to Toowoomba in 1867, and 40 kilometres to the east to Brisbane in the same year. Ten years later, the line reached 180 kilometres south from Toowoomba to Wallangarra, on the New South Wales border, to connect with trains running to Sydney.

Tasmania's first railway opened between Deloraine and Launceston in 1871, built by the Launceston and Western Railway. The 40-kilometre train service soon went bust and was taken over by the Tasmanian Government the following year. Four years later, in 1876, a 180-kilometre line was opened between Hobart and Evandale, near Launceston, thus effectively linking the colony's two largest towns.

It was not until 1879 that the first railway began operating in Western Australia. It was a privately operated timber-carrying railway that ran between Lockville and Yoganup, about 200 kilometres south of Perth. The same year, the Western Australian Government Railways built a 50-kilometre railway to link the copper mine at Northampton with the port of Geraldton. The line from Perth to the port of Fremantle was opened in 1881, and from Perth to Bunbury in 1893, and the 420-kilometre line from Perth to Geraldton in 1894. In 1896, a 650-kilometre line was completed from Perth to Kalgoorlie, where the gold rush had begun four years before. The rail connection from Western Australia to the rest of the country did not occur until a rail link was completed to South Australia in 1917.

Trains transformed Australia. Prior to the railway, apart from migrants who had sailed to the continent, most people died within walking distance of where they had been born. Most could not afford a horse or a coach, but the trains could carry large numbers of people much faster and further and at lower cost. Travelling overland from Sydney to Melbourne on a horse-drawn coach took six days and nights; the steam train took less than a day. No longer were people captive to their local town. The railways opened up the country and people could now more easily move to a new town or even another colony to find work or seek new business opportunities.

*

A major problem of the colonial railways building program was that the train tracks were built at different widths, or gauges, so that when they eventually reached the colony's border, the trains could not run on the neighbouring colony's tracks.

Different railway track gauges had been a problem earlier in Britain and America, where a number of different railways had been built on different gauges, but they were progressively standardised on mainline systems. In Britain, the earliest lines were built on gauges that ranged from the 'narrow gauge' of three feet six inches (1.07 metres) to seven feet (2.1 metres) on the line built by the brilliant engineer Isambard Kingdom Brunel from London to Bristol. Despite Brunel's argument that the optimum rail width was seven feet, the British Government moved to enforce a uniform-sized track and chose what became known as the 'standard gauge' of four feet eight and a half inches (1.4 metres).

However, because the wider gauge of five feet three inches (1.6 metres) was already the dominant gauge in Ireland, the *Railway Regulation Gauge Act* allowed for the Irish to keep what became known as the 'broad gauge' or the 'Irish gauge'.

This meant that, for the Australian colonies looking to Britain for guidance when starting their railways, there were two approved gauges: the 'standard gauge' of four feet eight and a half inches and the 'broad' gauge' of five feet three inches.

Historically, there has been much argument about who is to blame for the Australian colonies building different railway systems that did not allow trains to run on each other's tracks. But it was New South Wales – which adopted the British standard gauge – and not Victoria, which introduced the broad gauge – that should be held responsible.

When the Sydney Railway Company was formed in 1848, two years after the passing of the British *Railway Regulation Gauge Act*, the colonial secretary Earl Grey wrote specifying that all the Australian colonies should have the same four feet eight and a half inches standard gauge as in England. However, before construction of any Australian railways started, Francis Webb Shields, a new senior engineer from England who had joined the Sydney Railway Company in 1849, had persuaded both his company and the New South Wales Government that they should go with the five feet three inch broad gauge of his native Ireland. 'I do not concur in the propriety of fixing that gauge at four feet eight and a half inches,' he told a parliamentary inquiry, going on to say the broad gauge would increase the steadiness of the carriages, diminish the wear on the rails and reduce the cost of track maintenance.[16]

The governor of New South Wales applied in 1850 to London to have the 'standard gauge' policy changed, and in July 1851 the colonial secretary Earl Grey replied by saying it was 'his intention not to oppose the adoption of the [broad] gauge' if that was what the colonies wanted.[17]

However, the following year, Francis Shields was replaced by a new chief engineer, James Wallace, who arrived in Sydney from England in July 1852 and immediately disputed the claimed benefits of the broad gauge. 'In practice,' he said, within a month of taking up his appointment, the broad gauge 'had no advantage commensurate with the extra expense'. He argued that the standard gauge was better as it 'has been found to combine in a higher degree than any other the great commercial requisites for a railway, namely speed, safety, convenience and economy'.[18]

The views of Wallace prevailed and the Sydney Railway Company switched back to standard gauge, saying that the anticipated advantages from the broad gauge 'have not been realised'. However, the switch was too late for Victoria. Only a week before, the Victorian Parliament had passed legislation to follow New South Wales' preferred broad gauge, and orders had already been placed in Britain for locomotives to fit the five feet three inch track.

Meanwhile, in South Australia, the colonial parliament initially passed legislation to adopt the British standard gauge. It then followed the New South Wales decision and began building the colony's first line in the broad gauge, even though the broad gauge had now been abandoned by New South Wales. But not all South

Australian railways were built to the broad gauge. That colony also built some of the much cheaper 'narrow gauge' of three feet six inches, which was regarded as more suitable on short branch lines and on more mountainous terrains. The first 25-kilometre narrow gauge line opened between Port Wakefield and Balaklava in 1870, the 600-kilometre line from Port Augusta to Oodnadatta in 1879, and the 350-kilometre line from Port Pirie to Broken Hill, in western New South Wales, in 1888.

Eventually, in 1917, South Australia opened a standard-gauge line of four feet eight and a half inches from Port Augusta to Kalgoorlie, in Western Australia, and ended up with three different track sizes in its rail network. For passengers travelling through the colony, this could mean having to travel on three different trains. From Melbourne to Adelaide, the train was designed to fit the broad-gauge tracks. From Adelaide North to Port Augusta, the passenger would have to change onto a train that fitted the narrow gauge. Once at Port Augusta, it was necessary to change again to a train that fitted the standard gauge for the journey to Western Australia.

The decision of Queensland to become the first in the world to adopt the narrow gauge of three feet six inches for mainline rail operations had much to do with the influence of another Irish railway engineer, Abraham Fitzgibbon. In 1863, he was hired by the Sydney politician, farmer and businessman Robert Tooth, of the famous brewing family, to examine the prospects for building railways in Queensland. He reported that the British, European and American standard-gauge railways operated with locomotives weighing between 22 and 36 tonnes. The engines he proposed to run on a three foot six inch gauge rail weighed only 11 to 12 tonnes and could run on lighter steel rails. The lower cost of permanent line, bridges and superstructure, he argued, would reduce the overall cost of the railway to less than half that of the standard gauge:

> Such a railway, because of its cheapness is peculiarly adopted for a country such as Queensland, where an immense area has to be opened up. Many hundreds of miles of railway will have to be built in the next twenty or thirty years if the Colony is to progress and it is a serious consideration whether they should cost £6,000 or £7,000 per mile or £16,000. The more cheaply railways can be constructed the sooner can the Colony generally be furnished with railways. Let the country but make the railways and the railroads will make the country.[19]

There was widespread opposition to Fitzgibbon's proposal in the parliament and the press. William Coote of the new Brisbane Tram Company argued that, because of its narrower wheel base, the narrow gauge meant it was easier for trains to topple over at high speed on a bend than it would be for a train with a wider base or gauge:

> No engineer has ever before this time proposed a 3ft. 6in. gauge for a trunk line. No locomotives have ever been constructed for such a line. It is in opposition to the practice and theory of every known engineer and upon every railway since the railway system began . . . The 3ft. 6in. gauge is a dangerous innovation in locomotive gauges.[20]

But not only did Fitzgibbon's view prevail, after only four months in the colony, the Queensland Government hired him as chief engineer to build the narrow-gauge railway.

The narrow-gauge Queensland rail reached the border of New South Wales at Wallangarra Station in 1887. Nearly 130 years later, on the western side of Wallangarra

Station, the narrow-gauge trains from Brisbane still terminate, and on the eastern side, the standard-gauge trains from Sydney still end. There is an especially wide platform for the unloading of goods to be reloaded onto the train going to the other state and for passengers to cross when changing trains. The border between Queensland and New South Wales cuts across the southern end of the platform – the only known instance in the world where a railway station is in two separate territories.

Since Tasmania is an island, it did not matter at the time what gauge it used, but somehow it also managed to build different railway gauges within the colony. The first train line, opened in 1871 by Launceston and Western Railway, was a broad-gauge service, but subsequently narrow-gauge lines were also constructed there. However, in 1888, and at considerable expense, the government paid to convert the broad-gauge part of the line to narrow gauge, so there was only one gauge on the island.

*

The railways not only brought the mainland colonies and Tasmania closer together but also led directly to loud calls for them to unite as a nation. The most dramatic connection, which had the greatest symbolic impact, was the joining of New South Wales and Victoria. The Victorians had opened their broad-gauge track from Melbourne to the border town of Wodonga, 310 kilometres to the north, in 1873. Coming the other way on the standard gauge was the New South Wales line, which finally reached the nearby border town of Albury, 554 kilometres south of Sydney, in 1881.

The celebration to commemorate the linking of the colonies was one of the grandest events seen in Australia. It was planned for 14 June 1883 at Albury, where a magnificent stone station had been built. Designed by John Whitton, the grand, Italianate station had a large, 11-metre domed vestibule, a lofty clock tower and a 300-metre-long covered railway platform – to allow passengers to move across from the Victorian-gauge train to the New South Wales–gauge train in all weather. A public holiday was declared, the shops and post office closed, and the town's buildings decorated with flags and evergreens. Visitors poured in from surrounding districts, and a band paraded up and down the main street.

The first train that was part of the celebrations arrived in Albury from Sydney at about 1 am, and by 11.30 am another eleven trains had appeared. Shortly after noon, the official train, pulled by two locomotives, came in, carrying the most august officials who, 'having all had the advantage of sleeping cars, did not look much the worse for their journey'.[21]

The official party from Sydney included the New South Wales governor, Lord Augustus Loftus, and his wife, Lady Loftus, the premier Henry Parkes and his wife, and seventy-five parliamentary colleagues and official guests. As the governor stepped onto the platform, the local army band struck up with, 'God Save the Queen'.

After a short welcoming speech from the mayor of Albury, Mr G. C. Thorold, Lord Loftus, replied and, to the cheers of the crowd, made it clear that he thought the implications of these lines were enormous:

> I congratulate you on the junction today of the railway lines connecting New South Wales with Victoria, which cannot fail to be of the greatest importance to the interchange of traffic between Sydney and Melbourne. I feel confident that, with the increase of railway communication the necessity of free intercolonial trade will become

daily more apparent . . . and of establishing an intimate union among all the Australian colonies for their mutual welfare and common good.[22]

Shortly after 2 pm, the first trains began to arrive in Albury from Melbourne on the broad-gauge track that had been laid on the western side of the platform. According to the *Sydney Morning Herald*, the Victorian governor, the Second Marquess of Normanby, the premier James Service and his parliamentary colleagues were greeted with 'ringing cheers' by the locals. At the station, the Marquess of Normanby echoed the sentiments of his New South Wales counterpart:

> I have no doubt whatever that this union will tend greatly to the advantage of these two colonies, and we may before long see the same union between Victoria, South Australia, and New South Wales and Queensland. I am inclined to believe with you that before long this will be the first step towards the union of the Colonies.[23]

During the early afternoon, a special New South Wales train was laid on to take all the guests to the banquet, which was about a mile from the station in a giant new locomotive shed that had been 'floored and profusely decorated with banners and festoons of evergreens'. It was attended by more than 250 people, at an estimated cost of £2000, and included 'illumination of the entire building with electric lights, many of which were of beautiful variegated colours'.[24]

When it came to the speeches and the toasts, the Marquess of Normanby again spoke of the railways promoting national unity of the colonies: 'His Excellency, the Marquess of Normanby, in returning thanks, said that he thought the event of the day was pregnant with great results for Australia, for he believed it would be only the forerunner of that great ideal of Federation – the union of all colonies themselves.'[25]

The Victorian premier, James Service, was described as saying, '[Federation] was much nearer than most people supposed . . . There was nothing like the cowcatcher of the locomotive for sweeping away prejudices. They wanted federation and they wanted it now.'[26]

Despite this small chorus of support for national union, little happened for another six years, when the grand old statesman Sir Henry Parkes took more concerted steps to ignite the issue of Federation.

CHAPTER 11

'THE FATHER OF FEDERATION'

Australia [now has] a population of three and a half millions, and the American people numbered only between three and four millions when they formed the great commonwealth of the United States ... and surely what the Americans had done by war, the Australians could bring about in peace.

THE FIRST SERIOUS ATTEMPTS AT CREATING A NATION OF AUSTRALIA came from a grand old man of Australian politics, Sir Henry Parkes, when he was seventy-six years old and in the twilight of his career. Five times New South Wales premier, three times married, he sired a total of seventeen children with his first two wives, before he married for a third time at the age of seventy-nine to his twenty-three-year-old housekeeper.

Henry Parkes came from humble beginnings and showed great resilience throughout his life to overcome political defeats, personal disappointments and a succession of financial setbacks. Driven by 'social ideals and political passions',[1] he became what the London *Times* described as a 'most striking figure in public life in Australia'.[2]

Henry Parkes was born three weeks before the Battle of Waterloo, on 27 May 1815, in Warwickshire, England, the youngest of seven children. When he was eight years old, his indebted family lost their farm and his father, Thomas, was forced to work as a labourer and odd-job man near the city of Birmingham.[3] After limited schooling, Henry also worked in various labouring jobs. He later said of his time breaking rocks for the building of a Cheltenham road that he 'was cowed by the sneers and taunts of those who daily gazed upon my destitution'.[4] When he was twelve years old, his mother arranged for him to become apprenticed to a bone and ivory turner, which involved shaping wood, bone and ivory into ornaments and furniture.

By the time he was sixteen, Parkes was already showing an interest in politics: he was intrigued by the Chartist movement and galvanised by growing calls throughout England for social and economic reforms to improve the wellbeing of the working classes.[5] At twenty-one, he was married for the first time, to twenty-three-year-old Clarinda Varney, the daughter of a successful whip-maker, Robert Varney. Robert opposed the union, believing Clarinda was marrying 'beneath herself'.[6] Together, they eventually had twelve children, although only seven would reach adulthood.

After the bone and ivory business in which Parkes was working failed, he took his wife to London in 1838, where he continued to struggle. According to Parkes, he spent the winter of 1838–39 in London 'in the solitude which a friendless man feels in the crowded streets of a great city'.[7] Twice while they were in England, Clarinda had given birth, but both babies had died: Thomas Campbell, who was born in April 1837, lived for only seventeen days; and Clarinda Martha, born in June 1838, lived for less than twenty-four hours.

Eventually, in March 1839, Henry and Clarinda reluctantly migrated to Australia, where they hoped Henry's prospects might improve. Parkes was bitter about being, as he saw it, forced to migrate, and in a poem published in a Chartist magazine in March 1839 condemned the social injustices that made 'men like [me] compelled to seek the means of existence in a foreign wilderness'.[8]

He and Clarinda sailed on the *Strathfieldsaye*, and, during the voyage, Clarinda gave birth to a baby girl, on 23 July 1839, Clarinda Sarah. They reached Sydney on 25 July 1839. While waiting to disembark, Parkes pondered, as many migrants before and since have done, what the new land had in store for him:

> many hours of the early morning I spent hanging over the ship's side, looking out upon the monotonous, sullen and almost unbroken woods which then thickly clothed the north shore of the harbour, my thoughts busily employed speculating on the fortunes which that unknown land concealed for me. I knew no single creature in that strange new land; I had brought no letter of introduction to unlock any door to me; and in this state of absolute friendlessness I and my wife and child landed in Sydney . . .[9]

In Sydney, Henry admitted to 'fits of despondency' as he tried to secure a job, but eventually he found work as a labourer in an ironmonger's, then in an iron foundry. For a while, he worked alongside convicts on a farm beside the Nepean River to the west of Sydney.[10]

In 1845, he set up his own business in Sydney's Hunter Street as an ivory turner and importer of fancy goods.

After initially succeeding, the enterprise struggled to make profits. Parkes never made his fortune and throughout his life would lurch from financial crisis to financial crisis. Many years later, he admitted that he had never been ambitious to be wealthy and that lack of money didn't bother him:

> I feel no pride in place or position, or in possession of the gifts of fortune, which indeed have been few with me. I have never known what it is to feel envy of others more favoured than myself, and I have never withheld my last shilling from those who needed it more than I.[11]

During the 1840s in Sydney, Parkes became active in local politics and from 1842 wrote occasional political and literary articles, which were published in *The Sydney Chronicle*, *The Sydney Morning Herald* and the weekly *Atlas*. In 1848, he joined a 'tradesmen's committee' to help a colleague, Robert Lowe, in the city of Sydney council elections – Parkes later said it 'was the beginning of my political career'.[12] He also set up his own newspaper, the *Empire*, which ran from December 1850 till August 1858, when it became another of his failed businesses. Eventually, he was forced to sell the paper, which was later absorbed into the *Evening News*. Throughout this period, Parkes was a great fan of W. C. Wentworth, whom he described as 'beyond doubt the ablest man in the colony.[13]

In 1854, thirty-nine-year-old Parkes was elected to the New South Wales Legislative Council in what would be the start of a parliamentary career that would stretch over the next four decades, and two years later he was elected to the first Legislative Council created under the colony's new constitution. He rose through the ranks, and in 1866 became colonial secretary. During his tenure, he famously introduced the *Public Schools Act*, which for the first time provided for the establishment of state schools run by teachers who had been trained by the state. The new law enabled schools to be established in areas in which there were twenty-five or more children. No church-run school could operate within five miles of a public school. Church-run schools still qualified for government financial support but only if they used the same books and curriculum as the state schools, and limited religious teaching to an hour a day.[14] The Roman Catholics, for whom Parkes had no sympathy, raised a storm of protest against what they saw as state intervention in their methods of schooling, but he pressed on and the act was passed by parliament.

The following year, Parkes first called for the Australian colonies to be joined in national union. He was attending an intercolonial meeting in Melbourne to discuss the thorny issue of the customs duties that all the colonies collected on the import of goods that came across their borders. As guest speaker at the conference dinner, held at Scott's Hotel on 16 March 1867, Parkes unexpectedly urged the young colonies – 'the footprints of six giants in the morning dew' – to adopt the vision of Federation: 'I think that the time has arrived when these colonies should be united by some federal bond of connection . . . I regard this occasion, therefore with great interest because I believe it will inevitably lead to a more permanent federal understanding.'[15]

From the time of this first suggestion until his death nearly thirty years later in 1896, the story of Australian Federation is intertwined with the story of Henry Parkes.

Throughout the 1860s and 1870s, the colonies had regularly met to discuss issues of mutual concern, but the topic of federal union was always 'little more than a subject for after-dinner rhetoric at intercolonial meetings'.[16] There were some obvious benefits to be gained from national union. In addition to national defence, it was hoped Federation would enable the national coordination of postal, telegraphic and rail services. National union would also end the separate tariffs imposed on imported goods from other colonies. The 'free traders', which included Henry Parkes, saw the abolition of tariffs as a positive development since it would make goods cheaper and would increase the size of the market for all Australian industries. On the other hand, the 'protectionists' saw their abolition as a threat to local industries, which would suddenly be exposed to import competition. Tariffs were also an important source of revenue for each colony.

So, while there was growing support for Federation, there was also opposition. Many politicians in the colonies were reluctant to hand over their powers to a national parliament. There were also concerns that Federation would be expensive and that each individual colony would lose its character and the right to decide on its own laws, and local factories would lose the tariff protection they needed for their survival. Among the smaller colonies, there was a fear of domination by the larger colonies, and in the larger colonies a fear that the smaller colonies would become an economic burden.

Henry Parkes was a political opportunist who was able to exploit the public's mood, which he demonstrated early in his ministerial career following an assassination attempt on Queen Victoria's son in Sydney. On 12 March 1868, Prince Alfred, the Duke of Edinburgh, was shot and wounded at the popular Sydney beach picnic spot of Clontarf while on a royal tour of the colonies. The shooting was carried out by a mentally ill Irishman, Henry James O'Farrell, who fired a pistol at close range, the bullet striking the prince in the back before glancing off his ribs. As the police moved to quickly arrest O'Farrell, he was very nearly lynched by an angry mob.

The Prince fully recovered. However, after the shooting, people flocked to public meetings to express their loyalty to the throne, and to condemn the attempt on the Crown Prince's life. In Sydney the day after the shooting, 20,000 people attended a public meeting that saw an outpouring of patriotic fervour towards the British Empire and a great deal of anti-Irish and anti-Catholic sentiment.

Henry Parkes turned the attempted assassination to his own political advantage by capitalising on the nearly hysterical public mood.[17] Within a week, he had introduced new laws governing the crime of treason, which had provisions that went beyond anything seen before. Driven by the premier James Martin and Parkes as colonial secretary, the legislation was passed through both houses of the New South Wales Parliament in one day and the next day given assent by the governor, the Earl of Belmore. Under the new law, which survived for two years before its oppressive conditions were repealed, the police were given extraordinary powers to enter homes to look for incriminating evidence. It became a two-year jail offence to refuse to toast the Queen's health. It was also a jailable offence to 'use any language disrespectful' to the Queen, or 'to write or publish any words disrespectful to Her Most Gracious Majesty', or even to express sympathy for anyone 'suspected' of having broken the new law. Later, Parkes would criticise the legislation and the 'precipitous manner' in which it had been pushed through the parliament, but it was published under his name as colonial secretary.

In May 1872, after the collapse of the James Martin coalition government and some complex negotiations, Henry Parkes became New South Wales premier for the first of his five terms in office. (These were volatile times in colonial politics, and, during Parkes's nearly four decades in parliament, there were twenty-seven changes of premier in New South Wales.)

For nearly three years, he enjoyed a relatively successful period of government. However, in January 1875, he was forced to resign after the parliament passed a resolution condemning the government's bungling of the release from prison of the celebrated bushranger Frank Gardiner.

Ten years before, Frank Gardiner had led a gang that held up the armed escort carrying gold from the Forbes goldfields at Eugowra, about 70 kilometres west of Orange, in western New South Wales, and escaped with more than 5000 ounces (142 kilograms) of gold and thousands of pounds in banknotes. It was one of the biggest hauls in history. In the weeks that followed the hold-up, police chased the gang on horseback for more than 600 kilometres across western New South Wales. Most of the bushrangers were caught but Frank Gardiner got away. Eighteen months later, he was captured after being recognised running a store at Rockhampton near the recently discovered goldfields more than 1000 kilometres north of Sydney in north Queensland.

Brought back to Sydney, Gardiner was sentenced in June 1862 to thirty-two years' jail, but, after less than a decade, his sisters began a highly public campaign for his early release. Despite his obvious record of violence and robbery, Gardiner had become one of Australia's first hero-villains.

On 12 September 1874, a monster petition to His Excellency Sir Hercules Robinson seeking the release of Gardiner was 'so numerously and influentially signed, a few signatures more or less of persons of whom I had no knowledge'.[18] For the next eighteen months, the push for his release after ten years in prison stirred up public controversy and prompted petitions, counter-petitions and violent debates inside and outside the parliament.

During the heated debates about whether Gardiner should be paroled, Parkes called for a report from Gardiner's jailer, who said that he was a model prisoner and that a reduction in the prison sentence would be acceptable, particularly if it involved Gardiner being exiled to another country on his release. With the support of Parkes, Governor Sir Hercules Robinson subsequently approved the release of Gardiner on condition he leave the country. Gardiner left immediately for America and opened a bar in San Francisco's Barbary Coast red-light district. In the political furore that followed, a resolution condemning Parkes for supporting Gardiner's release was passed in the parliament and Parkes was forced to resign.

But, eighteen months later, following the failure of two more premiers, Parkes was back again, having negotiated enough support for his second premiership, which lasted less than five months. Two other short premierships followed (Sir John Robertson and James Farnell) before Parkes was back a little over a year later for his third and longest term as leader.

In 1881, three years into his third term, Parkes argued again for national union, at an intercolonial conference in Sydney:

> That the time is come for the construction of a Federal constitution, with an Australian Federal Parliament ... when a number of matters of much concern to all the colonies might be dealt with more effectively by some federal authority than by the colonies separately.[19]

He added that, while a national parliamentary system was being organised, there could be an interim Federal

Council that would 'accustom the public mind to federal ideas [and] would be the best preparation for the foundation of a federal Government'.[20]

In 1883, most of the Australian colonies agreed, and they formed a Federal Council of Australia to deal with issues of mutual concern, including tariffs, telegraphs, post and railways. However, by now Parkes was again out of office, and New South Wales refused to join. As a result, the council was 'fatally handicapped' throughout its existence by the absence of Australia's mother colony.[21] When the New South Wales Parliament had voted narrowly (22–21) to stay out of the Federal Council, Parkes surprised observers by also voting against joining. He later said that he voted 'no' because he felt the existence of a credible council would make it easier to avoid the reality of Federation.

The absence of New South Wales in the Federal Council caused great resentment in the other colonies. As Victorian premier James Service complained, 'We have gone out in the world, and made a house of our own, and are no longer children, and, when we rejoin the old mother colony . . . it must be in the shape of partners and not as children.'[22]

Parkes's third government fell in January 1883 after a relatively long term of more than four years. The end of the government came as a shock to him. A number of his close supporters had become disaffected with his leadership and 'ambushed' him by switching sides during a parliamentary vote, leaving Parkes without a majority.[23] He had no choice but to advise dissolution, which Governor Lord Loftus granted. In the subsequent election, now sixty-nine years old, Parkes lost office and his seat of East Sydney, and his long career appeared to be over. However, Edward Whereat, an admirer who occupied the seat of Tenterfield, near the north-east border of New South Wales with Queensland, agreed to resign and leave the seat open for Parkes at a by-election, which Parkes went on to win.

Shortly after becoming the member for Tenterfield, Parkes left Australia on a voyage to England to become a financial consultant for a Sydney company owned by George Murray. In Britain, Parkes established the Australasian Investment Company, with its headquarters in Edinburgh and a board in Sydney. But he had no real interest in business or money, and he soon resigned from the company without it making any significant profits. He was away for eighteen months, returning to Sydney in August 1884.[24]

Over the next four turbulent years, New South Wales would have four different premiers – Stuart Donaldson, George Dibbs, Sir John Robertson and Sir Patrick Jennings – until January 1887, when Parkes returned to parliament and managed to win office for his fourth and fifth terms, which ran for almost five years from January 1887 till October 1891, with a gap of two months early in 1889. He arrived back in office in plenty of time to organise the celebrations for Australia's Centenary, which commemorated the original British settlement of Sydney by Captain Arthur Phillip and the First Fleet of convicts in January 1788. The centre of the celebrations included the unveiling of a large statue of Queen Victoria at the eastern end of Sydney's King Street and the opening of Centennial Park – which was larger than London's Hyde Park and Regent's Park combined – by New South Wales governor Lord Carrington. The program stretched over a week so as to make it worthwhile for governors, politicians and other leading figures from the other colonies to make the journey to Sydney by train or by ship.

To coincide with the celebrations, Parkes audaciously introduced a bill into the parliament proposing the name of the colony of New South Wales be changed to Australia. It was his intention to bring this into force from 24 May 1888, Queen Victoria's birthday.[25] The proposal angered many of Parkes's colleagues as well as the other colonies – and London – and he was dissuaded from it with an offer of elevation to the highest order of knighthood, the Grand Cross, which no other colonial minister held at that stage.[26]

While the centenary celebration was an event shared by all the colonies, it very much focused on Sydney, which was not universally appreciated. In South Australia, *The Advertiser* pointed out that New South Wales, though 'senior', was not the 'parent colony' of the others, each of which had their own histories and significant dates. The *Brisbane Courier* went further, suggesting that the centenary marked a date that would 'best be forgotten' as it represented Australia becoming the 'cesspit of England with the first transportation of convicts'.

Only five days after the Australia Day celebration of 26 January 1888, Parkes's wife, Clarinda, died at the age of seventy-four, with Henry sitting at her bedside. At the time of their mother's death, the oldest surviving child, Clarinda, was almost fifty years old and the youngest, Lily, was twenty-six.

Parkes did not appear to have mourned for too long, however, as he was at the time in a relationship with Eleanor Dixon, who was thirty-one years old and had already borne him three children, all of whom were under five years of age when his wife died. It is believed that Parkes had met Eleanor eight years before on a visit to Melbourne. He subsequently set her up in a house in Sydney's Redfern with borrowed money, which added to his already significant financial problems. Barely a year after the death of Clarinda, he scandalised his family by marrying Eleanor and then having two more children. Having a mistress was one thing, but marrying her was another. Parkes's daughters – most of whom were many years older than their new stepmother – would have nothing to do with Eleanor. Nor would the New South Wales governor, Lord Carrington. When his wife was not also invited to Government House for dinner, Parkes refused to go himself:

> Sir Henry Parkes regrets that he cannot accept the invitation of his Excellency the Governor to dinner on the 24th May [1889]. He owes it to his wife, whatever may be the occasion, not to enter the door which is closed against her; but he desires at the same time to be understood as not seeking a reversal of her exclusion, while he insists upon sharing any indignity to which she is subjected.[27]

A year after the centenary celebrations, seventy-four-year-old Premier Parkes started the process that would eventually result in the creation of the nation of Australia. He did so in a speech he gave in Tenterfield on his way back from Brisbane, which he had visited to discuss federal union with Queensland political leaders.

He had gone to Queensland without consulting his New South Wales Government colleagues and reached Brisbane on 21 October 1889. He was unable to meet with the Queensland premier, Boyd Morehead, who was ill, but did manage to see the influential former premier Sir Thomas McIlwraith and Opposition Leader Samuel Griffith, both of whom backed his proposal for a meeting of colonial leaders to discuss federal union.[28]

Parkes's discussions with McIlwraith and Griffith centred on a report published a few months earlier on Australian military defence that suggested Australia was vulnerable and would be unable to defend itself properly if attacked.

The report had been carried out by a British major general, James Bevan Edwards, who had been to Australia to conduct the assessment the previous July. Edwards said some of the colonial defences were sufficient but that they would need to be coordinated to be able to withstand an attack: '[The colonies' forces] cannot at present be considered efficient in comparison with any moderately trained army, and without any cohesion or power of combination for mutual defence among the different colonies.'[29]

During the 1880s, the colonies had been increasingly sensitive to Australia's external security. The French had increased their presence on Tahiti and the Polynesian islands, and in 1884 Germany had annexed parts of New Guinea. Australia was a long way from the protection of the British Empire, and its leaders were aware that they had limited means to defend their huge continent were it ever to be attacked.

Parkes left Brisbane railway station at 7 am on 24 October 1889 to begin his journey home to Sydney and reached the Queensland–New South Wales border at about 5 pm. At Wallangarra Station, 150 kilometres further south-west, Parkes left the narrow-gauge Queensland railway and crossed the platform to board a special New South Wales train on the standard-gauge rail track on the eastern side of the station. Construction of the 700-kilometre railway line from Sydney to the border had only been completed the previous year.

About half an hour later, he reached the town of Tenterfield, about 19 kilometres to the south, where he had accepted an invitation to be special guest at a banquet that night because of his connection with the area. The visit of the veteran political leader and former local member Henry Parkes was a big event for the town. When he arrived, a brass band was playing, flags and banners

were flying, all the shops were closed and half the population of the district had turned out to greet the great man.

At Tenterfield Railway Station, the mayor gave a
welcoming speech and Parkes replied by referring to
Tenterfield as a beautiful town and reminding the people
of his gratitude in having been made their local member of
parliament. After the speeches, he was taken to Curley's
Commercial Hotel before heading to the Tenterfield School
of Arts Hall for a banquet attended by eighty local dignitaries, where he was to deliver his now famous address.

English writer David Christie Murray, who witnessed
the speech, said that despite his advancing years Parkes
was very impressive:

> The voice was a little veiled by fatigue and age. The massive
> shoulders were a little bowed, but the huge head, with its
> streaming wave of silver hair and beard was held as erect
> as ever. The rough homely features were as eloquent as
> the words he spoke and the instinct of a natural fighting
> man lit up the ancient warrior's eye.[30]

Parkes began by saying the defence of Australia needed to
be addressed and that it was 'absolutely necessary . . .
to have one central authority, which could bring all of the
forces of the different colonies into one army'. He attacked
the Federal Council, which still regularly met but without
New South Wales, to discuss issues of common interest to
the colonies. He pointed out that it 'sat in Tasmania and
held sessions which never appeared to interest anyone . . .
[it] has no power . . . it is not an elective body'. He
pointed out:

> Australia [now has] a population of three and a half
> millions, and the American people numbered only between

three and four millions when they formed the great commonwealth of the United States. The numbers were about the same, and surely what the Americans had done by war, the Australians could bring about in peace.[31]

Then he came to his proposal, which attracted cheers and applause: 'The great question which we have to consider is whether the time has not now arisen for the creation on this Australian continent of an Australian government and an Australian parliament.'

Parkes suggested that a Convention of 'leading men from all the colonies' should be organised:

> This convention will have to devise the constitution which will be necessary for bringing into existence a federal government with a federal parliament for the conduct of this great national undertaking . . . I believe . . . that the time has come . . . and all great national questions . . . will be disposed of by a fully authorised constitutional authority.

The story of Parkes's speech was published in a number of papers, including the *Sydney Morning Herald*. However, it met with some scepticism in the other colonies. After all, New South Wales had refused to sit with the other colonies on the Federal Council when Parkes had been premier. Four days after the oration, on 28 October, the Melbourne *Argus* suggested sarcastically that the speech signified that 'the colony of New South Wales is becoming discontented with her federal apathy'. Victoria's Alfred Deakin remarked upon Parkes's 'sudden adherence to the Federal cause which he had never opposed but which he had allowed to slumber for some ten years'.[32]

Parkes never explained why he took up the issue of national union when he did, in the twilight of his career and having allowed the matter to languish for so many years. According to the governor of New South Wales, Lord Carrington, it came as a result of a discussion the two men had had at Government House after a lunch the previous June. According to Carrington, they had been discussing Canada, where most of the provinces had confederated more than twenty years earlier, in 1867. Carrington said confederation of the Australian colonies made sense, and Parkes responded by saying he believed he could achieve it in 'twelve months'. Carrington replied, 'Then why don't you do it? It would be a glorious finish to your life.'[33]

Despite a lack of enthusiasm from his counterparts in the other colonies, Parkes pressed on and wrote to his premier colleagues suggesting a conference to progress the issue. Since the proposal was for a nation of Australasia, the invitation included New Zealand. Two days before the Tenterfield speech, Parkes had already telegraphed the Victorian premier, Duncan Gillies, suggesting they meet to discuss national defence following the Edwards report. Gillies had replied by suggesting that if Parkes wanted to discuss federal issues, he should join the Federal Council that New South Wales had boycotted for many years. Undaunted, Parkes persisted and asked Gillies and the other premiers to 'an informal meeting of the colonies for the purpose of preliminary consultation' to explore which colonies were prepared to seriously consider national union.[34]

Despite some misgivings, Gillies and the other representatives of the colonies finally agreed to meet in Melbourne early the following year. The conference was, according to Victoria's Alfred Deakin, 'in number, in quality and task, by far the most important representative gathering which had ever met in Australia'.[35] It opened during a sweltering hot summer on 6 February 1890 in the Victorian Parliament. Each colony sent two delegates, except Western Australia, which sent only one.

The two Victorians who came were the premier Duncan Gillies and the chief secretary Alfred Deakin. Fifty-six-year-old Duncan Gillies had been born in Scotland, the son of a market gardener. He had migrated to the Victorian goldfields in 1852 at the age of eighteen. He had been at Ballarat two years later at the time of the Eureka uprising and was a friend of the Irish radical Peter Lalor. Despite his youth and a limited education, young Gillies was first elected to the Victorian Parliament at twenty-six years of age as the member for Ballarat West in 1860 and became premier in 1886.

Victoria's second representative, thirty-four-year-old Alfred Deakin, would play a major role in the Federation movement. After Federation, he would serve as attorney general in the first Barton national government, before becoming prime minister himself in 1903. He was born in Melbourne in 1856, the son of English migrants who had arrived in Australia six years earlier. Deakin's father, Bill, had tried his hand on the Victorian goldfields before becoming a manager of the Cobb and Co. coach company and a respectable, if modest, middle-class suburbanite. Young Alfred was a brilliant scholar and a 'dreamer', and graduated in law from Melbourne University, where he had become actively involved in the debating society and developed what became a lifelong interest in spiritualism.

He entered parliament in 1879 at the age of twenty-three, and was 'six feet (about 183 cm) tall, dark haired and dark-eyed, his handsome, alert face fashionably bearded', speaking 'rapidly in a rich, baritone voice which, he claimed, bore no trace of "provincial" accent'.[36] Deakin always kept his deep spirituality from the public gaze. At nineteen years of age, he'd had his phrenology chart drawn up.[37] This involved the detailed measuring of the surface of the skull, from which it was believed mental and moral characteristics could be measured and diagnosed. Later, he began consulting 'sibyls' and other fortune tellers, and was told by one he would become a minister in the Victorian Government. Despite his diaries regularly recording self-doubt, Deakin was driven by a feeling of providence and destiny throughout his career.[38]

In 1882, he married Elizabeth 'Pattie' Browne, the daughter of a prominent spiritualist, and they had three daughters in their long and apparently happy marriage.

In the decade before the constitutional convention, Deakin served as minister for public works, solicitor general, chief secretary, commissioner for water supply and minister for health. From 1890, he refused any further ministerial appointments so he could concentrate on achieving a federated Australia, and despite being a dominant player in Victorian politics for more than twenty years, he never served as the colony's premier.

Deakin would later write a book about Federation called *The Federal Story*. It is a wonderfully candid and colourful 'behind the scenes' account by an insider who was deeply involved in the process over many years. No other record is anything like it. In contrast to the formal and overly polite official records, it is highly personalised, and includes brilliant and often unflattering portrayals of many of the key players in the story, some of them his close friends. He described his boss, Victorian premier Duncan Gillies as:

> short, stout, sturdy, florid, with clean-shaven face and close thin hair . . . clear-headed, and cold in temperament,

he was without even a tinge of . . . poetry . . . Not that in debate Gillies lacked force and fire or any quality of the successful party combatant . . . he was a good general either in victory or defeat, without intimate friends but loyal to his associates and enjoying the confidence even of his opponents in his judgment and fairness.[39]

In the book, Deakin also described Henry Parkes, whom he observed up close for the first time at this conference:

He had always in his mind's eye his own portrait as that of a great man, and constantly adjusted himself to it. A far away expression of the eyes, intended to convey his remoteness from the earthly sphere. Movements, gestures, inflections, attitudes harmonized, not simply because they were intentionally adopted but because there was in him the substance of a man he dressed himself to appear . . . Fond of books, a steady reader and a constant writer, his education had been gained in the world and among men . . . a life of struggle had found him self-reliant and left him hardened into resolute masterfulness . . . he was a born leader of men . . . He was jealous of equals, bitter with rivals and remorseless with enemies – vain beyond all measure, without strong attachment to colleagues and with strong animal passions . . . A doughty parliamentary warrior neither giving nor asking quarter . . .[40]

Parkes had with him in Melbourne William McMillan, the New South Wales colonial secretary. McMillan was a strong advocate of free trade and had been elected head of Sydney's Chamber of Commerce in 1886, entering the New South Wales Parliament the following year. The Irish-born McMillan was described by Deakin as 'narrow and cold . . . prudent but not wanting in courage'.[41]

Queensland was represented by Sir Samuel Griffith and Colonial Secretary John Macrossan. Forty-five-year-old barrister Griffith was, according to Deakin, 'lean, ascetic, cold, clear, collected and acidulated'.[42] Born in Wales in 1845, Griffith had come to Australia when his minister father, the Reverend Edward Griffith, had taken up a posting with the Colonial Missionary Society. Young Samuel graduated in law from Sydney University and became an articled clerk in Ipswich, Queensland. He first entered the Queensland Parliament as a twenty-six-year-old in 1871.

Queensland's second representative, fifty-seven-year-old John Macrossan, was described as a 'small rather shrivelled Irishman with a large forehead and a twinkling eye'.[43] He had migrated to the Victorian goldfields 1853 and followed the gold rushes into Queensland. He organised the Miners' Protection Association on the north Queensland Ravenswood goldfields in 1871 and two years later entered parliament as a member for North Queensland.

The South Australian delegation was led by its recently elected premier, forty-year-old John Cockburn. Cockburn had migrated to South Australia from Scotland in 1875 to practise medicine and less than a decade later was elected to parliament. Deakin's impressions of 'the young Premier' were mixed:

An extremely handsome man with regular features, dark hair and complexion and a well-proportioned figure, his enthusiasm glowed in his eye and overflowed in his fluent but not easy speech. A visionary by nature and a dreamer by habits, a professional man of miscellaneous reading and limited experience . . . weak in will and unstable in opinion . . .[44]

Cockburn was accompanied by his immediate predecessor as South Australian premier, sixty-three-year-old Thomas Playford. Deakin described Playford as a 'huge giant' who, by 'force of character and general disposition', pushed himself in front of his younger colleague John Cockburn at every opportunity during the conference.[45]

Tasmania sent its colonial secretary Bolton Stafford Bird and attorney general Andrew Inglis Clark. Clark was a lawyer who had studied the American constitution and was to play a major role in the later process of drafting the Australian constitution. Deakin described him as 'small, spare, nervous, active, jealous and suspicious in disposition, and somewhat awkward in manner and ungraceful in speech' but nevertheless a sound lawyer, who was 'keen, logical and acute'.

Stafford Bird, a tall, white-bearded, fifty-year-old farmer and religious minister from Tasmania's Huon district, was described by Deakin as 'sound and sober in thought'.[46] He was born in England, the son of a schoolteacher, and migrated with his family to the Victorian goldfields as a twelve-year-old. He became a minister in the congregational church in Victoria before moving with his wife to Tasmania, where he became an apple farmer and continued preaching.

Western Australia was not an active participant in the Melbourne conference and sent only one representative, Sir James George Lee Steere, as an observer. Steere was one of the few representatives at the conference to have come from a truly British establishment background. Politically conservative and with 'authoritative good looks . . . and a dignified . . . manner', Steere 'was the epitome of that type of Englishman for whom character is more important than brains'.[47] Born the third son of a fox-hunting squire and bred on the family's historic Surrey estates, Steere studied at Clapham Grammar School before joining the East India Company, where within ten years he had risen to the rank of captain. In 1860, at thirty years of age and newly married, Steere and his wife migrated to Western Australia, where he became a farmer and joined the property-owning elite of the colony.

Finally, New Zealand sent 'two cultured and wealthy gentlemen': colonial secretary Captain William Russell and veteran political leader Sir John Hall.[48] The seventy-six-year-old Hall had already been in the New Zealand Parliament for nearly half a century when he came to the Melbourne conference, having migrated from England to New Zealand in 1852, where he became a successful sheep farmer and then politician, becoming New Zealand's prime minister from 1879 to 1882.

His younger colleague, sixty-one-year-old William Russell, was born in Britain and had lived in New Zealand since 1861, first entering the New Zealand Parliament in 1871.

*

On the night before the start of the Federation conference, there was a welcome banquet for around 200 guests in parliament's Queen's Hall, which was located between the Legislative Council and the Legislative Assembly. On welcoming the guests, former Victorian premier James Service spoke of the widespread support for national union:

> The idea of united Australasia has sunk deep into the hearts of the Australian people. It has touched their imagination, and it has been approved of by their sober judgment. The idea has permeated the whole of society, and all classes in

society. The pulpit preaches federation, it is the theme of the poets and the ambition of the statesmen; our mechanics have engrafted the federal idea upon the trades unions, so have the churchmen on their ecclesiastical associations, while our merchants have done the same with their chambers of commerce. Our very Australian boys drink in federation with mother's milk ... We have among us federal banks and insurance companies.[49]

The conference lasted from Thursday 6 February to Friday 14 February 1890. At its opening, Parkes diplomatically moved that his host, Premier Duncan Gillies, chair the proceedings. Parkes then proposed his motion that would bind the colonies to pursue national union. The motion acknowledged the Federal Council, which had been ignored for years by New South Wales:

That, in the opinion of this conference, the best interests and the present and future prosperity of the Australasian Colonies will be promoted by their early union under the Crown, and, while fully recognising the valuable services of the Members of the convention of 1883 in founding the Federal Council, it declares its opinion that the seven years which have since elapsed have developed the national life of Australasia in population, in wealth, in the discovery of resources, and in self-governing capacity, to an extent which justifies the higher act, at all times contemplated, of the union of these Colonies, under one legislative and executive Government based upon principles just to the several Colonies.

During the seven sitting days, the discussion focused on whether national union was appropriate and how it might be achieved. There was little parliamentary-style debate:

each of the delegates spent their speaking time outlining their views as to whether Federation should proceed or not.

On the fifth day, the New Zealand representatives made it clear they wanted their own nation and did not want to be part of a united Australia. In his address to the conference, William Russell said they would happily join with Australia on issues of common military defence but not become part of the same country, because New Zealand was 'fundamentally different':

> We have had to struggle against not only a more boisterous climate than Australia, but against a dense vegetation; and we have had to carve our homes out of the wilderness, which, though marvellously prolific and fertile, nevertheless marks a country in which self-denial has had to be practised by its settlers to an extent of which the people of the Australian continent have no conception.[50]

Russell also pointed out that New Zealanders had managed their Indigenous problems better and did not want to risk the future by allowing an Australian federal authority any involvement:

> Not only have the settlers had to struggle against the forces of nature, but against a proud, indomitable, and courageous race of aborigines. That native race has been treated in a manner so considerate that the condition of no other native and savage race on the face of the globe can be compared to it. Their right to their lands was recognised from the first. I do not boast that our public men were more pure in spirit than those of other countries, but as the colonization of New Zealand was effected originally through missionary zeal, through that, to a large extent, our hearts and policy were softened. But in

addition to this feeling, the natives could defend their own interests and look down the sights of a rifle better than any other savage people. They were many, and the white settlers were few, and when our hearts were not softened by the missionary, we were controlled by the thought of the Maoris' numbers, and of their rifles. Therefore we recognised their right to their own land, and instead of confiscating it we admitted their claim to its full possession, administration, and disposal. Members of the Conference may perhaps ask, why am I giving this short historical sketch? It bears materially upon the question of federation. The whole of New Zealand politics for years hinged almost entirely upon the native question. That question destroyed more Governments than anything else in New Zealand. All turned upon the necessity for keeping the natives at peace, and yet obtaining enough of their lands to further colonization. I am happy to say, and I thank God for it, that the day is past in which there is any probability – nay, any possibility – of another native war occurring. But one of the important questions in New Zealand politics for many years to come must be that of native administration, and were we to hand over that question to a Federal Parliament – to an elective body, mostly Australians, that cares nothing and knows nothing about native administration, and the members of which have dealt with native races in a much more summary manner than we have ventured to deal with ours in New Zealand . . . It is extremely improbable that hostilities would again break out between the natives and the white settlers, but the advance of civilization would be enormously delayed if the regulation of this question affecting New Zealand was handed over to a body of gentlemen who knew nothing whatever of the traditions of the past.[51]

He concluded by saying that it had not been his intention 'to throw the apple of discord' into the conference but asked that New Zealand be taken out of the proposed resolution for the nation and that the name in the document be changed from 'Australasia' to 'Australia':

> I hope Sir Henry Parkes will consent to change the word 'Australasian' in his motion to 'Australian'. If he will consent to do that, I will propose a motion additional, as follows: – That to the union of the Australian Colonies contemplated by the foregoing resolution, the remoter Australasian Colonies shall be entitled to admission at such times and on such conditions as may hereafter be agreed upon.

If any offence was taken to Russell's comments by the delegates from other colonies, it was not recorded. On the last day of the meeting, a motion was unanimously carried that the Australian (not Australasian) colonies would agree to an 'early union' under 'one legislative and executive Government'. It provided that any colony, including New Zealand, that did not join at the start would be welcome to join later, as Russell had proposed. The conference also agreed that each of the colonies would the following year send up to seven delegates each to a 'national convention' to design the 'scheme for a federal Constitution'.

The conference was a victory. The colonies were now in agreement and on a clear path towards national union. Or so it seemed.

CHAPTER 12

'FEDERATION IS DEAD'

Believe me, it is as dead as Julius Caesar.

A YEAR AFTER THE BREAKTHROUGH IN MELBOURNE, FORTY-FIVE delegates, selected by their respective parliaments, met in Sydney for the serious task of designing the national political system of Australia.

The men who arrived in Sydney at the end of February and the beginning of March 1891 were the most impressive gathering of senior colonial figures ever to meet in Australia. Many would dominate the Federation process over the next ten years and play leading roles in the early days of the Australian Government:

Among the delegates, there was scarcely one, who at some time or another has not been a Minister of the Crown; and most of them have for many years been the most

279

prominent men in Australasia. There were, for instance, no less than twelve Premiers and ex-Premiers . . . nine . . . were lawyers . . . Seven bore titles conferred for distinguished services and . . . three were members of the Order of St Michael and St George, six in higher degrees and one in the lower . . . [and] four were wearers of the silk gowns of Queen's Counsel . . . Such an aggregation of eminent men has perhaps never before met . . . and it may be many years before . . . another such collection of humanity.[1]

Most of the delegates from Victoria, South Australia and Tasmania arrived on the Saturday morning before the convention began and were greeted at Sydney's Central Railway Station by Sir Henry Parkes and other senior New South Wales officials. In addition to their servants and administrative staff, many had brought their wives and, in some cases, children. After the welcome speeches, the delegates were taken to Sydney's best hotels, including the Grosvenor at the northern end of George Street and the Metropole on Phillip Street.

The visitors were concerned to see that seventy-six-year-old Parkes's health had declined since the meeting in January the year before. Three months after he had returned to Sydney from London, his horse-drawn cab had overturned on the corner of Sydney's York and Margaret streets, and he had badly broken his leg. It had taken fourteen weeks of recuperation before he could be assisted to his seat in parliament, and only eight weeks before the start of the Sydney convention he was still recording in his journal that his leg was causing him great pain.[2]

His health problems were noted by visiting newspaper reporters:

Those who had not seen Sir Henry since . . . twelve months ago noticed a very great change in his appearance. The accident by which he was so seriously injured has very much reduced him. He looks faded and weary, and quite fails to give the impression of revered force which his peculiar bearing has hitherto always strongly conveyed . . . On the day of the opening of the Federal Convention he looked stronger than he had done for some time, [but] had to use his stick and needed some help to get to his chair . . . as President of the convention.[3]

The Sydney contingent went to great lengths to be good hosts, and 'entertained their guests in a right royal fashion':

The hospitality offered . . . was large hearted and generous. The best that the land could produce was placed at the disposal of [the] visitors. There was no thought of paying for anything, and for the time being the Parliamentary refreshment rooms lost their character of a club and became a private house.[4]

Before the start of the conference, a Federation banquet was held in Centennial Hall (today's Town Hall) for more than 900 guests. During the dinner, *The Sydney Morning Herald* reported that each of the premiers was invited to respond to Parkes's toast, 'One people, one destiny'. The newly appointed governor of New South Wales, the Earl of Jersey, made Britain's position clear when he said that 'England desires that these Australian States should tread the path of peace and honour to unity and power . . . the constitution of Australia is now in the crucible'.[5] Britain had become a consistent supporter of Federation because they saw a united Australia as strengthening the British Empire.

The Federation convention opened on 2 March 1891 at 11 am at the Macquarie Street Legislative Assembly Chamber of Parliament House. The visitors from other colonies found the old chamber 'a rather badly-lighted and dingy building' and nowhere near as grand as the parliament buildings of either Melbourne or Adelaide'.[6] *The Sydney Morning Herald* described it as a 'patched up jumble of additions and alterations, of old and new buildings thrown together in confusion, and altered to suit the tastes of every succeeding government'.[7]

Parkes was appointed 'president' of the convention, nominated by Victorian premier James Munro not only as the Premier of the colony where the convention sat, but also as the immediate author of the present movement.[8] Creating the position of president gave special status to Parkes because it allowed him the opportunity to speak at the conference in a way he would not have been able to had he been elected to chair the meeting.

In opening the convention, he proposed the name of 'Commonwealth of Australia' for the new nation. When he rose to speak, he 'appeared weak and feeble' and needed to lean on his chair for support.[9] But despite his age and failing health, *The Advertiser* said he was still a commanding figure:

> He limped very slowly to that seat of honour . . . and [a] weary and fagged look . . . was still painfully apparent . . . His voice was weak, almost piping; an elongation of the uvula having joined the general bodily weakness . . . his lapses in pronunciation were also very marked . . . Nevertheless, behind all this bodily weakness and want of surface culture the dynamic power and great personal qualities of the man were evident . . . amid numberless defects and failures . . . Sir Henry Parkes [is] the most powerful of Australian statesmen.[10]

At the convention, Parkes had the support of Edmund Barton. The premier had won over Barton with his

Tenterfield speech, and their alliance would prove crucial in the years ahead, as Barton eventually became Parkes's chosen successor.

Victoria's Alfred Deakin, who became a close friend and ally of Barton's during the quest for nationhood, described him as an intellectual and a 'sound lawyer' who possessed a 'high sense of personal honour'. However, he also said his friend wasted much of his potential by excessive good living:

> This was largely due to the indolence which had contributed greatly during his political career to keep him out of the leadership of a party ... In later years his fine figure became too corpulent to be graceful so that his Apollo-like brow and brilliant capacities were to some extent chained to earth by his lazy love of good living ... his genial, affectionate nature made him so companionable that he spent many hours in his club chair which could have been more profitably spent in his [lawyer's] chambers or in his study ... he was at times an excellent debater ... but he could not be relied upon to rise regularly to his best level.[11]

Barton was born the third son and youngest child of William Barton and Mary Louisa in 1849. His accountant father had migrated to Australia in 1827 and had mixed fortunes in business as a financial agent and stockbroker. Young Edmund nevertheless had a good education: a brilliant scholar, he attended Sydney Grammar School and was the Sydney University medallist. At university, he earned first-class honours in classics and law before becoming a solicitor and barrister. He undertook his first major case at twenty-three years of age as junior counsel in the unsuccessful defence of Alfred Lester, who was hanged for his involvement in a high-profile murder.

In December 1877, the twenty-eight-year-old Barton married English-born Jane Ross Mason (Jeanie). Together, they would have three sons and two daughters. Two years later, he was first elected to the New South Wales Legislative Assembly for the seat of Sydney University, having lost two earlier attempts. When the university seat was abolished in 1880, he became the member for Wellington in western New South Wales. At thirty-three, he became the youngest speaker of any Australian parliament, a position he held from 1883 till 1887.

Barton enjoyed cricket and fishing, theatre, music and the arts, and was widely read. A member of the influential Freemasons' society, he was part of a group that established the Athenaeum Club on Castlereagh Street in Sydney, and it was here that it was widely believed he spent too much of his time. Other early members included Jules François Archibald, the owner and editor of *The Bulletin* magazine; the proprietor of the *Sydney Morning Herald*, James Fairfax; and the *Herald*'s editor, Andrew Garran. Barton's love of the good life and the time he spent at the Athenaeum meant he grew portly and was given the nickname of 'Toby Tosspot' by *The Bulletin* – a name that stuck.

Alongside Henry Parkes and Edmund Barton, the other New South Wales delegates were businessman and parliamentarian William McMillan, lawyer Joseph Abbott, former New South Wales premier George Dibbs, former speaker William Suttor and pastoralist Sir Patrick Jennings.

The Victorian delegation included Duncan Gillies, the host of the constitutional conference in Melbourne the year before, although he had since lost the premiership in a vote of no confidence the previous October. His replacement as the head of the delegation was the new premier, James Munro, who had previously been a supporter of Gillies but had turned and successfully moved a motion against him in the Victorian Parliament. The other members of the Victorian team were lawyer Henry Cuthbert, brewery owner Nicholas Fitzgerald and Henry Wrixon.

The South Australians were led by 'Honest Tom' Playford, who had been one of the two South Australian representatives at the Melbourne conference the year before with the then premier John Cockburn. This time, their roles were reversed: Playford was again premier, having won back the post after an election the previous August. The remaining five members were lawyers Charles Kingston, Sir John Downer, Richard Baker, Sir John Bray and John Gordon.

Adelaide-born Kingston was South Australia's attorney general and would later become its premier. He was another dominant player in the Federation story. Deakin said he was able to overcome a flawed character: 'A man of great physical size and strength, of fine features and large head with rather small eyes and compressed lips . . . strong passions had crippled his self-development and political career but his great ability, indomitable will, and fearless courage steadily surmounted all these barriers.'[12]

John Downer was born in Adelaide, and his son and grandsons would both become Cabinet ministers in the Australian Federal Parliament. Deakin had this to say about him:

Australian as he was, his appearance and character alike were thoroughly and typically English. Bull headed, and rather thick necked, clean shaven as a priest, and with the dogged set of the mouth of a prize fighter . . . of medium height and strongly built, his smallish eyes lit up with animation or twinkling of humour, only partly disclosed his combination of resolution with kindliness.[13]

Queenslanders Sir Samuel Griffith and John Macrossan led the Queensland delegation. Samuel Griffith would play a vital role at the Sydney convention as chairman of the constitution-drafting committee. Macrossan, who was in poor health, spoke only twice at the meetings, and died shortly before the conference finished. The other Queensland members were former railway engineer Sir Thomas McIlwraith, and lawyers Arthur Rutledge, Andrew Thynne, Thomas Macdonald Paterson and John Donaldson.

The Tasmanians took more than three months to decide on their delegation because of a dispute between their two houses of parliament about how many from each chamber should be chosen. Finally, from the Legislative Assembly, they selected Stafford Bird, Nicholas John Brown, Andrew Inglis Clark and William Henry Burgess. The Legislative Council selected William Moore, Adye Douglas and Philip Oakley Fysh.

The delegation was led this time by Fysh, who was in his second term as premier. Fysh's governments became well known for a range of progressive social policies, including the regulation of health, the legalisation of trade unions and the establishment of technical education.

Of course, Bird and Andrew Inglis Clark had been to the Melbourne conference the year before. Inglis Clark would play a big role at the Sydney convention, not so much in the debates but in the drafting of the constitution with Samuel Griffith. Before the convention, he had circulated his own draft Australian constitution bill. He was enthusiastic about the American constitution and had attracted criticism in Tasmania for being an 'ultra republican'. His draft was practically a transcript of relevant provisions from the United States constitution, the *British North American Act* and the *Federal Council Act*, arranged systematically. It was to be of great use to the drafting committee at the convention; out of the ninety-six sections in Inglis Clark's draft, eighty-six found a recognisable counterpart in the final constitution that came out of the Sydney convention.[14]

The biggest issue for the Tasmanians in the debates about a national system was the size of the Senate. As a small state, it would have fewer members of the lower house of parliament so it wanted the upper house to have equal numbers from each state.

It was in Sydney at the 1891 convention that Western Australia made its first full appearance in the nation-building process, when it sent six delegates headed by Premier John Forrest. Western Australia had only months before been granted self-government, sixty years after its official settlement in 1829. Development of the colony had been slow. By 1850, Australia's biggest colony, covering more than two million square kilometres and with almost 21,000 kilometres of coastline, had only a tiny population, leading Parkes to observe that 'There is something almost startling in the fact that the Western Australian Government, with its handful of 45,000 inhabitants, nominally holds one-third of Australia.'[15] The colony had experienced something of a boost with an intake of British convicts after 1850, when transportation was ending in the eastern colonies, but when the convicts stopped coming in 1868, economic growth and the colony's development slowed to almost nothing.

The colony's population jump following the 1885 gold discovery at Halls Creek had made the British Government more comfortable about granting Western Australia self-government in 1890. Western Australians had been granted limited representative government in 1870 when the British agreed to allow locals to elect twelve of the eighteen members of the colony's Legislative Council.

However, the British-appointed governor remained all-powerful and the new parliament was 'little more than an exclusive debating society'.[16] It was not until 1887 that the Legislative Council passed a resolution calling for self-government, which, after two years of delay, resulted in the British Government passing the enabling legislation in 1890.

Western Australia had kept abreast of the discussions of the eastern colonies about nationhood. In 1883, the Western Australian colonial secretary Malcolm Fraser had attended the Australasian Intercolonial Convention. He returned to Perth to report that the strength of support for Federation was growing in the eastern colonies, and predicted that Western Australians would find within themselves 'a germ of this movement in favour of Australian Federation'.[17]

Fifty-two-year-old John Forrest was a towering influence over the colony. He was a huge man with a striking physical presence. He was Western Australia's first premier and remained unchallenged at the head of the colony's government for eleven years – the longest term of any Australian premier in the nineteenth century. (Sir Henry Parkes was New South Wales premier over five terms, which totalled nearly thirteen years, his longest single term in office being just over four years, between 1878 and 1883.)

Forrest was born in 1847 in Bunbury, the fourth of ten children. His father, William, and mother, Margaret, both came from humble backgrounds in Scotland and had migrated to Western Australia as servants to the chief surgeon. After early schooling in Bunbury, John attended Bishop Hale's School in Perth before becoming an apprenticed surveyor as a sixteen-year-old. At twenty-one, he was appointed to survey the south-west of the colony while searching for evidence of the lost explorer Ludwig Leichhardt. For four months, from April till August 1869, he led a team of six men on horseback on a journey of more than 3000 kilometres as far east as Laverton, systematically surveying as he went. Forrest reported the absence of any decent farming land but could not have known that, within twenty years, the area's gold would attract tens of thousands of people.

The following year, Forrest led the first expedition overland from Perth to Adelaide, in the opposite direction to Edward John Eyre, who, thirty years before, had explored from South Australia to Albany. Travelling with a team of six men, which included his younger brother Alexander, Forrest was able to demonstrate that the telegraph could readily be connected along the coast, and seven years later it was done, connecting Perth to the eastern Australian colonies and also to London.

The expedition brought widespread recognition to John and Alexander. At a dinner in their honour in Perth, the governor, Sir Frederick Weld, spoke glowingly of the 'daring', 'enterprise' and 'pluck' of the expedition, which had raised awareness of Western Australia and brought it closer to the eastern colonies: 'Forrest's party did not leave South Australia without awakening a little public interest in the distant province. The "great unknown" had been traversed safely in little time, and Western Australia appeared closer to hand – appeared, in fact, a neighbour.'[18]

In 1871, now a senior surveyor for the north of the colony, Forrest led a further expedition from Geraldton, crossing the waterless western interior to Peak Hill and then going south to Adelaide. During the seven months, Forrest's party suffered a shortage of water, lost most of its horses and violently clashed with local Aboriginal people, before it triumphantly entered Adelaide on 3 November.

Back in Perth, Forrest was granted 2000 acres (809 hectares) of farming land and given leave to make his first visit to Britain, where he had also become famous as an explorer. In Scotland, he visited the birthplace of his parents and lectured in London about his expeditions. He was later awarded the Foundation Medal by the Royal Geographical Society.

Back in Western Australia, he was appointed government surveyor. In 1876, he married Margaret Hamersley, the daughter of Edward Hamersley, who had migrated to Western Australia in 1837 and founded the family pastoral dynasty. Margaret's wealth and social standing would be a great help to Forrest, who lacked the social and political connections of the Western Australian elite.

In 1883, Forrest was appointed to the colony's Executive and Legislative councils and with Alexander did his last field survey of the Kimberley region, where the colony's first gold rush would occur three years later.

Forrest was elected unopposed as the member for the town of his birth, Bunbury, in December 1890, just after Western Australia had been granted self-government. He was immediately made the colony's first premier, a position he held until 1901, when he became a federal member of parliament in the first Australian national elections.

Only three months after forming Western Australia's first government, Forrest led the colony's delegation to the Sydney convention. Before leaving Perth, he claimed that the issue was 'surrounded with very grave difficulties', but he felt it was better that Western Australia at least attend the convention.[19]

The group's departure with their wives, servants and staff for the long journey to the eastern colonies was a big event. On the evening of Saturday 28 February 1891, they left Perth Railway Station for the 400-kilometre overnight train trip to the southern port of Albany. A special train was provided by the Great Southern Train Company, which included a number of saloon cars and the governor's carriage 'for the comfort of the ladies'. According to a newspaper report, 'a large number of Ladies and Gentlemen were present at the platform and after . . . bidding the travellers goodbye, the train steamed off amid the cheers of the spectators'.[20]

At Albany, the delegation boarded the P&O steamship *Ballarat* bound for Adelaide, where they were 'accorded a hearty reception'[21] and lunch at Adelaide Town Hall, before taking the express train on 5 March for the rest of the journey to Sydney.[22] The journey took a total of ten days and the Western Australian group arrived in Sydney on 9 March 1891, a week after the start of the convention. Their late arrival did not matter a great deal as they were not major participants in the proceedings; in fact, some of the other colonies found them so 'solidly and stolidly conservative' that, Deakin reported, they felt it 'would have been better' if they had not come.[23]

New Zealand also sent a delegation of three to the Sydney convention: Captain William Russell, who had been at the Melbourne meeting the year before, Sir Harry Atkinson and Sir George Grey. But having made it clear in Melbourne the year before that they were not interested in seriously considering joining the nation of Australia – and although from the mid-1860s they had been part of intercolonial meetings to discuss matters such as post and telegraph – the Sydney convention of 1891 would be their last formal involvement in the building of the Australian nation.

*

For the first eleven sitting days of the conference, the discussion covered how the nation of Australia might function in terms of such matters as the rights of the colonies, or states, as they would become; also dominant was the argument for free trade and the abolition of interstate tariffs, and about the powers of the national parliament, the Executive, the judiciary and national defence.

On 18 March, about halfway through the convention, the delegates split into three groups to draft different parts of the constitution: the constitutional, financial and judicial. Much of the work of drafting the constitution was supervised by Samuel Griffith. With the long Easter weekend approaching, on which parliament would be closed, Griffith invited a number of colleagues on board the Queensland Government's magnificent yacht *Lucinda* to finish the draft. The *Lucinda* had been used to bring the Queensland delegation to Sydney and was anchored at the time in Sydney Harbour.

The chosen few who would finalise the writing of Australia's first full constitution included Griffith and Andrew Thynne, Charles Kingston and John Downer, Edmund Barton and Bernard Wise, and Victoria's Henry Wrixon. Tasmania's Andrew Inglis Clark was laid low in Sydney with influenza but managed to board the *Lucinda* on Easter Sunday for the completion of the work.

The *Lucinda* had been built for the Queensland Government in 1884 in Scotland and was designed for Cabinet meetings and government entertaining. It was 172 feet (52 metres) long, and was fitted with two dining rooms, a reception hall, a large promenade and two large smoking rooms. When it arrived in Brisbane, the *Brisbane Courier* described how it was the first ship to come to the city with electric lights rather than hurricane or gas lamps: 'From an external view of the steamer, no idea can be formed of the beauty and comfort of her internal fittings, which have been carried out on a scale quite new to Brisbane.'[24]

The yacht set off from Sydney's Port Jackson on Good Friday, 27 March 1891, and sailed out of Sydney Heads. Griffith said that they had planned to stay outside the Heads for the entire weekend but the sea was too rough so: 'On Friday we went to the Hawkesbury. There was too much swell on the outside for work. We did not get into smooth water till lunch time, and then we anchored in the most lovely place called Refuge Bay.'[25]

At Refuge Bay, the drafting committee worked through the next day, then the ship moved on to the Basin at Pittwater, where they spent the second night. On Easter Sunday, the *Lucinda* sailed back into Sydney and picked up the recovering Inglis Clark before going to Middle Harbour for another day's work. The completed draft was sent off to the printers that night.

Two days later, the convention resumed to consider the printed constitution, and the following week the delegates reconvened again to spend five days discussing the draft. Eventually, on 9 April, they had managed to agree on an outline.

The convention had met for more than a month, and at the end their draft constitution for the Commonwealth of Australia was in many ways similar to the final constitution adopted ten years later. An excited Parkes claimed 'This bill will be a document remembered as long as Australia and the English language exist'.[26] At the final session, the delegates gathered 'with the amended copies of the bill, fresh from the printers in their hands' and pledged support for the adoption of the constitution back in their own colonies. The meetings finally ended on the twenty-second day 'with three vigorous cheers . . . for the Queen'.[27]

The nation would be called the Commonwealth of Australia. The colonies would become states. There would be two national houses of parliament: one 'popular', or directly elected; the other, the Senate, to consist of an equal number of representatives from each of the colonies, which were to be chosen by each of the states. The Queen would remain the head of state, with the governor general her representative in Australia, who would give 'assent' to bills passed by the parliament. The national government would have the power to control certain matters concurrently with the states, such as immigration, post, telegraph and defence. Trade between the states would be 'absolutely free', with no tariffs on goods sold from one state to another. The Commonwealth would have exclusive power to collect duties on goods imported from other countries into Australia and would reimburse some of the money collected to the states.

At the conclusion of the Sydney convention, all the delegates agreed to take the constitution back to their colonies for ratification and then to the people for a referendum so they could decide on whether to form the nation.

Western Australia was the only colony that made it clear before leaving Sydney that it was unlikely to join the others in the push for national union. John Forrest said he 'failed to look hopefully' on Western Australians agreeing to be part of a united Australia unless his colony was 'especially favoured',[28] and his colleague Sir George Steere said he thought there was nothing to gain from Western Australia joining.

*

A week after the convention ended, Parkes had lunch with Edmund Barton, who had previously been his political opponent but had become his committed supporter and would eventually take over as the leader of the Federation movement. Parkes recorded in his diary that the two men agreed over lunch that Federation would involve a 'struggle', but that together they would fight 'strongly and steadily'.[29]

However, trouble had begun in New South Wales even before the convention had ended. Despite the commanding presence of Henry Parkes, Edmund Burton and five of the most powerful members of the New South Wales Parliament, there was still widespread political opposition in the colony to the idea of Australia becoming one nation. At the start of the convention, journalists from other colonies had reported the noisy dissent from some older New South Wales politicians, including Sir John Robertson, who had been five times the colony's premier between 1860 and 1886:

> While writing thus of federation . . . I am reminded that Sir John Robertson . . . is a bitter opponent of the Federal movement. From his chair at the Reform Club – where every day this splendid old man holds his court – he thunders forth anathemas upon those 'who would destroy the liberties of New South Wales'. It is worthwhile coming to Sydney to see this veritable old lion shake his silver mane and roar . . . and as he declares his intention of stumping the country against federation his opposition . . . may retard it for a while.[30]

At a banquet held during the convention, New South Wales parliamentarian Richard O'Connor rose to propose a toast 'to Australia as Nation'. According to *The Sydney Morning Herald*, Sir John Robertson 'took exception to it and made a vigorous speech against Federation, which, he contended, 'would destroy our nationality'.

On 21 April 1891, only weeks after the end of the convention, Sir John was again out on the attack. In a telegram to the Victorian premier James Munro, he said: 'We see published a statement that Sir Henry Parkes affirms that . . . federation is safe. Believe me, it is as dead as Julius Caesar.'[31]

George Reid, who would later become premier of New South Wales and, in 1904, prime minister of Australia, also joined the cries of opposition before the drafting of the constitution was complete. On 16 April, at a packed public meeting at the Protestant Hall in Sydney's Castlereagh Street, he mocked the New South Wales convention delegates and critically dissected the major aspects of the proposal. To the cheers of the crowd, he concluded by saying, 'In the interests of the future of this country . . . this great edifice of Government had better not be built in a hurry.'[32]

Forty-six-year-old Reid was something of a political opportunist: later, when times had changed, he also changed his position regarding Federation. He had first been elected a member of the New South Wales Parliament in 1880 and did not support a national union until 1894; even then, it was equivocal support.

According to Victoria's Alfred Deakin, he was a brilliant operator and a captivating public speaker:

As a platform orator he was unsurpassed. His voice could reach a great crowd and his deliberate drawl enabled the densest among them to follow him. At his best his arguments were well shaped and perspicuously expressed with admirable directness and in the plainest words, often in slang, but always so as to be understood.[33]

However, he was also widely disliked and even despised by his contemporaries, who saw him as 'vain and resolutely selfish . . . cunning' and a shameful opportunist. In one of his more colourful descriptions, Deakin described Reid, whom he despised, as:

> physically as remarkable as his predecessor Parkes, but without his dignity . . . his immense, unwieldy, jelly-like stomach, always threatening to break his waistband, his little legs apparently bowed under its weight to the verge of their endurance, his thick neck rising behind his ears rounding to his many-folded chin. His protuberant blue eyes were expressionless until roused or half hidden in cunning, [and] a blond complexion and infantile breadth of baldness gave him an air of insolent juvenility. He walked with a staggering roll like that of a sailor, helping himself as he went by resting on the backs of chairs as if he were reminiscent of some far-off arboreal ancestor. To a superficial eye his obesity was either repellent or else amusing. A heavy German moustache concealed a mouth of considerable size from which there emanated a high, reedy voice rising to a shriek or sinking to a fawning, purring, persuasive orotund with a nasal tinge.[34]

Reid's manners, Deakin said, were no more appealing:

> he . . . [was in the] habit of dropping asleep at all times and places in the most ungraceful attitudes and in the most impolite manner . . . He never slept in a public gathering more than a moment or two, being quickly awakened by his own snore. He would sleep during the dealing of cards for a game of whist and during the play too if there was any pause . . . In the Assembly or in a train he indulged with the same facility both of sleeping and waking if necessary with an appropriate retort upon his tongue. His extreme fatness appeared to induce this state and for that his self-indulgence was chiefly responsible since he denied

himself nothing that he fancied, sucking ice or sweetmeats between meals and then eating and drinking according to his fancy.

Henry Parkes later pointed to Reid as 'the arch-plotter against federation', who 'had made up his mind not to allow, as far as he had power, an open and unprejudiced discussion of the momentous question'.[35]

In Reid's opposition to national union, he was supported by fellow member of parliament John Want, whose protests, according to Deakin, were 'as wild and virulent' as Mr Reid himself:

> Mr. Want . . . was equally frantic in his utter condemnation of the draft bill and in the enunciation of the narrow prejudices of provincialism. He saw in federation 'not the birth of a nation, but the strangulation of a great colony'; he declared that those who signed the bill in the Convention 'were traitors to their country' . . .[36]

The opposition to Federation did not abate, despite being branded by the newspapers as 'neither patriotic nor statesmanlike', and 'unworthy' and 'wanting in dignity'.[37] Three months after the Sydney convention, in June 1891, Parkes's position was further weakened when he faced an election. He was returned to office but with a reduced majority and having depended on the support of the emerging Labor Party members, who were at the time more focused on social and industrial change and less on the issue of Federation.[38] Then, in October 1891, and now seventy-six years old, tired and in ill health, Parkes resigned as premier, and the Federation bill languished.

*

In Victoria, the delegates arrived home to a 'storm of criticism' about the undemocratic nature of the draft constitution.[39] At a fiery public meeting at Fitzroy Town Hall on 9 June, Alfred Deakin was interrupted by angry interjectors who 'were anxious to cram the constitution down [the Victorian delegates'] throats'.[40] The most consistent opposition came from those shouting 'one man, one vote' in objection to the proposal to give each colony the same number of federal senators irrespective of the size of their population.

Alfred Deakin later wrote that the delegates had been carried away with optimism at the convention and lost sight of the reality back in their home colonies:

> The probability that those present were engaged in drafting a constitution for a great country led to a certain amount of posing for photographers and in the Hansard. Indeed the success of the undertaking was generally assumed on all hands . . . at the close . . . the convention seemed to be launching its bark upon a halcyon sea.[41]

The Victorians kept their promise made in Sydney and the bill was 'debated and amended by both Chambers of the Legislature',[42] but within a month it had effectively been shelved.

In 1891, a great economic depression began in Australia with the collapse of the banking system: Victorian banks and financial companies started to founder, and, by the end of the year, the bottom had fallen out of the land market.[43] Widespread unemployment followed as shops and businesses closed. As the depression deepened, particularly in Melbourne, Alfred Deakin and others unsuccessfully tried to argue that Federation would be 'a solution to all their difficulties'[44] and help restore investor confidence in Australia. Few believed him, and while the economic

outlook remained so bleak, the more realistic felt that federating was no longer 'within the range of practical politics'.[45]

The South Australian delegates were not expecting the
same difficulties when they reached Adelaide, but they
were looking for a lead from New South Wales, and when
it did not come they found themselves in difficulty. The
necessary constitution bill was introduced to both South
Australian houses of parliament in July but was then
sent off to be examined by committees. They made slow
progress. Premier Thomas Playford remained dedicated
to the process but was replaced in the middle of 1892.
Later, John Downer became premier, and he renewed the
undertaking to pass the bills in July 1893, but was himself
replaced by Charles Kingston, who, by mid-1894, was still
unable to make any progress. All these administrations
were theoretically committed to Federation, but the turbulence of local politics and, more importantly, the failure
of New South Wales to act, stymied their intentions.[46]

In Queensland, despite the pivotal role played by
Premier Griffith in the success of the Sydney Convention,
there was still no strong push in the colony for Federation
in the early 1890s. There was a feeling that the 1891 convention had fallen flat – it was seen as a politicians' bill,
'which had not come from the people'.[47] There was again
a widespread view that Federation could not progress
unless it was first embraced by New South Wales.

Tasmania was also hoping to follow the lead of the
larger colonies, particularly New South Wales. The following September, Andrew Inglis Clark drew up a bill to
ratify the constitution, which was passed in the Tasmanian
House of Assembly on 15 September 1891. However,
when it was introduced into the Legislative Council, it
languished. In November, the Hobart *Mercury* announced
the death of the Federation movement:

Federation is dead, or at any rate, the Commonwealth Bill is dropped for the year, so far as Tasmania is concerned. It had reached the Legislative Council upon the order paper of which chamber it remained for some weeks. Then seeing how matters stood in other colonies, and what a difference of opinion existed in them in regards to the functions of the branches of the Federal legislature, it was thought better to let the matter rest for the present year. So the bill was discharged from the paper, which means the closing of the subject so far as the present session is concerned.[48]

Deakin summarised it well:

The Convention having been Parliamentary in its origin required to submit its work to its parents. In a short time its fate became manifest. New Zealand at once made it plain that no such Union would be acceptable [and] from this time she disappeared altogether from the Federal stage . . . Western Australia indicated the role she intended to follow as one of dependence on her elders. When they had agreed to terms of partnership she would be prepared to come in, but until then remained quiescent. South Australia and Tasmania commenced to consider the measure but on realisation of the fact that they too could accomplish nothing of themselves, hung back waiting for a lead. Queensland though ready for action allowed herself to be paralysed by the uncertain attitude of New South Wales. Victoria alone and as usual fulfilled her obligations. The bill was debated and amended by both Chambers of the Legislature and though their views were not brought into harmony, a compromise could have been agreed upon if the situation had encouraged them to complete their work.[49]

CHAPTER 13

THE PUBLIC MOVEMENT

[It is] an important step, because it is the first taken by the people, as distinct from the politicians.

AFTER THE PUSH FOR NATIONHOOD WANED, THE ISSUE REMAINED IN the political void: politicians were preoccupied with immediate problems of a distressing economic kind. By the late 1880s, the colonial economies were overheated from excessive borrowing, spending and unprecedented rises in property values. When the bubble burst and property values began to fall, many of the banks and finance houses did not have the capital reserves to survive. On top of an already fragile situation, a drop in prices in the vitally important wool industry (by 1892, it had become one of Australia's largest industries, with more than a hundred million sheep, according to the Australian Bureau of Statistics) helped to send the economy into a downward spiral. By the early 1890s, the Australian colonies had slumped into the worst economic depression the country had ever seen. In 1892, twenty-one Melbourne and twenty Sydney building, land and mortgage companies went bust, and later in the year and early in 1893 many of the largest and previously secure banks collapsed.

Throughout these difficult times, several factors began to reshape the political landscape in New South Wales. The period saw the beginning of the emergence of the trade-union movement to give workers representation within the colonies' parliaments, which eventually led to the foundation of the Australian Labor Party. The rise of vigorous unionism in the 1880s and 1890s also contributed to workers in the rural, agricultural, manufacturing and coal industries pushing for higher wages, which was strongly resisted by employers. Major strikes in the maritime and shearing industries broke out between 1890 and 1894: some involved particularly bitter and violent clashes, with armed police escorting non-union labour to shearing sheds to break the strikes.

In August 1890, the great maritime strike started in Melbourne and quickly spread to include miners, shearers, carters, drivers and other trades.[1] This strike pitted the principle of unionism against freedom of contract. Most trading activity ceased during this time, a lot of the commercial operations of the eastern states became paralysed, and when, in January 1891, financial distress hit the wool industry, 'tension between squatter and shearer reached breaking point.[2] The great shearers' strike started in the Darling Downs of Queensland and quickly spread through the shearing sheds of Queensland and New South Wales. It lasted a good six months.

This emerging Australian identity was now articulated in a far more distinct kind of arts and literature. Much of the new Australian ethos of egalitarianism was being expressed by Henry Lawson, who wrote in 1887, 'The only protection Australia needs is from landlordism, the title-worship, the class distinctions and privileges, the oppression of the poor, the monarchy, and all the dust-covered customs that England has humped out of the middle ages where she properly belongs.'[3]

Four years later, Lawson wrote his famous poem 'Freedom on the Wallaby', in support of striking shearers. On 15 July 1891, the conservative parliamentarian and clergyman Frederick Brentnall read the last two stanzas in the Queensland Parliament, which resulted in calls for Lawson to be arrested and charged with sedition:

> So we must fly a rebel flag,
> As others did before us,
> And we must sing a rebel song
> And join in rebel chorus.

> We'll make the tyrants feel the sting
> O' those that they would throttle;
> They needn't say the fault is ours
> If blood should stain the wattle!

Henry Lawson's father was a Norwegian seaman, Neils Larsen, who jumped ship in Melbourne to dig for gold in 1856 and anglicised his name to Lawson with the birth of his first son, Henry, the following year. Henry had attended a bush school at Eurunderee and later a Catholic school in nearby Mudgee. After school, he worked in a number of labouring jobs while studying at night but failed the exams that would have taken him to university. His first poem was published by *The Bulletin* when he was twenty years old. Two years later, *The Bulletin* paid for him to trek the outback of New South Wales, which, along with his childhood on the goldfields, helped shaped the harsh realism of those he wrote of – typifying the persevering, humanist, sad and laconic character, and the underprivileged, itinerant, social outcast.

The Bulletin spoke to both city and country people with a distinctly Australian voice, and was described by Warren Fahey in his history of the publication as the magazine that 'reshaped the Australian identity'.[4] Launched in Sydney in 1880 by accountant, journalist and miner Jules François Archibald and his journalist and politician partner John Hayes, and calling itself 'The Bushman's Bible', the magazine was radical for its times. It promoted the Australian values of mateship and trade-union solidarity, and was anti-wowser, anti-authority and egalitarian. It was pro-Federation, anti-imperialist and pro-republic. It was unashamedly xenophobic, and the masthead 'Australia for the White Man' was printed on the front cover of the magazine until the 1950s.

Also writing for *The Bulletin* was Andrew (Banjo) Paterson. Born in 1864 near Orange, in New South Wales, to Scottish migrant Andrew Bogle Paterson and his Australian-born wife, Rose Barton, Paterson spent his early years on farms in the Orange district being taught by governesses. At ten years of age, he was sent to Sydney Grammar School and then became a lawyer. Although he lived most of the time in Sydney, he became famous as a romantic bush poet. His first poems were published in *The Bulletin* in 1885 using the pseudonym 'Banjo'. His poem 'The Man from Snowy River' was first published in the magazine in April 1890. In his lifetime, in Australia, Paterson was second only to Rudyard Kipling in popularity among poets writing in English.

By the late nineteenth century, a more defined Australian style was also apparent in the colonies' paintings. Most notable was the emergence of the Heidelberg School, named after a camp set up by the impressionist painters Tom Roberts and Arthur Streeton on the rural outskirts of Melbourne. Their paintings, and those of others such as Frederick McCubbin and Charles Conder, captured the raw emotion and the stark reality of the Australian landscape, and moved away from the idyllic green that typified European painted scenery. Their most recognised paintings involve scenes of pastoral and outback Australia, with its distinctive colours, pale and glowing shadows, and heat-haze from Australia's brilliant sunlight.

*

After several years, a renewed push for nationhood came not from the politicians or parliaments but from the people – and specifically from a little border town between New South Wales and Victoria on the Murray River.

At the end of July 1893, more than two years after the drafting of Australia's first constitution, a local 'Federation League' organised a public conference in the town of Corowa to promote the idea of federal union. The Federation Leagues had first begun to appear after it had become apparent that parliaments were failing to follow through with the issue. They were non-official, public organisations acting as pressure groups, campaign centres and event organisers with the aim:

> to advance the cause of federation of the Australian colonies by an organisation of citizens owning no class, distinction or party influence, which shall use its best energies to assist parliamentary action ... to advocate, promote and (after its attainment) to defend the federal union of Australia ...[5]

The Corowa conference was organised by John Quick, a forty-one-year-old lawyer from Bendigo, 200 kilometres further to the south-west, on the Victorian side of the border. Quick, who was described by Deakin as 'handsome, sturdy and intelligent',[6] was born in Cornwall in 1852 and had been brought to Australia by his parents when he was two years old. His father had gone directly to the Bendigo goldfields but soon became ill and died. Young John was brought up by his mother but left school at ten years of age to work in a variety of labouring jobs, including in an iron foundry, in the mines, and in the print room of the *Bendigo Evening News*, where he developed a love of journalism. In 1874, he matriculated and, with the help of a scholarship, graduated in law at Melbourne University in 1878. Two years later, he first entered the Victorian Parliament as a member for Bendigo and became an early advocate of Federation. In 1893, he established the Bendigo Federation League and became its president.

The seventy-two delegates who attended the two-day conference came almost entirely from Victoria and New South Wales, and included Victoria's premier, James Patterson, plus a number of other senior politicians. On the first day, the League met in Corowa's Globe Hotel, where it was welcomed by William Lyne, the minister for public works in the New South Wales Parliament. In the evening, there was a large public meeting in the town's Oddfellows Hall, where motions were passed calling for Federation, and the following day the conference resumed in the town's courthouse.

On the second day, when the meeting resumed, John Quick put forward what became known as the 'Corowa Plan'. He called for a new approach: no longer was national union to be left in the hands of politicians.

Quick proposed that elections be held in each colony so that the public could select delegates to frame a new constitution, which would then be put back to the people for a vote:

> Each Australian colony should pass an Act ... for the election of representatives to attend ... a ... convention ... to establish a federal constitution for Australia ... [which] should be submitted by some process of referendum to the verdict of each colony.[7]

At the Corowa conference, Quick met and became good friends with twenty-six-year-old Robert Garran from Sydney – another law graduate and a strong advocate of Federation. Garran was the son of Dr Andrew Garran, the editor of *The Sydney Morning Herald*, himself a long-time supporter of the union of the colonies. Later, Quick and Garran wrote the 'Annotated Constitution of the Australian Commonwealth', which was published in 1901 and became a classic, used by constitutional scholars and Federation historians – and both were later knighted for their contribution to the Federation process.

Quick's Corowa Plan was embraced by the meeting, and newspapers covering the conference immediately recognised it as an important event that could not be 'lightly dismissed':[8]

> The Corowa Conference is a step, to some extent an important step, because it is the first taken by the people, as distinct from the politicians ... Once popular interest is aroused, once the politicians see there is capital in the cry, apathy will disappear, and something like a fight to become the chosen champions of the movement will take place among the political leaders of the colonies.[9]

Immediately following the conference, Quick returned to Bendigo and drafted the 'Australian Federal Congress Bill', which he took to present to the Central Federation League that had recently been established in Sydney. In essence, the bill proposed that each colony commit to holding elections for delegates to draft a new national constitution, since there had been no firm commitment to the 1891 version (although no proposal that it be ignored).

When Quick reached Sydney, he met with a number of leading politicians and later said he was surprised to find many in New South Wales less resistant to Federation than people in Victoria believed. With the help of South Australia's premier, Charles Kingston, the Federation League managed to bring on board George Reid, who had become the New South Wales leader in August 1894.

Reid, who had replaced Sir Henry Parkes, was to be both a champion and villain in the story that followed. 'Having previously been a strong opponent to Federation, Reid was cynical enough to see that the tide of public opinion was now running strongly in favour of nationhood.'[10] Deakin suggested that Reid was also forced to run with the issue because it would otherwise mean 'the complete isolation of New South Wales'.[11]

After meeting with the Federation League in Sydney on 12 November 1894, Reid agreed to approach all the other premiers, suggesting they meet to discuss the issue in Hobart early the following year. The four colonies that were still members of the old Federal Council (Queensland, Tasmania, Western Australia and Victoria) were scheduled to meet in Hobart anyway, and Reid was able to persuade the premiers to meet 'informally' at the same time. They agreed, despite being sceptical about New South Wales, whose representatives had of course refused for many years to participate in the regular Federation

Council meetings. South Australia had also stayed out of the Federal Council, because its Legislative Council had rejected a government motion to join some years before, in 1886.[12] However, when George Reid suggested meeting the other four colonies in Hobart, South Australia's pro-Federation premier Charles Kingston readily agreed, saying his colony would 'not fail to be represented at any federal gathering'.[13]

The following January, Reid travelled by train to Melbourne and with the other mainland premiers caught the steamship *Pateena* to Launceston.[14] When they arrived, they were officially welcomed by the Tasmanian treasurer, Philip Fysh, and former premier, Adye Douglas. That afternoon, the entire party, which included all the visiting premiers, their servants and some of their wives, caught the train to Hobart, and the following Tuesday morning the premiers began their discussions in the Tasmanian chief secretary's office while the Federal Council met separately in the nearby Legislative Council.

On Tuesday 29 January 1895, they met at the exclusive, 'gentlemen only' Tasmanian Club to finalise their historic resolution, which, based on the 'Corowa Plan', would allow for the people to decide who shaped the nation's constitution.[15]

In anticipation of a momentous decision, journalists from all the colonies and from the international news agency Reuters 'besieged the clubhouse'.[16] However, given the conservative nature of the club, the press were denied 'the offer of the common hospitality of a room and chair each'[17] and were forced to wait throughout the day and into the evening outside on Hobart's Macquarie Street until late that night.

At around 10.30 pm, Reid appeared at the front door of the club and from the top of its steps read out the premiers' resolution. Popular elections were to be held in the colonies to decide who would draft a national constitution, and after it was drafted it would be submitted to the people for a vote.[18] The detailed, five-point resolution stated that, if acceptable to three or more colonies, the constitution would be sent to the Queen for the necessary laws to be passed by the British Parliament.

There were some important qualifications from Western Australia and Queensland that would have a major bearing on later developments. Queensland's premier, Hugh Nelson, said that, while he supported the resolution, it should be left to each colony to decide how the delegates should be elected or appointed. Western Australia's John Forrest said he agreed that Federation 'was the great and principal question' but he was opposed to the idea of a popularly elected convention and believed the colonies' parliaments should have the first and final say in a national constitution.

The premiers made one important change to Quick's Corowa plan, which had called for the process to be left entirely in the public's hands. They added a new provision: the elected delegates, having drafted their constitution, should submit the draft to each of the colonial parliaments, which could then suggest changes before it was put to the public for a vote.

At last, there was an agreed path to nationhood. However, this time, the premiers secured a promise from George Reid that his colony would commit first:

Messrs. Turner [Victoria], Nelson [Queensland], Kingston [South Australia], and Sir Edward Braddon [Tasmania] intimated that as soon as New South Wales had passed the bill their Governments would introduce measures providing for the same objects, Mr. Nelson reserving the right to dispense with the direct reference to the electors required by the second object of the bill.[19]

George Reid agreed, claiming he expected little difficulty because the issue was 'almost past the point of speechifying'.

In fact, back in Sydney there was still a great deal of antipathy being expressed, particularly among conservative politicians, and it would be another nine months before the matter reached parliament. The bill to allow for the election of delegates to draft the constitution was first debated on 23 October and was eventually passed two days before Christmas. During the debate, the leader of the parliamentary opposition, William Lyne, attacked Premier Reid, pointing out that Reid had been a constant opponent of Federation and had been personally responsible for the failure of the earlier attempt in 1891:

> If there was anyone in the community who had delayed Federation and had been a block in the way it was the present Premier . . . it was only about four years ago that the Premier had declared in the most unmistakable terms that he would attempt to destroy the government . . . if an attempt was made to go on with the Commonwealth Bill . . . The Premier had been an unmistakable opponent of Federation in any shape or form, and, despite any effort he might now make to the contrary, he could not be looked upon seriously.[20]

Reid later admitted he had been 'one of the strongest opponents to the bill' but said that previously it had the fatal flaw of not being embraced with any enthusiasm by the public at large, as they would a 'cricket match or a boat race':[21]

The Bill of 1891, whatever our opinions might be as to the merits of its provisions, was a very able measure, splendidly drafted, but the movement had lacked one essential element, and that was the earnest adherence to the Federal movement by the great body of the people.[22]

*

For several years after the 1891 conference, Henry Parkes had tried to keep the flame of Federation alive by travelling around the country giving speeches. In 1895, he stood again for parliament against George Reid but lost. Shortly afterwards, on 11 July, his second wife, Eleanor, died of cancer, aged only thirty-eight. Parkes was devastated, yet within four months, aged eighty-one, he married for a third time – to his late wife's maid who had served the past four years as a domestic in his house, twenty-three-year-old Julia Lynch. The new Mrs Parkes was described as 'tall in stature, probably about 5ft. 4in., and of fine figure, with a pleasant homely face, bright blue eyes, with dark nut-brown hair . . . wonderfully healthy', and 'possessing all the physical qualities and disposition of a lady, well-educated, mild-mannered, with none of the predilections of the ordinary domestic'.[23] She was said to be very attractive. According to press reports, the Parkes children were very upset about him marrying Julia, who was nearly sixty years his junior:

Sir Henry Parkes was married to Miss Julia Lynch, at Parramatta yesterday. The bride had for years been employed in Sir Henry's house. She is 23 years of age, and is very prepossessing in appearance. Sir Henry, who is 82 [sic] years of age, lost his second wife on July 11 last. Sir Henry's family are disgusted with the marriage. Two of his daughters have left home and the family governess has resigned her situation and left the house.[24]

Just under a month after Eleanor had died, Parkes had spoken in Adelaide about the women's vote, saying, 'We cannot term ourselves a democracy as long as we exclude half the human race from the franchise ... I admit women's claim to the franchise because of their common humanity as intelligent, responsible members of the community.' (A year and a half later, South Australia became the second place in the world after New Zealand to grant women the vote.) Soon afterwards, Parkes caught a chill that quickly developed into pneumonia, and on 27 April 1896 the great man passed away, a month short of his eighty-first birthday, 'with his hand clasped in that of his wife', Julia.[25]

At the news of his death, the newspapers in Britain as well as throughout the colonies applauded his achievements. The *Illustrated London News* said he was 'the most remarkable product of Australian development'; the London *Morning Post* said he was Australia's 'foremost statesman'; and the London *Daily Graphic* labelled him, 'the Gladstone of Australia'. Even Parkes's old adversary George Reid was generous in his praise, describing him as 'the greatest, so far as an Australian statesman' and 'the one colossal figure in public life in Australia'.[26]

*

Despite the passing of the legislation to elect delegates to draft another national constitution, there was no move to set a date for their election until the following year, when the people spoke out again. This time, it was at a public conference calling itself the Peoples' Federal Convention, which was held between 16 and 21 November 1896 in the New South Wales town of Bathurst, some 200 kilometres from Sydney, on the western side of the Blue Mountains. It was now almost three years since the Corowa convention and almost two since the premiers' Hobart agreement.

Organised in only six weeks by a newly established 'Bathurst People's Federation League', the convention attracted 200 delegates, including George Reid, Edmund Barton and Alfred Deakin, who crowded into the town and 'taxed the local hotel accommodation to its utmost capacity'. At the opening, the mayor of Bathurst, Dr Thomas Machattie, spoke of 'the spontaneous effort of a people crying aloud for more light, and refusing to rest until it was granted'.[27]

According to the newspapers, Bathurst was successful in 're-oxygenating' Federation and restoring it 'to a robust and energetic life'.[28] Within weeks, four colonies – New South Wales, Victoria, Tasmania and South Australia – finally committed to hold the public elections in March 1897 for delegates to be sent to a convention to draft the constitution.

Western Australia, as Forrest had warned at the Hobart premiers' conference, did not agree to an election but would have the parliament decide on their representatives to the convention. Queensland, where there was still a lower level of enthusiasm in the community about the idea of nationhood, did not hold an election either, and nor did its politicians agree to send a delegation to help draft the constitution.[29]

Tasmania was the first to pass the legislation for the popular election of delegates. Within months of the Hobart meeting, and without waiting for New South Wales, the bill was introduced into the parliament in August 1895 and had passed through all stages by 9 January 1896. The colony then waited more than a year for New South Wales and the other parliaments to catch up.

Of the thirty-two candidates who nominated for the ten elected Tasmanian positions, twenty-five were parliamentarians: twelve from the House of Assembly and thirteen from the Legislative Council. Former premier Philip Fysh, now the colonial treasurer, and veteran of the constitutional convention in Sydney, topped the poll. In second spot was the current premier, sixty-eight-year-old Sir Edward Braddon, about whom Alfred Deakin commented:

Sir Edward Braddon, brother of the lady novelist of the same name and himself author of a book of sporting adventure ... slight, erect, stiff, with the walk of a horseman and the carriage of a soldier, he had the manner of a diplomat and the face of a mousquetaire. An iron-grey lock fell artistically forward upon his forehead, bright grey eyes gleamed from under rather bushy eyebrows, a straight nose leading to a heavy moustache and a Vandyke beard. If his locks had been longer his whole appearance would have admirably suited a Cavalier costume ... He was a most amiable cynic, an accomplished strategist and an expert administrator ... An admirable negotiator, a devoted whist player, an indefatigable sportsman and thorough man of the world ...[30]

The election in New South Wales was announced soon after Christmas and held on 4 March 1897. The poll caused great excitement as the voters decided which of the forty-nine candidates would take the ten positions. During the campaign, public meetings attracted the 'largest gatherings in years',[31] and supporters of both sides made bold claims at these gatherings and in letters to the newspapers. Advocates of Federation claimed it would protect white

Australians from 'Asiatic incursions', bring 'unparalleled success' to Australia, 'rid all sorts of bitterness' between the colonies and 'bring happiness and the blessing of God'.[32] Opponents claimed that hard-fought liberties would be lost, that 'Federamania' had become a 'raging mental' epidemic and that the populace was allowing itself to be 'led like lambs to slaughter'.[33]

More than half of those eligible turned out to vote, well exceeding expectations,[34] and on the night of the election *The Bulletin* reported that 'half of Sydney turned out to watch the results as they arrived, and where the figures were exhibited, the streets were practically impassable'.[35]

In a pattern that would be followed in all of the colonies' elections, the 'people's' delegates came overwhelmingly from the ranks of serving and former politicians. Edmund Barton, who had assumed the role of leader of the Federation movement following the death of Henry Parkes, topped the poll and became the first person in any Australian colony to attract more than 100,000 votes.

The other successful New South Wales candidates were also well-known public figures, and three – William McMillan, Joseph Abbott and former New South Wales premier George Dibbs – were veterans of the constitutional convention of 1891. It was a formidable team, which Deakin described as 'absolutely one of dominance and supremacy from first to last'.[36]

The South Australian election was marked by having the first woman candidate to stand for office in Australia now that the colony had granted women the vote. Seventy-one-year-old preacher, writer and feminist Catherine Helen Spence was born in Scotland in 1825 and had migrated with her family to Adelaide when she was fourteen years old. In the election, she campaigned on the sole issue of a change in the voting system for 'proportional representation'.

At the election, she failed to poll among the top ten but came a creditible twenty-second out of thirty.

The successful South Australian candidates were a mixture of liberals and conservatives. At the top of the poll was the forty-seven-year-old premier, Charles Kingston. He was followed by the colony's treasurer Frederick Holder and former premier John Cockburn. Alfred Deakin said that 'on all-round ability the South Australian delegation was undoubtedly the strongest', and five of their team had been at the constitution convention in 1891 – Charles Kingston, John Cockburn, Richard Baker, John Gordon and John Downer. He also pointed out that, at the next convention, which was held in Adelaide, South Australia was able to play a valuable role as a broker between the two most populous colonies (Victoria and New South Wales) and the two least (Tasmania and Western Australia).

As was the case in the other colonies, the election race in Victoria was contested entirely by a field of politicians. Of the twenty-nine candidates, twenty-five were current or former members of parliament, and the remainder were mayors or shire presidents. During the election, most of the candidates were promoted on 'tickets' run by the *Age* and *Argus* newspapers and Trades Hall, which promoted the Labor candidates. *The Age*'s recommended 'ticket' picked all ten winners, including Victorian premier Sir George Turner, who topped the ballot. Turner had become the first Australian-born premier of Victoria in 1894.[37] His Victorian colleague Alfred Deakin described him as a hard worker and a good lawyer but an 'average man . . . the ideal bourgeois who married early and who was in dress, manner and habits exactly on the same level as the shopkeepers and prosperous artisans who were his ratepayers and constituents'.[38]

In addition to Turner and Deakin, the Victorian delegation included John Quick, Isaac Isaacs, the son of an immigrant tailor, and the relatively unknown Henry Higgins, who had only been a member of the Victorian Legislative Assembly for three years. Both Isaacs and Higgins would later serve on Australia's High Court; Higgins would be centrally involved in drafting the Australian constitution, and would later be a member of the first national parliament before becoming a judge on the bench of the first High Court.

On 7 May 1896, Western Australia's premier John Forrest wrote confidentially to his ministers saying that, if Western Australia was to think about joining the union at a later date, it should try to have 'a large influence in guiding its proceedings' at the forthcoming convention. But if they did not like the outcome, he said, 'we need not proceed any further'.[39]

As Forrest had indicated in Hobart, the colony did not hold a public election for its delegates. John Forrest had decided Western Australia's delegates would be chosen by the colony's forty-six members of parliament. Thirty men nominated for the ballot held in March 1897. All ten of the successful candidates were current or past parliamentarians, were reasonably well off, and most had extensive pastoral and other business interests. Most were born in the colony or had lived there for some years.

Unsurprisingly, Forrest topped the poll, with forty-five of the possible forty-six votes, having presumably not voted for himself. The next highest votes went to George Steere and opposition leader George Leake. The tenth and final slot, with only seventeen of the forty-six votes, went to John Taylor, a young Englishman who had amassed a fortune as a gold stockbroker on the Western Australian goldfields. It is believed Forrest worked for his election to ensure some representation of the growing population on the diggings.

Queensland was the only colony that did not select or elect candidates and did not send delegates to the subsequent meetings to design the national constitution. Premier Hugh Nelson had attended the 1895 Hobart conference called by George Reid, and agreed with the other premiers that Federation was 'the great and pressing question of Australian politics'.[40] However, he did not believe the delegates should be chosen by popular vote and was unable to get agreement about proceeding from the Queensland Parliament: his proposal to the parliament to send a delegation was defeated by a vote of twenty-one to nineteen.[41]

*

The fifty delegates from New South Wales, Victoria, Tasmania, South Australia and Western Australia met in Adelaide on 22 March 1897 to begin the task of writing the new constitution. At the last minute, Queensland had sent a message to say that if the convention could be postponed they may be able to participate at a later date, but the assembled delegates decided to go ahead anyway.

At first, Melbourne had been the favoured location for the convention – not only by the Victorians but also by Reid, because Melbourne was where he enjoyed taking his holidays. However, Kingston made a claim for Adelaide as no federal gathering had yet taken place there.[42] He had already secured the support of Tasmania's Edward Braddon, as Adelaide was on the way to London where Braddon and other premiers planned to go after the convention for Queen Victoria's Diamond Jubilee celebrations. Western Australia's John Forrest also threw its weight behind South Australia's claim. Reid persisted with the argument that Adelaide was 'an inconvenient place' but relented when he realised the majority would be happy to meet there.[43]

The Western Australians travelled by train to Albany and then by steamboat to Adelaide. The delegates from New South Wales and Tasmania joined the Victorian delegates in Melbourne on a special train to Adelaide, consisting of 'three boudoir cars, a Victorian department car and two long carriages fitted up with sleepers'.[44] At Murray Bridge the next morning, the delegates were given a 'capital breakfast' and an Adelaide *Advertiser* newspaper, a copy of the South Australian Railway Guide, and two free tickets to Adelaide Zoo.[45]

When they arrived on Sunday morning, they were met by a large crowd and an official welcoming committee that included Charles Kingston and other leading South Australian figures. As George Reid and Edmund Barton got off the train with George Turner and Edward Braddon, the crowd cheered. Adelaide's John Downer described the scene as 'almost like the home-coming of the Australian [cricket] eleven'.[46]

As the week began, the South Australians went to great lengths to demonstrate they were elegant hosts. On the Monday, after the convention's official opening, the delegates were invited to Government House to witness 'the performance of Hindoo jugglers, listened to the strains of the police band and partook of afternoon tea on the east lawns'.[47]

All of the men wore the customary dark suits but each wore bright buttonholes of flowers in their lapels to distinguish them as delegates to the convention:

Nearly all the representatives wore bright bouquets in their button holes ... in a style which made known to the spectators how fully the duly accredited constitution builders recognize the dignity and responsibility of the momentous task on which they are engaged.[48]

The following night, a lavish banquet was held at Jubilee Exhibition Hall for 200 male guests, including the 'leading lights' of Australasia:

> Its walls have witnessed many brilliant scenes and surrounded many great gatherings, but probably none so notable as that which took place on Tuesday evening. Flowers, flags and foliage had completely transformed the internal appearance of the hall and its brilliant lighted and heavily loaded tables were as pleasing to the sight as the temptingly displayed victuals and viands subsequently proved acceptable to the palate.[49]

When the delegates got down to business, Edmund Barton was elected 'leader of the convention', and was asked to 'shepherd' the meeting.[50] Deakin said there were antagonisms within several of the delegations, and within the New South Wales team, Premier Reid 'cherished some resentment' towards his rival Barton: 'Reid could not forget that although Premier of New South Wales he held but the second place to Barton in the national poll, watching events with an evident determination to attain what he considered his due position in the convention.'[51]

However, Reid reluctantly accepted Barton's 'selection as inevitable' and Deakin conjectured that Reid 'knew perfectly well that he had neither the constitutional knowledge, capacity as draftsman nor unwearying industry that were essentials in a leader. He would only have exposed his own weakness and have been at the mercy of better qualified critics.'[52]

There were even greater tensions within the South Australian delegation, particularly between Premier Kingston and the president of the colony's Legislative Council, Richard Baker. Five years before, Kingston had challenged Baker to a duel and had been arrested walking with a loaded revolver in his pocket on the way to the site he had nominated. The dispute had started when Baker had denounced Kingston as 'a coward, a bully and a disgrace to the legal profession'. Kingston had responded by describing Baker as 'treacherous', 'mendacious' and 'utterly untrustworthy in every relationship of public life'. Kingston had then procured a pair of matched pistols, one of which he sent to Baker accompanied by a letter appointing the time for a duel in Victoria Square, Adelaide, on 23 December 1892. Baker had informed the police, who arrested Kingston shortly after he arrived, carrying a loaded revolver. Amid widespread publicity, he was tried and bound over to keep the peace for twelve months. The sentence was still in force when Kingston became premier in June 1893.[53]

George Reid of New South Wales later made the observation that Kingston seemed to 'arouse ridiculous hatreds amongst his political opponents' but was 'a delightful companion for everyone else'.[54]

Alfred Deakin admitted there were also tensions within his own Victorian delegation and that he had a poor opinion of his leader, Premier George Turner:

> [he is] bourgeois in his uprightness, straightforwardness, domestic happiness and regularity of habits . . . he never read a book and . . . had no hobbies, no amusements and no diversions. He ate, slept and worked . . . He had no enthusiasms and no vices . . . Ambitious, secretive and impressionable, he was timid and inclined to be envious.[55]

Early in the convention's proceedings, Charles Kingston read a message he had received from Joseph Chamberlain, the secretary of state for the colonies in London, which made the British Government's wishes clear:

> I have received Her Majesty's command to desire you to acquaint the Federal Convention that she takes a special interest in their proceedings and hopes that under Divine guidance their labours will result in practical benefit to Australia. I desire to add my own cordial wishes for a successful result, which will conduce to the dignity and strength of the Empire.[56]

On the same morning, South Australia's John Cockburn read out a resolution from the 8000-strong Women's Christian Temperance Union, calling for the constitution to include votes for women: 'That this executive representing the Women's Christian Temperance Union ... earnestly urges the Federal Convention of Australasia to secure in the Federal Constitution the provision that all voting by electors for Federal Parliaments be upon the basis of equal voting rights for both sexes.'[57]

Not all the delegations agreed with women's suffrage, but when Tasmania's Sir Edward Braddon told the convention 'women have no right to take part in parliamentary elections', there was a 'shower of interjections' from other delegates who disagreed with his views.[58]

Once the convention got down to business, its delegates decided to write a completely fresh constitution. However, seventeen of the fifty delegates in Adelaide had been at the 1891 convention, which gave the Adelaide meeting a source of great experience and knowledge, and in reality the 1891 draft was used as the point of departure.

The men met for twenty-five days from Monday 22 March 1897, starting on most days at 10.30 am and finishing at 5.30 pm, with a break for lunch between 1 and 2 pm. The sessions were suspended on 23 April (formally adjourned on 5 May) because the premiers and many of the other delegates had to travel to London to be part of the British Empire's first Intercolonial Conference. The conference was timed to coincide with Queen Victoria's Diamond Jubilee – the seventy-eight-year-old monarch was celebrating being on the throne for sixty years on 20 June 1897, during which time the British Empire had become the greatest power the world had ever seen. In the previous year, 1896, she had surpassed her grandfather George III to become the longest-reigning monarch in British history.

The Adelaide sessions were productive: the delegates were able to take back a complete draft constitution to their parliaments and it was agreed to resume the convention in Sydney the following September, after the jubilee celebrations.

In England, the leaders of all the Empire's self-governing dominions joined the Australian premiers for the jubilee procession through London. Ten minutes ahead of Queen Victoria, each was carried in a carriage 'drawn by four richly-caparisoned horses' and escorted by a contingent of their own colony's troops, from Buckingham Palace to St Paul's Cathedral. Once at the cathedral, they were given front-row seats with 'a splendid view', where they were 'able to salute the sovereign'.[59]

The premiers were caught up in the swirl of the pomp and ceremony of the Great British Empire at its zenith. The Australian colonial press was effusive about the celebrations and the reception given to the colonial representatives:

Words cannot adequately describe the celebration. The good old queen had a magnificent reception all along the line of the procession. Next to the queen the most enthusiastic greetings were given to the Colonial premiers and the Colonial troops. In fact it has been a noticeable feature ever since they began to reach England that no welcome could be too hearty. In the case of the premiers they have been feted in all parts of the kingdom and have been presented to the Queen.[60]

Among the many highlights of the jubilee was a banquet for the premiers at the Mansion House attended by the prime minister, the Third Marquess of Salisbury, the secretary of state for the colonies Joseph Chamberlain and other senior British figures. As premier of the senior colony, New South Wales, George Reid gave a speech in which he said he hoped at the next conference back in Australia that the colonies would agree to unite and that 'federation of the Australian colonies would strengthen the ties with Empire'.[61]

When the premiers sailed back to Sydney to resume the constitutional convention, expectations of the talks were high, and the local press urged Reid to get on with the job of federal union:

He returns just in time to take his place in the coming session of the Federal Convention. Whatever else the Premier may have learnt during his stay in London . . . the supreme lesson . . . must be that of the strength and security derived from union . . . If the Premier went away a federationist, he must come back with his federal faith strengthened and justified by all that he has seen . . .[62]

Reid arrived back on 1 September aboard the Royal Mail steamship *Miowera*. The bulk of the other convention delegates had arrived earlier in the day on a special overnight train from Melbourne, 'and a very large crowd was present to catch a sight of the distinguished visitors. The government had arranged for special carriages to convey the delegates to their hotels, and as they departed, the crowd sent up some hearty cheers.'[63] That evening, there was a torchlight procession and a citizens' demonstration in Sydney Town Hall in support of federal union. Most of the premiers attended and, after the lord mayor of Sydney spoke, George Reid responded, 'to a great ovation' from the crowd.

The Sydney convention opened the following morning in the New South Wales Legislative Assembly in Macquarie Street, with Edmund Barton again the leader of proceedings. For the event, new carpet had been laid, new gaslights installed, and the benches and tables re-polished to make the 'dingy Chamber look bright and comfortable'.[64]

Again, before they started there was another request from Queensland to defer the conference. Sir Samuel Griffith had written seeking the deferral but, after considering a suggestion that the meeting be held over to early the following year to give time for Queensland to vote to participate, the delegates decided to press on.[65]

Alfred Deakin said that when the convention resumed, the discussions were very different: 'it was not only a change of scene and of climate but of the whole spirit, temper and attitude of the convention'.[66] The first matters to consider were the suggested changes from the colonies to the bill that had come out of the Adelaide meeting. While the premiers had been in London, all the colonial legislatures had deliberated on Adelaide's draft constitution and had suggested a total of nearly 300 amendments.

For three weeks, debate was dominated by arguments about what limits should be put on the power of the Senate to decide on federal income and expenditure matters – the so-called 'money bills'. In the last week, the focus was on how differences between the Federal House of Representatives and the Senate might be resolved. Then the session was again adjourned because the Victorian delegation had to go home for a general election. Before winding up, it was agreed, after some argument, to meet again early in the new year in Melbourne to finish the job.

The Victorian election was held on 25 October, and George Turner's government, campaigning on the promise that, if re-elected, they would ensure Victoria a period of 'rest and quiet', was returned to office, though with a reduced majority.

On 20 January 1898, the convention resumed in Melbourne for what was to be the longest session of all: thirty-seven days. The official record of the eleven weeks of deliberations of the three sessions held in Adelaide, Sydney and Melbourne ran into more than 5000 pages. Much of the arguments in Melbourne concentrated on the distribution of specific powers between the new national, or Commonwealth, government and the colonies, which would become states. There was also considerable debate about how surplus revenue raised by the new national government would be given over to the states. During the discussions, the issue of the national government's powers over the colonies was again debated; old age and invalid pensions were also added, as were industrial-relations arbitration powers. There was no argument about who would be responsible for defence – it had always been accepted that national defence would become a federal responsibility. Most significantly, the convention reached agreement that, in the event of a deadlock between the proposed House of Representatives and the Senate, there would be a double dissolution of both chambers.

One of the major issues left unresolved in Melbourne was the site of the nation's new capital. The New South Wales representatives were adamant it should be in the 'mother' colony, but in the end it was resolved to leave the matter for the first national parliament to decide.

Women were not given the right to vote in the constitution, but women from South Australia and Western Australia were eligible to vote for the first Australian national parliament, which used the voting system of each of the colonies. (All women were given the right to vote in 1902 in Australian national elections with the passing of a new law in the Federal Parliament – one of the first countries to do so. Shortly afterwards, all the states granted women the vote, and by 1911 all states had universal suffrage.)

After all the work and extensive redrafting, the result was similar to the structure of the 1891 constitution, but with some significant changes. The national Senate would be directly elected rather than appointed by state parliaments. Ministers would be required to be members of parliament. There were further provisions for breaking a deadlock between the House of Representatives and the Senate. The new draft constitution defined clearer powers for the Commonwealth in interstate arbitration. The Australian High Court was a creation of the constitution. The 1897 draft constitution more clearly describes the powers of parliament.

The meeting worked through until 4 am on Saturday 12 March 1898 and reconvened at 11 am to finish the draft.[67] Almost exactly ten years after Sir Henry Parkes had started the process with his Tenterfield oration, a relieved Alfred Deakin recorded, 'after an all-night's sitting and under conditions of great nervous exhaustion and irritability we have practically completed the draft Bill for the Constitution of the Australian Commonwealth'.[68]

At a banquet in Melbourne Town Hall during this final session, Reid spoke for everyone when he pledged:

> We have now come to the most critical stage of our great work. Now ... it will be possible for me and the other leaders ... to go to our respective colonies and to use every influence we possess in recommending the constitution for the adoption of the people of the colonies'.[69]

There was little celebration. The process had been exhausting, and most of the delegates were relieved and happy to be going home. *The Sydney Morning Herald* summed up the mood by describing Premier Forrest as he boarded a train in Melbourne bound for Adelaide: 'The only expression to which he would give an unrestricted utterance was one of thankfulness that the convention was over.'[70]

The delegates must also have felt satisfied. The 'stern and eventful moment', as *The Argus* described it, had come to Australia.[71] The men had reached agreement on the plan for the nation and they were all committed to ensuring their colonies adopted the constitution.

However, all was not as well as it seemed.

CHAPTER 14

VOTING FOR NATIONHOOD

*Mr. Reid['s] ... rotund figure and indispensable
eyeglass provoked groans, loud and deep, each time
they appeared on the screen.*

THREE MONTHS AFTER THE CONVENTION WOUND UP, NEW
South Wales, Victoria, Tasmania and South Australia took
the new constitution to referenda to be voted on by their
people. New South Wales, Victoria and Tasmania called
the poll for Friday 3 June 1898; South Australia the following day.

Queensland and Western Australia were still lagging
behind. In Queensland, there remained an absence of
enthusiasm or any sizeable groundswell of support for
uniting with the other colonies; in Western Australia the
conservative political leadership was still deeply suspicious
that Federation would be more harmful than beneficial to

the colony, and its premier John Forrest would still not agree to put the matter to the public for a vote.[1]

Campaigning was passionate for both the 'yes' and the 'no' vote in each of the colonies. A new feature of the referenda campaigns was the emergence of women in the political arena. It was now three years since women had been given the right to vote in South Australia, and for the last decade most colonies had had branches of the Women's Christian Temperance Union, which was a strong advocate of Federation and petitioned for governmental controls on alcohol and the recognition of God in the constitution. By the mid-1890s, there was a proliferation of such women's benevolent, charitable and literary societies: other prominent ones were Women's Suffrage Leagues and, by 1898, in Sydney, the Women's Federation League. The Woman's Suffrage Leagues generally supported Federation but some of their branches and members campaigned for the 'no' vote. Most notable among these was Rose Scott in New South Wales. A fifty-two-year-old suffragette, Scott was born in 1847 in Singleton in the Hunter Valley, north of Sydney. Well educated by her mother, she was a renowned beauty who remained single and later claimed life was too short to waste in service to one man.[2] In Sydney, she became quite a social celebrity, and her house in Woollahra a well-known salon that attracted intellectuals, artists, philosophers, judges and politicians. During the referendum campaign, her speeches were enthusiastically reported by the anti-Federation *Daily Telegraph*. Scott argued that Federation would expose Australia to a greater risk of war, would result in increased taxation and mean a higher cost of living in New South Wales. Federation would be a financial disaster, Scott concluded, unless, of course, the federal treasurer was a woman.[3]

Scott's was not the only prominent opposition to Federation in the colony, and the supporters of the 'no' vote – the so-called 'anti-Billites' – were well-organised and campaigned effectively. The 'yes' campaigners in New South Wales faced an added difficulty: the conservative parliamentarians of the colony had successfully persuaded the parliament to attach a condition that, in addition to achieving a majority, the 'yes' vote had to exceed 80,000.

The 'yes' campaign in New South Wales got off to a bad start when George Reid addressed a meeting at Sydney's Town Hall on 28 March, ten days after coming home from Melbourne. The widely reported meeting attracted a huge crowd: *The Sydney Morning Herald* reported that between 4000 and 5000 people attended, and claimed it was 'one of the largest political meetings ever'.[4]

The delegates were warmly received by the large audience, but the loudest cheers were for Reid, who was at the time at the height of his political popularity: 'The audience rose and cheered again and again, hats and handkerchiefs being waved in the air. The Premier politely bowed his acknowledgments, [as] the mayor at once proceeded to introduce Mr. Reid.'[5]

Reid held the audience for over two hours, going through the proposed constitution section by section, explaining what it meant. Rather surprisingly, considering he had pledged at the Melbourne meeting to use every influence he could to recommend the constitution to his people, Reid then began to highlight what he thought were the flaws of the bill. He said it was 'not perfect': it was not democratic enough and Federation would be especially financially injurious to New South Wales because they would have to pay 'above a fair share' of the cost of nationhood. He also said the national House of Representatives would not have 'sufficient superiority' over the Senate on taxation and spending decisions, and the Senate would become too powerful. Nor did he like the 'rigidity' of the provisions for amending the constitution. He concluded by saying that he would vote 'yes' in the referendum: 'So far as I am concerned, with all the criticisms I have levelled at this Bill, with all the fears I have for the future, I feel I cannot become a deserter from the cause of federation.'

But, at the same time, he told the audience they were entitled to something better:

> I cannot take up this bill with enthusiasm. I see serious blots in it which have put a severe strain upon me . . . Because after all, great as a nation's worth is, great as an Australian union is . . . in a continent as free as this, we ought to have, I admit a more democratic constitution.

At the conclusion of the speech, he not only failed to call for a 'yes' vote but also made it clear that people should not feel they had to vote for the bill: 'Having shown you the dark places as well as the light places of this constitution, I hope every man in this country, without coercion from me, without any interference from me, will judge for himself . . .'[6]

Reid had reneged on public commitments to do everything within his power to support the 'yes' vote. His mixed message was to prove a major problem in the referendum in New South Wales and would earn him the nickname of 'Yes–No Reid' and the distrust of his intercolonial colleagues. Within days of his Sydney Town Hall speech, rumours were published in some of the other colonial newspapers suggesting that Reid deliberately undermined the 'yes' vote:

> One of the tales being told in Sydney in connection with the anti-Federation campaign, of which Mr. Reid is said

to be the author, is highly sensational, and very credible to the inventor. It is, that there is a conspiracy in the convention to keep the Federal capital not only in Victoria, but actually in Melbourne . . . the keen eyes of the opponents in Sydney have discerned the plot, and what is more, they have discovered that Mr. Reid knew all about it when he made his now celebrated speech, in which he did all that was in his power to damage the cause he finally pledged himself to support.[7]

For the next two months, the campaign raged between supporters of national union and the 'anti-Billites'.

Supporting the 'yes' vote was the Federal Association, which raised money for campaigning and for the production of special supplements that were circulated with the daily newspapers. The New South Wales Government Printer produced copies of the proposed constitution, with annotated explanations, for every eligible voter in the colony. With Edmund Barton leading the campaign, and with the backing of prominent newspapers, it was increasingly expected that the 'yes' vote would prevail. *The Sydney Morning Herald* ran pro-Federation editorials almost every day before the election, and most of the other newspapers and magazines, including *The Bulletin* and the Melbourne journal *The Review of Reviews*, were strongly in support.

At the head of the 'no' campaign was the 'Anti-Convention Bill League', which had been formed the year before and included among its supporters a number of prominent conservative bankers and businessmen. Many of the anti-Billites said they were in favour of the principle of Federation but strongly opposed 'the present constitution Bill'. In the launch of their 'manifesto', the anti-Billites claimed Federation would be undemocratic and mean the 'birth of minority rule in Australia' because each colony would have the same number of senators in the upper house of the proposed Federal Parliament:

THE DEATH-KNELL OF MAJORITY RULE

The fatal and unchangeable defect of the Convention Bill is that it does not provide for this ... The Senate – or States House ... each state, large or small, is represented by six senators. That is to say, New South Wales, with 1,323,000, Victoria with 1,173,000 ... and Western Australia with 161,000 persons are all placed on a precisely equal footing. The effect of constituting the Senate in this way is to impose an insuperable obstacle in the way of majority rule, and implant in the constitution the seeds of inevitable discord. Seven hundred thousand people in the three smaller states will possess between them 18 senators, whilst two million and a half in the two larger states will be represented by only 12 senators.[8]

The 'no' campaign was also supported by a number of newspapers in Sydney and across the colony. The Sydney *Daily Telegraph* pioneered the use of large, bold headlines, urging anti-Billite supporters 'NO SURRENDER'.[9] Victoria's Alfred Deakin said *The Daily Telegraph* 'shrank from no suggestion, insinuation or assertion that could stimulate hate, fear, cupidity, jealousy, envy or animus of its readers' in its opposition to Federation.[10]

Premier George Reid made two other decisions during the campaign that would further undermine the 'yes' vote. Two months before the referendum, he appointed a committee to examine the financial implications of Federation. The committee included well-known anti-Federationist, doctor, businessman and Sydney University chancellor Sir Henry MacLaurin. It was no surprise when

MacLaurin's committee reported on the eve of the vote that the financial burden of Federation would fall disproportionately on New South Wales.[11]

Reid also made it easier for one of his own government ministers to work full-time promoting the 'no' vote. John Want, Reid's close friend and attorney general, became president of the 'Anti-Convention Bill League'. Reid gave Want permission to stand down from his portfolio to campaign full-time against nationhood, promising to reinstate him as minister immediately after the poll. Want was the member of parliament for the country seat of Gundagai and passionately anti-Federation. He saw it as a 'hydra-headed monster' and said his purpose was to protect New South Wales 'and not sell it into bondage'.[12]

Such was the intense interest in the poll that a public holiday was called on Friday 3 June 1898 and special trams were arranged:

> to bring the people in to the city, and also to convey them back to their homes at night. The steam trams will be run up till midnight or 1 o'clock in the morning if this course should prove necessary.[13]

It was also planned that if the crowds were too dense the trams running up and down Sydney's King Street would be suspended. There was a great deal of interest in the other colonies in the New South Wales result, where it was known that the vote might be close: 'Naturally the interest of all the other colonies was centred on the contest . . . for it is recognised by all Australian statesmen that unless New South Wales accepts the measure there can be no Federation.'[14]

On election night, large crowds gathered outside the *Sydney Morning Herald* office in Sydney's Hunter

Street, and there were also large crowds in Melbourne and Hobart, where voting had taken place on the same day. As the results were telegraphed in from the polling booths and posted on the giant hoarding, it looked like the 'yes' vote would win. At one stage during the evening, the *Herald* incorrectly posted the figure of 80,284 'yes' votes. 'For twenty golden minutes euphoria reigned', as the enthusiastic crowd began celebrating.[15]

When the correct figure of 67,500 'yes' votes was posted, it produced a 'hideous chill'.[16] And, as the evening progressed, it became obvious that the 'yes' vote would not reach the required level of 80,000: 'Then at 8.50 pm Mr. Crichett Walker, the chief returning officer says the convention bill party cannot get more than 72,000, and their chance is hopeless.'[17]

The final count was 'yes': 71,595, or 52 per cent; and 'no': 66,228, or 48 per cent.

*

On the same night in Melbourne, huge crowds gathered to witness the outcome of the Victorian poll. Outside the *Argus* newspaper office, an 'immense hoarding . . . brilliantly illuminated by several arc electric lights' was built and the results posted as the numbers were telegraphed in from the polling booths.

The Argus reported that heavy rain did not dampen the enthusiasm of the crowd:

The scene in front of the *Argus* office last night will be long remembered by all who saw it. In spite of a drizzling, soaking rain, which fell during a greater part of the evening, an enormous crowd collected, and at 9 o'clock, it formed one unbroken mass, extending from the Town

Hall corner to the Baptist church. Viewed from above, the sea of upturned faces presented a striking spectacle. Umbrellas were not allowed, except on the outskirts of the crowd, yet thousands of people were willing to put up with the discomfort in order to watch the progress of the federal fight.[18]

A highlight of the evening was the projection of lighted images onto a big screen, which was on top of the tally board. When Queen Victoria's picture was shown, the 'national anthem was sung from 30,000 throats, and was followed by round after round of cheering'. Pictures of the pro-Federation leaders were also shown, and Edmund Barton 'was the hero of the night' and attracted most cheers. *The Argus* reported Barton was followed in popularity by Deakin and Premier Turner. When a picture was shown of a leading opponent to Federation, Henry Higgins, 'it was greeted with mingled boo-hoos and cheers'. (Though Higgins had been a Victorian delegate to the constitution convention, he campaigned against the bill in 1898.) But the worst response was for George Reid: 'Mr. Reid, whose rotund figure and indispensable eyeglass provoked groans, loud and deep, each time they appeared on the screen.'[19]

The first returns began to come in at 7.15 pm, and from the very start it was clear the 'yes' vote would prevail with a big majority, and the result became a foregone conclusion. At 8.30 pm, the 50,000 minimum was announced, amid great cheering. By 10 pm, Sir George Turner's 'tip' that there would be a four to one majority of 80,000 votes to 20,000 was reached and passed, and thereafter the Federal position was steadily improved.

The final vote in Victoria was 'yes': 100,520, or 82 per cent; and 'no': 22,090, or 18 per cent. Victoria had also easily exceeded the additional requirement it had set for the poll, that the 'yes' vote number more than 50,000.

Every polling booth in Victoria recorded a majority vote, and in some Melbourne suburbs, including St Kilda, Toorak, Hawthorn and Brighton, the 'yes' vote outnumbered the 'no' vote by more than ten to one. Even in the 'strongholds of the opposition' of Collingwood, Fitzroy and Richmond, the majority voted 'yes'.

In Tasmania, the vote was also overwhelming. During the campaign, the 'yes' vote was 11,797, or a little over 80 per cent; and the 'no' vote 2716, or a little under 20 per cent.

In South Australia, a victory for the 'yes' vote was never seriously doubted. The 'yes' vote was 35,950, or around 65 per cent; and the 'no' vote was 17,328, or 35 per cent.

Despite the successes of the 'yes' campaigns in Victoria, Tasmania and South Australia, the failure of the referendum in New South Wales meant the Australian colonies could not federate.

In the days after the debacle in New South Wales, George Reid telegraphed the other premiers, suggesting a meeting. Having all driven successful campaigns in their own colonies, they were outraged at Reid's equivocation, which they believed explained much of the failure in New South Wales. However, they were also well aware that no New South Wales meant no Federation, so eventually they reluctantly agreed to try to sort something out.

But before the premiers could discuss the problem, in the month after the poll, New South Wales faced a general election. Reid's opponent was Edmund Barton and, unsurprisingly, Federation became the driving issue of the campaign. No doubt aware of public opinion, Reid campaigned strongly for a union of the colonies and called his team of candidates the 'Liberal Federal Party'. Barton led a team of candidates called the 'National Federal Party'.

The newspapers portrayed Barton as genuine and Reid as the political opportunist:

> It has been said that Mr. Reid and Mr. Barton both advocate the same policy. If that were so, though it is not, then why does he not follow the federal leader, Mr. Barton – leader in New South Wales, and elected leader of the convention. The differences in policy of the two great men are – Mr Barton has one aim only – Federation; Mr Reid fights for power first, and the federation is his shield.[20]

The Sydney *Evening News* ran a damning chronicle of Reid's opposition to and lack of support for national union, going back more than a decade. It pointed out that, as far back as May 1890, Reid had attacked Henry Parkes's calls for Federation in the parliament. The following year, when the 1891 convention was held, he had accused Parkes of jumping 'from the cliffs of our self-government and independence into the unknown sea of federation'.[21]

Reid was also widely accused of stymying the 1898 referendum by unnecessarily agreeing to the 80,000 minimum 'yes' vote and for giving speeches in Sydney and other major towns highlighting the flaws of the Federation bill. He was criticised as 'insincere' for allowing Federation's greatest critic, John Want, to temporarily leave Cabinet to campaign for the 'no' vote and then readily admitting him back into the government.

In the election held on 27 July 1898, Barton ran head to head against Reid in Reid's seat of East Sydney. Despite all the criticism levelled at him, Reid was a clever and popular politician, and he managed to stave off Barton's challenge to narrowly hold onto his seat. A number of Reid's colleagues lost their seats in the election, but with a reduced majority Reid managed to cobble together a coalition government, which he formed with the help of the emerging Labor Party.

Any satisfaction that Reid might have had about beating Barton was short-lived. Less than two weeks after the election, a Barton supporter, parliamentarian Francis Clarke, announced he would quit his seat of Hastings and Macleay, 400 kilometres north of Sydney, so Barton could win it in a by-election.

Barton gratefully accepted the lifeline and, five days later, in the early morning of Monday 12 September, left Sydney on the steamer *Burrawong*, arriving late the following night at Port Macquarie to run his campaign. The locals were thrilled to have him as their candidate:

> The great event of to-day was the arrival of Mr. Barton. He came up by the steamer *Burrawong* . . . about two hundred persons assembled to meet him, and he addressed a few words from the steamer . . . The public meeting . . . did not begin until 9 o'clock. It was held in the Theatre Royal which was crowded to excess. Mr. Barton met with a magnificent reception, and was accorded a splendid hearing, whilst a vote declaring him to be a fit and proper person to represent the constituency in Parliament was carried with great enthusiasm.[22]

Desperate to keep Barton out of parliament, Reid ran his own candidate, Sydney Smith, and sailed to Port Macquarie on Barton's heels to campaign for his politician. But a week later, in the by-election, Barton beat Smith comfortably, 960 votes to 658.

Barton was immediately elected as leader of the opposition, from which position he could agitate to get Federation back on the agenda. With the election out of the way, Reid wrote another 'eminently friendly letter to his brother premiers asking them to meet him for the purpose of consultation'.[23] So, in Melbourne in January 1899, Reid and the premiers had what was called the 'secret' meeting (because, unlike with earlier conferences and conventions, the public and press were kept from the meeting and no transcript was taken of proceedings) to discuss how New South Wales might ensure a sufficient 'yes' vote in a second referendum.

The premiers knew each other well by now. George Turner, Edward Braddon and Charles Kingston had all been at the constitutional convention with Reid. The only newcomer was the Queensland premier, James Dickson. After an absence from Federation talks for almost a decade, he announced at the Melbourne meeting that he thought Queensland might also join the union.

The sudden re-emergence of Queensland was something of a surprise. Sixty-seven-year-old Dickson was a prosperous and patriarchal retired merchant and a political conservative that the pro-Labor local newspapers nicknamed 'Oily Jimmy'.[24] He had become what many regarded as a stopgap Queensland leader only three months earlier, following the sudden death from pneumonia of Hugh Nelson's replacement, the very popular premier Thomas Byrnes.

Dickson was familiar with federal issues, having been a Queensland delegate to the largely toothless Federal Council more than a decade before. However, he had not at any stage been such a strong advocate of joining a national union before this 1899 meeting. At the end of the meeting, he caused some surprise when he said, 'As it now stands, I think the measure has a good prospect of being accepted by the Queensland people.'[25]

A local newspaper rather unkindly suggested the parochial Dickson had 'converted to Federation as a provincial politician who had never been able to project himself very far from [Brisbane's] Queen Street throughout his political life'.[26]

Turner consulted Deakin throughout the conference, and also the highly regarded thirty-two-year-old Robert Garran, who had helped draft the constitution bill since emerging as a significant player at the People's Convention in Corowa three years before.

Edmund Barton was not invited to the conference. But he was greatly admired by all the other premiers and, while on holiday in Adelaide and then Melbourne, managed to meet up with them discreetly for talks.

The premiers continued to be suspicious of Reid, and Deakin said Reid came to the conference 'trembling' and 'at the mercy' of the others.[27] Nonetheless, during the meeting, Reid managed to persuade the others that New South Wales needed something to offer the voters at another referendum. The concessions included a change to how differences could be settled between the national House of Representatives and the Senate, and a time limit of ten years on surplus revenue raised by the national government being paid back to the states. But the big concession involved the location of the national capital. In earlier negotiations and conferences, no agreement had been reached and it had been decided that it would be left to the new national parliament to determine. Now the premiers were persuaded to agree that:

The seat of Government of the Commonwealth shall be determined by the Parliament and shall be within territory that shall have been granted to or acquired by the Commonwealth and shall be vested in and belong to the Commonwealth, and shall be in the state of New South Wales and be distant not less than one hundred miles from Sydney.[28]

So sensitive was the issue that the deal had to be locked into the Australian constitution. Reid then tried unsuccessfully to persuade the other premiers that they need not have a second referendum so the people could decide on the changes. Kingston wrote to Turner to say:

> It would be absolutely indefensible I think to alter the popular decision by Parliamentary vote without direct confirmation by the people by fresh referendum . . . Reid's proposal [is] to set aside the verdict of the people for the purpose of, behind their backs, securing better terms for New South Wales at the instance of a minority in that State. We will have nothing to do with it.[29]

He also wrote directly to Reid accusing him of sabotaging the referendum in order to secure further concessions from the other colonies for New South Wales:

> you were unable to cordially support the Bill for which you voted and no doubt your powerful influence considerably reduced the majority by which it was carried . . . I would never have contemplated reducing the majority in favour to secure better terms for MY colony.[30]

The premiers accepted they had no authority to change the constitution bill that had now been passed by the people at the first referenda in Victoria, Tasmania and South Australia. The best they could do was reach a 'gentlemen's agreement' about changes, which they could then take back to all of the colonies for a second referendum. But this time, New South Wales would hold its referendum first and, if passed, the others would follow. Victoria's George Turner made his feelings clear:

> While I am not altogether satisfied with the compromise, I think on the whole the decisions are so reasonably fair that I am prepared to recommend the people of Victoria to accept them as soon as New South Wales has accepted the draft constitution in its amended form . . . We will do nothing in Victoria till New South Wales has shown its desire to enter the federation by accepting the constitution in its altered form.[31]

When Reid returned to Sydney, his government made the task of winning the second referendum easier by dropping the requirement for at least 80,000 voting 'yes', which had doomed the poll the year before. Reid also publicly pledged: 'I am quite prepared to ask my colony to accept this bill . . . I am prepared to make the bill, as amended, a vital part of my Ministerial policy, and to fight for it heart and soul.'[32]

The newspapers, although still sceptical, saw that, with an end to Reid's equivocation, Federation was now likely:

> the premier's declarations are clear and unmistakable, and bind him in the most emphatic way to a definite course. He says he is now determined to throw his utmost strength into the task of carrying the measure as it is amended. That is explicit, and marks the attainment of a definite stage on the road to federation. For the first time Mr. Reid commits himself directly and unreservedly to the work of carrying a definite measure of federation . . .[33]

While the other colonies had said they would not go back to the people with a second referendum until it was passed in New South Wales, the South Australian premier Charles Kingston, with the support of opposition leader John Downer, in the end did decide to do so six weeks before New South Wales, on 21 April 1899. When the matter was debated in the South Australian Parliament, not all members were happy with the concessions made to New South Wales, particularly the location of the national capital. When Kingston tried to point out that the issue was 'non-negotiable' from New South Wales' point of view, a number of members of parliament interjected, calling, 'What of South Australia?' and, 'Why not Port Augusta?'[34]

Despite the misgivings of some members of parliament, the 'yes' vote in the second South Australian referendum was almost double that in the first, up from 35,800 to 65,990. At the same time, the 'no' vote stayed almost the same, at a little more than 17,000. There was also more than a 50 per cent increase in voter turnout, from 53,120 in the first poll to 83,043 in the second.

Dickson also brought forward a bill into the Queensland Parliament for a constitutional referendum. The bill had a rough ride before being passed by the Legislative Assembly, and a rougher ride in the Legislative Council, where it finally scraped through with a 14–12 vote at midnight on 15 June. Dickson's government did not survive long after this, but he was the incumbent long enough to steer Queensland towards scheduling a referendum on Federation for later in the year.

All eyes were now on New South Wales for the second referendum, which was held on 20 June 1899, a little more than a year after the first. The government printed enough copies of the amended constitution for every elector in the colony and again announced that polling day would be a public holiday.

Despite all the concessions and increased support, the campaign leading up to the second referendum was every bit as intense as the one the year before. Supporting the 'yes' campaign, a new 'United Federal Executive' was formed. It systematically canvassed the entire colony and raised a campaign war chest of more than £2000. The money paid for publications and for hundreds of speakers to travel around the colony. The executive included the old 'Federation League' and 'Federal Association', and had both Reid and his opponent Barton as its vice presidents.

The opposition was led by sixty-five-year-old former premier George Dibbs, who argued that, if there was to be national union, New South Wales should be the dominant player. Dibbs was offended that it had already been agreed that Melbourne would be used as a temporary capital city until a spot for the final national capital was decided upon: 'A greater piece of impertinence could not have been offered to this colony. Is Sydney the leper spot?'[35] During the campaign, he distributed an estimated half a million copies of speeches, leaflets and posters, at a cost of £1800 for postage alone.[36]

Though, at last, George Reid was indeed unequivocal in his support for the bill, only three days before the poll, at a meeting in Goulburn, he was still trying to explain his previous about-face, as reported by a local newspaper:

He spoke here a year ago and he put before them a number of very serious defects in the 1898 bill, and he wanted to explain to them why it was that while he threw cold water on that Bill he now came before them to warmly and strongly urge them to accept the bill of 1899.[37]

On the night of the ballot, large crowds gathered to watch the result. The railways again announced special trains to the city from the suburbs of Liverpool, Homebush, Parramatta and Hurstville:

> Very great interest was manifested in watching the numbers as they were posted at the *Herald* office in Hunter-street, and at the branch office in King Street, both localities being crowded with spectators, who cheered enthusiastically as the majority in favour of Australian union continued to swell.[38]

The *Herald* reported 'an unparalleled burst of enthusiasm' and 'ringing and prolonged cheering' when Premier Reid, then Edmund Barton, appeared at the window of the Empire Hotel, opposite the *Herald* offices in Hunter Street, after it became clear that the 'yes' vote had won.

This time, the majority supporting Federation increased from 52 per cent to 56 per cent, and the total 'yes' vote was 107,420, easily passing the 80,000 minimum that had been required in the first referendum. There was also an almost 39 per cent increase in the number of people voting, up from 137,000 in the first referendum to 190,161 in the second.

The result was eagerly awaited around Australia and around the world. As soon as news reached London, the British secretary of state for the colonies, Joseph Chamberlain, telegraphed Reid with 'heartiest congratulations'.[39] When the result was read out in the House of Commons, it was 'received with cheers'. The House immediately sent a message to 'cordially congratulate New South Wales upon result of referendum on federation question, and rejoice in political unification of Australia'. Similar telegrams came from the other Australian colonies, which were relieved that at last the bill was passed.

Victoria had waited for the New South Wales poll before agreeing to a second referendum, which was held five weeks later, on 22 July 1899. Many Victorians felt bitter about this second poll. Victoria had delivered an overwhelming vote for Federation the first time around, and now they had to go back a second time, and had had to make more concessions to New South Wales. In the days leading up to the second Victorian poll, there had been some concern that many voters had become complacent and wouldn't bother turning up to vote.[40] However, on election day, the voter turnout was more than 30 per cent higher than at the first referendum, and the 'no' vote dropped from 22,090 to less than 10,000. The majority 'yes' vote was up more than 50 per cent, from 100,520 to 152,653, accounting for 94 per cent of the total ballot – the highest of any colony in any poll.

The next day The Argus echoed the pride of the colony, with its claim 'Victoria Leads': 'The Federal poll in Victoria yesterday was all that was anticipated . . . It was a magnificent demonstration of loyalty to the Australian idea, transcending hope in its magnitude.'[41]

In Tasmania on the day of the second poll, the premier ordered that the major post offices throughout the colony stay open and post the voting figures every half-hour.[42] As the votes were counted, it became apparent that there was a slight reduction in the number of people voting (14,513 down to 14,280), but the support for Federation was even more emphatic. Around 90 per cent voted 'yes' (13,437) in the second poll, compared with around 80 per cent (11,797) in the first. In the second poll, the number voting 'no' dropped from 2716 to 791, prompting the Melbourne Argus newspaper to report, 'Gallant little Tasmania has . . . faithfully done her share of the battle.'[43]

Four of the six colonies had 'now formally repudiated the policy of hostile isolation' and committed to unite to become the nation of Australia.[44] Now Queensland decided to hold its own referendum after its 'long and acrimonious' debate and its close result in the colony's Legislative Assembly.[45]

Prominent in the two-month campaign were the 'Queensland Federation League' and the 'Anti-Federation League'. During the campaign, most of the Queensland newspapers came out for Federation, but there were some significant exceptions, including Brisbane's *Telegraph*, the *Rockhampton Morning Bulletin*, the *Ipswich Times* and *The Toowoomba Chronicle*.[46]

There were also big regional differences across the vast colony of Queensland. Those against Federation tended to be concentrated in the small farming communities of the south-east of the colony, such as Toowoomba and the Logan Valley.[47] In Brisbane and these southern areas, there was a fear of the competition that might come from New South Wales with Federation and the abolition of protective tariffs. Those in the centre and north felt they would gain from intercolonial free trade.[48]

A number of local issues impacted on the campaign. Many of the interests in the north and the centre of the colony wanted to secede from the south-east and become separate colonies. To attract enough support from these regions, Premier Dickson had to promise to leave open the possibility that each would have their own quota of senators from their local area – rather than have all the senators from Queensland determined by a state-wide poll, which would be dominated by the more densely popu-lated south-east corner around Brisbane.

Another problem that caused Queensland to baulk at national union was the race issue. Since the gold rushes, all the colonies had attempted to limit the immigration of non-white people – particularly the Chinese – into Australia. However, at the same time, Queensland had for as many years been dependent on the importation of cheap Pacific Island labourers (then called Kanakas) to work on the farms and sugar-cane plantations. They feared a national government would force a limit on the number of Kanakas who could come into Queensland.

Leading the Federation campaign was the former Queensland premier Sir Samuel Griffith, a key player in drafting the first constitution. To help with the campaign, Deakin, Barton and Reid spoke at public meetings across Brisbane and the Darling Downs. On the night before the vote, Barton was mobbed after speaking to a huge audience in Brisbane. During the meeting, he had upset sections of the crowd by saying that if they had such terrible opinions of the people in other colonies, they should vote 'no', 'and 'take the shame of it'.[49] According to Barton, he and his colleagues were pushed and shoved by a disorderly crowd before managing to reach the safety of his hotel.

The next day, 2 September, Queensland recorded a comfortable but not overwhelming win. The 'yes' vote of 38,488, or 56 per cent, was similar to the winning ratio in New South Wales but much less than the majorities recorded in Victoria (94 per cent), Tasmania (90 per cent) and South Australia (79 per cent).

There were marked differences between the different parts of the colony. Brisbane voted almost two to one against it, with 5765 'yes' votes and 10,170 'no's. The south of the colony, including the Darling Downs, was closer to three to two against: 'yes', 8520; 'no', 12,228. The result was carried by the big majorities in the north and west of the colony. In the centre and the west, the 'yes' vote was almost twice the 'no' vote: 12,132 to 6862. In the north, the 'yes' vote won by a margin of nearly four to one: 12,376 to 3332.

Finally, with Western Australia still sitting on the sidelines, the other five colonies had agreed to national union. But, before it could happen, the premiers had to travel to London to steer the approval through the British Parliament, and there they would encounter an entirely new set of obstacles.

Chapter 15

London, 1900

Mr. Barton is now the foremost man in Australia.

New South Wales, Victoria, Tasmania, South Australia and Queensland now had agreement to form the nation, but they could not enact it. Australia was still a British territory, so, short of following the American example of a Declaration of Independence, a law had to be passed in the British Parliament to allow its federation.

While the five colonies were planning their trips to London to steer the new Australian constitution through the House of Commons and the House of Lords, the sixth, Western Australia, was at last starting to stir towards joining the union.

Before now, Western Australia had not been a serious player in the process. It had not participated in the design of the first constitution in 1891, sending only an observer.

It had sent delegates to the constitutional conventions in Adelaide in 1897 and Sydney and Melbourne in 1898, but had never agreed to put the matter to a vote of the people as the other colonies had. During the conventions of 1897 and 1898, Alfred Deakin had complained that Forrest 'was to the fore as leader of the stalwart Conservatives in resisting with undaunted courage and inexhaustible persistency common-sense objections to every innovation'.[1]

Yet only a week before the eastern colonies had voted in their referenda in 1898, Forrest had made positive comments about the proposed constitution. Addressing a newly established Western Australia Federation League meeting at Perth's St George's Hall on 27 May 1898, he said that even if it was started all over again, it was unlikely the constitution could be improved on:

> Now that the Bill has been decided upon, and we have done all we could have done to obtain the fairest terms possible, I see no reason to be other than satisfied with the result that has been achieved . . . [The proposed constitution] is a really good one, and quite as good as we are likely to get if we had to go over the work again.[2]

Forrest's comments in favour of Federation alarmed his ministerial colleagues and many of his supporters. Six of the ten Western Australian delegates who had attended the constitution conventions came out at odds with him.[3] Prominent among Forrest's opponents was Sir John Hackett, the powerful editor of the *West Australian* newspaper. Hackett did in fact regard himself as a Federationist at heart, but he believed Western Australia needed more time to strengthen its 'embryo' industries before joining the other colonies to form one nation.

When New South Wales fell short of the required number of votes in its first referendum in June 1898, Forrest had admitted to Edmund Barton that the failure in the east had doomed his plans for the west:

> I am unable to go with the bill here, after New South Wales threw it out. It would have been difficult enough for me if you had passed it, but without that it is impossible. The chief support here is from [gold-mining] newcomers and the Opposition members. The Government supporters, old settlers, farmers, graziers and such like being against it, particularly owing to the free trade clauses and all these latter are my principal supporters – you will therefore see my position.[4]

So although Premier John Forrest did not want Western Australia to be left out of the nation-building, he could not find enough support from his conservative colleagues to commit the colony to join the others. Forrest had also made it clear to the other premiers as far back as 1891 at the Sydney constitutional convention that he believed Western Australia should be granted 'especial benefits' to join the other colonies in the national union. Over the next two years, he had unsuccessfully tried to extract some of these special concessions.

It was generally accepted that the vast colony had unique problems. It had only a small population so its government had a limited capacity to raise taxes. It was in the midst of a gold rush and the government depended heavily on the tariffs on goods imported from the other colonies, which were paid for from gold. However, there was a feeling in the other colonies that two-thirds of the continent could satisfactorily form a nation without having to make any special concessions to pull in the isolated west. It was also felt that, if the draft constitution was amended to accommodate Western Australia, it would be necessary to go back yet again for a vote of the people. When the possibility of special concessions for Western Australia was discussed at the Melbourne convention in 1898, Charles Kingston scoffed at the idea:

> I cannot help saying that Western Australia is greatly indebted to us. We have peopled her wilderness, we have developed her resources, we have discovered her gold mines, we have fed her people, and in return for that it seems to me that we have had to bear heavy burdens in the shape of taxation.

Forrest had also sought a commitment that under Federation a national government would build a railway line connecting Perth to the eastern states across the vast Nullarbor Plain. The other colonies agreed only that the new national government would have the power to build it, not the obligation.

Premier Forrest was in an increasingly difficult position. His conservative colleagues were opposed to Federation without special concessions, which the other colonial premiers were not prepared to give. Forrest was beginning to realise this. He also knew that the other colonies were prepared to join the union without Western Australia.

But, since 1892, the gold miners on the rapidly growing goldfields in the waterless wastelands about 600 kilometres east of Perth, at Kalgoorlie and Coolgardie, had been strongly supportive of national union; and by the late 1890s the population of the gold regions had begun to outstrip that of the rest of Western Australia.

In November and December 1898, after the eastern colonies had voted for the constitution, a petition in

Western Australia calling for a large part of it to become a separate colony, which would federate with the other eastern colonies, attracted 5000 signatures. The idea of the goldfields becoming a separate colony for this purpose had first been mooted in 1894 and had grown in strength in the years since.[5]

On 3 December 1899, at a public meeting in the gold-mining town of Kalgoorlie, the local mayor, Charles Sommers, called for the petition to be sent to Queen Victoria. Later in the same month, a meeting in the port town of Albany unanimously resolved to join with the goldfields. To be called Aurora, the new colony was to extend from Eucla to Cape Leeuwin, and from the 25th parallel to the South Australian border, taking in all of the goldfields.

Forrest was well aware of the political danger. In September 1899, he had been warned by the parliamentary opposition leader George Leake that the goldfields would split from Western Australia unless it agreed to federate. He now had an ultimatum, and time was running out for Western Australia. Forrest had to decide in which direction to steer his colony.

*

On 25 January 1900, the premiers met to decide on who from each of the five colonies would go to London. Victoria had already chosen Alfred Deakin. New South Wales selected Edmund Barton. South Australia picked Sir Charles Kingston and Queensland James Dickson. Tasmania opted for their former premier Philip Fysh because he was already in England, having become Tasmania's resident agent general in London the year before.

The British colonial secretary Joseph Chamberlain said he wanted the Australians 'to assist and explain when the [British] Parliament is considering the Federation Bill'. But as the Australians going to London saw it, their task was 'to secure the passage of the bill without amendment'. This fundamental difference in expectations between the British and the Australians did not seem an auspicious start. And at a farewell speech at Sydney's Town Hall a few days before leaving for London, Edmund Barton said that it would not be 'reasonable', 'just' or 'proper' for the British to change the bill:

> Not one of the five delegates would like to say that the bill, having been submitted to the people and accepted by an overwhelming majority in a certain form, should now be amended. He acknowledged that the Imperial Parliament, being the sovereign body of the realm, had a technical right, a legal right, to make any amendments in the bill, but he contended that it had not a constitutional right to do so; because the bill was the expression of the will of a large majority of the people, who would be affected by it.[6]

Barton very nearly missed the ship to London for the talks. Having caught the overnight train from Sydney to Melbourne and then Adelaide, he spent too long eating his supper at Moss Vale Railway Station, where the train had stopped, about 130 kilometres south-west of Sydney. When the train left without him, Barton was lucky there was another express locomotive nearby and, after a long and uncomfortable ride on the footplate, he managed to catch up with the passenger train. When he finally reached Adelaide on 7 February, he boarded the *Orizaba* with Kingston and Dickson. They stopped briefly in Perth, where they were entertained by Premier Forrest, before continuing the voyage to London, where they met up with Alfred Deakin and Philip Fysh.

In London, the five Australians were joined by Western Australia's London-based agent general Stephen Parker and New Zealand's agent general William Pember Reeves – who both attended in an unofficial capacity since neither of their colonies had committed to becoming members of the new national union.

At the Australians' first meeting together, they elected Barton as their senior spokesman for the negotiations with the British, led by Colonial Secretary Joseph Chamberlain, which were to begin at the Colonial Office in March.

Sixty-four-year-old Joseph Chamberlain was a tough negotiator. He was not from the traditional British aristocracy that typified British leadership of the times, but was nevertheless an ardent imperialist. Born the son of a prosperous shoe manufacturer in London, he had gone into the family business when he was sixteen years old, before joining a cousin the following year manufacturing screws in Birmingham. At the age of thirty-seven, he became the mayor of Birmingham and a year later retired, having made a substantial fortune. The following year, he became a Liberal member of parliament and a supporter of William Gladstone. In 1895, he switched sides to the Conservatives and under the prime minister the Third Marquess of Salisbury was appointed colonial secretary with responsibility for Australia.

While the Australians found Chamberlain 'iron-willed',[7] he found them equally tough, describing them as 'some of the stoutest negotiators he had met in his life'.[8] At the first meeting, the Australians were advised that the constitution was unacceptable as it stood. The British sought a number of minor changes that were easily agreed to by making small adjustments to the wording. However, a major sticking point was clause 74, which dealt with the proposed new High Court of Australia. According to clause 74, the High Court of Australia would effectively replace the British Privy Council. Although the Australian state Supreme Courts would still have a right of appeal to the Privy Council, constitutional matters would have their final hearing in the High Court. Chamberlain argued that, as with all other members of the British Empire, the highest appeal court should remain the Judicial Council of the Privy Council. He was supported by an influential coalition of forces in Australia, including all the British-appointed governors to each of the colonies, a number of chief justices and the Chambers of Commerce, backed by investors and bankers in the colonies.[9]

The Australians spent several months lobbying around London to avoid being stuck with the Privy Council as the ultimate legal course of appeal, but with little success. At the time in Britain, Chamberlain was at the height of his powers and the British Empire at its zenith. The British were hardly going to be pressured by a small gaggle of relatively unknown colonials into having different rules from all the other dominion states.

The deputation was nevertheless graciously entertained by the British hosts. On 26 March, the Australians lunched at Windsor Castle and were granted an audience with Queen Victoria. On 3 April, they were presented at Buckingham Palace to the Prince of Wales (who, less than a year later, would become King Edward VII on the death of his mother); on 30 April, they were guests at a banquet in the House of Commons and on 12 May they dined with the Countess of Warwick at Warwick Castle. On 24 May, they were special guests of the Colonial Club at a dinner for around 350 people. They also attended a raft of other functions, including the Easter Banquet at

Mansion House given by the lord mayor of London, the Worshipful Company of Ironmongers' Dinner and the secretary of state for war's banquet at the Anglo-Saxon Club. On Derby Day, they were taken to the horse races at Epsom in the Prince of Wales' train and given a special box at the racecourse.

Back in London, they were the special guests at a dinner for 450 people at the National Liberal Club, and they were given the royal box at Her Majesty's Theatre for a performance of A Midsummer Night's Dream. They even went to Cambridge, where Edmund Barton was awarded an honorary doctorate.[10]

Throughout all the entertaining, the Australians stuck to their guns in refusing to accept any significant changes to their hard-won constitution. In late April, Barton, Deakin, Kingston and Fysh presented Chamberlain with a memorandum that insisted that any alteration to the bill would be distasteful and harassing to the colonies.[11] James Dickson, however, broke ranks with his colleagues and refused to sign the memorandum on the ground that 'further controversy would militate against the speedy passage of the bill'.[12] Over the next weeks, he made speeches and press statements in agreement with Chamberlain. Also, while neither Western Australia nor New Zealand were yet part of the plan, they both supported Chamberlain's viewpoint that the Privy Council should remain the highest court of appeal.

On 27 April, the London Times urged 'that Australian statesmen and people should recognise the wisdom of the arguments of the Imperial Government', but the rest of the Australian delegation stuck to its guns, despite pressure to concede. Finally, on 14 May, with no prospect of agreement, and to the grave disappointment of the Australians, Chamberlain introduced the Commonwealth of Australia Bill into a crowded House of Commons – but without clause 74. Later the same evening, he invited the remaining Australian delegates to dinner to try once more to persuade them to agree with his proposal. When he failed, he finally offered a compromise: the Australian High Court would remain the ultimate court of appeal in constitutional matters unless the Australian Government and states involved consented to a British Privy Council appeal. (The following month, this was changed so that the High Court had to be the party that agreed the matters would be referred to the Privy Council.)

A few days later, on 20 May, in further discussions with Chamberlain and the British attorney general, both sides agreed to a rewriting of clause 74.[13] Thus, both could claim a partial victory. The Australians could point to the fact that the High Court would review constitutional matters and only with the High Court's consent would they go to the British Privy Council; and Chamberlain would point to the fact that all non-constitutional matters would go before the Privy Council.

According to Deakin, the Australians were so excited and relieved after the deal was done that he, Kingston and Barton closed the door, 'seized each other's hands and danced hand in hand in a ring around the centre of the room to express their jubilation'.[14] When news of the breakthrough reached Australia, the delegates were widely praised, particularly Edmund Barton:

This year Mr. Barton proved that Australia had a scholar, a constitutional lawyer, a negotiator and a debater who rose to the level of the best that Great Britain possesses. Truly, Mr. Barton is now the foremost man in Australia. The establishment of the Australian Commonwealth is largely his work, and the moulding of its early career will without doubt be his task if he cares to undertake it. The launching of a great nation? – and who doubts, that Australia will be a great nation one day – is an important event in the history of mankind . . . As to the coming Commonwealth, its history for many years will probably be the history of Edmund Barton. His position is unique. He is perhaps the only man now above the political horizon who is acceptable as a leader to the majorities in all the colonies of the continent. That he will be the first man sent for to form a Federal Government goes without saying.[15]

The Commonwealth of Australia Constitution Act 1900 became law on 9 July 1900 after finally being passed by the British Parliament. The proclamation of the nation of Australia would take place on 1 January the following year, when New South Wales, Victoria, South Australia, Queensland and Tasmania would cease to be colonies and become states. However, the law had been cleverly drafted so as to make it possible at the last minute for Western Australia to join:

It shall be lawful for the Queen, with the advice of the Privy Council, to declare by proclamation that . . . after the passing of this Act, the people of New South Wales, Victoria, South Australia, Queensland, and Tasmania, and also, if Her Majesty is satisfied that the people of Western Australia have agreed thereto, of Western Australia, shall be united in a Federal Commonwealth under the name of the Commonwealth of Australia.

*

In Western Australia, by February 1900, when the delegates from the other colonies were on their way to

London, another petition – this time signed by 27,000 Western Australians wanting 'separation for Federation' – attracted considerable publicity in England. In March, Joseph Chamberlain asked the delegates from the eastern colonies if they could offer any further concessions to Western Australia, but they said no.[16] However, South Australia's Charles Kingston was in constant contact with Forrest and continued to urge him to call a referendum on Federation.[17]

Chamberlain now had nothing left to offer, but, still wanting Western Australia on board, the following month he cabled Forrest via the acting governor of Western Australia threatening that the British Government might well agree to allow the goldfields to secede from Western Australia unless the whole colony agreed to federate: '[Britain would] of course take into consideration effect of agitation of the Federalist party, especially on gold fields if Western Australia does not enter as an original state.'[18]

Forrest had finally run out of options, so, on 17 May 1900 – as agreement was being reached in London on the Australian Constitution – he told the parliament of Western Australia that there would be a referendum on Federation on 31 July 1900.

The campaign both in support and opposition of the union was vigorous. According to *The West Australian*, by the day of the vote, the referendum dominated all conversation:

Little else was talked about in the streets but Federation. You heard it at the street corners and along the footpaths. In the trains the chief topic was the result of today's poll. The tram cars, which were full of passengers throughout the day, as a rule, were also full of Federation, and anti-Federation ... In the shops you talked Federation and made your purchase ... the same topic stared you in the face from different hoardings and out of the shop windows.[19]

The result was a resounding vote of more than two to one to join the other colonies: 44,800 voted 'yes' and 19,691 voted 'no'. Over 67 per cent of those eligible voted, which was the highest rate of voter turnout of any colony, including South Australia, the only other colony where women had the vote.

As expected, most of the farming districts, which feared unreasonable competition from the eastern states, and a number of coastal towns, including Bunbury and Geraldton, voted 'no'. In Perth, the 'yes' vote was passed by barely 7000 votes to nearly 5000 who voted 'no'.

However, it was the overwhelming vote from the goldfields that gave Western Australia its huge vote in favour of the union. In the Kalgoorlie region, more than 95 per cent of the 24,000 votes cast agreed with Federation, swamping the other results and ensuring an almost 70 per cent majority.

Western Australia was finally on board, having joined the union just in time for the momentous inauguration of the Commonwealth of Australia five months later.

CHAPTER 16

THE NATION IS BORN

*Everything is now ready for the swearing in of the first
Federal Ministry tomorrow.*

AFTER THE COMMONWEALTH OF AUSTRALIA CONSTITUTION
Act had passed in London in July 1900, and with the
subsequent addition of Western Australia, preparations
began in earnest for the official launch of the new nation
of Australia on 1 January 1901.

Some months after the inauguration, an election would
be held to choose the first parliament, but in the meantime
an interim government had to be appointed. The man with
this responsibility was Adrian Louis Hope, the Seventh
Earl of Hopetoun, who had been made the nation's first
governor general.

Hopetoun was no stranger to Australia. He had been
educated at Eton and Sandhurst Military College, then

selected in 1889 at twenty-nine years of age to be governor of Victoria. As governor, he was noted for his passion for hunting and horseriding, and for the unusual habit of powdering his hair. Before leaving the post to return to England in 1895, he had implored the colonies to make the union 'the goal of your desires'.[1]

Hopetoun's appointment was announced in London on 13 October 1900, only four days after Queen Victoria had signed the *Commonwealth of Australia Constitution Act* into law. It was well received in the colonies. When news of the posting reached Australia, the premiers shot off telegrams: New South Wales premier Sir William Lyne, who had replaced George Reid the previous year, congratulated Hopetoun as 'eminently fitted for the position';[2] South Australia's Sir Frederick William Holder wired to say Hopetoun would be 'in every way pleasing to the Australians'. Queensland's Robert Philp said he would 'make a very good Governor General' and Victoria's Sir George Turner said that 'the Imperial Government could not have made a happier choice'.[3]

With his wife and large entourage, Hopetoun sailed on the *Victoria* to Australia via India. En route, he caught typhoid and at Bombay was so ill he had to be 'carried aboard on a dhooly'.[4] At the same time, his wife contracted malaria and both were still in poor health when they reached Sydney on 15 December.

Hopetoun brought with him the same pomp as he had to Victoria the decade before. His staff included a private secretary, assistant private secretary, military secretary, aide-de-camp, house steward, twenty house servants and thirteen stable hands for his thirty horses.[5] He had barely two weeks to familiarise himself with the local scene and appoint the interim government before the New Year. On Tuesday 18 December, he met in Sydney with Premier Lyne.

With very little consultation with anyone else in the city, and none of the other premiers, the next day Hopetoun invited Lyne to form the interim national government.

Lyne was not originally a New South Welshman. He was born in Tasmania but left the island at twenty years of age with his cousin to work as a sheep farmer in western Queensland. He returned to Tasmania and then moved to New South Wales and became a successful sheep farmer near Albury, in the south of the colony. He was elected to the New South Wales Parliament in 1880, and had attended the 1897 and 1898 federal conventions as a New South Wales delegate, but had campaigned vocally in both of the New South Wales referenda against Federation. He had been the premier of New South Wales for a little over a year.

The public and the press expressed 'blank surprise' at Hopetoun's appointment of Lyne.[6] Just about everyone had expected Edmund Barton to be asked to form the government. Barton was the undisputed leader of the Federation movement and only a few months before had returned a hero to Australia from London. Indeed, the day before Hopetoun announced the appointment, the Sydney *Evening News* had pointed out:

> it is generally recognised that the governor-general will not only lose no time in making the appointment . . . but that the first Premier of Australia will in all probability be Mr. Edmund Barton . . . Of Sir William Lyne, without wishing to disparage him, it may be said that he is impossible as first Federal Premier. He is the Premier of New South Wales, certainly, but, if outside this he represents anything, it is the anti-Federal movement of 1898 and 1899.[7]

Undeterred by any forthcoming criticism, Lyne telegraphed the other colonial premiers, telling them, 'Lord Hopetoun has asked me to form a Ministry,' and inviting them to be part of it. He also wanted to meet his old adversary Barton to ask him to join, but Barton responded quickly:

> If your object is to ask me to join you in a Federal Administration it will be of little use for us to meet and discuss the matter. It would be a contradiction of my whole career in relation to Federation if I served under a Prime Minister who throughout opposed the adoption by the people of the measure of which he is now asked to be the first constitutional guardian.[8]

The same day, Barton also telegraphed his old friends and colleagues Alfred Deakin in Melbourne and Charles Kingston in Adelaide. A shocked Deakin responded on 19 December by saying that Hopetoun's decision to appoint Lyne risked bringing down Federation 'like a house of cards': 'Who could have believed that Hopetoun would make such a blunder. To choose *the* anti-federalist of NSW and *the* least effective member of the convention in place of yourself . . . it passes all comprehension.'[9]

Even the British Government was shocked. On 22 December, the colonial secretary Joseph Chamberlain sent a terse telegram to Hopetoun saying, 'Great surprise expressed at choice of Lyne instead of Barton. Please give reasons.'[10]

The next day, Deakin, still upset, wrote again to Barton from the Australia Club in Melbourne's Collins Street to say, 'I have not recovered yet. Could scarcely write to you yesterday . . . the whole business makes me sick with disgust.'[11] Deakin assured Barton that he would not accept any invitation to join Lyne's ministry and said he doubted he'd even go to Sydney for the inauguration. Deakin's view was that he would 'not be disposed to enter a Cabinet which Mr. Barton has specifically declined to join'.[12]

Lyne pressed on, and invited the premiers to Sydney for a meeting on Saturday 22 December. Given the short notice and the distances involved, neither John Forrest nor Tasmania's premier, Neil Elliott Lewis, were able to reach Sydney in time. However, Queensland's Philp, South Australia's Holder and Victoria's Turner attended the meeting.

There is no record of what was discussed there, but afterwards Philp issued a statement that said he had no intention of leaving public office in Queensland to join the federal sphere. Turner and Holder waited till they got back to Melbourne and then issued a similar statement:

> Their advice to Sir William Lyne was that the first Federal Cabinet should be one that was likely to be stable and strong ... Their advice had been sought and given, and they did not know if Sir William Lyne would act upon it or not, but they could say that neither of them was prepared to join a Federal Ministry with Sir William Lyne as its head ...[13]

Lyne was also unsuccessful when he tried to invite Richard O'Connor from New South Wales and Bernard Wise from South Australia, though both men were strong supporters of Federation, had been delegates at the 1897–98 conventions and had been involved in the drafting of the constitution.

On Christmas Eve, having failed to attract any prominent leaders to join him, Lyne advised the governor general he could not form a government, and returned his commission. To the relief of everyone, Hopetoun then turned to Edmund Barton. As the *West Australian* newspaper said on 2 January 1901:

No man today, as far as Australia is concerned, is more famous than Edmund Barton . . . For Edmund Barton this means the realisation of the hopes and the crowning of the labours of many years – which have served to bring him more and more prominently before the eyes of his fellow and neighbouring colonists as one whom they could all trust to deal honourably and act impartially, as one who could forgive and forget petty State jealousies, and look steadfast towards the glory of a just, righteous, and loving union. His reward is that, with the approval of all Australia, he is now called upon to take the chief position in the political affairs of the new nation. To direct the first years of that national life which he has been so instrumental in calling into being upon no one could the task more befittingly have fallen; upon no one could the honour have more justly been bestowed.

Barton contacted the premiers and other senior figures over Christmas to invite them to join his ministry. George Turner and John Forrest accepted immediately. So did William Lyne, to whom Barton felt he was obliged to offer a position. In the case of South Australia, Barton did not end up offering a position to Premier Frederick Holder but instead invited his old friend and Federation colleague Charles Kingston. Holder found out he had been passed over by Barton when the Cabinet list was announced in the newspapers and was reportedly 'much aggrieved at his exclusion'.[14]

Queensland premier Robert Philp declined his invitation, telling Barton what he had told Lyne a week before: he did not want to leave public office in Queensland. Barton then felt free to ask James Dickson, who had been at the first constitution convention a decade before, as well as the later ones of 1897–98, and had been with Barton in

London the year before when negotiating with the British to pass the *Commonwealth of Australia Constitution Act*. Barton could have chosen Sir Samuel Griffith, but Griffith had lobbied 'behind the backs' of Barton and the Australian delegation in London against the proposed reduced role of the Privy Council with the advent of the Australian High Court.[15] The appointment of Dickson upset Griffith, who recorded in his usually moderate diary that Barton was a 'fathead' and Dickson a 'prating cockatoo'.[16]

Sadly, Dickson would soon be dead. Having accepted his appointment to the first ministry, he took ill the following week in Sydney during the inauguration celebrations and died on 10 January 1901. He had been a diabetic for many years.

As well as undertaking the prime ministership, Barton also took on the external affairs portfolio with responsibility for foreign affairs. Deakin was made attorney general and minister for justice, and Turner was appointed treasurer. Lyne was made minister for home affairs, Kingston minister for trade and customs, Dickson minister for defence and Forrest postmaster general.[17]

There was considerable relief that 'a strong Cabinet' had been formed in the nick of time for the New Year's Day inauguration:

> It is satisfactory to find that the negotiations of the past few weeks ... have had so successful an issue, that the initial difficulty in selecting a Premier has been overcome, and that everything is now ready for the swearing-in of the first Federal Ministry tomorrow.[18]

There were bitter complaints from Tasmania that it had been left out of the ministry. Premier Lewis was in Sydney, having been invited the week before by Lyne to discuss

Tasmania's inclusion in the first Australian government. However, it was explained to Lewis that, with Barton's appointment, the 'whole situation had changed' by the time he reached Sydney:

> the claims of Tasmania have been overlooked. I had an interview with Mr. Barton this morning, and find there is no likelihood of a representative of Tasmania being included in the government . . . I scarcely think that the arrangement which has been made will be satisfactory to the people of Tasmania. There will be a great deal of disappointment at their being left out in the cold.[19]

Barton further inflamed the sensitivities of Tasmanians by favouring Western Australia's inclusion, in the form of Forrest, and suggesting that Tasmania could be represented by Victoria:

> What influenced me in the decision was this. Western Australia is at the extreme end of the continent, and is an important and growing community. Unless Western Australia was represented in the Government, we should know little concerning her requirements. Tasmania, on the other hand, is a more settled community, and is in close proximity to Victoria. The Victorian ministers will really represent Tasmania in the Cabinet.[20]

Tasmanians responded by pointing out that they had been the first to support Federation and were now being treated disrespectfully:

> There is much adverse comment throughout Tasmania . . . Considering that Tasmania was one of the original federating colonies in the first referendum, New South

Wales, Queensland and Western Australia only coming in after much diplomatic persuasion, it is maintained that Tasmania's reasonable claim to recognition has been contemptuously heard, and that this sorry commencement does not augur well for future fairplay.[21]

Eventually, at the eleventh hour, Barton bowed to their pressure, and on the night of New Year's Eve, just in time for the next day's inauguration, Barton 'waited on the governor-general and submitted the name of the Hon N. E. Lewis of Tasmania [who] has accepted the position as a ... member of the Federal executive to represent Tasmania'. At the same time, Barton added another member from New South Wales, his lifelong friend and Federation supporter Richard O'Connor, which brought the number of the first Australian Cabinet to be sworn in the next day to nine.

*

The national inauguration took place in Sydney's Centennial Park, three kilometres from the edge of the city. A giant procession began at 10.30 am on New Year's Day and included horse-drawn carriages and floats, soldiers, police, firefighters, stockmen, trade unions, church leaders, the senators of Sydney University, representatives of foreign governments, and premiers and officials from the other Australian states. An estimated 250,000 people lined the route, which started near Sydney Harbour in the Domain and wound its way along Macquarie Street, down Bridge, along Pitt, King, George, Park, College and Oxford streets to Centennial Park.

In Centennial Park, a large, white, timber pavilion had been built for the occasion. During the ceremony, which began at noon, the Anglican archbishop of Sydney, William Smith, read the Lord's Prayer. This caused some controversy, as *The Sydney Morning Herald* reported:

> The celebrations were regarded as an outstanding success but there were some embarrassing issues. Australia's Catholic Cardinal Patrick Moran was allocated a position in the procession behind the Anglican Archbishop William Smith, although his position was technically the senior one. Moran was also offended that the role of reading the prayers had been given to his Anglican counterpart so he withdrew from the procession and stood among a choir of Catholic school children as it passed by St Mary's Cathedral.[22]

After Lord Hopetoun had been sworn in as the governor general of the new nation, he read out a message from Queen Victoria, which was also delivered to each of the other colonies by the governors who were being sworn in on that day: 'The Queen commands me to express through you to the people of Australia her Majesty's heartfelt interest in the inauguration of the Commonwealth, and her earnest wish that under Divine Providence it may ensure the increased prosperity and well-being of her loyal and beloved subjects in Australia.'[23]

The oath of office was then administered to Edmund Barton and to each member of his first Commonwealth ministry. In the evening, there was a banquet in Sydney Town Hall attended by those who had played the most significant roles in the Federation journey: Edmund Barton, George Reid, Sir John Forrest, Charles Kingston, Sir John Downer, Robert Philp, Sir James Dickson, Sir Samuel Griffith, Sir George Turner and Alfred Deakin.

Sydney had no difficulty in congratulating itself on a splendid celebration:

Sydney has reason to be proud of its Commonwealth inauguration. The scenes in the city yesterday when the procession passed through the streets, at the Centennial Park when the governor-general was sworn in and the Commonwealth proclaimed, and in the evening when a blaze of illuminations transformed night into day, will not lightly pass from the memories of those who witnessed them. It will not be often in the history even of the Commonwealth that an occasion so important will be so brilliantly celebrated, and the citizens of this metropolis have cause to congratulate themselves on the manner in which they have represented the States of the Commonwealth, and demonstrated loyalty to the federation on behalf of the whole continent. Considered simply as a series of spectacles the demonstration left nothing to be desired.[24]

The official program of celebrations in Sydney stretched over eight days. The day after the inauguration, there was a swimming carnival and a Highland Gathering at the Sydney Cricket Ground. On Thursday 3 January, the program included a military tattoo and a cycling carnival, and on Friday there was an athletics carnival, an aquatic demonstration and a fireworks display. On Saturday, the trade unions and friendly societies paraded through the city streets and a cricket match was played between New South Wales and South Australia. On Sunday, there was a military church parade, on Monday a military sports carnival and an evening harbour cruise. On the final day, Tuesday 8 January, there was a military athletics carnival and a banquet for the press at Sydney Town Hall.

While the inauguration celebrations were being held in Sydney on 1 January 1901, the occasion was also being celebrated in other towns and cities around Australia, although not necessarily with the same level of pomp:

> Quiet joyousness is the dominant note of Commonwealth Day in Melbourne. Everybody felt happy, but nobody felt inclined to make a noise about it. The mild warmth of the sun and the light pressure of a north-west wind lent that delicious physical sensation which makes people feel it is good to live, and which was in true harmony with the glad spirit of the holiday-makers. Even the flags and banners as they lazily and silently corrugated the yellow sunlight seemed to be conscious of a sense of quiet enjoyment . . . Their enjoyment was quiet, but it was very full, and none of them will forget the first Commonwealth Day in Melbourne . . . Flags and streamers were the principal decorations in the streets . . . Parliament House was festooned with flags and evergreens . . .[25]

At noon, there was a firing of a 101-gun salute, 'which was accompanied by the rhyming and chiming of the bells in St Paul's Cathedral'.[26]

In Queensland, the main celebrations began in Brisbane at nine in the morning and continued till after ten in the evening.[27] During the morning, there were special services in a number of churches and a procession by naval and military forces, the fire brigades, the police and the friendly societies. In the afternoon, the public were invited to 'a program of military events, such as tent-pegging, cutlass and bayonet drills' in the Queen's Park and the Domain. In the evening, there was a fireworks display sent up from gunboats and other craft on the Brisbane River.

The nation's inauguration was also celebrated in towns and villages spread throughout the state, including Warwick, Roma, Cunnamulla, St George, Mackay, Maryborough, Cairns, Barcaldine and Longreach. In Gympie, a reported 8000 people attended the inauguration celebrations and were a very enthusiastic crowd at a giant fireworks display that followed.

In Perth, the city's apparent reluctance to federate only months earlier did not prevent it from holding major celebration show. The local newspaper boasted that, 'for its size, no city in Australia more fittingly welcomed the proclamation of the new nation than the capital of the Golden West':

> In all its history Perth has never given itself up so thoroughly and completely to the enjoyment of the hour as it did yesterday. From all parts of the colony visitors had come to the metropolis, and day and night all the leading thoroughfares were crowded with holiday-makers ... The earliest token of the great holiday was the crowding of the tramcars ... They literally swarmed down street and lane, as the hour for the reading of the Proclamation approached and ... there must have been fully 10,000 people gathered on the slopes of the Esplanade Recreation Reserve ... The processions of the military forces and the friendly societies helped to satiate the appetite for spectacles that the populace had turned out to see, but the most interest was centred in the illuminated procession of the evening ...[28]

In Tasmania, many people were still unaware that Lewis had finally, the night before, been appointed to the ministry, and the Hobart *Mercury* reported that the celebrations were quieter than they might have been. In Hobart a 'representative gathering' assembled in the Supreme Court in Hobart's Macquarie Street for the:

> eventful occasion . . . [of] the first official act performed in connection with the new Commonwealth, but the crowd was not a large one, nor was it very demonstrative . . . Mr. Barton having ignored our strong claim to have a Tasmania Minister included in his Cabinet, is being keenly felt by all classes and this seemed to have completely damped the ardour of all assembled, including the more prominent leaders of the Federal League, giving rise to feelings that prompted such remarks as 'We would have stood out of it if we could; but unfortunately we could not afford to.'[29]

In Adelaide, the celebrations began with a parade of 900 members of the military to St Peter's Cathedral. At noon, there was an official ceremony in the city's town hall, which was filled 'by a large and enthusiastic assemblage' to hear a speech from the governor Lord Tennyson and music from the 'organ galleries and the Adelaide Choral Society'.[30] The Adelaide *Advertiser* joined the celebrations by asserting that the Australian Federation was unique:

> 'A nation for a continent and a continent for a nation.' For the first time in recorded history has that aspiration been realised. 'The long wash of Australasian seas' beats now upon the coast of a country with no imaginary barriers to separate its citizens into antagonistic communities . . . Never since Captain Cook first planted the British flag upon Australian soil has any other ensign floated over it, and every colony which has been founded within its limits formed from the beginning an integral part of the one Empire. Europe, Asia, and America have from time

immemorial been parcelled out by hostile tribes, and the spread of the higher civilisation in each has been behind the broadsword, the spear, the rifle, and the bayonet . . . The six States of the Australian Commonwealth were, however, cradled in peace, nurtured in liberty, and developed under political institutions which are the flower and fruit of all that is best and noblest in the art of popular government. What wonder, then, that though a hundred years ago a little patch of red on the eastern coast was all that spoke of settlement on a vast terra incognita, the rising sun of the present century smiles on a map fully filled in from ocean to ocean, and . . . the honourable rivalries which have existed between them have hastened the dawn of the day of harmonious union. The Commonwealth has been built from within. No external force has had influence in its creation. It has not been hurriedly fabricated in stress of threatened war or serious political commotion. It has come from the people by the people to the people.[31]

At last! Australia could now enter the new century with a new kind of country, a new constitution and a new government.

But there was still a great deal to be done to make the country a nation.

CHAPTER 17

UNFINISHED BUSINESS

I have planned a city [Canberra] that is not like any other in the world.

AUSTRALIA BEGAN ITS LIFE AS A NATION WITHOUT A CAPITAL CITY, without a national Parliament House, without a national currency, without an official flag and without its own national anthem.

The nation's search for territory in which to house its capital would take three years; it would take seven more to enshrine the choice into law; and it would take twenty-six years before the Parliament House opened. In the meantime, the business of the Australian Government was run out of Melbourne in the Victorian Parliament. So it was there, five months after the proclamation of Australia, on 9 May 1901, that the first Australian parliament was officially opened by Prince George (who later would become King George V).

Even before the Commonwealth had been inaugurated, the New South Wales Government had been trying to decide where the national capital territory should be situated. In 1899, following the 'yes' vote for Federation, the colony had appointed Land Appeal Court judge Alexander Oliver to examine which New South Wales towns would be considered. Forty towns put themselves forward. They included major centres such as Armidale, Orange, Albury, Bathurst and Goulburn; and also a number of much smaller hopefuls, including Barbers Creek (current-day Tallong), Bowna, Sassafras and Molong.[1] Oliver ended up recommending three possible sites: Orange to the west, Bombala to the south and Yass, also to the south and near the eventual site of Canberra.

However, the new Federal Government ignored this New South Wales initiative and appointed its own royal commission on 14 January 1903 to endorse a suitable territory. The commission investigated a number of major towns but eventually recommended the tiny town of Dalgety in the mountains close to the Victorian border, because of its water supply, climate and food supply, and thus its ability to support a large population. The Federal Parliament accepted that Dalgety was to be Australia's national capital and passed the *Seat of Government Act 1904* to make it law, but the choice was then blocked by the New South Wales Government, which would not agree to make the land available because, according to the premier, Joseph Carruthers, the town was too far from Sydney.[2]

Negotiations and assessments of the various other options continued for the next three years, until finally the area surrounding and including Canberra was chosen because it had what was believed to be enough water from the nearby Molonglo River. But it was a close-run thing: Canberra only narrowly won over Dalgety, with a vote of 39–33 in October 1908 in the Federal House of Representatives. The vote was even closer in the Senate a few weeks later. The Senate looked at six sites (Dalgety, Armidale, Albury, Tumut, Lyndhurst [near Orange/ Bathurst] and Yass–Canberra) and was deadlocked on a vote of 18–18 between Tumut and Yass–Canberra. It was only when Victorian senator James Hiers McColl changed his vote that Canberra won by the narrowest of margins: 19–17. In a lengthy speech to the Senate on 29 October 1908, McColl said the matter had dragged on too long:

> It is a large national question, and we ought to discuss matters in connection with it in a manner becoming the dignity of the Senate. It is most unfortunate that incriminations and insinuations should have been hurled at those who intend to vote against Dalgety . . . My simple desire is to do what is best for the Commonwealth. I have endeavoured to look at the whole question in a common-sense light, and with a view to the solution of it . . . These visits have cost a good deal of money. I suppose that if we do not settle the question there will still be more trips and more expense in connection with them . . . We have now been playing with the question for eight years, and the request on the part of New South Wales that we should make an honest attempt to settle it now is, I think, fair and reasonable.

In voting for Canberra, McColl said it had plenty of water and good soil:

> If we have any idea of making the Seat of Government self-supporting it seems to me that we cannot select a finer site than that of Canberra . . . As one who has had a great deal to do with water questions during a parliamentary

career of twenty years, I do not think that in Australia there is any district which has a finer water supply than has Canberra. It contains so many different sources of supply that water is of excellent quality, and the quantity is so great that it could be used for ordinary and power purposes without any fear of impurity or deficiency. If we are to have a Federal Capital, let us have one which we can be proud of, and which persons from other countries will appreciate. Let us have a Capital which our own people will be glad to go to and settle in, with territory in which agricultural industries, as well as others, can be carried on. Let us have a Capital where people will care to live, and delight in bringing up their children.

McColl was criticised for his vote by his Victorian Senate colleagues and the Melbourne newspapers, which had supported Tumut, being closer to the Victorian border. The Melbourne *Argus* said he was naive: 'The age of romance is not past when a mature senator can fall so deeply and hopelessly in love at first sight with a poor and ordinary virgin site, and proclaim himself her fearless champion.'[3]

Not wishing to risk any further changes or machinations, the *Seat of Government (Yass–Canberra) Act* was hastily passed in both chambers of the Federal Parliament and given royal assent a week later, on 14 December 1908.

So, on 1 January 1911 – exactly ten years after the nation of Australia had been proclaimed – the Federal Capital Territory, of 2360 square kilometres, came into being, after both the New South Wales and Australian parliaments passed the requisite legislation. (Four years later, New South Wales added Jervis Bay, on the coast, to the federal capital territory. In 1915, Australia's first national naval college was established at Jervis Bay.)

In 1908, the decision was made for the Yass–Canberra area, but a decision had to be made as to where the actual capital city would be built within the federal capital territory area. In 1908, the prime minister, Queenslander Andrew Fisher, had New South Wales' chief surveyor Charles Scrivener examine where is the city was going to be within the Yass–Canberra area, and where the territorial border would run. His examination included the areas around Yass, Hall, Gundaroo, Mahkoolma, Queanbeyan and Lake George. Eventually, after negotiation with New South Wales premier Charles Wade, the area was decided, its shape a 'sort of like a mutant ear, perhaps with a cigarette stuck behind it pointing out towards Bungendore. But it's water that explains that shape because the bulk of our border follows watersheds'.[4] Scrivener indeed favoured the site for its availability of water, and for the fact that the flood plain of the Molonglo River could be dammed to form an ornamental lake in the centre of the site.

For thousands of years, the Canberra region had been home to the Ngunnawal people and other Aboriginal clans, including the Ngarigo, Wiradjuri, Wolgalu, Gundungurra and Yuin people. It had first been occupied by Europeans in the form of sheep and cattle farmers in the 1820s. It is widely accepted that Canberra is an Aboriginal name, but discussion still rages about whether it means a 'meeting place' or a 'woman's breasts' – the latter being the correct meaning, according to Ngunnawal elder the late Don Bell, as it was the Aboriginal name for Black Mountain and Mount Ainslie, which lie almost opposite each other with a plain between.[5] As with almost all European settlement in Australia, the Indigenous people's traditional ownership of the land was simply not considered when the building of Canberra began.

Now that the nation had a site for the capital, the government's attention turned to building it. On 30 April 1911, an international contest was announced for its design. The competition attracted 130 entries from North America, Europe and Australia, and was won by Walter Burley Griffin, a thirty-six-year-old architect from Chicago, who had never been to Australia.

Griffin's winning design showed a chain of lakes along the Molonglo Valley and a triangular framework for a central national area laid out along major vistas from Mount Ainslie and Black Mountain. On the southern side of the central lake, Griffin proposed a terraced group of government offices leading to the 'Capitol', his place of the people (now the site of Parliament House). Lower hills in the valley were reserved for other government and national institutions, a university, military college and municipal buildings, including a city hall. It was a simple concept, laid out in a geometric pattern intricately developed from the topography of the valley, with long, tree-lined avenues and boulevards. Griffin said he had designed the city on an unprecedented scale:

It [is] the first time such a thing has been attempted on any large scale ... George Washington employed Major Pierre (Peter) Charles L'Enfant to plan our capital at Washington, but this work was on a small scale, for no one had the slightest inkling of what the growth of the City of Washington would be ...

The plan I have prepared for the Australian capital will cover an area of twenty-five square miles [65 square kilometres], and is intended to provide for an immediate population of 75,000, with ample provision for the growth of the city as gauged by the increase in population of other foreign capitals. The plan is complete in every detail and covers everything that the city will need – street railway system, steam railway line, business and manufacturing districts. I have planned the city so that the three mountain peaks about it will close its principal vistas and form a splendid background for its architectural beauty.

The central district of the city will contain three centres – a centre devoted to government buildings, the municipal centre, and the mercantile centre. The outlying district will contain five additional centres. Three of these will be agricultural centres, one a manufacturing centre, and another a suburban residence centre.[6]

Griffin thought his design would be too radical for government and was surprised that it had won the competition: 'I have planned a city not like any other city in the world. I have planned it not in a way that I expected any governmental authorities in the world would accept . . . a city that meets my ideal of the city of the future.'

He came to Australia a year later with his wife and took up the position of director for the design and construction to of the new city. The cost of building the vision soon blew out, and the outbreak of the First World War forced cuts to the scope of the project. The city's main Northbourne Avenue was built but not the proposed Eastbourne, Southbourne and Westbourne avenues. Construction of the artificial lakes was deferred and the proposed railway connecting north and south Canberra across the lake was scrapped.

Griffin's relationship with the civil servants he was working with, and with the government, became increasingly acrimonious, and in 1920 he was forced to resign with much of his city still under construction. He remained in Australia for another fifteen years and designed a number of prominent buildings, including

Newman College at Melbourne University, the Capitol Theatre in Melbourne, the towns of Leeton and Griffith in southern New South Wales, and houses and large-scale incinerators in Sydney. He left Australia for India in 1935, having been invited to design the library at Lucknow University. He died of peritonitis eighteen months later, on 11 February 1937.

For its first two decades, Canberra grew slowly, and had the feel more of a small country town than a national capital. Uniquely in Australia, it was a dry town in which alcohol was outlawed. Prohibition was introduced in 1911 by King O'Malley, a zealous American teetotaller who was a member of the first Australian Parliament and Australia's minister for home affairs in 1910. O'Malley said he was born in Canada, in order to qualify as a British citizen and run for parliament in Australia; in fact, he was almost certainly born in Kansas, in the United States, around 1858. In America, he had been involved with fundamentalist religious churches, and had become a passionate advocate of temperance and a hater of what he termed 'stagger juice'. He arrived in Melbourne in 1888, before moving to Tasmania, then Adelaide, where he was first elected in 1896 to the South Australian Colonial Parliament (by declaring he was a British citizen). To the surprise of many, O'Malley was elected to the first Australian Parliament in 1901.

O'Malley was unable to keep the new national capital completely dry. His prohibition made it illegal to sell alcohol in Canberra but did not make it unlawful to possess alcohol, and residents could legally buy alcohol across the border and bring it back into the federal territory. By the 1920s, around 70,000 empty beer bottles were collected every six months from those who brought alcohol into the territory.[7] Prohibition was officially in force for seventeen years, until it was abolished in 1928, and was resented by many in Canberra:

> Canberra does not take it seriously. Canberra laughs at the idea as scornfully as the rest of Australia would laugh if any authority endeavoured to isolate this thin strip of country, set in a frontier 150 miles long from the rest of the Commonwealth ... [Across the New South Wales border] Queanbeyan is always crowded on Saturday afternoon [and in] Canberra ... everywhere one goes one finds pantries well and thoughtfully stocked ... the Capital has no sympathy with the cause ... People in Canberra resent the idea that they should be expected to conduct their lives with a virtue demanded of no citizen anywhere else in Australia.[8]

*

On 30 June 1914, another public competition was announced: for the design of Canberra's new Parliament House, which still hadn't moved from its temporary base in Melbourne:

> The Australian Government announces an international architectural competition for the purpose of selecting the architect of the Parliament House and possibly incidentally additional architect for other government structures of the new Federal Capital City, Canberra. Only tentative outline sketch designs for the building are requested and eight (8) prizes are offered aggregating £6,000, the first being £2,000, in addition to commission for service at the scale of the Royal Institute of British Architects.[9]

But the First World War began only two months later, and the competition was abandoned in September 1914. A new one was announced two years later, but was abandoned again in 1916. The work was eventually given to Scottish-born John Smith Murdoch, the Federal Government architect, and to the Commonwealth Department of Public Works. Eager to avoid great expense, the government decided to build a less costly temporary, or 'provisional' parliament house, and a grander building when the economic outlook was better:

> If . . . in Canberra we are to have the world's most beautiful city . . . in forty to fifty years' time, the work of building a Parliament House worthy of such a city is too big a job for us to tackle at the present time, and might well be left to posterity. The Government desires that Canberra shall not be a sink for the pouring out of public money, but shall be run on business lines. It does not desire to overload the Federal City with a huge capital cost at the expense of the taxpayers.[10]

Construction of the temporary parliament started in 1923 and was completed in 1927. It cost £600,000, which was three times the original budget, and was built using labourers from all over the country. One was Harold Lasseter, who died five years later in remote central Australia while trying to rediscover a reef of gold he claimed to have found years before.

The building consists of three levels, with the main floor on the middle level, reached by steps that lead to the centre of the building. The main entrance opens on to King's Hall, which was named after King George V, the reigning monarch. To the left of King's Hall is the chamber of the House of Representatives and to the right the Senate chamber. Interestingly, both chambers were designed to be the same size, despite the requirement of section 24 of the Australian Constitution that the House of Representatives have 'as near as practicable' twice the number of members as the Senate. This design flaw was a serious source of over-crowding until a larger chamber was built in the permanent Parliament House just over sixty years later.

The provisional Parliament House was officially opened on 9 May 1927 by the Duke and Duchess of York, the later King George VI and Queen Elizabeth, the Queen Mother. The opening was a grand event: the building was extensively decorated with British and Australian flags, and stands were built on the grass lawns outside for the attending dignitaries. At the beginning of the ceremony, Dame Nellie Melba, now sixty-six years old, sang the national anthem, which was, of course, 'God Save the King'. The Duke unlocked the doors with a golden key and led the official party into King's Hall, where he unveiled the statue of his father, King George V.

It was not until 1978 that Australian prime minister Malcolm Fraser announced a design competition for the new, 'permanent' Parliament House. The contest was won by Italian architect Romaldo Giurgola, who worked out of New York. His winning design involved burying most of the building under Capital Hill and capping it with a giant spire that flew an enormous Australian flag.

The new Parliament House, like the old one, was finished over time and over budget. It was officially opened by Queen Elizabeth II on 9 May 1988, which was the anniversary of her grandfather King George V's opening of the first Australian parliament in Melbourne, and of the opening of the 'provisional' Parliament House in Canberra on 9 May 1927 by her father.

*

The first national currency was not introduced into Australia until 1913, more than twelve years after

Federation. For most of the first decade after the federal inauguration, Australia continued to use myriad colonial currencies and other monies.

The new Australian currency was modelled on the British pound, which was made up of twenty shillings. Each shilling was made up of twelve pennies, and each penny could be made up of either two halfpennies or four farthings. A 'crown' was five shillings, and half a crown was two shillings and sixpence. A 'guinea' was twenty-one shillings, or one pound and one shilling. The currency was officially pegged to sterling so that one Australian pound was of the same value as one British pound.

From the time of the settlement of Sydney Cove in 1788, the official currency had been British sterling. However, there had been practically no money in the new colony to facilitate commerce and trade. Of all the detailed planning for the British settlement in Australia, the question of currency was never considered. Apart from 300 pounds issued to Arthur Phillip, the only other currency on First Fleet were the coins carried in the pockets and purses of individual officers and marines – and maybe a little secreted away by the convicts.

In the early years, everyone relied on the government stores for the issue of food and provisions. As the first settlement struggled to survive, Captain Phillip bought whatever he could from the occasional merchant ships that visited Sydney, paying with promissory notes that could be redeemed from the British Treasury when the ship returned to England. In 1789, with the settlement starving, Arthur Phillip sent his deputy, John Hunter, on the *Sirius* to Cape Town for a shipload of grain that was paid for by the issue of these Treasury bills.

One of the earliest alternative currencies used in Sydney was the Spanish dollar, which was spread widely around the world since Spain had been a dominant trader for several hundred years. It had also become widely accepted to cut the dollar coins into smaller denominations, first in half, then into quarters and finally into eight pieces, which became known as 'pieces of eight'. The American term 'two bits' is derived from two of these pieces being equal to 25 cents, or a quarter of a dollar. In the early days of the New South Wales colony, the Spanish dollars were worth about five British shillings, or four dollars to the pound.

For the first decades of settlement, in the absence of enough official currency, bartering became the main source of exchange. Foodstuffs became the obvious circulating medium, including flour, pork, tobacco and tea, and particularly, of course, rum.

By 1800, the population of the New South Wales colony had passed 5000 people, and the currencies in circulation included British guineas, crowns, half-crowns, shillings, pennies, halfpennies and farthings, Dutch guilders, Spanish dollars and their 'bits' and 'pieces', ducats, Portuguese Johannes, and Indian mohurs, pagodas and rupees.

In 1813, Governor Lachlan Macquarie addressed the continuing money problem by issuing the first Australian currency. He purchased 40,000 Spanish dollars from the visiting merchant ship the *Samarang* and turned them into 'colonial dollars' and 'dumps', the latter of which had the words 'New South Wales' stamped around the edge.

The first colonial banknotes were issued by Australia's private banks, starting with the Bank of New South Wales, which was created at the instigation of Macquarie. During the course of the next ninety years, a wide variety of banknotes were issued by the emerging banks and helped to lubricate the growing Australian economy.

On the initiative of Andrew Fisher's Labor government, the first Commonwealth of Australia ten-shilling banknote was issued on 1 May 1913. It was met with widespread scepticism by the public, who had previously been used to metal coins. The paper currency was soon nicknamed 'Fisher's Flimsies', described as 'dirty and smudgy' and believed to be disease-carrying and even life-threatening:

> No one objects to Fisher's Flimsies as long as they are clean. A report from Ballarat, Victoria however, states that five bank officials have become fever stricken this month, and fears are being expressed that some typhoid carrying banknotes are in circulation. Two deaths occurred this week. Constant handling of the banknotes will make them dirty, and then they may become a menace to public safety.[11]

Of course, everyone soon became accustomed to the paper notes. Australia continued with pounds, shillings and pence until February 1966, when it changed to a decimal system. The new dollar was made up of 100 new cents and was equal to half a pound, or ten shillings. The old shilling coin, which was made up of twelve old pence, was replaced by a ten-cent piece. Then, in 1996, Australia became the first country in the world to introduce plastic banknotes to replace notes made of paper.

*

Despite the abundant banners, bunting and flags flying in every city and town of Australia on 1 January 1901, Australia began its nationhood without an official flag. It was not until nine months later that Edmund Barton launched the officially approved flag, and even then there were two versions of it for more than half a century, until a single national flag was proclaimed in the *Flag Act* in 1954.

A section of all the earlier flags flown in Australia carried the Union Jack, and until the emergence of the self-governed colonies, the Union Jack was the only flag flown in Australia. During the Boer War, when the different colonies committed troops to fight alongside the British in South Africa, the Australians fought under the Union Jack.

In the lead-up to Federation, there was a multiplicity of flags, all attempting to represent Australia as part of Britain. One of the most popular ones, which was flown for more than thirty years until Federation, was a flag with the usual Union Jack in the top corner and a thick, blue St George's Cross with five white stars, one on each arm of the cross and a fifth in the centre. The constellation represented the Southern Cross, which, after the Eureka rebellion in 1854 at the Ballarat goldfields, had also become associated with Australian republicanism and was therefore unsuitable for a country that remained a dominion of imperial Britain.

On the occasion of the inauguration of Australia, in the absence of an officially agreed standard, much of the official material displayed no flag at all. At the opening of the Federal Parliament at Exhibition Hall in Melbourne on 9 May 1901, a large and colourful invitation card was sent to all the official guests. It had symbols of each the colonies and, in the top centre, a white crest with a red St George's Cross, and at the bottom a navy-blue crest with five white stars – but nowhere on it was a flag.

On 29 April 1901, the new Australian Government announced a competition to design an Australian national flag. The year before, *The Review of Reviews* had launched its own public flag-design competition and the government included their entries in the national competition. The contest attracted 32,823 entries from men, women and children across Australia, and a panel of judges was appointed to assess the designs based on their distinctiveness, history, heraldry and cost of manufacture.

The winning design was the same as the Australian flag of today – with the Union Jack in the top corner and the six stars of the constellation of the Southern Cross. The competition was won jointly by five people, who all submitted almost identical designs and shared the prize of about £40 each. They included a fourteen-year-old schoolboy from Melbourne, Ivor Evans; an eighteen-year-old Sydney student, Leslie John Hawkins; a thirty-five-year-old Melbourne architect, Egbert John Nuttall; a thirty-five-year-old Perth artist, Annie Dorrington; and a thirty-five-year-old ship's officer from Auckland, William Stevens.[12]

The winners were announced and the flag first flown in a special ceremony at Melbourne Exhibition Hall on 3 September 1901. The *Argus* was carried away by the occasion, in which Edmund Barton, in the presence of the governor general's wife, Lady Hopetoun, raised the flag for the first time:

> In years to come the flag which floated yesterday in the Exhibition building over Her Excellency the Countess of Hopetoun, who stood for Great Britain, and the Prime Minister (Mr. Barton), who stood for Australia, will, in all human probability, become the emblem upon which the millions of the free people of the Commonwealth will gaze with a thrill of national pride.[13]

Few people who witnessed Edmund Barton unveil the flag that day realised it would not become the official Australian flag until it was given royal consent in 1903 by King Edward VII.

For the next half-century, there were two official versions: one blue and the other red. For major celebrations and official occasions, the red ensign was flown alongside the Union Jack, including the official ceremony for the opening of the new federal capital of Canberra in 1913 and the opening of the new Parliament House in 1927. In both the First and Second World Wars, Australian troops fought under a red Australian ensign. As recently as the royal tour of Queen Elizabeth after her coronation in 1953, most of the hundreds of thousands of Australian schoolchildren were given red ensigns to wave as she went past.

Then, in late 1953, Prime Minister Robert Menzies introduced legislation for one flag, declaring to the parliament on Friday 20 November that 'the precise form of the flag or the circumstances of its use' had never been properly determined.[14] This flag was to be blue rather than the more popular red, and in future the blue ensign was indeed used on most occasions. The red ensign was still used, however, for official events and by the merchant navy. In a later explanation for choosing the blue over the red as the official colour, Menzies wrote in his memoir that red had become unpopular as the chosen colour of Australia's cold war communist enemies, including the Soviet Union and China.[15]

*

Australia did not have its own national anthem for more than seventy years after it became a nation, and it was not until 1984 that the matter was finally and officially resolved. For almost three-quarters of a century after 1901, most Australians were happy to continue singing 'God Save the Queen' (or King) as if it were theirs.

There were many early suggestions for an Australian anthem but none were adopted until the 1970s. John Dunmore Lang, a Scottish-born writer, politician and advocate of Australian independence, argued for a distinctly Australian national hymn in 1826 when he published an 'Australian Anthem' with eight verses:

> O be it then thy care,
> From Superstition's snare
> And Slavery's chain,
> To set the wretched free;
> 'Till Christian liberty,
> Wide o'er the Southern Sea,
> Triumphant reign![16]

Another suggestion was 'Song of Australia', written in 1859 by South Australian Caroline Carleton, who had migrated to Adelaide twenty years before with her doctor husband.[17] South Australia's Charles Kingston was so impressed by it that he had it taught in the state's schools, but it never made it to becoming the national anthem:

> There is a land where summer skies
> Are gleaming with a thousand dyes,
> Blending in witching harmonies, in harmonies;
> And grassy knoll, and forest height,
> Are flushing in the rosy light,
> And all above in azure bright –
> Australia!
>
> There is a land where honey flows,
> Where laughing corn luxuriant grows,
> Land of the myrtle and the rose,
> On hill and plain the clust'ring vine,

Is gushing out with purple wine,
And cups are quaffed to thee and thine –
Australia! . . .

There is a land where, floating free,
From mountain top to girdling sea,
A proud flag waves exultingly,
And freedom's sons the banner bear,
No shackled slave can breathe the air,
Fairest of Britain's daughters fair –
Australia![18]

In 1956, when Melbourne became the first city in the southern hemisphere to host the Olympic Games, an earnest search was made to find an anthem that reflected Australian identity, but 'God Save the Queen' remained.

It was not until 1974 that 'Advance Australia Fair' was chosen to become the national anthem of Australia. The government of the then prime minister Gough Whitlam ordered in 1974 a sample poll of 60,000 people to pick one of three options. They were Caroline Carleton's 'Song of Australia', 'Waltzing Matilda' and 'Advance Australia Fair'.

'Waltzing Matilda' (walking with a bag, or 'swag', over the shoulder) was written by the Australian-born poet Banjo Paterson in 1895 and published with sheet music in 1903. The poem narrates the story of an itinerant 'swagman' making tea at a bush camp and capturing a lamb to eat. When the sheep's owner arrives on horseback with three police to arrest the man for theft, he throws himself into a waterhole and drowns himself, after which his ghost haunts the pool.

'Advance Australia Fair' was composed in the 1870s by Scottish-born schoolteacher Peter Dodds McCormick, who had migrated to Australia as a twenty-one-year-old in 1855. The song was instantly very popular when performed on 30 November 1878 at a St Andrew's Day concert, and *The Sydney Morning Herald* wrote: 'the music in the song is bold and stirring and the words decidedly patriotic'.[19] At the inauguration ceremony for the new nation of Australia on 1 January 1901, a version of the song was sung by a choir of 10,000 in Melbourne.

Years later, McCormick explained what inspired him to write what became the Australian national anthem:

One night I attended a great concert in the Exhibition Building, when all the National Anthems of the world were to be sung by a large choir with band accompaniment. This was very nicely done, but I felt very aggravated that there was not one note for Australia. On the way home in a bus, I concocted the first verse of my song and when I got home I set it to music. I first wrote it in the Tonic Sol-fa notation, then transcribed it into the Old Notation, and I tried it over on an instrument next morning, and found it correct. Strange to say there has not been a note of it altered since. Some alteration has been made in the wording, but the sense is the same. It seemed to me to be like an inspiration, and I wrote the words and music with the greatest ease.[20]

In the 1974 survey, 'Advance Australia Fair' attracted the most votes – 51.4 per cent – and Prime Minister Whitlam announced it would be the Australian national anthem but that 'God Save the Queen' would be played at royal occasions. Some of the words of the original song have been changed for the official version. For example, the first line of the original, 'Australia's sons let us rejoice' was changed to 'Australians all let us rejoice' in the 1980s.

But that was not the end of the matter. In 1976, after a change of government, 'God Save the Queen' was reinstated for not only royal but also vice regal, defence and all loyalty toasting occasions, with 'Advance Australia Fair' to be played on other occasions. In May 1977, coinciding with the national election, a plebiscite was held where the seven million voters had their say about the three options, but also whether they wanted to hang on to 'God Save the Queen'. The results were: 'Advance Australia Fair' 43.2 per cent; 'Waltzing Matilda' 28.3 per cent; 'God Save the Queen' 18.7 per cent; and 'Song of Australia' 9.6 per cent.

So 'Advance Australia Fair' remained the national anthem. However, it was not until 1984 that the governor general issued a proclamation making it clear that McCormick's song was to be the anthem for all Australian occasions, and that 'God Save the Queen' would only be played at public engagements in Australia attended by the royal family.

*

Many people still feel the process of making Australia remains incomplete and will not be finished until the country is fully independent. According to Australia's 'constitutional monarchy', the head of state is still the Queen (or King) of Great Britain, and her representative in Australia, the governor general, is appointed by the British monarch.

Supporters of a republic argue that our head of state should be Australian and should be appointed by Australians. There were calls for an Australian republic decades before Federation, and they have continued ever since. However, it was only towards the end of the twentieth century that public support for a republic was in the majority, and on 6 November 1999 Australian voters were asked to vote 'yes' or 'no' to the question:

'Do you approve of an Act to alter the Constitution to establish the Commonwealth of Australia as a republic with the Queen and Governor-General being replaced by a President appointed by a two-thirds majority of the members of the Commonwealth Parliament?' The referendum failed – largely because many supporters of a republic did not want the Australian head of state being appointed by parliament but directly elected by the people.

Until the constitution is changed so that the governor general must be an Australian and be appointed by Australians, many will feel that the making of Australia is not quite complete, that it is not quite a sovereign state, and that the nation's business remains unfinished.

NOTES

CHAPTER 1: BEFORE THE BRITISH

1 Flinders, Introduction, p. 18
2 McClymont, pp. 442–4.
3 Richardson, p. 2.
4 Fitzgerald, 'Chinese', www.dictionaryofsydney.org.
5 Juxian, quoted in *Who Got to Australia First?*.
6 Stevens, p. 221.
7 Royal Society of Tasmania's Manuscript Collection. Map number 53: http://eprints.utas.edu.au/11107/1/rsa_mp_Royal_Society_of_Tasmania_Maps.pdf
8 The cove was later named Cygnet Bay by explorer Captain Phillip Parker King in 1818, after Dampier's ship, but it was renamed King Sound by Lieutenant John Stokes – who also named the Fitzroy River – in 1838.
9 Dampier, p. 463.
10 'Cook's Voyage 1768–1771: Copies of Correspondence', National Library of Australia, MS 2; nla.ms-ms2-s56-e-cd.
11 Coleville to Admiralty Secretary, letter, 30 December 1762, 1/482, Public Records Office, Kew.
12 Cook, April 1770.
13 Ibid., 22 August 1770.
14 Ibid.
15 Journal of the House of Commons, Public Records Office, RB F342.4206/1.
16 Banks, *Endeavour* Journal, April–May 1770.
17 Gilbert, 'Banks, Joseph (1743–1820)', http://adb.anu.edu.au.
18 Clark, M., Vol. I, p. 62.
19 Westervelt, p. 111.

20 Clark, M., Vol. I, p. 67.
21 Lord Sydney to Treasury, letter, 18 August 1786, *Historical Records of New South Wales*, Vol. 1, Part 2, pp. 14–16.
22 Lord Howe to Lord Sydney, letter, 3 September 1786, *Historical Records of New South Wales*, Vol. 1, Part 2, p. 22.
23 Tench, *Expedition*, chapter I.
24 Ibid., chapter II.
25 White, J., July 1787.
26 Bowes Smyth, January 1788.
27 Tench, *Expedition*, chapter VIII.
28 Cook, May 1770.

CHAPTER 2: THE EARLY DAYS OF STRUGGLE

1 Tench, *Settlement*, chapter XVII.
2 Phillip to Lord Sydney, letter, 15 May 1788, *Historical Records of New South Wales*, Vol. 1, Part 2, p. 127.
3 White, J., May 1788.
4 Phillip to Sydney, letter, 15 May 1788, *Historical Records of New South Wales*, Vol. 1, Part 2, p. 126.
5 Phillip to Sydney, letter, 28 September 1788, *Historical Records of New South Wales*, Vol. 1, Part 2, p. 188.
6 Phillip to Nepean, letter, 9 July 1788, *Historical Records of New South Wales*, Vol. 1, Part 2, p. 155.
7 Ross to Stephens, letter, 10 July 1788, *Historical Records of New South Wales*, Vol. 1, Part 2, p. 173.
8 Lord Sydney to the Admiralty, letter, 29 April 1789, *Historical Records of New South Wales*, Vol. 1, Part 2, p. 230.
9 Tench, *Settlement*, chapter VI.
10 White to Skill, letter, 17 April 1790, *Historical Records of New South Wales*, Vol. 1, Part 2, p. 332.
11 Tench, *Settlement*, chapter VII.
12 Phillip to Nepean, letter, 13 July 1790, *Historical Records of New South Wales*, Vol. 1, Part 2, p. 354.
13 Phillip to Nepean, letter, 15 April 1790, *Historical Records of New South Wales*, Vol. 1, Part 2, p. 330.
14 Grenville to Phillip, letter, 15 February 1791, *Historical Records of New South Wales*, Vol. 1, Part 2, p. 463.

15 Grose to Dundas, letter, 16 February 1793, *Historical Records of Australia*, Series I, Vol. II, pp. 14–15.

16 Hughes, p. 326.

17 Steven, Margaret, 'Macarthur, John (1767–1834)', http://adb.anu.edu.au

18 Banks to Hunter, letter, 1 February 1799, British Museum, NH DTC, 11.187.

19 Auchmuty, 'Hunter, John (1737–1821)', http://adb.anu.edu.au

20 Macarthur to Portland, letter, 15 September 1796, *Historical Records of Australia*, Series I, Vol. II, pp. 89–93;

21 Hunter to Portland, 14 September 1796, *Historical Records of Australia*, Series, I, Vol. I, pp. 661–3.

22 Hunter to King, letter, 1 June 1797, *Historical Records of Australia*, Series I, Vol. II, p. 11.

23 Hunter to Portland, letter, 25 July 1797, *Historical Records of Australia*, Series I, Vol. II, p. 171.

24 Portland to Hunter, letter, 26 February 1799, *Historical Records of Australia*, Series I, Vol. II, p. 338.

25 Ibid.

26 Portland to Hunter, letter, September 1799, *Historical Records of Australia*, Series I, Vol. II, p. 392.

CHAPTER 3: THE SETTLEMENT OF THE SOUTH

1 Clark, M., Vol. I, p. 161.

2 P. G. King to J. King, letter, 3 May 1800, *Historical Records of Australia*, Series I, Vol. 2, p. 505.

3 Shaw, 'King, Philip Gidley (1758–1808)', http://adb.anu.edu.au

4 Horner, p. 377.

5 Flinders, p. 181.

6 Ibid., p. 199.

7 King to Baudin, letter, 23 December 1802, *Historical Records of New South Wales*, Vol. 4, p. 1007.

8 Baudin to King, letter, 23 December 1802, *Historical Records of New South Wales*, Vol. 5, p. 830.

9 Ibid., p. 831.

10 Ibid.

11 King to Nepean, letter, 9 May 1803, *Historical Records of New South Wales*, Vol. 4, p. 249.

12 King to Bowen, letter, 28 March 1803, *Historical Records of New South Wales*, Vol. 5, p. 76.

13 Ibid.

14 King to Portland, letter, 21 May 1803, *Historical Records of Australia*, Series I, Vol. IV, p. 776.

15 Clark, M., Vol. I, p. 83.

16 Phillip to Sydney, letter, 28 September 1788, *Historical Records of New South Wales*, Vol. 1, Part 2, p. 190.

17 Shaw, p. 12.

18 Hobart to Collins, letter, 7 February 1803, *Historical Records of New South Wales*, Vol. 5, p. 16.

19 Collins to King, letter, 5 November 1803, *Historical Records of New South Wales*, Vol. 5, p. 248.

20 Collins to King, letter, 16 December 1803, *Historical Records of New South Wales*, Vol. 5, p. 313.

21 Nicholls (ed.), Knopwood entry of 6 February 1803.

22 Ibid., 12 February 1803.

23 Ibid., 16 February 1804.

24 Ibid., 15 February 1804.

25 Hughes, p. 125.

26 Darwin, chapter XIX, 5 February 1836.

27 Hughes, p. 621.

28 General Statement of the Inhabitants in His Majesty's Settlement, Hobart Town, 30 June 1806, *Historical Records of Australia*, Series I, Vol. III, p. 371.

29 Clark, M., Vol. I, p. 195.

30 Ibid., p. 194.

31 Ibid., p. 195.

32 Paterson to King, letter, 14 November 1805, *Historical Records of Australia*, Series III, Vol. I, p. 644.

33 Enclosures Nos 4, 5 in King to Windham, 12 August 1806, *Historical Records of Australia*, Series I, Vol. V, pp. 778–9, 780–2.

CHAPTER 4: WILLIAM BLIGH AND AUSTRALIA'S COUP D'ÉTAT

1 Kennedy, p. 1.

2 Ibid., p. 13.

3 Ibid., p. 14.

4 Bligh, April 1789, p. 163.

5 Kennedy, p. 285.

6 Bligh to Sir Joseph Banks, letter, 21 March 1805, Mitchell Library, State Library of New South Wales.

7 Seale, 'Mary Bligh O'Connell', www.hawkesburyhistory. net.au.

8 *Sydney Gazette*, 8 August 1796.

9 Bligh to Windham, 5 November 1806, *Historical Records of Australia*, Series I, Vol. VI, p. 27.

10 Kennedy, p. 289.

11 Ibid.

12 Bligh to Windham, letter, 31 October 1807, *Historical Records of Australia*, Series I, Vol. VI, p. 150.

13 Seale, 'Mary Bligh O'Connell', http://www.hawkesbury history.net.au.

14 Johnston to Castlereagh, letter, 11 April 1808, *Historical Records of Australia*, Series I, Vol. VI, p. 212.

15 Petition, *Historical Records of Australia*, Series I, Vol. VI, p. 240.

16 Quoted in Seale, 'Mary Bligh O'Connell', www.hawkesbury history.net.au.

17 Bligh to Castlereagh, letter, 1 June 1808, *Historical Records of Australia*, Series I, Vol. VI, p. 421.

18 Johnston to Castlereagh, letter, 26 January 1808, *Historical Records of Australia*, Series I, Vol. VI, p. 241.

19 Johnston to Castlereagh, letter, 11 April 1808, *Historical Records of Australia*, Series I, Vol. V, p. 212.

20 Macarthur Onslow (ed.), p. 153.

21 Watson, Paterson, Bartrum and Bladen, www.gutenberg. net.au.

22 Foveaux to Castlereagh, letter, 4 September 1808, *Historical Records of Australia*, Series I, Vol. VI, p. 624.

23 Foveaux to Paterson, letter, 16 August 1808, *Historical Records of Australia*, Series I, Vol. VI, p. 634.

24 Paterson to Castlereagh, letter, 12 March 1809, *Historical Records of Australia*, Series I, Vol. VII, p. 18.

25 Kennedy, p. 295.

26 Bligh to Castlereagh, letter, 10 June 1809, *Historical Records of Australia*, Series I, Vol. VII, p. 128.

27 Watson, Paterson, Bartrum and Bladen, www.gutenberg.net.au.

28 Ellis, p. 178.

29 Kennedy, p. 299.

30 Bligh to Elizabeth Bligh, letter, 11 August 1810, Mitchell Library, State Library of New South Wales, ML MS 1/45.

31 Watson, Paterson, Bartrum and Bladen, www.gutenberg.net.au.

32 Ritchie, p. xviii.

33 Watson, Paterson, Bartrum and Bladen, www.gutenberg.net.au.

34 Castlereagh to Macquarie, 14 May 1809, *Historical Records of Australia*, Series I, Vol. VII, p. 81.

35 Steven, 'Macarthur, John (1767–1834)', http://adb.anu.edu.au.

36 Macquarie to Castlereagh, letter, 10 May 1810, *Historical Records of Australia*, Series I, Vol. VII, p. 331.

CHAPTER 5: LACHLAN MACQUARIE: 'THE FATHER OF AUSTRALIA'

1 Ellis, p. 166.

2 Ibid.

3 Macquarie, Journal, 20 August 1804.

4 Ibid.

5 Macquarie, Journal , 26 March 1805.

6 Ibid.

7 Macquarie to Charles Forbes, 13 February 1809, Macquarie papers, Mitchell Library, State Library of New South Wales, ML MS 15/5.

8 *Sydney Gazette*, 7 January 1810.

9 Castlereagh to Macquarie, letter, 14 May 1808, *Historical Records of Australia*, Series I, Vol. VII, pp. 80–3.

10 Ellis, p. 177.

11 *Sydney Gazette*, 7 January 1810.

12 Ibid., 28 April 1810.

13 Ellis, p. 195.

14 Ibid.

15 Ibid., p. 192.

16 Liverpool to Macquarie, letter, 4 May 1812, *Historical Records of Australia*, Series I, Vol. VII, pp. 477–8.

17 Liverpool to Macquarie, letter, 5 May 1812, *Historical Records of Australia*, Series I, Vol. VII, p. 481.

18 Liverpool to Macquarie, letter, 19 May 1812, *Historical Records of Australia*, Series I, Vol. VII, pp. 486–8.

19 Ellis, p. 219.

20 Macquarie to Liverpool, letter, 9 November 1812, *Historical Records of Australia*, Series I, Vol. VII, p. 525.

21 Ellis, p. 220.

22 Macquarie, Journal, 23 November 1811.

23 Macquarie, Journal of Tour to and from Van Diemen's Land, New South Wales, 4 November 1811 – 6 January 1812, p. 36, and 2 December 1811, quoted in Ellis, p. 208.

24 Macquarie, Journal, 27 November 1811.

25 Macquarie, Journal of Tour to and from Van Diemen's Land, New South Wales, 4 November 1811 – 6 January 1812, p. 48, and 8 December 1811, quoted in Ellis, p. 209.

26 Macquarie, Journal, 10 December 1811.

27 Ibid., 25 December 1811.

28 Macquarie to Bathurst, letter, 31 July 1813, *Historical Records of Australia,* Series I, Vol. VIII, p. 84.

29 Macquarie to Bathurst, letter, 31 July 1813, *Historical Records of Australia*, Series I, Vol. VIII, p. 3.

30 Ibid., pp. 1, 4.

31 House of Commons, 25 March 1812.

32 Blaxland, p. 36.

33 Macquarie to Bathurst, 19 January 1814, *Historical Records of Australia*, Series I, Vol. VIII, p. 149.

34 Ellis, p. 265.

35 Macquarie to Bathurst, letter, 19 January 1814, *Historical Records of Australia*, Series I, Vol. VIII, pp. 123–4.

36 Ellis, p. 271.

37 Ibid.

38 Macquarie, Journal, 25 April 1815.

39 Ibid., 4 May 1815.

40 Macquarie, *A Letter to the Right Honourable Viscount Sidmouth*, p. 79.

41 Macquarie to Castlereagh, letter, 30 April 1810, *Historical Records of Australia*, Series I, Vol. VII, p. 276.

42 Macquarie to Bigge, letter, 6 November 1819, *Historical Records of Australia*, Series I, Vol. X, p. 222.

43 Yarwood, 'Marsden, Samuel (1765–1838)', http://adb.anu.edu.au.

44 Marsden.

45 Ellis, p. 227.

46 Ibid., p. 325.

47 Macquarie to Bathurst, letter, 4 December 1817, *Historical Records of Australia*, Series I, Vol. IX, p. 502.

48 Macquarie to Marsden, letter, 8 January 1818, www.sl.nsw.gov.au.

49 Spigelman, 'A Reappraisal of the Bigge Reports', http://historycouncilnsw.org.au.

50 Bathurst to Bigge, letter, 6 January 1819, *Historical Records of Australia*, Series I, Vol. X, pp. 7–8.

51 *Sydney Gazette*, 15 February 1822.

CHAPTER 6: THE ABORIGINAL PEOPLE

1 Phillip's instructions, 25 April 1787, *Historical Records of New South Wales*, Vol. 1, Part 2, p. 89.

2 George Worgan, Journal, 27 January 1788, Library Council of New South Wales in Association with the Library of Australian History, Sydney, 1978.

3 Bowes Smyth, January 1878.

4 Nagle, p. 12.

5 Tench, *Expedition*, chapter XI.

6 Phillip to Stephens, letter, 16 November 1788, *Historical Records of New South Wales*, Vol. 1, Part 2, p. 214.

7 Quoted in Connell (ed.), p. 76.

8 Newton Fowell, letter to father, John Fowell, PRO CO 201/4, MLMSS 4895/1/18, Mitchell Library, State Library of New South Wales.

9 Phillip to Nepean, letter, 13 February 1790, *Historical Records of New South Wales*, Vol. 1, Part 2, p. 308.

10 Phillip to Lord Sydney, letter, 12 February 1790, *Historical Records of New South Wales*, Vol. 1, Part 2, p. 299.

11 Blainey, p. 30.

12 Tench, *Settlement*, chapter II.
13 Ibid., chapter III.
14 Ibid.
15 Ibid.
16 Ibid.
17 Ibid.
18 King to Lord Hobart, 20 December 1804, *Historical Records of Australia*, Series I, Vol. V, p. 166.
19 Turbet, p. 127.
20 Kohen, 'Pemulwuy (1750–1802)', http://adb.anu.edu.au.
21 Heaton, p. 3
22 Roth, p. 3.
23 Darwin, chapter XIX, 12 January 1836.
24 Parliamentary Select Committee on Aboriginal Tribes, report, https://archive.org.
25 George Murray to George Arthur, letter, 5 November 1830, republished House of Commons, report, *Colonies and Slaves*, p. 56, Bodleian Museum, Oxford, July 1831.
26 Blackstock, p. 83.
27 Ibid., p. 84.
28 Australian Bureau of Statistics, Australian Historical Population Statistics, 2008, 3105.0.65.001.

CHAPTER 7: THE FOUNDING OF THE OTHER AUSTRALIAN COLONIES

1 Barnard, p. 53.
2 Darling to Wright, letter, 4 November 1826, *Historical Records of Australia*, Series I, Vol. XII, p. 701.
3 Ibid.
4 Shaw, p. 36.
5 Ibid., p. 36.
6 Ibid., p. 37.
7 Clark, M., Vol. III, p. 89.
8 Flannery, p. 144.
9 Ibid., p. 129.
10 Anderson, 'Fawkner, John Pascoe (1792–1869)', http://adb.anu.edu.au.
11 Clark, M., Vol. III, p. 90.
12 Bourke to Glenelg, letter, 11 September 1836, *Historical Records of Australia*, Series I, Vol. XVIII, p. 541.

13 Penny, 'Lonsdale, William (1799–1864)', http://adb.anu.edu.au.

14 Shaw, p. 69.

15 Bassett, 'Gisborne, Henry Fyshe (Fysche) (1813–1841)', http://adb.anu.edu.au.

16 Sturt, chapter VIII.

17 Ibid.

18 *South Australian Gazette and Colonial Register*, 18 June 1836.

19 Clark, M., Vol. III, p. 51.

20 Manning, 'Kangaroo Island: Early History in Nepean Bay and the Settlement on Kangaroo Island', www.slsa.sa.gov.au.

21 Ibid.

22 Ibid.

23 Clark, M., Vol. III, p. 55.

24 Royal Australian Historical Society, 'Australia's First Northern Port', www.rahs.org.au.

25 Pike, p. 325.

26 Ibid.

27 Murray to Darling, letter, 1 November 1828, *Historical Records of Australia*, Series 1, Vol. XIV, pp. 410–11.

28 Pike, p. 339.

29 *The Sydney Morning Herald*, 26 March 1846.

30 *Illustrated Australian News*, 22 February 1869.

31 Rolls, p. 260.

32 Ibid.

33 Bathurst to Darling, letter, 1 March 1826, *Historical Records of Australia*, Series I, Vol. XII, p. 498.

34 Darling to Lockyer, letter, 4 November 1826, *Historical Records of Australia*, Series I, Vol. XII, p. 700.

35 Crowley, 'Stirling, Sir James (1791–1865)', http://adb.anu.edu.au.

36 Welsh, p. 135.

37 Ibid.

38 Ibid., p. 136.

39 Barrow to Hay, Robert, undersecretary of the War and Colonial Office, letter, UK Public Records Office, CO 323/152.

40 Welsh, p. 135.

41 Clark, M., Vol. III, p. 21.
42 *Sydney Gazette and New South Wales Advertiser*, 8 December 1829.
43 Ibid.
44 Cook, June 1770.
45 Harrison, 'Moreton Bay Convict Settlement', http://www.archives.qld.gov.au.
46 *The Sydney Monitor*, 17 July 1830.
47 *The Sydney Morning Herald*, 20 January 1851.
48 Labouchere to Denison, letter, 21 July 1856, UK Public Records Office, Commonwealth Office, CO 201/494.

CHAPTER 8: W. C. WENTWORTH AND SELF-GOVERNMENT

1 Clark, M., Vol. III, p. 452.
2 *The Sydney Morning Herald*, 7 May 1872.
3 *The People's Advocate*, 25 August 1849.
4 Persse, 'M. Wentworth, William Charles (1790–1872)', http://adb.anu.edu.au.
5 Ellis, p. 231.
6 Wentworth, preface.
7 Clark, G., 'Farm Wages and Living Standards in the Industrial Revolution', www.econ.ucdavis.edu.
8 Persse M., 'William Charles Wentworth (1790–1872)', http://adb.anu.edu.au.
9 Ibid.
10 Parliament of New South Wales, 'History of the Parliament of New South Wales', www.parliament.nsw.gov.au.
11 Tink, p. 117.
12 *The Sydney Morning Herald*, 27 May 1847.
13 *Australian*, 25 November 1826.
14 Darling to Hay, letter, 16 December 1826, *Historical Records of Australia*, Series I, Vol. XII, pp. 762–3.
15 Darling to Goderich, 10 October 1827, *Historical Records of Australia*, Series I, Vol. XIII, p. 547.
16 Wentworth to Murray, 1 March 1829, *Historical Records of Australia*, Series I, Vol. XIV, pp. 801, 805.
17 Goderich to Darling, letter, 11 July 1827, *Historical Records of Australia*, Series I, Vol. XIII, pp. 439–40.
18 *Australian*, 21 October 1831.

19 King, 'Bourke, Sir Richard (1777–1855)', http://adb.anu.edu. au.

20 Gipps to Glenelg, letter, 3 April 1839, *Historical Records of Australia*, Series I, Vol. XX, pp. 81–2.

21 Gipps to Russell, letter, 16 August 1840, *Historical Records of Australia*, Series I, Vol. XX, p. 160.

22 *The Sydney Morning Herald*, 13 July 1840.

23 Fletcher and Elias, 'A Collusive Suit', www.victoria.ac.nz.

24 Select Committee on Transportation, report, http://trove. nla.gov.au

25 *The Sydney Morning Herald*, 27 December 1842.

26 Ibid.

27 Ibid., 28 December 1842.

28 Ibid., 16 June 1843

29 Ibid., 4 July 1843.

30 Tink, p. 175.

31 *The Sydney Morning Herald*, 21 June 1844.

32 Grey to FitzRoy, letter, 31 July 1847, *Historical Records of Australia*, Series I, Vol. XXV, p. 694.

33 *The Sydney Chronicle*, 20 January 1848.

34 FitzRoy to Grey, letter, 11 August 1848 (received by Grey 19 January 1849), *Historical Records of Australia*, Series I, Vol. XXVI, p. 540.

35 Ibid., 4 December 1848, *Historical Records of Australia*, Series I, Vol. XXVI, pp. 609–10.

36 *The Argus*, 4 August 1853.

37 *The Bathurst Free Press*, 13 August 1853.

38 *The Sydney Morning Herald*, 17 August 1853.

39 Ibid., 19 April 1861.

40 Ibid., 21 April 1861.

41 Ibid., 12 November 1862.

42 Ibid., 7 May 1873.

43 *The Sydney Morning Herald*, 7 May 1873.

44 Ibid.

CHAPTER 9: GOLD AND THE EUREKA REBELLION

1 Evidence before the Select Committee on the claims of Reverend W. B. Clarke, New South Wales Legislative Assembly, Votes and Proceedings, Vol. 2, 1861, p. 1186.

2 *The Maitland Mercury*, 28 May 1851.

3 Mundy, p. 562.

4 Godley, pp. 332, 335.

5 Mundy, p. 572.

6 *The Sydney Morning Herald*, 23 July 1851.

7 La Trobe to Grey, letter, 25 August 1851, Mitchell Library, State Library of New South Wales.

8 Ibid., 10 October 1851.

9 Hall, p. 10.

10 Letter from 'gentleman', quoted in Australian Journalist, *The Emigrant in Australia, or Gleanings from the Gold-fields*, Addey and Co., London, 1852, p. 59.

11 Ibid., p. 62.

12 'Correspondence Relative to the Recent Discovery of Gold in Australia', Thomas, 2 February 1852.

13 Cecil, p. 10.

14 Ibid.

15 Howitt, p. 19.

16 *The Argus*, 11 April 1855.

17 *The Sydney Morning Herald*, 7 May 1855.

18 Young, p. 19.

19 Ibid.

20 Ibid., p. 24.

21 *The Argus*, 23 May 1855.

22 Ibid., 12 October 1854.

23 Victorian Parliamentary Papers, 'Report from the Commission Appointed to Inquire into the Conditions on the Gold Fields', Legislative Council, Votes and Proceedings, A76/1854–55, Vol. II.

24 Smeaton, 'Our Invasion', Robe Public Library.

25 Young, p. 213.

26 *The Sydney Morning Herald*, 2 and 4 July 1861.

27 *Geelong Advertiser*, 26 August 1851.

28 Carboni, p. 3.

29 Hotham to Bart, 18 September 1854, dispatch no. 112, Public Record Office of Victoria, 1085/PO, unit 8.

30 Carboni, p. 13.

31 *Ballarat Times*, 18 November 1854.

32 Hotham to Bart, 18 November 1854, dispatch no. 148, Public Record Office of Victoria, VPRS 1085/PO, unit 8.

33 Carboni, p. 35.

34 *The Argus*, 10 April 1855.
35 Ferguson, pp. 284–6.
36 *The Age*, 5 December 1854.
37 FitzSimons, p. 616.
38 Blainey, p. 56.
39 Traill, p. 56.
40 'Early Gympie Incidents', *The Gympie Times*, 16 October 1917, republished in *Gympie's Jubilee*, 1867–1917, special issue, 1917.
41 Weitemeyer, p. 168.
42 Holthouse, p. 7.
43 Ibid.
44 *The Queenslander*, 27 November 1875.
45 Holthouse, p. 88.
46 *Cooktown Herald*, May 1876.
47 Cecil, p. 9.
48 Marshall, pp. 22–3.
49 Keesing, p. 330.

CHAPTER 10: LINKING THE COLONIES

1 *South Australian Register*, 23 August 1872.
2 Ibid.
3 Ibid., 16 November 1872.
4 *Western Australian News*, 28 December 1877.
5 Ibid.
6 *The Argus*, 13 September 1854.
7 Ibid.
8 Ibid.
9 Gunn, p. 16.
10 Annual Report of the New South Wales Railway Commissioner, 30 September 1865, quoted in Gunn, p. 25.
11 Gunn, p. 40.
12 *The Sydney Morning Herald*, 27 September 1855.
13 *Empire*, 27 September 1855.
14 Gunn, p. 46.
15 Ibid.
16 Ibid., p. 18.
17 Thompson to Cowper, letter, 11 July 1851, Votes and Proceedings of the Legislative Council (VPLC).

18 Wallace to the Sydney Railway Company, letter, 20 September 1852, quoted in Gunn, p. 28.

19 Cole, A. E., 'Early History of the Queensland Railways', Royal Historical Society of Queensland, 27 April 1944, p. 295.

20 Ibid., p. 296.

21 *The Sydney Morning Herald*, 15 June 1883.

22 Ibid.

23 Ibid.

24 *The Sydney Morning Herald*, 16 June 1883.

25 *South Australian Register*, 20 June 1883.

26 Ibid.

CHAPTER 11: 'THE FATHER OF FEDERATION'

1 Dando-Colllins, p. 3.

2 *The Times* (London), 29 April 1896.

3 Martin, 'Parkes, Sir Henry (1815–1896)', http://adb.anu.edu.au.

4 Dando-Collins, p. 11.

5 Ibid., p. 14.

6 Ibid.

7 Parkes, *Fifty Years*, p. 9.

8 Martin, 'Parkes, Sir Henry (1815–1896)', http://adb.anu.edu.au.

9 Parkes, *Fifty Years*, pp. 1–2.

10 Ibid., p. 4.

11 Ibid., p. 382.

12 Ibid., p. 12.

13 Dando-Collins, p. 40.

14 Ibid., p. 232.

15 Irving, *Centenary Companion*, p. 25.

16 De Garis, 'How Popular was the Popular Federation Movement?', www.aph.gov.au.

17 Dunn, 'The Attempted Assassination of Prince Alfred at Clontarf 1868', www.historyaustralia.org.au.

18 White, C., p. 341.

19 Parkes, *Fifty Years*, p. 336.

20 Irving, *Centenary Companion*, p. 26.

21 *Australian Encyclopaedia*, p. 115.

22 *The Argus*, 11 December 1883.

23 Dando-Collins, p. 316.

24 Ibid., p. 322.

25 Roderick, p. 43.

26 Dando-Collins, p. 343.

27 Lyne, p. 258.

28 Dando-Collins, p. 350.

29 Clark, C., p. 464.

30 Murray, p. 277.

31 *The Sydney Morning Herald*, 25 October 1889.

32 Deakin, *Federal Story*, p. 28.

33 Dando-Collins, p. 348.

34 Quick and Garran, p. 119.

35 Deakin, *Federal Story*, p. 38.

36 Norris, 'Deakin, Alfred (1856–1919)', http://adb.anu.edu.au.

37 Clark, M., Vol. IV, p. 373.

38 Ibid., pp. 372–3.

39 Deakin, *Federal Story*, p. 36.

40 Ibid., p. 24.

41 Ibid., p. 44.

42 Ibid., p. 18

43 Ibid., p. 35.

44 Ibid., p. 29.

45 Ibid., p. 30.

46 Ibid.

47 Bolton, 'Steere, Sir James George Lee (1830–1903)', http://adb.anu.edu.au.

48 Deakin, *Federal Story*, p. 37.

49 *The Sydney Morning Herald*, 7 February 1890.

50 Official Record of the Proceedings and Debates of the Australasian Federation Conference, Melbourne 1890, http://adc.library.usyd.edu.au.

51 Ibid.

CHAPTER 12: 'FEDERATION IS DEAD'

1 *Newcastle Morning Herald and Miners' Advocate*, 9 March 1891.

2 Parkes, Diary, 9 January 1891, http://acms.sl.nsw.gov.au.

3 *The Sydney Morning Herald*, 3 March 1891.

4 Ibid., 11 April 1891.

5 Ibid., 3 and 9 March 1891.

6 *The Advertiser* (Adelaide), 3 March 1891.

7 *The Sydney Morning Herald*, 11 April 1891.

8 http://parlinfo.aph.gov.au/parlInfo/search/display/display

9 *The Advertiser* (Adelaide), 5 March 1891.

10 Ibid., 7 March 1891.

11 Deakin, *Federal Story*, p. 32.

12 Ibid., p. 41.

13 Ibid., pp. 12–13.

14 Irving, p. 345.

15 Parkes, *Fifty Years*, p. 258.

16 De Garis, 'Representative Government: The First Elections', www.constitutionalcentre.wa.gov.au.

17 Western Australia Parliamentary Debates, Vol. 11, 1884, p. 32.

18 *The Inquirer and Commercial News* (Perth), 2 November 1870.

19 Crowley, p. 288.

20 *The Western Mail* (Perth), 7 March 1891.

21 Ibid.

22 *The Sydney Morning Herald*, 6 March 1891.

23 Deakin to Pearson, letter, 25 March 1891, quoted in De Garis/ Irving, p. 290.

24 *The Brisbane Courier*, 8 May 1885.

25 Royal Historical Society of Queensland.

26 *The Sydney Morning Herald*, 11 April 1891.

27 Ibid., 10 April 1891.

28 *Illustrated Australian News*, 1 April 1891.

29 Parkes, Diary, 15 April 1891.

30 *The Advertiser* (Adelaide), 7 March 1891.

31 *The Sydney Morning Herald*, 21 April 1891.

32 Ibid., 17 April 1891.

33 Deakin, *Federal Story*, p. 66.

34 Ibid., p. 65.

35 Parkes, *Fifty Years*, p. 373.

36 *The Brisbane Courier*, 26 May 1891.

37 Ibid.

38 Irving, p. 33.

39 Quartly/Irving, p. 239.

40 *The Age*, 10 June 1891.
41 Deakin, *'And Be One People'*, p. 51.
42 Ibid., p. 55.
43 Quartly/Irving, p. 240.
44 *The Age*, 27 January 1893.
45 Ibid., 7 February 1893.
46 Bannon/Irving, p. 148.
47 Bolton Waterson/Irving, p. 100.
48 *Mercury* (Hobart), 21 November 1891.
49 Deakin, *Federal Story*, p. 57.

CHAPTER 13: THE PUBLIC MOVEMENT
 1 *The Mirror* (Perth), 20 December 1924.
 2 Roderick, p. 116.
 3 Ibid., p. 39.
 4 Fahey, 'The Bushman's Bible: The History of the Bulletin', http://warrenfahey.com.
 5 *The Morning Bulletin* (Rockhampton), 11 August 1893.
 6 Deakin, *Federal Story*, p. 61.
 7 Quartly/Irving, p. 243.
 8 *Wagga Wagga Advertiser*, 3 August 1893.
 9 *The Morning Bulletin* (Rockhampton), 11 August 1893.
10 Glynn, Patrick, quoted in McMinn, p. 277.
11 Deakin, *Federal Story*, p. 62.
12 Irving, *Centenary Companion*, p. 362.
13 Bannon/Irving, p. 157.
14 *Mercury* (Hobart), 23 January 1895.
15 Ibid., 30 January 1895.
16 Ibid., 1 February 1895.
17 Ibid.
18 Ibid.
19 Conference of Premiers, p. 2.
20 *The Sydney Morning Herald*, 24 October 1895.
21 Ibid.
22 Reid, p. 84, http://setis.library.usyd.edu.au.
23 *The Western Champion* (Barcaldine, Queensland), 5 November 1895.
24 *Daily News* (Perth), 25 October 1895.
25 *South Australian Register*, 28 April 1896.

26 *The Brisbane Courier*, 28 April 1896.
27 Proceedings of the Bathurst People's Federal Convention, p. 78.
28 *The Daily Telegraph* (Sydney), 21 November 1896.
29 Bolton Waterson/Irving, p. 107.
30 Deakin, *Federal Story*. p. 74.
31 *The Sydney Morning Herald*, 1 March 1897.
32 Ibid., 27 February 1897.
33 Ibid., 3 March 1897.
34 Irving, *Centenary Companion*, p. 66.
35 *The Sydney Morning Herald*, 6 March 1897.
36 Deakin, *Federal Story*, p. 81.
37 Serle, 'Turner, Sir George (1851–1916)', http://adb.anu.edu. au.
38 Deakin, *Federal Story*, p. 70.
39 Crowley, p. 109.
40 Stephen and Quick, p. 74.
41 Bolton Waterson/Irving, p. 107.
42 Bannon/Irving, p. 162.
43 *The Chronicle* (Adelaide), 13 March 1897.
44 Ibid., 27 March 1897.
45 Ibid.
46 Ibid.
47 Ibid.
48 Ibid.
49 Ibid.
50 Irving, *Centenary Companion*, p. 68.
51 Deakin, *Federal Story*, p. 76.
52 Ibid., p. 79.
53 Playford, 'Kingston, Charles Cameron (1850–1908)', http:// adb.anu.edu.au.
54 Reid, p. 71, http://setis.library.usyd.edu.au.
55 Deakin, *Federal Story*, p. 70.
56 *The Chronicle* (Adelaide), 27 March 1897.
57 Ibid.
58 Ibid.
59 *The Daily Mail and Empire* (Toronto), 20 June 1897.
60 Ibid.
61 *South Australia Register*, 3 July 1897.

62 *The Sydney Morning Herald*, 1 September 1897.

63 Ibid., 2 September 1897.

64 Ibid.

65 Ibid.

66 Deakin, *Federal Story*, p. 86.

67 *The Argus*, 13 March 1898.

68 Deakin, *Federal Story*, p. 11.

69 *The Argus*, 21 January 1898.

70 *The Sydney Morning Herald*, 17 March 1898.

71 *The Argus*, 15 March 1898.

CHAPTER 14: VOTING FOR NATIONHOOD

1 De Garis/Irving, p. 303.

2 Allen, 'Scott, Rose (1847–1925)', http://adb.anu.edu.au.

3 Irving, 'Who Are the Founding Mothers?' www.aph.gov.au.

4 *The Sydney Morning Herald*, 29 March 1898.

5 Ibid.

6 Ibid.

7 *Illawarra Mercury*, 12 April 1898.

8 *The Sydney Morning Herald*, 25 April 1898.

9 *The Daily Telegraph* (Sydney), 23 June 1899; Irving, *Centenary Companion*, p. 79.

10 Deakin, *Federal Story*, p. 98.

11 Irving, *Centenary Companion*, p. 76.

12 Finn, 'Want, John Henry (1846–1905)', http://adb.anu.edu. au.

13 *The Sydney Morning Herald*, 1 June 1898.

14 *The Chronicle* (Adelaide), 4 June 1898.

15 *The Review of Reviews*, 15 June 1898.

16 Reid, p. 170, http://setis.library.usyd.edu.au.

17 *The Advertiser* (Adelaide), 4 June 1898.

18 *The Argus*, 4 June 1898.

19 Ibid.

20 *The Queanbeyan Age*, 27 July 1898.

21 *Evening News* (Sydney), 22 July 1898.

22 *The Sydney Morning Herald*, 14 September 1898.

23 *South Australian Register*, 4 January 1899.

24 Bolton and Waterson/Irving, p. 111.

25 *The Examiner* (Launceston), 4 February 1899.

26 *The Progress*, 11 February 1899.

27 Deakin, *Federal Story*, p. 79.

28 Section 125, Australian Constitution.

29 Kingston to Turner, letter, 5 June 1898, quoted in Bannon/ Irving, p. 176.

30 Ibid., 8 June 1898.

31 *Launceston Examiner*, 4 February 1899.

32 Ibid.

33 *The Sydney Morning Herald*, 3 February 1899.

34 Bannon/ Irving, p. 177.

35 *The Daily Telegraph*, 7 March 1899.

36 *The Sydney Morning Herald*, 23 June 1899.

37 *Goulburn Evening Penny Post*, 17 June 1899.

38 *The Sydney Morning Herald*, 21 June 1899.

39 *Evening News* (Sydney), 21 June 1899.

40 *The Argus*, 22 July 1899.

41 Ibid., 28 July 1899.

42 Ibid., 25 July 1899.

43 Ibid., 28 July 1899.

44 Ibid.

45 *The West Australian*, 2 June 1899.

46 Bolton Waterson/Irving, p. 113.

47 Ibid., p. 115.

48 Ibid., p. 113.

49 Ibid., p. 117.

CHAPTER 15: LONDON, 1900

1 Deakin, *Federal Story*, p. 90.

2 *The West Australian*, 28 May 1898.

3 De Garis/Irving, p. 303.

4 Forrest to Barton, letter, 9 July 1898, Barton Papers, National Library of Australia, MS 51.

5 Baston, pp. 77–8.

6 *The Advertiser* (Adelaide), 3 February 1900.

7 Reynolds, p. 174.

8 Garvin, Vol. 3, p. 557.

9 Bolton Waterson/Irving, p. 119.

10 *The Advertiser* (Adelaide), 28 May 1900.

11 *The Sydney Morning Herald*, 30 April 1900.

12 Ibid.

13 *The Inquirer and Commercial News* (Perth), 25 May 1900.

14 Deakin, '*And Be One People*', p. 156.

15 *The Freeman's Journal* (Sydney), 8 September 1900.

16 Irving, *Centenary Companion*, p. 317.

17 Ibid., p. 180.

18 Chamberlain to Onslow, letter, 27 April 1900, WA Votes and Proceedings, 1900, Vol. 1, pp. 8–9.

19 *The West Australian*, 31 July 1900.

CHAPTER 16: THE NATION IS BORN

 1 *The Sydney Morning Herald*, 17 December 1900.

 2 *The Sydney Morning Herald*, 5 October 1900.

 3 *The Examiner* (Launceston), 17 July 1900.

 4 *The Sydney Morning Herald*, 23 November 1900.

 5 Carroll, p. 34.

 6 *Mercury* (Hobart), 21 December 1900.

 7 *Evening News* (Sydney), 17 December 1900.

 8 Reynolds, p. 183.

 9 Ibid., p. 185.

10 Chamberlain to Hopetoun, telegram, 23 December 1900, http://vrroom.naa.gov.au.

11 Papers of Alfred Deakin, National Library of Australia, Collection number MS 1540.

12 *The Argus*, 21 December 1900.

13 Reynolds, p. 188.

14 *Mercury* (Hobart), 1 January 1901.

15 Irving, *Centenary Companion*, p. 378.

16 Bolton and Waterson/Irving, p. 120.

17 *The Sydney Morning Herald*, 31 December 1900.

18 Ibid.

19 *Mercury* (Hobart), 31 December 1900.

20 Ibid.

21 *The Sydney Morning Herald*, 31 December 1900.

22 Irving, *Centenary Companion*, p. 385.

23 *The Examiner* (Launceston), 5 January 1901.

24 *The Sydney Morning Herald* and *The Daily Telegraph* (Sydney), 2 January 1901.

25 *The Argus*, 2 January 1901.

26 Ibid.
27 *The Brisbane Courier*, 2 January 1901.
28 *The West Australian* (Perth), 2 January 1901.
29 *Mercury* (Hobart), 2 January 1901.
30 *The Advertiser* (Adelaide), 2 January 1901.
31 Ibid.

CHAPTER 17: UNFINISHED BUSINESS
 1 For the complete list, see State Records New South Wales, Digital Gallery, 'Canberra: The Contest to Become our Federal Capital', http://gallery.records.nsw.gov.au.
 2 Pegrum, p. 122.
 3 *The Argus*, 31 October 1908.
 4 Higgins, 'Surveyors at the Snowline'.
 5 Frei, 'Discussion on the Meaning of Canberra', www.canberrahistoryweb.com.
 6 Reps (ed.), 'American Designs Splendid New Capital for Australia', http://urbanplanning.library.cornell.edu.
 7 National Archives of Australia, 'Prohibition in Canberra: King O'Malley and the "Dry" Capital', http://yourmemento.naa.gov.au.
 8 *The Sydney Morning Herald*, 3 November 1927.
 9 Hogan, p. 9.
10 Minister for Works and Railways Mr P. G. Stewart, *Hansard*, 26 July 1923, pp. 1668–9.
11 *The Braidwood Dispatch and Mining Journal*, 31 January 1914.
12 Ausflag, 'History of the Australian National Flag', www.ausflag.com.au.
13 *The Argus*, 4 September 1901.
14 *Hansard*, No. 49, 2 December 1953, second session
15 Menzies, p. 187
16 Lang, 'Australian Anthem', www.poetrylibrary.edu.au.
17 Australian Government, Department of Foreign Affairs and Trade, 'National Anthem', www.dfat.gov.au.
18 http://www.southaustralianhistory.com.au/song.htm.
19 *The Sydney Morning Herald*, 5 December 1878.
20 McCormick to Fuller, letter, 1 August 1913, MS 1347, National Library of Australia, Canberra.

BIBLIOGRAPHY AND FURTHER READING

BOOKS

Australian Encyclopaedia, Vol. 4, first edition, Angus & Robertson, Sydney, 1925–26

Barnard, Edwin, *Capturing Time: Panoramas of Old Australia*, National Library of Australia, Canberra, 2012

Blainey, Geoffrey, *A History of Victoria*, second revised edition, Cambridge University Press, Cambridge, 2013

Blaxland, Gregory, *A Journal of a Tour of Discovery across the Blue Mountains in New South Wales*, B. J. Holdsworth, London, 1823

Bligh, William, *Log*, Hutchinson, Melbourne, 1979

Bowes Smyth, Arthur, *The Journal of Arthur Bowes Smyth: Surgeon, Lady Penrhyn 1787–1789*, Australian Documents Library, Sydney, 1979

Carboni, Raffaello, *The Eureka Stockade: The Consequence of Some Wanting on Quarter-deck a Rebellion*, Melbourne University Press, Melbourne, 1963

Carroll, Brian, *Australia's Governors-General: From Hopetoun to Jeffery*, Rosenberg Publishing, Sydney, 2004

Cecil, Lord Robert, *Lord Robert Cecil's Gold Fields Diaries* (edited by Ernest Scott), Melbourne University Press, Melbourne, 1935

Clark, C. M. H., *Select Documents in Australian History, 1851–1900*, Angus & Robertson, Sydney, 1955

Clark, Manning, *The History of Australia Volumes 1 and 2 From Earliest Times to 1838*, Melbourne University Press, Melbourne, 1995

Connell, J. (ed.), *Sydney: The Emergence of a Global City*, Oxford University Press, Oxford, 2000

Crowley, Francis Keble, *Big John Forrest 1847–1918: A Founding Father of the Commonwealth of Australia*, Vol. 1, University of Western Australia Press, Perth, 2000

Dando-Collins, Stephen, *Sir Henry Parkes: The Australian Colossus*, Knopf, Sydney, 2013

Darwin, Charles, *The Voyage of the Beagle*, John Murray, London, 1839

Deakin, Alfred, *'And Be One people'*, *Alfred Deakin's Federal Story* (introduction by Stuart Macintyre), Melbourne University Press, Melbourne, 1995

Deakin, Alfred, *The Federal Story: The Inner History of the Federal Cause* (edited and with an introduction by John Andrew La Nauze), Melbourne University Press, Melbourne, 1963

Ellis, Malcolm Henry, *Lachlan Macquarie: His Life, Adventures and Times*, Angus & Robertson, Sydney, 1978

Farrell, Frank, *Themes in Australian History: Questions, Issues and Interpretation in an Evolving Historiography*, New South Wales University Press, Sydney, 1990

Ferguson, Charles, *The Experiences of a Forty-Niner, during Thirty-Four Years' Residence in California and Australia*, Williams Publishing Co., Cleveland, Ohio, 1888

FitzSimons, Peter, *Eureka*, Random House, Sydney, 2013

Flannery, Tim (ed.), *The Life and Adventures of William Buckley*, Text Publishing, Melbourne, 2002

Flinders, Matthew, *A Voyage to Terra Australis*, Vol. 1, G. and W. Nicol, London, 1814

Garvin, J. L., *The Life of Joseph Chamberlain*, Macmillan, London, 1934

Gunn, John, *Along Parallel Lines: A History of the Railways of New South Wales 1850–1986*, Melbourne University Press, Melbourne, 1989

Hall, William, *Practical Experiences at the Diggings of the Gold Fields of Victoria*, Effingham Wilson, London, 1852

Harris, H. M., *Asiatic Fathers of America*, Warwick House Publishing, Virginia, 2006

Heaton, J. Henneker, *Australian Dictionary of Dates and Men of the Time*, George Robertson, Sydney, 1879

Holthouse, Hector, *River of Gold: The Story of the Palmer River Gold Rush*, Classics edition, Angus & Robertson, Sydney, 1967

Horner, Frank, *Looking for La Perouse: D'Entrecaseaux in Australia and the South Pacific, 1792–3*, Melbourne University Press, Melbourne, 1995

Howitt, *William, Land, Labour, and Gold: Or, Two Years in Victoria, with Visits to Sydney and Van Diemen's Land*, Longman, Brown, Green and Longmans, London, 1855

Hughes, Robert, *The Fatal Shore*, Collins Harvill, London, 1987

Irving, Helen Dorothy, *The Centenary Companion to Australian Federation*, Cambridge University Press, Melbourne, 1999

Keesing, Nancy (ed.), *History of the Australian Gold Rushes by Those Who Were There*, Angus & Robertson, Melbourne, 1981

Kennedy, Gavin, *Captain Bligh: The Man and his Mutinies*, Duckworth, London 1979

Lyne, Charles, E., *The Life of Sir Henry Parkes G.C.M.G., Australian Statesman*, T. Fisher Unwin, London, 1896

Macarthur Onslow, Sibella (ed.), *Some Early Records of the Macarthurs of Camden*, Angus & Robertson, Sydney, 1914

McClymont, James Roxburgh, *The Theory of Antipodal Southern Continent during the Sixteenth Century*, Australasian Association for the Advancement of Science, Hobart, 1892

McMinn, W. G., *George Reid*, Melbourne University Press, Melbourne, 1989

Marshall, John, *Battling for Gold: Or Stirring Incidents of Goldfields Life in West Australia*, E. W. Cole, Melbourne, 1903

Menzies, R. G., *Afternoon Light: Some Memories of Men and Events*, Cassell, Melbourne, 1967

Mudie, James, *The Felonry of New South Wales being a faithful picture of the Real Romance of Life in Botany Bay with Anecdotes of Botany Bay Society and a Plan of Sydney*, Whaley and Co., London, 1837

Mundy, Godfrey Charles, *Our Antipodes; Or, Residence and Rambles in the Australian Colonies: With a Glimpse of the Gold Fields*, British Library Historical Print Editions, London, 2011

Murray, David Christie, *The Cockney Columbus*, Downey, London, 1898

Nagle, Jacob, *Diary of the Life of Jacob Nagle, Sailor, from the Year 1775 to 1841* (edited by J. C. Dann), Weidenfeld & Nicolson, London, 1988

Nicholls, Mary (ed.), *The Diary of the Reverend Robert Knopwood, 1803–1838: First Chaplain of Van Diemen's Land*, Tasmanian Historical Research Association, Hobart, 1977

Parkes, Sir Henry, *Fifty Years in the Making of Australian History*, Vol. 1, Longmans, Green & Co., London, 1892

Pegrum, Roger, *The Bush Capital*, Hale & Iremonger, Sydney, 1983

Quick, John and Garran, Robert Randolph, *The Annotated Constitution of the Commonwealth of Australia*, Angus & Robertson, Sydney, 1901

Reynolds, John, *Edmund Barton*, Angus & Robertson, Sydney, 1948

Richards, Thomas, *An Epitome of the Official History of New South Wales, from the Foundation of the Colony, in 1788, to the Close of the First Session of the Eleventh Parliament under Responsible Government*, Government Printer, Sydney, 1883

Richardson, William A. R., *Was Australia Charted before 1606? The Java la Grande Inscriptions*, National Library of Australia, Canberra, 2008

Ritchie, John, *A Charge of Mutiny*, National Library of Australia, Canberra, 1988

Roderick, Colin, *Henry Lawson: A Life*, Angus & Robertson, Sydney, 1991

Rolls, Eric, *Sojourners: The Epic Story of China's Centuries-old Relationship with Australia*, Queensland University Press, Brisbane, 1992

Roth, Henry Ling, *The Aborigines of Tasmania*, F. King & Sons, Halifax, UK, 1899

Scott, Ernest, *The Life of Captain Matthew Flinders, R.N.*, Angus & Robertson, Sydney, 1914

Shaw, Alan George Lewers, *A History of the Port Phillip District: Victoria before Separation*, Melbourne University Press, Melbourne, 1996

Stevens, H. (ed). *New Light on the Discovery of Australia as Revealed by the Journal of Captain Diego de Prado y Tovar*, (translated by George F. Barwick), Hakluyt Society, Liechenstein, 1930

Tink, Andrew, *William Charles Wentworth: Australia's Greatest Native Son*, Allen & Unwin, Sydney, 2009

Traill, W. H., *Historical Sketch of Queensland*, Lansdowne Press, Sydney, 1886

Turbet, Peter, *The First Frontier: The Occupation of the Sydney Region*, Rosenberg Publishing, Sydney, 2011

Weitemeyer, Thorvald, *Missing Friends: Being the Adventures of a Danish Emigrant in Queensland (1871–1880)*, T. Fisher Unwin, London, 2011

Welsh, Frank, *Great Southern Land: A New History of Australia*, Penguin, London, 2004

Wentworth, William Charles, *A Statistical, Historical and Political Description of the Colony of New South Wales and its Dependent Settlements in Van Diemen's Land: With a Particular Enumeration of the Advantages Which These Colonies Offer for Emigration, and Their Superiority in Many Respects over Those Possessed by the United States of America*, G. and W. B. Whittaker, London, 1819

Westervelt, D., *Hawaiian Historic Legends*, Revell & Co., New York, 1923

White, Charles, *History of Australian Bushranging*, Vol. 1, Angus & Robertson, Sydney, 1862

Young, Reverend William, *Report on the Condition of the Chinese Population of Victoria*, Census of Victoria, Melbourne, 1868. Reprinted in McClaren, Ian F. (ed.), *The Chinese in Victoria: Official Reports and Documents*, Red Rooster Press, Melbourne, 1985

LIBRARY COLLECTIONS AND PAPERS, JOURNALS

Annual Report of the New South Wales Railway Commissioner, New South Wales State Records, 30 September 1865

Arthur, George Sir, Copies of all Correspondence between Lieutenant-Governor Arthur and His Majesty's Secretary of State for the Colonies, on the Subject of the Military Operations Lately Carried on Against the Aboriginal Inhabitants of Van Diemen's Land (introduction by A. G. L. Shaw), Tasmanian Historical Research Association, Hobart, 1971

Banks, Sir Joseph to Governor John Hunter, 1 February 1799, The Dawson Turner Copies (DTC) of Sir Joseph Banks's Correspondence in the British Museum Natural History (NH) Botany Library, 11.187

Barton Papers, Manuscript Collection 1968–70, 1996 and last amended 2001, 1290a from Arthur J. Reynolds, National Library of Australia, MS 51 (nla.ms-ms51)

Baston, John, 'The Western Australia Separation for Federation Movement', *Australian Quarterly Review*, Vol. 27, No. 1, March 1955

Blackstock, Michael, 'The Aborigines Report (1837): A Case Study in the Slow Change of Colonial Social Relations', *Canadian Journal of Native Studies*, Vol. XX, No. 12000, pp. 67–94.

Clark, Gregory, 'Farm Wages and Living Standards in the Industrial Revolution: England, 1670–1869', *Economic History Review*, Vol. 54, No. 3, August 2001

Colville, Alexander, Lord Colville of Culross, letters to Admiralty, 10 April 1761, 25 October, 30 December 1762, PRO Adm 1/482, Public Records Office, Kew

Conference of Premiers, Held at Hobart, 1895, Minutes of Proceedings, Government Printer, Sydney, 1895

'Correspondence Relative to the Recent Discovery of Gold in Australia', 1852–57', H. M. Stationery Office, Great Britain, 1852

Fowell, Newton, Letters to his Family, 1786–90, manuscript, MLMSS 4895/1/18, Mitchell Library, State Library of New South Wales

Harrison, Dr Jennifer, Moreton Bay Convict Settlement, Queensland State Archives, June 2012

Higgins, Matthew, 'Surveyors at the Snowline: Surveying the ACT–NSW Border 1910-15', (introduction by David Arnold), National Museum of Australia, 12 April 2013

Historical Records of Australia, Series I, Vols II, III, IV, V, VI, VII, VIII, IX, X, XII, XIII, XIV, XX, XXVI; Series III, Vol. I

Historical Records of New South Wales, Vol. 1, Part 2 (edited by F. M. Bladen, Frank Murcott), 1858–1912, Government Printer, Sydney, 1892–1901

Irving, Helen, 'When Quick Met Garran: The Corowa Plan', Papers on Parliament, No. 32, Parliament of Australia, Canberra, December 1998

Macquarie, Lachlan, Journals 1787–1824, together with memoranda and selected letters, A768 to A786, Mitchell Library, State Library of New South Wales

Marsden, Samuel, Marsden Papers, MS 8, Mitchell Library, State Library of New South Wales

Parkes, Sir Henry, Diary, 1 January–31 December 1891, A1018, Mitchell Library, State Library of New South Wales

Pike, Glenville, 'Early Attempts at Settlement in the Northern Territory', Royal Historical Society of Queensland, 27 August 1959

Proceedings of the Bathurst People's Federal Convention, Gordon & Gotch, Sydney, 1897

Smeaton, Thomas Drury, 'Our Invasion by the Chinese', Local History Collection, Robe Public Library, 1865, D7477 (T), State Library of South Australia

Stephen, Sir Ninian and John Quick, 'A True Founding Father of Federation', Senate Occasional Lecture Series, Australian Parliament House, 21 May 2004

Victorian Parliamentary Papers, 'Report from the Commission Appointed to Inquire into the Conditions on the Gold Fields', Legislative Council, Votes and Proceedings, A76/1854–55, Vol. II

Wentworth Family Papers, 1783–1827, A751–A755; A756–A761; A762–A765; A767, Mitchell Library Manuscripts index card catalogue, State Library of New South Wales

Western Australia Parliamentary Debates, Vol. 11, *Hansard*, 1884

Worgon, George Bouchier, 'Journal on a Voyage to NSW with the First Fleet, by George Bouchier Worgon, Surgeon on the *Sirius* in November 1786', ML C830, Mitchell Library, State Library of New South Wales

ONLINE ARTICLES AND RESOURCES

About Australia, Our National Symbols, Australian Government, http://australia.gov.au

Allen, Judith, 'Scott, Rose (1847–1925)', *Australian Dictionary of Biography*, National Centre of Biography, Australian National University, 1988, http://adb.anu.edu.au

Anderson, Hugh, 'Fawkner, John Pascoe (1792–1869)', *Australian Dictionary of Biography*, National Centre of Biography, Australian National University, 1966, http://adb.anu.edu.au

Auchmuty, J. J., 'Hunter, John (1737–1821)', *Australian Dictionary of Biography*, National Centre of Biography, Australian National University, 1966, http://adb.anu.edu.au

Ausflag, 'History of the Australian National Flag', www.ausflag.com.au

Australian Government, Department of Foreign Affairs and Trade, 'National Anthem', February 2011, www.dfat.gov.au

Banks, Joseph, *The Endeavour Journal*, http://gutenberg.net.au/ebooks05/0501141h.html

Bassett, Marine, 'Gisborne, Henry Fyshe (Fysche) (1813–1841)', *Australian Dictionary of Biography*, National Centre of Biography, Australian National University, 1966, http://adb.anu.edu.au

Bolton, G. C., 'Steere, Sir James George Lee (1830–1903)', *Australian Dictionary of Biography*, National Centre of Biography, Australian National University, 1990, http://adb.anu.edu.au

Chamberlain to Hopetoun, telegram, 23 December 1900, National Archives of Australia, Virtual Reading Room (Vrroom), A6661, 1055, 2010, http://vrroom.naa.gov.au

Clark, Gregory, 'Farm Wages and Living Standards in the Industrial Revolution: England, 1670–1850', University of California, Davis, Department of Economics, 2001, www.econ.ucdavis.edu

Cook, Captain James, *Captain Cook's Journal during His First Voyage round the World Made in* H.M. Bark Endeavour *1768–1771*, http://www.gutenberg.org

Crowley, F. K., 'Stirling, Sir James (1791–1865)', *Australian Dictionary of Biography*, National Centre of Biography, Australian National University, 1967, http://adb.anu.edu.au

Dampier, William, *A New Voyage round the World*, www.gutenberg.net.au

De Garis, Brian, 'How Popular was the Popular Federation Movement?', Papers on Parliament No. 21, Parliament of Australia, Canberra, December 1993, www.aph.gov.au

De Garis, Brian, 'Representative Government: The First Elections', from *A History of Western Australia*, 1981, The Constitutional Centre of Western Australia, Government of Western Australia, December 2010, www.constitutional centre.wa.gov.au

Dunn, Cathy, 'The Attempted Assassination of Prince Alfred at Clontarf 1868', Internet Family History Association of Australia, 1998, www.historyaustralia.org.au

Fahey, Warren, 'The Bushman's Bible: The History of the Bulletin', Australian Folklore Unit, Colloquial Sayings and Slanguages, 2005, http://warrenfahey.com

Finn, Paul, 'Want, John Henry (1846–1905)', *Australian Dictionary of Biography*, National Centre of Biography, Australian National University, 1990, http://adb.anu.edu.au

Fitzgerald, Shirley, 'Chinese', Dictionary of Sydney, 2008, www.dictionaryofsydney.org

Fletcher, Ned and Elias, Rt Hon. Dame Sian, 'A Collusive Suit to "Confound the Rights of Property Through the Length and Breadth of the Colony"?: *Busby v White* (1859)', *Victoria University of Wellington Law Review*, Vol. 41, No. 3, 2010, www.victoria.ac.nz

Frei, Patricia, 'Discussion on the Meaning of "Canberra"', Canberra History Web, 2014, www.canberrahistoryweb.com

Gilbert, L. A., 'Banks, Joseph (1743–1820)', *Australian Dictionary of Biography*, National Centre of Biography, Australian National University, 1966, http://adb.anu.edu.au

Godley, Charlotte, *Letters from Early New Zealand*, private printing, 1936, Victoria University of Wellington, New Zealand Electronic Text Collection, 2014, http://nzetc.victoria.ac.nz

Harrison, Dr Jennifer, 'Moreton Bay Convict Settlement', Queensland State Archives, Queensland Government, June 2012, http://www.archives.qld.gov.au

Hogan, Gay, 'Parliament House, Canberra 1927: Records Relating to the Design, Construction and Opening of the Provisional Parliament House', Research Guide 6, National Archives of Australia, 1997, http://guides.naa.gov.au

Irving, Helen, 'Who are the Founding Mothers? The Role of Women in Australian Federation', Papers on Parliament, No. 25, Parliament of Australia, Canberra, June 1995, www.aph.gov.au

Juxian, Wei, *The Chinese Discovery of Australia*, Hong Kong, 1960, quoted in *Who Got to Australia First?*, National Library of Australia Gateways, http://pandora.nla.gov.au/pan/11779/20070524-0000/www.nla.gov.au/pub/gateways/issues/83/story01.html

King, Hazel, 'Bourke, Sir Richard (1777–1855)', *Australian Dictionary of Biography*, National Centre of Biography, Australian National University, 1966, http://adb.anu.edu.au

Knowles, J. W., 'Adoption of the 3ft. 6ins. Gauge for Queensland Railways', University of Queensland, eSpace, 1981, http://espace.library.uq.edu.au

Kohen, J. L. 'Pemulwuy (1750–1802)', *Australian Dictionary of Biography*, National Centre of Biography, Australian National University, 1966, http://adb.anu.edu.au

Lang, John Dunmore, 'Australian Anthem', 1826, Australian Poetry Library, www.poetrylibrary.edu.au

McLachlan, Noel, 'The Extraordinary Frenzy of both Imperial Loyalty and Mad Sectarianism: The Effects of the Prince Alfred Shooting at Clontarf', Internet Family History Association of Australia, Perspectives on Australian History http://www.historyaustralia.org.au

Macquarie to Marsden, letter, 8 January 1818, Marsden and Macquarie Collection, State Library of New South Wales, 2007, www.sl.nsw.gov.au

Manning, Geoffrey H., 'Kangaroo Island: Early History in Nepean Bay and the Settlement on Kangaroo Island', taken from *A Colonial Experience*, The Manning Index of South Australian History, State Library of South Australia, www.slsa.sa.gov.au

Martin, A. W., 'Parkes, Sir Henry (1815–1896)', *Australian Dictionary of Biography*, National Centre of Biography, Australian National University, 1974, http://adb.anu.edu.au

Moreton Bay convict settlement, Queensland State Archives, Queensland Government, http://www.archives.qld.gov.au

National Archives of Australia, 'Prohibition in Canberra: King O'Malley and the "Dry" Capital', *Your Memento*, Issue 10, April 2013, http://yourmemento.naa.gov.au

Norris, R., 'Deakin, Alfred (1856–1919)', *Australian Dictionary of Biography*, National Centre of Biography, Australian National University, 1981, http://adb.anu.edu.au

Official Record of the Proceedings and Debates of the Australasian Federation Conference, Melbourne 1890, University of Sydney, Australian Digital Collections, http://adc.library.usyd.edu.au

Parliament of New South Wales, 'History of the Parliament of New South Wales', Fact Sheet No. 02, September 2009, www.parliament.nsw.gov.au

Parliamentary Select Committee on Aboriginal Tribes, 'Report', William Ball and Hatchard & Son, London, 1837, Internet Archive, 2007, https://archive.org

Penny, B. R., 'Lonsdale, William (1799–1864)', *Australian Dictionary of Biography*, National Centre of Biography, Australian National University, 1967, http://adb.anu.edu.au

Persse, Michael, 'William Charles Wentworth (1790–1872)', *Australian Dictionary of Biography*, National Centre of Biography, Australian National University, 1967, http://adb.anu.edu.au

Playford, John, 'Kingston, Charles Cameron (1850–1908)', *Australian Dictionary of Biography*, National Centre of Biography, Australian National University, 1983, http://adb.anu.edu.au

Reid, George Houstoun, *My Reminiscences*, Cassell, London, 1917, University of Sydney Library, SETIS, 2000, http://setis.library.usyd.edu.au

Reps, John W. (ed.), 'American Designs Splendid New Capital for Australia', Urban Planning, 1794–1918: An International Anthology of Articles, Conference Papers, and Reports, 2002, http://urbanplanning.library.cornell.edu

Royal Australian Historical Society, 'Australia's First Northern Port', History Resources, www.rahs.org.au

Seale, Shirley, 'Mary Bligh O'Connell', The Hawkesbury Historical Society, www.hawkesburyhistory.net.au

Select Committee on Transportation, House of Commons report, 3 August 1838, National Library Australia, http://trove.nla.gov.au

Serle, Geoffrey, 'Turner, Sir George (1851–1916)', *Australian Dictionary of Biography*, National Centre of Biography, Australian National University, 1990, http://adb.anu.edu.au

Shaw, A. G. L., 'King, Philip Gidley (1758–1808)', *Australian Dictionary of Biography*, National Centre of Biography, Australian National University, 1967, http://adb.anu.edu.au

Spigelman, J. J., 'A Reappraisal of the Bigge Reports', History Council of New South Wales, Annual History Lecture, 4 September 2009, http://historycouncilnsw.org.au

State Records NSW, Digital Gallery, 'Canberra: The Contest to Become our Federal Capital', http://gallery.records.nsw.gov.au

Steven, Margaret, 'Macarthur, John (1767–1834)', *Australian Dictionary of Biography*, National Centre of Biography, Australian National University, 1967, http://adb.anu.edu.au

Sturt, Charles, *Two Expeditions into the Interior of New South Wales*, http://gutenberg.net.au

Sydney Gazette, 7 January 1810, The Lachlan and Elizabeth Macquarie Archive, Macquarie University Library, 2011, www.library.mq.edu.au/digital/lema

Tench, Watkin, *A Narrative of the Expedition to Botany Bay*, London, 1789, web edition, eBooks@Adelaide, University of Adelaide Library, South Australia

Tench, Watkin, *A Complete Account of the Settlement at Port Jackson*, University of Sydney, Australian Digital Collections, 1998, http://adc.library.usyd.edu.au/data-2/p00044.pdf

Watson, F., Paterson, G., Bartrum, J. and Bladen, F. M., *Mutiny and the Trial of Lt Col Johnston: An Outline of the Rum Rebellion*, (edited by Ned Overton), 2013, www.gutenberg.net.au

Whitaker, Anne-Maree, 'Castle Hill Convict Rebellion 1804', Dictionary of Sydney, 1970, www.dictionaryofsydney.org

White, John (Surgeon-General to the Settlement), *Journal of a Voyage to New South Wales July 1787*, J. Debrett, London, 1790. Web Edition eBooks@Adelaide, University of Adelaide Library, South Australia

Yarwood, A. T., 'Marsden, Samuel (1765–1838)', *Australian Dictionary of Biography*, National Centre of Biography, Australian National University, 1967, http://adb.anu.edu.au

LIST OF ILLUSTRATIONS

Captain James Cook by Nathanial Dance-Holland, *c.* 1775
National Maritime Museum, Greenwich, London

Sir Joseph Banks by Sir Joshua Reynolds
National Library of Australia

Captain Arthur Phillip by Henry Macbeth-Raeburn
National Library of Australia

The First Fleet in Sydney Cove by John Allcot
National Library of Australia

Lieutenant John Bowen by unknown artist, *c.* 1890
La Trobe Picture Collection, State Library of Victoria

David Collins Esq. by Antoine Cardon
National Library of Australia

John Macarthur by unknown artist
Dixson Galleries, State Library of New South Wales

Rear-Admiral William Bligh by Alexander Huey, 1814
National Library of Australia

Lachlan Macquarie by Richard Read, 1822
State Library of New South Wales

Convicts building road over the Blue Mountains, New South
   Wales by Charles Rodius, 1833
National Library of Australia

'The looking glass, no. 5' by William Heath
National Library of Australia

The Proclamation of South Australia 1836 by Charles Hill,
   c. 1856–76, Adelaide

Oil on canvas, 133.3 × 274.3 cm
Morgan Thomas Bequest Fund, 1936
Art Gallery of South Australia, Adelaide

Frescoes for the new Houses of Parliament, no. V [picture];
    'The first land sale'
Wood engraving published in Melbourne *Punch* by Edgar Ray
    and Frederick Sinnett, 1856
State Library of Victoria

W. C. Wentworth by James Anderson, 1872
Mitchell Library, State Library of New South Wales

Mr E. H. Hargraves by Thomas Balcombe
National Library of Australia

Eureka Stockade by B. Ireland
State Library of Victoria

'Celestial Happiness' by Frederick Grosse
Wood engraving published in Melbourne *Punch*, 1855
State Library of Victoria

'An interruption on the overland telegraph line' by G. E.
    Charlton
Wood engraving published in the *Illustrated Australian News*,
    1889
State Library of Victoria

Albury Railway Station – opening of the Albury–Wodonga link
New South Wales State Records

'Intercolonial travellers passing the customs' by Alfred Martin
    Ebsworth
Wood engraving published in *Australasian Sketcher*, 1887
State Library of Victoria

Sir Henry Parkes by P. Spence, 1887
State Library of New South Wales

Australasian Federation Conference, Melbourne, 1890
National Library of Australia

National Australasian Convention, Sydney, 1891
National Library of Australia

Sir Edmund Barton by Sir Leslie Ward, 1902
National Library of Australia

Alfred Deakin, 1868
National Library of Australia

Captain William Russell
Alexander Turnbull Library, Wellington, New Zealand

Andrew Inglis Clark by Vandyck Photographers, 1909
National Library of Australia

Sir Samuel Walter Griffith
National Library of Australia

Lucinda by unknown artist, *c.* 1897
State Library of Queensland

Sir George Reid
National Library of Australia

John Quick, 1898
National Library of Australia

Premiers' conference on Federation, Hobart, 1895
National Library of Australia

Catherine Helen Spence by unknown artist, 1890s

Federal Convention in session Parliament House, Adelaide,
    10 April 1897
National Archives of Australia

Sir John Forrest, 1874
National Library of Australia

Sir Edward Braddon
Allport Library and Museum of Fine Arts, Tasmanian Archive
    and Heritage Office

Charles Kingston
National Library of Australia

'How to Vote'
State Library of South Australia

'Referendum Day', 4 June 1898
State Library of South Australia

Australian Federation poster, 1901
National Library of Australia

Sir George Reid
National Library of Australia

Hon. Edmund Barton addressing a meeting in Martin Place, Sydney
National Library of Australia

'Combine, Australia' published in London *Punch*, 28 June 1899
National Museum of Australia

'Three men in a boat' published in *Quiz*, 8 February 1900
State Library of South Australia

Federal poll, 31 July 1900
State Library of Western Australia

Swearing-in ceremony, Centennial Park, Sydney, 1901
National Library of Australia

Duke and Duchess of York open the new national parliament, 9 May 1927
Fairfax Syndication

ACKNOWLEDGEMENTS

The nature of researching history is radically changing as fewer books are made readily available by the major libraries. While researching and writing this book, many invaluable sources, such as the *Historical Records of New South Wales* and the *Historical Records of Australia*, became more difficult to access in places like New South Wales's Mitchell Library. At the same time, vast amounts of historical information and books now exist online. This is particularly so with the National Library of Australia's Trove website, which provides an increasingly rich source of historical material, including copies of most of the colonial newspapers.

I would like to thank Random House for their terrific support, particularly from my publisher Nikki Christer. I am especially grateful (again) for the great help of my editor Catherine Hill, whose persistence and professional guidance has made this (yet again) a far better book than it otherwise would have been. Thanks, too, to Kevin O'Brien for his copy-editing.

I am also greatly indebted to Linda Atkinson for her help with the research and editing of the book. *The Making of Australia* required a vast amount of research of primary source material (more than was the case for all four of my previous books put together!) and Linda's acumen, knowledge, stamina and hard work have been invaluable.

The *Making of Australia* covers a large span of modern Australian history, traversing well over 100 years of British settlement, as well as some of the pre-British European exploration of Australia. In telling the story of how the tiny convict settlement of 1788 evolved to become the nation of Australia, I have drawn on some of the pivotal events and stories covered in more detail in earlier books I wrote, including *1788, The Gold Rush* and *The Great Race*.

Finally, as I did in *The Great Race*, in this book, wherever possible, I have avoided the word 'discover' in relation to European expeditions around and within Australia. Where I have used the word, I do not mean to indicate that I believe Australia or any other lands were undiscovered before Europeans settled them.

INDEX